THE ILLUSTRATED HISTORY OF
MILITARY
MOTORCYCLES

THE ILLUSTRATED HISTORY OF
MILITARY
MOTORCYCLES

DAVID ANSELL

OSPREY
AUTOMOTIVE

To Jean, for her patient help.

Published in Great Britain in 1996 by Osprey,
an imprint of Reed Books Limited,
Michelin House, 81 Fulham Road, London SW3 6RB
and Auckland, Melbourne, Singapore and Toronto

ISBN 1 85532 584 5

Editors: Charles Davidson and Dennis Baldry
Managing Editor: Shaun Barrington
Layouts: Gwyn Lewis

Set in 10pt on 11.5pt Monotype Bembo.

Typeset by Dorchester Typesetting Group Ltd.

Printed in Hong Kong.

Title page: **May 1940, a column of Indian 1200cc 340-B sidecar outfits,
recently delivered to the French Army. With the fall of France the
remaining machines were supplied to the US Army and other Allied armed
forces. The model was also made available to domestic police
departments. Note the mixture of leaf sprung front wheel and plunger
type rear suspension.** *(ECPA)*

Page 6: **December 1941, mechanics of the Australian No.3 Squadron,
R.A.A.F., working upon various captured motorcycles; the WH number
plates of the *Wehrmacht* can be clearly seen.** *(Australian War Memorial)*

ACKNOWLEDGEMENTS

The author would like to thank the numerous individuals, manufacturers, museums, government agencies, and other organizations that kindly provided the reference material to prepare this book.

Archives & Museums
Australian War Museum, Canberra, Australia
Centre d'Archives de l'Armenent, Paris, France
Centre of Military History, Washington, USA
Hadtorteneti Intezet es Muzeum, Budapest, Hungary
Imperial War Museum, London, England
Museum of Army Transport, Beverly, England
Musée Royal de l'Armée et d'Histoire Militaire, Brussels, Belgium
Museo Storica della Motorizzazione Militare, Rome, Italy
Royal College of Military Science, Swindon, England
US Army Transportation Museum, Virginia, USA
Vehoniemi Car Museum, Finland
Verbehrsmuseum, Dresden, Germany

Embassies
Austrian, Australian, Belgian, Czechoslovak, Danish, French, German, Hungarian, Italian, Netherlands, Norwegian, Russian, Swedish, Swiss, South African, United States, Embassies in London.

Manufacturers
Benelli SpA, BMW GmbH, Bombardier Ltd, BSA Co Ltd, Bultaco SA, Condor SA, CCM-Armstrong, CZ-Jawa, Fabrique Nationale Herstal, Hagglund SA, Harley-Davidson International, Hercules-Werke GmbH, Husqvarna AB, Jonas Øglaend As, Maico GmbH, Moto Guzzi SpA, Motorradwerke Zschopau, Polar Metal Plast AB, Steyr-Daimler-Puch GmbH, Zündapp Werke GmbH. (Alas, some are no longer working companies.)

Importers & Exporters
Avtoexport, Moscow
Heron Suzuki GB Ltd, London
Honda (GB) Ltd, London
Motokov Foreign Trade, Prague
Transportmaschien, Berlin

Military Procurement
Australian Army GHQ, Melbourne
Belgian Army GHQ, Brussels
Canadian Army GHQ, Ottawa
Danish Army GHQ, Hjørring
Finnish Army GHQ, Helsinki
French Army GHQ, Paris
Swiss Army GHQ, Bern

With a particular thank you to the following for providing individual answers, photographs, or translating original material; Tibor Almassy, Graeme Brown, David Bullivant, Sgt Callum Davey, Henry Davis, François Dumas, Rob East, Doug Frost, Jacek Gorski, Doug Jackson, Bror Jauren, Barry Jones, Hannu Lindell, Harry Ljungdahl, Alan Magness, Tals Melkis, Andrew Morland, Frank Nyklicek, Sven-Olof Persson, Tony Silvey, Miroslav Sochor, Garry Stuart, Bart Vanderveen, Stig Wilderberg, Mick Woollett and Finn Yding.

CONTENTS

CHAPTER ONE

Early Years 1900–18

I: German Empire . . . 12
Imperial Manoeuvres, Kaisermanövern, NSU, Wanderer, Triumph/TWN

II: Austro-Hungary . . . 15
Laurin & Klement, Puch

III: British Development . . . 18
Early Motorcycles, Standardisation, Douglas, Triumph, Clyno, Phelon & Moore/Panther, Scott

IV: Britain Supplies Allies . . . 23
BSA, Rudge-Whitworth, Royal Enfield, Matchless, Sunbeam, Other Manufacturers

V: The Rest of Europe . . . 26
France, Italy, Belgium, Netherlands, Sweden, Switzerland

VI: American Beginnings . . . 31
The Big Three (Harley-Davidson, Indian & Excelsior)

CHAPTER TWO

Interwar Years 1919–38

I: Germany Strategy . . . 39
Victoria, BMW, Zündapp, NSU, DKW & Triumph, Austria

II: Eastern Europe . . . 43
Forged-steel design, Military Potential, Poland, Czechoslovakia, CZ, Jawa, Ogar, Praga, Itar & Walter

III: False Expectations . . . 58
Italy, Denmark, Sweden. Husqvarna, Suecia, France, Prototypes, General Production, Belgium

IV: Once and Future Allies . . . 71
Great Britain, Manoeuvres, Procurement, Triumph, BSA, United States, General Decline

CHAPTER THREE

Second World War 1939–45

I: Germany Re-arms . . . 78
Kradschützen, BMW & Zündapp, Additional machines

II: Italian Diversity . . . 89
Moto Guzzi, Gilera, Moto Benelli, Folding Airborne Motorcycle

III: Unprepared Britain . . . 95
Norton, AMC, Triumph, BSA, Royal Enfield, Flying Flea, Clockwork
Mouse & Welbike, Final Request

IV: American Models . . . 103
Servi-Cycle, Cushman, Harley-Davidson, Indian, Japanese copies

V: France, Belgium & USSR . . . 119

VI: Neutrals . . . 121
Sweden, Switzerland

CHAPTER FOUR

Post-War Production 1946–66

I: Warsaw Pact . . . 126
Communist Nationalisation, East Germany, Czechoslovakia, USSR

II: North Atlantic Treaty . . . 131
American Policy, Indian, Harley-Davidson

III: British Domination . . . 133
Flat-Twins, Triumph, New Models

IV: New Models . . . 137
Condor, BMW revived, Swiss Boxer, Finland, Sweden, Norway

V: The New Generation . . . 149
Zaibatsu

CHAPTER FIVE

Contemporary Design

I: Italian Alternative . . . 150
Military Tricycle, The V7 Model, The 850T3 Model, The V-1000
Convert, Lightweights

II: German Design . . . 155
Hercules & Maico, BMW Heavyweights, BMW Boxer, BMW K Series

III: The Japanese Four . . .159
Europe, Australia, Limitations

IV: British Production . . . 170
Armstrong, Bombardier

V: American Programme . . . 171

VI: Scandinavian Independence . . . 173
Winha, Hägglund, Sweden, Two-Stroke Dominance

Specification Tables 178

Arranged in chapter order

Introduction

Military expectations have often been inconsistent with standard production; demanding specifications and performance beyond any readily available technology. While pushing against recognised and accepted standards of design, occasionally resulting in innovation, the majority of military motorcycles remained a compromise of the original specifications or brief.

Armed forces, worldwide, required service availability throughout the year, in all possible conditions, demanding special attention to overall finish. All running-gear components had to remain easily accessible for routine maintenance, with the minimum of dismantling, while being completely protected from the worst of the elements. These demands promoted additional problems for the brakes, carburettor air-filter and cable operated controls. Not too surprisingly, very few manufacturers were able to maintain a continuous, or even occasional, military contract, and any factory that gained a second order had established a reputation worthy of mention.

Such standards were not always in-line with current trends or fashion, but during later years, factories with success in off-road competition became a major influence upon motorcycles designed for military service; providing valuable experience for multi-terrain liaison and reconnaissance duties. Each chapter of this book is indexed to specification tables compiled in the final section of the more popular motorcycles specially designed or adapted for service within each period covered. Any repetition of a factory name is a clear indication of success!

As the role of the military motorcycle continued to be defined, experience provided a clearer and more mutual understanding between production possibilities and the changing role of the armed forces. While procurement groups may have differed in their demands to suit specific terrain or climate for example, some of the greatest challenges to the diversity of these machines come at the hands of unskilled riders.

Throughout the history of the military motorcycle, both social and economic conditions have of course transformed the suitability of the average recruit. The motorcycle has declined in general popularity, but at the height of the industry during the inter-war period, every other soldier had a motorcycle licence, and considerable maintenance experience. Those days have long since passed, and without this personal knowledge or participation, many soldiers objected when transferred from four- to two-wheeled vehicles.

To combat this situation, most armed forces have introduced motorcycle training programmes, for officers and new recruits alike, in order to maintain the maximum effective backup and reserve. With a history approaching a century of unbroken development, the military motorcycle remains an essential, if more specialised, part of military service worldwide.

CHAPTER ONE

Early Years 1900–18

I: GERMAN EMPIRE . . .

In January 1871, the North German Federation was dissolved, and with Kaiser Wilhelm of Prussia as Emperor, an army of the first German Reich was created. With the union of 26 States, this formation was of considerable size. By 1914, these different military units had become a single highly trained fighting force. Peacetime strength in 1914 was some 840,000, but within three years this figure had risen to more than six million.

The German High Command was quick to realise the potential of automatic weapons, and a number of machine-gun detachments were formed during the early stages of the war. Elite units arrived at the Western Front in the Spring of 1916, and a number of motorcycles were attached to machine-gun sections for quicker manoeuvrability.

Mechanical transport was gradually deployed throughout the German forces, and during the war numerous units were formed to manage these expanding requirements. Communication troops had formally managed the Railway & Mechanical Services, but when the Air Service and Signal Corps gained their independence in 1916 (originally considered part of the Communication troops), all transportation in the field became the responsibility of the Quartermaster General's Department.

In December 1916, all mechanical transport and the railways were re-organised again, as separate units, and each Army in the field had a Mechanical Transport Park, to maintain a pool of staff cars, trucks, an ambulance convoy, tractors for the artillery, and a motorcycle detachment. As the conflict continued, and spares became more difficult to obtain, mechanical transport was greatly restricted, and largely only used when the railway was unavailable.

Imperial Manoeuvres
Kaisermanövern

In 1885, Karl Benz produced the first motor-car of any practical design in Mannheim, and Gottlieb Daimler the first motorcycle in Cannstatt, near Stuttgart, but it was a further 13 years before the first motor vehicle was adopted by the German military; a Daimler truck was borrowed by the Army.

The following year, in 1899, the *Kaisermanövern* were held, and a number of cars (Benz, Cudell, Daimler, Eisenach, and Marienfeld) underwent trials, and on 1st October the *Inspektion der Verkehrstruppen* was founded to test and study vehicles for military service. Without any motoring associations, and very little automotive experience, it was important to adopt machines of technical simplicity, with a robust and reliable design. That year, the first two German military trucks were ordered from Daimler, and following the *Kaisermanövern* of 1904, the first NSU 2¾hp

(p 179) and Triumph 4¼hp motorcycles were procured.

Little more than powered bicycles these machines had a single-cylinder inlet-over-exhaust valve engine, of 375cc (NSU) and 489cc (Triumph) mounted vertically within a tubular frame without front or rear suspension. With a direct belt drive to the rear wheel, auxiliary cycle pedals provided some help for steep hills. A fuel tank was mounted between the top two frame tubes, with a total-loss oil supply and hand pump action. The NSU had a contracting band brake upon the front wheel hub, while the Triumph featured a block brake upon the belt wheel rim. Military conversion centred upon a rear carrier rack and overall service livery (Emperor Grey).

By 1914, a total of 64,000 motor vehicles existed in Germany; three quarters were under military control. During the course of the war this number continued to increase, and by 1918, the *Reichswehr* (German Army) had some 12,000 cars, 3200 ambulances, 25,000 trucks, 1600 trailers and 5400 motorcycles at their command.

The German forces largely restricted their motorcycles to solo despatch duties, but shortly before the war experimented with sidecar designs (attached to either side of the machine), and a number of these outfits were used as personnel carriers. These machines were rapidly accepted as an inexpensive alternative troop carrier, providing a lightweight three seater vehicle to carry men and equipment. A limited number were modified to carry medical supplies or to provide an ambulance service.

In 1914, the German Army adopted a wide range of vehicles to carry arms and ammunition, and the motorcycle and sidecar was widely thought more able to travel to the front line; the destruction of surfaced roads often stopping heavier four wheeled transport. From 1915, an NSU 7½hp sidecar outfit was often used in action with a demountable machine-gun and tripod located on a flat-bed sidecar with ammunition and spares.

NSU

For some pre-war years, NSU pursued a policy of continued development, and by 1914 had established export agencies across Europe (Austria, Belgium, France, Italy, Great Britain, Netherlands, Russia and Switzerland). As early as 1901, NSU made their debut in Britain at the Stanley Show, held at Crystal Palace, London, as manufacturers of cycle components. That year the Neckarsulm factory assembled their first motorcycle, with a Belgian made Minerva 1¼hp engine of 211cc (62 x 70mm). The following year NSU assembled a similar model with a Swiss made Zedel 1¾hp unit of 240cc (66 x 70mm), and later that year the first complete NSU motorcycle was introduced with a 2¾hp single-cylinder 375cc engine of their own design mounted vertically within a tubular frame. In 1904 the NSU 2¾hp model took part in the *Kaisermanövern*, and

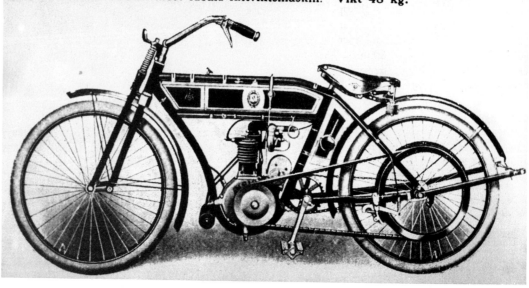

Neckarsulmer 1½ hkr. 1-cyl. motorvelociped
Den mest ideala lättviktsmaskin. Vikt 48 kg.

the first contract to supply the *Reichswehr* was placed.

From 1905, the NSU 2-speed pulley gear was adopted by factories worldwide; a simple epicyclic design to give greater flexibility to the single speed motorcycle. The NSU unit replaced the engine pulley normally used, without any structural change. By 1914, NSU offered 2hp, 2¼hp, 2¾hp & 3hp single-cylinder and 3hp & 5hp V-twin models, and the next year the 7½hp (p 179) V-twin was produced.

Alongside continued engine development, NSU transmission and frames were also improved; the original belt drive and auxiliary cycle pedals were largely replaced by chain drive, and front and rear suspension adopted. Many years ahead of their time, by 1915 all new NSU models featured leading link front forks and a helical sprung rear sub-frame assembly. With the declaration of war, NSU lost all but their Austrian export market, and although military orders continued, the factory mainly concentrated on munitions.

Widely used throughout the war, NSU supplied the majority of motorcycles adopted by the German Army before 1918. From 2-speed models, little more than powered bicycles with a single or V-twin engine, to the advanced 7½hp V-twin model, with a 3-speed gearbox and full chain drive, these sturdy machines were deployed for solo or sidecar use; and included full lighting. Following the Armistice, NSU rapidly returned to full motorcycle production, and unable to meet demand, NSU pioneered German 'production line' techniques. By 1922, the Neckarsulm factory employed more than 3,000 people.

Wanderer

The second major motorcycle supplier of the German Forces, Wanderer of Schonau, near Chemnitz was also able to manufacture all major components required for motorcycle production. The first machine was assembled in 1902; very similar to many of the period, with a single-cylinder 1½hp engine of their own design. Within six years Wanderer developed a 3hp model (p 179) with an unusual 408cc V-twin engine: the rear cylinder was vertical, but the forward cylinder was inclined 45°. The two cylinders, however, had horizontal cooling fins, giving an unusual appearance. The engine was mounted within a tubular frame, with a reinforced tube beneath the power unit, with leading link front forks and ingenious double-sprung rear sub-frame assembly.

Transmission was limited to belt final drive and auxiliary cycle pedals, but further advanced features included an internal expanding rear drum brake, automatic lubrication system and full acetylene lighting. The model also introduced a unique wedge shaped fuel tank, sloping rearwards, retaining the greater volume of fuel to the rear.

By 1913, Wanderer had discarded auxiliary cycle pedals, and the 408cc engine was remounted in a more central position. The belt drive was retained, but the two cylinders were both mounted at an angle, with horizontal cooling fins (with a similar appearance to a number of NSU models). The Wanderer motorcycle was expensive to produce, but their components could be assembled from mass production without much special machining. As with NSU, Wanderer

established a good reputation during pre-war years, and the 3hp V-twin model was widely procured by military, including the *Reichswehr* and police departments across Europe.

During the early 1920s, the Wanderer V-twin was re-introduced with an increased engine capacity of 616cc (70 x 80mm). The machine had a 3-speed gearbox, free-wheel clutch and chain final drive.

In 1926, the sv layout was replaced with an exposed ohv design, some with eight valves, and the capacity increased to 708cc (70 x 92mm) and 744cc (71 x 94mm). The pistons were made of light alloy and the chrome-nickel steel crankshaft ran on roller bearings. The following year Wanderer began work upon a completely different design; a vertical single-cylinder 498cc (84 x 90mm) ohv engine with a shaft final drive, mounted within a pressed steel frame with leaf sprung front suspension.

Despite its modern concept and clean appearance, the workmanship and reliability was below standards, and within two years or so, the design was sold to the Prague arms factory of F. Janecek, and became the first Jawa motorcycle (see chapter two). This marked the end of Wanderer motorcycles, but the works signed an agreement with NSU to assemble motorised bicycles during the 1930s.

Triumph/TWN

In 1887, the two Germans, Siegfried Bettman and Maurice Schulte founded the British company of Triumph in Coventry, to produce bicycles of their own design. Some ten years later Schulte began to develop a motor-powered bicycle, and in 1902 adopted a Belgian 1¼hp Minerva engine (also used by NSU) of 211cc (62 x 70mm). Further proprietary engines from Fafnir and JAP were tried until the first Triumph power unit was introduced in 1905; a vertical single cylinder 3hp sv engine of 363cc (78 x 76mm), which laid the foundation for the Triumph reputation for reliability. By 1907, the unit increased to 453cc (82 x 86mm), and in 1908 became 476cc (84 x 84mm). Two years later it grew to 499cc (85 x 85mm), and in 1914 to 550cc. The 363cc model remained classified as 3hp, the three 500's as 3½hp, and the 550cc as 4hp respectively.

Triumph officially began motorcycle production in 1903, and that year founded a German sister factory in Nuremburg. The German-built Triumphs were almost identical to the British machines, and while the situation was restricted during World War 1, this arrangement would continue until 1929. From 1904, the Nuremburg factory began to supply machines to the German Army, but with the parent company in Britain,

continued German military orders were disrupted during the war.

While both factories used the Triumph name (some German-built models were badged Orial) within their domestic market, the British works were known as TEC (Triumph Engineering Co.) in Germany, and the German business adopted the name TWN (Triumph Werke Nuremburg) for export sales. While the British factory's 'Trusty Triumph' became synonymous with British military motorcycles during World War 1. TWN models became important motorcycles within the *Wehrmacht* in World War 2 (see Chapter Three).

II: AUSTRO-HUNGARY . . .

Among the oldest manufacturers in the world, the Austro-Hungarian automotive industry quickly formed a close relationship with the armed forces; developing some of the first purpose-built military vehicles ever produced. As in Germany, the Austro-Hungarian Army began a motorisation programme in 1898, when a licence-built Daimler truck was procured. It was not long before a number of advanced fwd machines were assembled, and the well-known Austro-Daimler armoured car with the revolving gun turret was built. With a mixture of initiative, ingenuity and military support, by 1914, very few Austro-Hungarian motor vehicle factories were not actively engaged in some form of military development or production.

By 1914, the Austro-Hungarian Army had a total of 54 passenger cars and nine artillery command cars, but as military demands continued to increase, within just two years, some 830 assorted military vehicles were being assembled each month. The first motorcycles were however, of only limited interest for military use, but as reliability improved a growing number of manufacturers supplied two- and three-wheeled vehicles to the armed forces.

Laurin & Klement

In the winter of 1894–95, Vaclav Laurin and Vaclav Klement rented a small workshop in Mlada Boleslav, to produce bicycles of their own design, but in common with many small factories across Europe, L & K became interested in powered cycles. Following extensive development work and prototypes, promising results began to take shape, and finally the first L & K Slavia motorcycle was assembled in 1898. Rather than attach an engine to an existing frame, Laurin and Klement developed a machine around the engine; the result providing the arguably world's first practical motorcycle for everyday use.

Maintaining the initiative, within four years L & K prepared three different single-cylinder motorcycles for mass production: the BZP and BZN 2½hp, the L 2¾hp and LW 3hp models. With another first for motorcycle design, the LW 3hp had a water cooled engine, with a simple radiator coiled around a frame section. In 1903, the factory built their first V-twin model, designated the CC 3hp, and in 1904, the V-twin CCD 4hp, CCR 5hp, and water-cooled CCRW 5hp models.

The following year L & K introduced the model CCCC, one of the first motorcycles with an in-line 4-cylinder engine.

As production increased L & K sought new markets; exports were readily accepted worldwide. The business became a limited company and grew into a vast industrial concern, supplying two-, three- and four-wheeled vehicles.

At this time one-third of all L & K production was exported to Russia, with agencies in Kiev, Moscow, St. Petersburg and Rostov. Exports were also made to Australia, China, Germany, Great Britain, Japan, and Mexico. The Japanese Government sent officials to report upon European automotive works, and after visiting the L & K sales office in London, the Mlada Boleslav models were highly recommended. Japan became the third country, after Austro-Hungary, and Montenegro, to procure the majority of their motor vehicles from Laurin & Klement Ltd, many of which were adapted for military service.

Laurin & Klement Ltd became an important influence upon the automotive industry of Europe. At a time when powered vehicles were more a novelty than a practical form of transport, it was very difficult to gain the financial backing required to develop new designs, but L & K were

able to expand upon their excellent reputation. Producing machines of sound design and finished to the highest standards, L & K made a major contribution to the industrial interests of Austro-Hungary.

Quality alone, however, could not save the company, and with insufficient investment, a number of competitors were able to improve upon the L & K production figures. In 1925, Laurin & Klement amalgamated with the Skoda factory of Pilsen, and the distinctive L & K badge was replaced by the Skoda emblem forever.

Puch

Austro-Hungary provided the conditions for numerous factories to develop and improve upon the newly created powered transportation, and while many only lasted a few years, others successfully introduced new standards of reliability and design. Johann Puch was an engineer able to take advantage of the new technology. During his national service in the Austro-Hungarian Army, he served an apprenticeship making bicycles at the Styria Fahrradwerke, and in 1889, set up his own repair business in Graz. After some success, Puch founded the *Johann Puch & Co. Fabriksmässige Erzeugung von Fahrrädern* in 1891, and began to manufacture bicycles; this company was bought out in 1897 by the forerunner of the German Durkopp business.

Two years later, Puch founded the *Johann Puch Erste Steirmärkische Fahrradfabrik AG*, and began to work on various motorised vehicles; a prototype car was introduced in 1901, followed by a number of tricycles. The first production Puch motorcycle was built in 1903, with a vertical single-cylinder engine, mounted centrally and low within a simple cycle frame. The machine followed the generally accepted design principles of the period, with a 2¾hp inlet-over-exhaust valve layout, larger 3¼hp and 3½hp models followed. These machines all had magneto ignition, hand-operated oil pump and a single brake, with a contracting band acting on a dummy rear-wheel rim.

Until 1914, Puch continued to develop a number of single-cylinder and V-twin models, by which date the Graz factory was also interested in four-wheeled vehicles. Johann Puch, however, had driven himself too hard and died in July 1914. The business was reorganised in May 1914, and renamed Johann Puch AG: with an outstanding team of designers and a workforce of some 1200. The Austro-Hungarian Army had started to investigate the suitability of powered transport, and with the declaration of World War 1, Puch motorcycles were widely deployed for solo despatch and general liaison; in particular the 2hp (p 178) model R-1 and 2½hp model R-2. These were very similar single-cylinder lightweights, but the R-2 was widely used for gear-change and front fork experiments.

With the exception of a prototype (10 only) introduced in 1916, with an in-line horizontally opposed twin-cylinder engine, the majority of war-time Puch motorcycles had a vertical single cylinder four-stroke engine. Puch V-twin machines were largely restricted to limited edition deluxe or specialist racing models. Puch motorcycles proved so popular, however, that the factory discontinued their car production after 1918. Under the guidance of Ing. Giovanni Marcellino, post-war Puch models centred upon 2-stroke designs, and as they gradually grew in capacity, the factory was destined to become a major European motorcycle supplier, exporting worldwide.

Leichtes „Puch"-Motorrad, Type R 2 (2½ HP).

Left: **1914 Puch type R2; virtually identical to type R1, with an increased engine capacity and revised engine ratio. Both models were adopted in limited numbers by the Austrian Army during the First World War.** *(Steyr-Daimler-Puch)*

III: BRITISH DEVELOPMENT . . .

Under the guidance of Edward Cardwell, Gladstone's Secretary of War, between 1869–74, the British Army underwent major changes of restructure and modernisation, and by 1914, had become a professional fighting force. Control of the Artillery and Royal Engineers passed to the Commander in Chief, Transport and the Commissariat moved from civilian to army control, and the Army Service Corps and Ordnance Stores Department were introduced. The long established commission purchase system was abolished and the well tried Prussian method of dividing the country into military areas was adopted.

For some years troops were drilled and deployed as before, but gradually, tactics gained during the Boer War, largely fostered by Lord Roberts, placed a greater emphasis on being mobile and taking full advantage of surrounding terrain. New methods of attack, defence and withdrawal, and greater emphasis on shooting fast and straight were introduced. The new Lee-Enfield magazine rifle was excellent for the individual soldier, while the Maxim, and later Vickers, machine guns completely changed warfare. In 1914 the infantry had one machine-gun per 500 men; by 1918 one machine-gun was deployed for every 20 men.

Early Motorcycles

In 1899, the Simms/Vickers machine 'Motor Scout' made its public debut at Richmond Park, London. Designed by Frederick Simms for Vickers & Maxim Ltd, this motorquadricycle had a 1½hp single-cylinder engine, mounted between the two rear wheels, while an air-cooled Maxim machine-gun and armoured shield was positioned in front of the single rider. Spare ammunition lay in a tray, mounted between the two front wheels. Little more than a pair of bicycles held side-by-side, the machine was not adopted by the military, but in 1902, the larger 'Motor War Car' was presented by the same designer; this project did not gain an order either. Following trials, however, the British Army began using bicycles and early motorcycles; with some of the first purpose-built machines supplied by A. W. Wall Ltd, of Guildford, in 1906.

In 1910, Autocars & Accessories Ltd, of West Norwood, London, three-wheeler manufacturers, supplied four Autocarrier models to the 25th County of London Cyclists Regiment. A tiller-type arm for steering controlled the single rear wheel, while a large wooden frame (ash members reinforced with birch) provided a carrying capacity of 4-5 cwt between the two front wheels. Two machines were equipped with a Maxim machine-gun, facing forward in front of the rider/driver, the other two were equipped as support vehicles with spare ammunition boxes and mechanical spares. A single-cylinder 650cc (90 x 102mm) sv engine provided 5.6hp to the rear wheel, via an exposed chain drive, and a 2-speed gear assembly within the rear-wheel hub. The engine was fully enclosed behind wooden panels, and two soldiers could sit, facing rearward, upon the wide wooden wings over the two front wheels.

AC with a fuel capacity of 2¼g, a service range of up to 100 miles was achievable, dependent upon load and type of terrain. While not the most adaptable military model, the machine was a commercial success and the factory became AC Cars Ltd, of Thames Ditton, Surrey, named after

the Autocarrier model. By the armistice in 1918, the British military had a total of 12 of these AC Autocarriers in their possession, these having mainly been used in London and the home counties region.

Scott. In the pre-war years, the machine-gun continued to interest British motorcycle manufacturers, looking to produce a means of carrying guns and ammunition into action or providing a mobile machine-gun tripod. In 1912, Scott Engineering, Bradford, exhibited a solo Scott 3¾hp model (p 180) at the Olympia Show, with a lightweight (16lbs) Laird-Menteyne machine-gun mounted on the handlebars. The L-M machine-gun had a long magazine, projecting downwards, and only a model with an open frame, such as the legendary Scott, could permit the full turning circle with this magazine in position. While in use, a special stand lifted the front wheel off the ground, permitting the gun to be fired throughout the full movement of the handlebars. The gun was retained in the barrel-downwards position, while the motorcycle was being ridden. The model however, had been developed too early to rouse any real interest from the War Office, and did not go into production.

As interest continued to grow, manufacturers were invited to the first British military trials in 1912, and official observers were sent to many principal racing events; but large orders were not placed until the declaration of World War 1. Two military observers were present at the Isle of Man TT races in 1912, and Harry Bashall's win in the Junior race probably had a strong influence on the vast numbers of Douglas machines adopted during the war. Frank Applebee (Scott) had won the 1912 Senior TT, followed by Jack Haswell (Triumph) and Harry Collier (Matchless) in third place.

With the outbreak of war, Vickers Ordnance contacted the Scott works to supply a motorcycle machine-gun outfit. (Triumph Engineering became second only to Douglas Bros. for supplying solo despatch machines, and H. Collier & Sons – Matchless – were contracted by the Ministry of Munitions to produce war materials and aircraft parts.)

On the 12th November 1914, the Motor Machine Gun Corps was founded, to provide a battery for every infantry division, the Royal Horse Artillery and Royal Field Artillery. Each battery was to have 64 men, with six machine-gun teams, each team having three motorcycle outfits; one with a gun, one with gun mountings only, and one for spares only. Six solo riders and six mechanics/gunners were allocated to each battery, with the addition of nine cars and their drivers. The Clyno 5-6hp model (p 180) was widely adopted by the Motor Machine Gun Corps, and the P & M 3½hp (p 180) supplied to the Royal Flying Corps; both maintained by their respective mechanics.

Standardisation

All British divisions expanded during World War 1, but the support troops, the Service Corps, Signals, and Ordnance grew beyond all recognition; placing greater demand on the recently procured motorised transportation. The motorcycle was originally adopted to support, and eventually replaced, the traditional cavalry Signal Corps despatch rider. As the conflict escalated, with almost incessant bombardment and the hazards of shell holes and ever deeper mud, the motorcycle offered an effective alternative to the horse.

Irrespective of make or model, a large wooden box was mounted on a rear carrier rack to carry spares, inner tubes, drive belts, valves, and a tool kit. Further accessories included acetylene lighting and a bulb horn. The box was often removed during service, the additional weight proved too much to handle. The contents were generally carried by the rider; spare tube worn as a collar, and a back-pack or larger coat pockets provided space for many smaller items. Standard issue clothing included a special mackintosh coat, and leather gaiters or high boots to replace ankle boots and puttees. Neither warm or waterproof, very few riders were pleased with the clothing, and various additional more suitable civilian items were adopted.

Despite the introduction of far more sophisticated radio equipment, many messages were sent by carrier pigeon during the war. The British Army adopted motorised pigeon-lofts (heavy trucks with a wooden 'loft' constructed on a flatbed) to transport them close to the battlefield, and motorcycles were used for the more inaccessible areas or when a return message was required more quickly. The solo 'Don R' (Despatch Rider) carried the pigeons within large cane baskets, frequently strapped to the rider's back; the wooden accessory box officially discarded. These machines proved a welcome sight for many distant or surrounded positions, providing their only means of communication.

With a growing number of vehicles, by 1916, the British Army established a large Motor Transport base at St Omer, Northern France, to repair worn-out or damaged machines. Unlike their colleagues in the trenches, many soldiers gained an additional trade there during this period, and remained in the automotive industry after the war. While there are no records of war-time losses, by the end of the war, the British Forces had

Below: **1914 Douglas 2.75hp; the most widely procured motorcycle of the British armed forces during the First World War. A total of 13,471 of these machines were in British service at the end of the war, with a further 4,816 of the larger 4 hp models adopted for sidecar service. With such popularity the 2.75hp model remained in production for a number of years post-war, retaining the belt drive and exposed flywheel to the end.** *(Mick Woollett)*

more than 48,000 motorcycles (from 54 different factories) in active use, and similar workshops had been set up abroad. From 1912, civilian riders had been encouraged to join the Army with their own motorcycles, and during 1914 a wide range of impressed motorcycles were also used. The vast majority of British military motorcycles, however, were standardised Army models from Douglas Brothers, 2¾hp (p 180) & 4hp and Triumph Engineering, 3½hp & 4hp (also see German Empire–Triumph p. 15), and all repairs centred upon these; any other machines were rejected at the end of their useful life.

Douglas

By 1914, Douglas Bros., Kingswood, Bristol, had manufactured and sold some 12,000 motorcycles, and for the first two years of the war, the factory remained faithful to basically the same design. Apart from changing from German Bosch to the American Dixie magneto, the same 2¾hp model remained in production until 1916. From the first days of the war, the British Army adopted the Douglas 2¾hp for solo despatch and general liaison duties, and by the armistice in 1918, had a total of 13,477 in their possession, second only to the Triumph model H. With a war-time output of some 25,000 machines, Douglas also supplied the Belgian Government and the Australian Expeditionary Forces in France.

Based upon the 1912 Junior TT winner, the Douglas had a 2-cylinder 348cc sv engine, mounted in-line within the tubular frame, with girder-type Douglas front forks and a rigid rear wheel. By 1914, many British manufacturers had adopted a complete chain drive transmission, but Douglas retained the original V-belt drive throughout the war. This dated appearance was further emphasised with an exposed flywheel, and a chain primary drive located behind, driving a 3-speed gearbox mounted below the rear cylinder; a further development from the single speed direct drive model. Renamed the Douglas WD21, the popular 2¾hp model remained in production for many post-war years, retaining the original chain and belt drive throughout.

In 1915, Douglas introduced a 4hp model, for military sidecar service. This was an updated version of the proven 3½hp model; the engine enlarged to 593cc (74.5 x 68mm). As many British sidecar machines, the larger Douglas was mainly used to transport senior Army staff, but a number also carried mobile radio equipment for the Royal Naval Air Service. By 1918, the British Forces had a total of 4816 in their possession.

Triumph

Triumph Engineering (of Anglo-German ownership) remained the largest British motorcycle manufacturer of the war, their robust and reliable machines gaining the name 'Trusty'; a popular name that was well used by the works for many post-war years. Initially the factory provided their successful 3½hp 500cc (85 x 88mm) model, with either a direct drive or 3-speed hub gear, but these were replaced by the new 4hp (p 180) 550cc model H, with a separate unit Sturmey-Archer 3-speed countershaft gearbox, controlled by a long lever directly onto the box. Both models had a V-belt final drive.

The 3½hp had auxiliary cycle pedals with an additional chain drive to the rear wheel, while the 4hp discarded the pedals and introduced a fully enclosed primary chain case on the left. The two machines featured a vertical single-cylinder engine, the traditional British layout for many post-war years, with a magneto mounted forward of the single front down-tube. The frame was a weldless tubular construction, with the maker's own pivoted front fork suspension.

Neither designed nor prepared for military duties, apart from an overall service livery and wooden accessory box, Triumphs provided excellent service throughout the war wherever

Left: **Signal Office and Headquarters of 4th Australian Divisional Signalling Company on Vaulx-Beugny road. A despatch rider is leaving upon a Triumph model H, with a basket containing carrier pigeons. Note the spare inner-tubes around the handlebars.** *(AWM neg no E646)*

they were deployed. With a reputation for reliability, by 1918, orders for more than 30,000 of the model H alone had been placed. In reality, the factory supplied some 20,000 machines to the British military, and a further 10,000 to the Allies.

At the time of the armistice, the British Forces had a total of 17,998 Triumph machines (306 equipped with a sidecar) at their service, including some 17,000 of the model H. The British machines were deployed in almost equal numbers between home and abroad with a total of 9813 stationed overseas and 8185 deployed in Britain at the end of the war.

Clyno

Following extensive trials, the Clyno works supplied the majority of sidecar outfits adopted by the Motor Machine Gun Corps; most other machines were produced by Matchless, Royal Enfield and Scott. With an easy to remove 744cc (76 x 82mm) V-twin sv engine, interchangeable wheels, enclosed chain drive and three point sidecar suspension, the Clyno 5-6hp model (p 180) provided an excellent basis for the required machine-gun carrier. A water-cooled Vickers machine-gun and armoured shield was tripod mounted, with spare ammunition, spares, a cooling water container, fuel and oil tanks, positioned on the flat-bed sidecar.

While rarely, if ever, fired when the machine was moving, the gun was normally pointing forwards, but could be reversed if required; the gun

Above: **1915 Triumph model H. At the time of the armistice in 1918, just over 17,000 of these machines had been standardised for the British armed forces, gaining the name of 'Trusty' Triumph.** *(Sven-Olof Persson)*

could also be detached from its sidecar mounting for a ground firing position. The Clyno 5-6hp model was also used for personnel transportation and ambulance duties, and in 1917, a further 1500 outfits were assembled with the larger JAP V-twin 8hp engine for the Russian Army, but very few of these arrived before the Bolshevik Revolution. At the time of the armistice, the British Forces had a total of 1792 of the 5-6hp model in their possession, with 642 deployed overseas.

Phelon & Moore/Panther

With only a fraction of either Douglas or Triumph production, the P & M 3½hp model (p 180), became the third most numerous British military motorcycle of the war. By the early 1910s, the P & M factory was manufacturing one of the most advanced motorcycles in the world, and following the War Office manoeuvres of

Coventry, but after the death of his partner, Harry Rayner, in 1903, Phelon went into partnership with Richard Moore the following year, and these machines were built under the P & M name in Cleckheaton.

One of the first developments of the P & M partnership included the introduction of a 2-speed gear system, involving two primary chains and a selective clutch. Within a few years the auxiliary cycle pedals were discarded, and the chain drive was fully enclosed. Further improvements included a leading link front fork suspension, a contracting band rear brake, and magneto ignition. Limited military modifications centred upon revised front forks, for additional strength, full acetylene lighting, and overall service livery.

During the war, the Yorkshire factory became increasingly involved with military production, and by 1918, the RFC had a total of 3383 machines (and 150 P & M sidecars) at their service. Although further military contracts were not placed in any quantity, during the early

1913, P & M were awarded a contract to supply the newly established Royal Flying Corps, with machines for solo despatch and sidecar duties.

Jonah Phelon had assembled his first motorcycle in 1900, with a single-cylinder De Dion type engine; positioned as an integral part of the cycle frame, replacing the front down tube. This was a feature that became a continuing characteristic of P & M (Panther) design.

The first commercially offered machines were assembled at the Humber-Beeston factory,

1920s, the P & M 3½hp became the standard model for the RAC (Royal Automobile Club) patrolman, in Britain.

Scott

A Scott/Vickers machine-gun carrier was prepared in 1914, and taken to London, where Winston Churchill, then First Lord of the Admiralty, approved the design, and a contract was placed for 300 Scott machines (200 machine-gun carriers, 100 solo despatch models), to be divided

between the Admiralty and the War Office. During November, three of the first outfits were presented to King George V, in the grounds of Buckingham Palace.

The sidecar provided a tripod mounting to withstand the recoil of the Vickers machine-gun; the gun was designed so it could be fired while the machine was moving. The gunner sat behind an armoured shield (the rider/driver remained fully exposed), able to fire 300 rounds per minute. As was the case with other machines adopted by the Motor Machine Gun Corps, these outfits were prepared to be used in teams of three; one with a gun, one with gun mountings only, and one for spares only. In addition to the rider/driver and passenger, mechanic and gunner respectively, the spares carrier was intended to carry 2250 rounds, spare tyres, four gallons of fuel and a gallon of oil, tins of calcium carbide for the lights, water for the engine radiator, and various smaller engine parts.

During trials at Bisley, the water-cooled 2-cylinder 3¾hp Scott engine was found far too vulnerable, without frost protection for the radiator; lower winter temperatures causing serious problems. Despite the lower gearing, the 486cc (70 x 64mm) engine could not offer the required performance when the machine was fully loaded. The armour shield also restricted the machine-gun line of fire. The Scott machine-gun carrier remained in production, but a repeat order was not placed, and the majority of these machines stayed in Britain during the war. It would be fascinating to know if this configuration was *ever* fired in battle: unlikely.

Realising the shortcomings of his Scott/Vickers model, Alfred Scott, founder of Scott Engineering, dissociated himself from the machine, and began working on a completely new project to meet the demands of the machine-gun carrier. While retaining a triangulated tubular construction, a well proven Scott feature, the machine also had a three wheeled configuration of a sidecar outfit, for maximum manoeuvrability. Known as the Scott Gun Car, this unique machine, when fully loaded, was still half the weight of a comparative four wheeled vehicle.

This lopsided model had a 578cc (76 x 63mm) 2-cylinder water-cooled two-stroke engine, mounted in-line with the two off-side wheels. Transmission ran through a friction band clutch, counter-shaft 3-speed gearbox and enclosed shaft drive. The interchangeable wheels were heavily dished, fully enclosed by discs, and supported by stub axles. Scott, however, did not gain the anticipated military contract. Renamed the Scott Sociable, a civilian version made a limited post-war appearance, but could not compete with the small family car boom.

IV: BRITAIN SUPPLIES ALLIES . . .

BSA

In August 1914, the British requirement for armaments was alarming; the War Office had let stocks dwindle, and the situation required massive orders. The Birmingham Small Arms Company – BSA – returned to its original production, and with the introduction of 24 hour shifts all week, output increased from 650 to 4360 rifles a week. Within two years this rose to 8000, with a peak of 10,000 at the end of the war.

By 1918, BSA had produced more than 1½ million Short Lee-Enfield rifles, and enough spares to assemble a further 500,000. As the only makers of the Lewis gun, BSA would produce a total of 145,397 during the war, and supplied British, Belgian and Russian Forces.

By the end of the war, BSA's Small Heath, Redditch, and Sparkbrook factories had increased from some 3500 to over 13,000 employees, becoming one of the world's largest light engineering concerns.

During this period of expansion the BSA bicycle and motorcycle workshops had of course been working overtime, producing both civilian and military machines.

In accordance with the Ministry of Munitions ban in November 1916, all civilian machines were suspended until the end of hostilities, but BSA military models continued to be sought wherever possible. The British Army Cyclist Corps' demand (cycles were also widely adopted by the Royal Engineers and Signal Corps), and

Above: **3 Dec 1914, Scott 3.25hp; prepared for service in the Motor Machine Gun Corps. While offering a mobile machine gun platform, the Vickers gun was very rarely fired while the sidecar outfit was moving. The motorcycle rider has no protection at all. A column of three machines would provide a mounted machine gun, a spare tripod position without a weapon, and a sidecar for spare ammunition.** *(Mick Woollett)*

following requests for a lightweight model that could be carried over rough terrain, BSA prepared a folding cycle that could be carried on a soldier's back.

While maintaining only a restricted output, BSA motorcycles were also able to prove their military worth, from the mud and cold of Europe to the heat of East and South Africa. The 4¼hp model H became the most numerous military BSA, while the 3½hp model was also supplied between 1912 and 1917. By the end of the war, the British Forces had a total of 537 of the 4¼hp, and 551 various other BSAs at their service; 766 deployed at home, 322 in Europe, and a further 245 in East Africa. BSA had also supplied some 400 machines to the South African Motor Cycle Corps early in the war.

BSA began motorcycle production in 1911, with a 3½hp model with a 499cc (85 x 88mm) sv engine, direct belt drive and auxiliary cycle pedals. By 1914, the cycle pedals had been discarded and a 3-speed countershaft gearbox adopted; a number of both models were adopted by the British Army. After only two years motorcycle production, BSA introduced the 4¼hp model H, with fully enclosed all-chain transmission, and a pedal operated 2-speed hub gear. By 1915, the model H also featured a 3-speed countershaft gearbox, and once again both versions were procured for military use. With a reputation for reliability, these machines were widely used for solo despatch and general liaison.

Rudge-Whitworth

From the turn of the century, the British motorcycle industry began to export worldwide, and while the War Office restricted their interest to only a few manufacturers, a large number of British factories continued to export. In some pre-war years, Rudge-Whitworth, Coventry, exported at least half their production, to Europe and the Empire. Their largest European customer was Veladini in Milan, but many machines were also exported to Australia, Austria, France, Latvia, New Zealand, Russia and South Africa.

With the declaration of war, the Austrian sales were lost, but the Russian Army placed an order of 400 for the Rudge 3½hp Multi model (p 180). The contract was signed on 2nd October; the first machines left Coventry seven days later and the last on the 20th that month. The military conversion consisted solely of repainting, but to meet this order in such a short time (with only 20 machines produced a day), every unsold machine in and around the works was commandeered. A contract for 400 of the same model was received from the Belgian Army, and this was completed and despatched in early 1915. Although the British Army did not place an order with Rudge-Whitworth, a number of despatch riders, recruited before 1914, brought their own Rudge machines into British service. In addition, a small number were requested by the Admiralty, for Royal Navy shore patrol, and the Royal Naval Air Service.

With the Bolshevik Revolution and fall of Belgium, Rudge production began to fall. In 1916, the War Office considered the introduction of a standard motorcycle, assembled from the best of British components. Rudge contributed wheels, frames and front forks, but by this time the factory output had dropped to just five military export machines a day. On 3rd November 1916, by order of the Ministry of Munitions, all production of cars and motorcycles for civilian sales was terminated, and Rudge restricted manufacture to supplying their strong, but light, aircraft wheels, and to ammunition manufacture.

Royal Enfield

In accordance with the Ministry of Munitions ban, all motorcycles were discontinued at Royal Enfield, Redditch, with the exception of one. The 6hp sidecar model was prepared in limited numbers for the Motor Machine Gun Corps, with a sidecar-mounted Vickers machine-gun, or supplied with a medical sidecar, for transporting wounded to field hospitals. The medical sidecar had a large locker at the front, folding pram-style hood and a spare wheel mounted at the rear. Throughout this period the factory also supplied a number of these heavyweight outfits to the Swiss proprietary engine manufacturer MAG (Motosacoche of Geneva), often without the engine, for eventual Swiss Army service. Although the Royal Enfield name was cast on the magneto chain cover, the 6hp model had a JAP V-twin 771cc (76 x 85mm) sv engine and 3-speed gearbox, mounted within a tubular frame with girder-type front forks. At the end of the war, the British Forces had a total of 161 of these machines in service.

Matchless

A similar situation existed at H. Collier & Sons (Matchless) factory, Plumstead, London. Within months of the war starting, the Ministry of Munitions contracted the works to assemble aircraft parts and armaments; all motorcycle production was restricted to the Model 8B.

The Matchless Model 8B had a MAG 976cc (85 x 85mm) inlet-over-exhaust valve engine and 3-speed countershaft gearbox, mounted within a tubular cycle frame with girder-type front forks and rigid rear wheel. Transmission ran through a fully-enclosed all-chain drive. Further advanced features included a kick start and internal expanding rear hub brake. For the 1915 season, the

Left: **1917 Matchless 976cc Model 8B/2; while Matchless of South London were contracted to assemble aircraft parts and armaments, all motorcycle production was restricted to the Model 8B (solo) or 8B/2 (with sidecar). Ready and waiting for service, surprisingly the War Office did not place an order for a military version, and the project had to be abandoned.** *(Mick Woollett)*

Model 8/B was introduced as a sidecar machine, with quickly detachable and interchangeable wheels. This machine provided the basis for the Matchless military sidecar model of 1917, with a reversible (forward or rearward facing) Vickers machine-gun, mounted on a flat-bed sidecar. Surprisingly, this advanced model did not receive a military order, and the project was abandoned. However, the British Forces had a total of 161 Matchless motorcycles (and 8 Matchless sidecars) in their possession at the end of the war.

Sunbeam

Although John Marston Ltd (Sunbeam), Wolverhampton, had a good reputation for quality and had modified their 3½hp model for military use, in 1914 the War Office considered their vehicle and aircraft radiators more vital to the war effort. The Sunbeam Catalogue of 1915, however, presented the 3½hp military model (including a new heavyweight gearbox, clutch and mountings, etc), with the addition of 6hp and 8hp utility sidecar outfits prepared for military service.

The 6hp model had an AKD (Abingdon King Dick) 795cc (73 x 95mm) V-twin sv engine, mounted within a tubular frame with Brampton Biflex front fork suspension, and quick-release interchangeable wheels. The previously used JAP units were being supplied to 'official' WD works. The 8hp model had a MAG 996cc (82 x 94mm) V-twin engine, and revised 3-speed gearbox, squeezed into the same 6hp frame. With an inlet-over-exhaust valve layout, the taller MAG unit had to be set lower in the frame, which reduced the ground clearance and restricted the model to sidecar service only.

The Sunbeam's price, however, prohibited British military orders (only 79 machines in British service in 1918), but a number were sold to different Allied Forces, with the majority supplied to France, Italy, and Russia. The French Army, in particular, adopted the 6hp model for ambulance work, with a pram-style hood over a standard army stretcher, while the 8hp model was supplied with a sidecar mounted machine-gun to the Russian Army. The Russian Government had a permanent representative at the Sunbeam factory until the Revolution in 1917.

For some years, Sunbeam had produced their 3½hp model with a fully enclosed all-chain drive, but French military specifications had required a belt final drive, and with the addition of 50cc to overcome any belt drag, the Wolverhampton factory prepared the unique 4hp FMM (French Military Model). With a production run of less than 1000, the machine remained very similar to the 3½hp, but with both primary and final drive on the near-side, a new gearbox was developed. The clutch and kick-start were fully enclosed. Further

Above: **Official photograph of 1915 Sunbeam 8hp military sidecar model, with Swiss made MAG 996cc V-twin engine. This taller inlet-over-exhaust valve unit was replaced as soon as possible by the more practical JAP 976cc side valve engine.** *(Bob Currie)*

major changes included a French-made internal expanding drum brake to replace the mechanical caliper on the front wheel. Supplied throughout 1916 (with a French language instruction book), the 4hp FMM (p 180) was used both solo or with a sidecar attached, providing despatch and liaison, or personnel transportation and ambulance duties respectively.

During 1916, the Sunbeam ambulance sidecar was re-designed, becoming a wood and canvas construction to hold two stretchers; handles pushed through holes at the front and tied down at the rear. These heavier designs were mainly used with the 6hp model, but as the war progressed, the Motor Machine Gun Corps did not have the success intended, and contracts for more machines were terminated. Once again, JAP engines became more readily available, and the Sunbeam 8hp model adopted the JAP 976cc (85 x 85mm) V-twin sv engine, to replace the taller MAG unit. With a return to its former position, a ground clearance of some 4in was available, and the model remained in production until 1922. Sunbeam motorcycles were not procured by the British Forces (limited numbers were in service with their civilian owners), but Sunbeam sidecars were bought independently. By 1918, the British Army had 326 Sunbeam sidecars available for suitable machines, and a further 646 Sunbeam sidecars specifically for the New Imperial 8hp military model.

Russian Collapse

With varying degrees of success, several other British motorcycles were also selected by Allied Forces. Major models included: Ariel 3½hp, James Model 7, New Imperial 8hp, Norton Big Four, Premier 3½hp and Rover 3½hp. Some of which were destined for Russia.

The Russian war economy had been entirely dependent upon Allied imports, and eventually became a victim of its own internal collapse. With some eight billion roubles outstanding, the Tsarist government would eventually pay the ultimate price for its increased dependence upon foreign powers, and was forced to send part of its gold reserves to the Allies. A bureaucratic nightmare (amongst other kinds of nightmares); goods ordered by Russia were piled high at American, British and French ports before their despatch, as the situation deteriorated in Russia, with a revolution developing across the country and chaos on the railways.

During this turbulent period, little is known of the vast supply of military materials that arrived in Russia, but for some two years a steady stream of British motorcycles were crated and despatched. In the early months of 1917, Russia declared its intention to withdraw from the war, and these shipments were diverted to other Allied Forces. But in reality crates remained in storage at ports, and many were broken open and the machines reduced to spare parts. After 1918, these stockpiles were widely bought back by manufacturers, and the machines re-assembled for an eager civilian market. British motorcycles originally procured by Allied Forces were also widely bought by civilians abroad, priming a wider market for post-war sales and thus having an important influence upon domestic industry.

V: THE REST OF EUROPE . . .

From the early 1900s, the armed forces of France and Italy experimented with the internal combustion engine; developing new machines to meet military demands. The French Government, in line with Austro-Hungary, Germany and Great Britain, introduced a subsidy system, as less costly than direct purchase. Even so, with the declaration of the World War, large numbers of different machines were either requisitioned or procured from both home and abroad. In complete contrast, Italian industry produced a wide range of vehicles for domestic and foreign Governments alike. Unlike most other countries involved in World War 1, Italy imported only a few machines.

Moreover, the majority of Italian factories were located within the two northern cities of Turin and Milan, and no more than a 20-hour journey from the most distant front lines, so the Italian Army had a prompt supply of vehicles and spares throughout the war.

Below: **French military repair depot during the First World War; the majority are single-cylinder Peugeot models of the immediate pre-war years.** *(ECPA)*

France

It is widely accepted that the French introduced the first motor vehicle for military service. In 1769, Joseph Gugnot assembled a steam-driven tricycle for artillery towing, unsuited for general use, and it was not until 1867 that a similar machine was produced by Lotz in Nantes and successfully towed a gun and limber. With, however, the development of the first practical four-stroke engine in the late 1890s, the French military were quick to procure various cars and trucks. While not deployed in quantity, the French Army were also interested in motorcycles for despatch and general liaison. Supplied by a wide number of domestic works (Griffon, Rene-Gillet, Peugeot (p 179), Werner, etc), the majority were produced by Terrot, Dijon.

After some years preparing a number of auxiliary engines for bicycles, Terrot assembled their first motorcycle in 1901, to become one of the largest motorcycle manufacturers in France. Little more than civilian models with a coat of service livery, single cylinder Terrot machines were used for solo and sidecar duties throughout the war.

In general, French industry could not provide sufficient vehicles to meet active service demands, but Terrot (p 179) gained a good reputation that lasted many years, and although the name became better known on the race track during the 1920s, these machines continued to provide military service for many post-war years. Retaining their elegant French style and advanced, robust design, Terrot models were widely used by French military and police departments worldwide.

During the war period, Rene-Gillet, Paris, also continued to develop public service machines; centred upon their 748cc (70 x 97.7mm) and 996cc (80 x 97.7mm) V-twin sv models. Unlike Terrot, while never considered a sporting machine, Rene-Gillet became known for producing 'unbreakable' touring models, with outstanding reliability to match; adapted both for solo or with a sidecar attached, a number of different purpose-built designs for ambulance, radio equipment, or machine-gun mountings were developed. As with Terrot, Rene-Gillet machines continued to be deployed throughout the inter-war years; both factories producing military models in addition to their commercial machines.

Italy

Italian military motorisation began in 1903, with a single Fiat 12hp car for general service. During the Italo-Turkish war of 1911–12, the Italian Army had a large number of trucks and tractors, and by 1914 some of the first motorcycles had been procured for Italian service. Italy did not declare war on Germany until 1915, but with some knowledge of motor vehicles on active duty, Italian manufacturers were more able to meet military requirements. While many factories had to increase their production output, manufacturers became specialist organizations. By 1917, it was claimed Fiat had produced more military vehicles than any other European factory; by October 1918 more than 36,000 vehicles had been supplied to the Italian Army, some 25,000 of which were trucks.

While not purchased in large numbers, the Italian Army acquired a diverse range of motorcycles during World War 1 (Benelli, Bianchi, Frera, Garelli, Gilera, etc), providing solo despatch and general liaison, and also sidecar

Top: **Early 1916, on the outskirts of Rousbrugge in Belgium, a French despatch rider upon a Peugeot 2½hp. Note the spare drive belt on the rear carrier rack.** *(ECPA)*

Above: **A French military ambulance; little more than a stretcher upon a sidecar frame. Note the spare wheel beneath the stretcher.** *(ECPA)*

27

Top: **1914 Bianchi type A. One of the most numerous motorcycles procured by the Italian armed forces during the First World War. Bianchi also supplied a wide range of pedal cycles especially prepared for the Italian Army; folding model for easy carrying, reinforced model for machine gun transport, etc.**
(Museo Storico della Motorizzazione Militare)

Above: **1905 FN Four model. The 362cc (45 x 47mm) engine had four independent cylinders upon a single crankcase, with an enclosed shaft final drive to the rear wheel.**
(Sven-Olof Persson)

personnel transportation, ambulance, and machine-gun mounting. From 1914, the Bianchi type A (p 180) remained one of the most numerous Italian military motorcycles of the war, with a single cylinder 500cc sv engine and belt final drive. The Frera factory, Tradate, also provided a number of popular machines; a single-cylinder 499cc solo model (p 180), and V-twin 795cc and later 1140cc sv machines for sidecar service. Further factories supplied military motorcycles in smaller numbers; by the end of the war the Italian Army had a total of 6420 motorcycles. Following the war, the Italian Army was allowed to decline, and many of these machines remained in service until the late 1920s, and the rise of Mussolini (see chapter two).

Belgium

While maintaining a policy of neutrality, from the turn of the century, the Belgian armed forces began to experiment with various powered vehicles. The Belgian Army did not deploy any quantity of military motorcycles until the late 1930s, but the Fabrique Nationale des Armes de Guerre SA (now FN; *Fabrique Nationale Herstal SA*), Herstal, Liege, assembled their first car in 1889 and introduced their first motorcycle in 1901.

Three years later, the FN factory would set

new standards in motorcycle design with the introduction of the first production motorcycle with a four-cylinder engine, at the Paris Automobile Show in 1904. The model retained standard auxiliary cycle pedals, but the flexible 362cc (45 x 57mm) power unit was not matched to a gearbox for some years (p 178). Mounted within little more than a modified pedal-cycle frame, the inlet-over-exhaust valve engine was positioned in-line and below a duplex cradle, with an enclosed shaft final drive on the rear wheel hub.

In 1909, a similar transmission was adopted with the introduction of an FN single-cylinder 249cc (65 x 75mm) 10E model, held in a similar cycle frame, but with a leather-lined cone clutch connected to a 2-speed gearbox, and exposed shaft drive. Both models had an advanced girder-type telescopic sprung front fork suspension, and internal expanding rear wheel drum brake.

The FN Four grew from 362cc in 1904 to 493cc in 1910, and became 747cc in 1915, but apart from the original layout had become a quite different machine, in both performance and construction. By 1912, the FN single model had a 285cc engine (p 179); retaining the transverse layout with a Bosch magneto at the front (on the FN Four) and shaft drive. The two machines had a single FN carburettor, controlled by a handlebar lever and Bowden-type cables. A hand-pump, incorporated within the oil tank, provided lubrication to the crankcase; oil within the four-cylinder engine could be seen through a row of small mica windows in the cast-iron crankcase.

Quickly gaining a reputation for reliability, both FN machines were widely procured by a number of European (Belgian, German, Russian, Swiss, etc) armed forces during the pre-war years, and remained in active service during the early war years; consolidating a military tradition that FN retained for many years.

Netherlands

In contrast, the Netherlands did not develop a motorcycle industry of major size, and during the early 1920s imported American (Excelsior, Harley-Davidson and Indian), British (BSA and Douglas), Belgian (FN), German (BMW and DKW), and Switzerland (MAG) motorcycles for military service. The Netherlands remained neutral during World War 1, but the Netherlands Army adopted a number of motor vehicles during the war; including domestic Omnia cars, Spyker trucks, and Eysink motorcycles (p 181). Many were commandeered civilian models, but a number of Eysink 365cc and 425cc motorcycles were prepared for the armed forces. Some 425's were modified to carry a machine-gun mounted

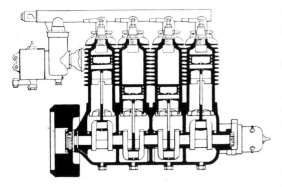

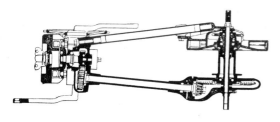

Sweden

Since their military involvement at Leipzig in 1814, Sweden has also followed a policy of strict neutrality, and the country developed a highly efficient defence industry to maintain this tradition. In 1867, the Royal Arms Company was reorganised and became Husqvarna Vapenfabriks AB, and prospered as a major international arms supplier. After the Franco-Prussian war, however, the demand for muskets began to fall, and the factory widened their production range in the early 1870s; including such domestic items as sewing machines, timber saws, lawn mowers, and eventually motorcycles.

After tests with a number of imported engines, Husqvarna chose an FN 1½hp engine for their first motorcycle. Introduced in 1903, the single cylinder engine was mounted vertically in a cycle

above the front wheel. With heavyweight suspension units and additional support legs, and the option to carry an ammunition case each side of the front wheel, these machines were designed as a mobile tripod.

While the motorcycle was moving, the machine-gun was mounted pointing forward and down, but once the machine was stationary, the weapon could be swung into virtually any firing position required; turning back to front for maximum elevation. The Eysink factory, Amersfoort, introduced its first motorcycle in 1901 (and continued production until 1956), and with the exception of the carburettor (AMAC), magneto (Bosch), and tyres (Dunlop), manufactured most components themselves; but with the return of peace, the Netherlands Army began to acquire imported machines.

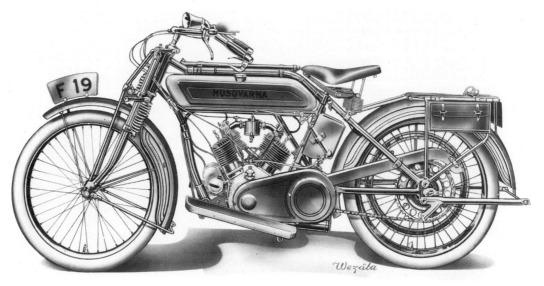

frame. Transmission ran via a leather belt from the engine pulley, providing a single speed to a wooden pulley on the rear wheel. With auxiliary cycle pedals and caliper brakes, little changed until 1909, when the Belgian engine was replaced by a V-twin 548cc design supplied by the Swiss factory of Moto-Reve. Close collaboration followed, and between 1909 and 1919, Husqvarna assembled ten different twin-cylinder models with the Moto-Reve engine.

Well suited to the climatic conditions and character of the Swedish terrain, Husqvarna received their first military order for motorcycles in 1916, when five machines were delivered to the Arms Supply Administration, Stockholm, on 20th December. An immediate success, a further 139 machines were procured before the end of the year, providing solo despatch and general liaison duties. Designated the Model 145A (A for Army), these machines were based on the civilian entries that had taken the first three places in the *Novemberkasen* (November Trophy) the previous month; Sweden's oldest reliability trial dating from the early 1900s.

By this date, the 548cc Moto-Reve V-twin (p 181) was coupled to a 3-speed gearbox, multi-plate clutch and full chain drive. Further advanced features included a kick-start acting on the gearbox mainshaft, automatic oil pump and a gear-driven Bosch magneto. Proving both robust and reliable, a further 315 machines were supplied in 1917, and another 27 in 1918.

Switzerland

Similarly to Sweden, Switzerland also maintained a fully equipped military force to preserve their neutrality, and from the turn of the century experimented with motorised transportation.

In 1907, a Volunteer Automobile Corps was formed within the Swiss Automobil Club. Very few motor vehicles were procured before 1914, when insufficient machines were available for requisition. Trucks and tractors were mainly supplied by the domestic factories of Berna and Saurer, and have since built many thousands more for the Swiss Army and export markets. Before 1918, Swiss military motorcycles were mainly imported, and it was not until the early 1920s that the domestic works of Condor and Motosacoche began to supply motorcycles to the Swiss Army (see chapter two).

VI: AMERICAN BEGINNINGS

Prior to 1910, the US Army did not have any particular policy for motor vehicles, and procure–

Above: **Early 1915, a Swiss despatch rider upon a Motosacoche 500cc V-twin model. Note the ski conversion for all-year military service.** *(Office Federal des Troupes de Transport)*

Left: **Early war years, Swiss mobile soldiers equipped with 1915 FN Four 500's (Belgian) and 1913 Wanderer 408's (German), in Romont, France. These well proven machines were both widely deployed by various armed forces throughout the First World War.** *(Office Federal des Troupes de Transport)*

ment lacked any order; by 1914, the US Army Quartermaster Corps had 35 trucks, 27 cars, and three ambulances, a further 26 trucks and ten cars were purchased that year. In addition the QMC had 15 trucks, eight cars, and one ambulance in the Philippines. During 1915 the QMC bought another 30 trucks. By this time the Navy had some 68 vehicles and the Marine Corps 72 machines, and an unspecified number of motorcycles. Between 1910 and 1916, the first attempts towards standardisation was introduced, but vehicles continued to be procured with little regard for spares, maintenance, or training procedures.

By 1916, US Marines stationed in Port-Au-Prince, Haiti, were using Indian motorcycles in their despatch and police duties in accordance with US foreign policy. These single-cylinder 500cc Indian machines, with auxiliary cycle pedals and rigid rear wheel, were some of the first motorcycles to be procured by the Marines. While troops were keeping order in Haiti, US Marines were also ordered ashore in the Dominican Republic in 1916 (also undergoing a revolution). Based upon the Gendarmerie d'Haiti, on 7th April 1917, the Guardia Nacional Dominicana (Dominican Constabulary) was formed. Ten Dominican towns were garrisoned, including Santiago, where the motorcycle squad of the 29th Marine Company also served. Providing despatch and police duties, these troops deployed the better known Indian 1000cc Power Plus model; widely used during the World War.

America declared war on Germany and Central Powers on 6th April 1917, but the US Army was still quite unprepared for any immediate service. During the Spring of 1916, Gen. Pershing had been sent into Mexico in pursuit of the revolutionary Doroteo Aranga (better known as Pancho Villa), and a small number of motor vehicles were hurriedly bought to give chase to the Mexican bandit. With a mixture of trucks, cars and motorcycles, this limited campaign marked the first occasion any US Army combat unit used motor vehicles under military field conditions.

A number of these early motorcycles were equipped with a sidecar mounted machine-gun, and the US Army was introduced to the advantages and limitations of powered transport. Deployed under harsh conditions and with the bare minimum of maintenance, Harley-Davidson, Indian, and a smaller number of Excelsior machines, offered a new form of mechanised warfare. While military modifications were largely restricted to fitting a lower gear ratio, for multi-terrain service, these heavyweight V-twin machines provided robust and reliable performance. (They never caught up with Pancho, but H-D were quick to use the expedition in advertising.)

The Big Three. Harley-Davidson, Indian & Excelsior

Following the Mexican campaign, the American Big Three took the initiative and began developing various military prototypes. Hendee Manufacturing (later known as the Indian Motorcycle Company), virtually abandoned their civilian market, with the intention to secure the maximum military work. In cooperation with the armed forces recruiting office, Hendee Manufacturing also trained some 3000 mechanics to service and repair motorcycles; not just Indians, but also Excelsior and Harley-Davidson machines.

Hendee Manufacturing decided it would be more economical to concentrate their production, at least for the duration of the war, rather than divide their military and commercial interests. They offered to supply 20,000 machines (their entire annual output) at the cut down price of $187.50 for a solo, and an additional $49.50 with a sidecar; these figures cut any profit thin,

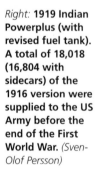

Right: **1919 Indian Powerplus (with revised fuel tank). A total of 18,018 (16,804 with sidecars) of the 1916 version were supplied to the US Army before the end of the First World War.** *(Sven-Olof Persson)*

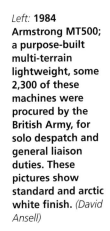

Below: **Graeme Brown's 1948 Douglas 600cc DV60;** a unique experimental design that did not reach production, with fully enclosed rear chain drive. *(David Ansell)*

Bottom: **1939 BSA 490cc M20;** a prewar machine of basic design, the M20 provided service in most parts of the world; an excellent compromise. *(Andrew Morland)*

Right: **1939 Matchless 350cc G3;** vertical ohv engine and 4-speed Burman gearbox, a combination developed until the mid 1950s. *(Andrew Morland)*

Above: **1939 BSA 490cc M20: widely used throughout the world, this machine has been prepared for military service in the deserts of North Africa. Note the pillion pad on the rear mudguard, a feature often adopted before a sprung saddle in the British services.** *(Andrew Morland)*

Left: **1980 Bombardier 250cc; designed and produced in Canada, with an Austrian engine and assembled in Britain, this multi-terrain lightweight was eventually adopted throughout the world. This is the Belgian version.** *(Forces Armées)*

Right: **1944 Excelsior 98cc Welbike; a droppable lightweight carried within a cylindrical container. A total of 3,840 were produced between 1942-45.**

Below: **1912 Triumph 3.5hp; with belt final drive and exposed electrics – how did these machines keep going through the mud of Flanders?** *(Both François-Marie Dumas)*

and Hendee remained alone in this decision. In direct response, while announcing their contribution to the war effort, Harley-Davidson began a massive sales campaign to recruit new dealers, with a particular interest in areas where Indian had been strongest. As civilian Indian machines began to dwindle, a large number of Indian dealers switched their allegiance to Harley-Davidson. At this time Harley-Davidson offered to supply 7000 machines to the US Army, while planning 10,000 for private owners, but by late 1917, the Milwaukee works offered half their production for military service.

Left: **Indian 1000cc Powerplus. April 1918, 2230, Pickens Street, Augusta, Georgia. The rider, an enlisted man from the 103rd Sanitary Train, a part of the 28th Infantry Division (Pennsylvania National Guard). In the sidecar, 1st Lt (Dr) Henry B Davis, also of the 103rd, and on his lap his son, Henry B Davis Jr, who kindly supplied this photograph.**

Left: **1921 Harley-Davidson 74, the first of a new series, set new standards in public service. The 74 was based upon the similar 987cc model widely adopted during the First World War.** *(Vehoniemen Automuseon)*

Below left: **A detailed view of Tony Silvey's Excelsior engine, clearly showing the exposed inlet-valve pushrods.** *(Tony Silvey)*

By the time peace was declared in 1918, the American motorcycle industry had received contracts to supply some 2600 Excelsior, 26,500 Harley-Davidson, 40,000 Indian (p 181), and 1500 Cleveland machines for the armed forces. With the exception of the Cleveland lightweight 221cc 2-stroke, virtually all machines were ordered with a sidecar attached, but even working at maximum capacity, by 31st December 1918, the US Forces had only received a total of 14,666 (14,332 sidecars) Harley-Davidson, 18,018 (16,804 sidecars) Indian and 1476 Cleveland machines, and all outstanding orders were cancelled. A limited number of Excelsior machines were supplied, but this figure has not been officially recorded.

The vast majority (some two thirds) of these machines remained in the USA, deployed in training and internal despatch duties, but some found their way to Europe and further afield. Many of these survived active service only to be left in vehicle dumps and eventually found by local civilians, while a large number in better condition were declared war-surplus and sold through civilian agents. A smaller number remained in various armed forces worldwide, and were seen in regular use well into the 1930s. The American V-twin motorcycle established an outstanding reputation, and provided a strong influence upon many manufacturers worldwide.

The military requirements of 1917–18 encouraged the American 'Big Three' to expand their facilities, improve efficiency and introduce better quality control, but the war years proved quite disastrous for Hendee Manufacturing. With the termination of all US military contracts in January 1919, the three factories had to re-direct their production towards civilian markets. Military profits had been disappointing (inflation wiped out Hendee's nominal profits), and having let their commercial dealer network collapse during the war, Hendee had neither the funds nor the support to maintain their pre-war position.

Excelsior and Harley-Davidson were on a far stronger footing and immediately began to take full advantage of the situation; Excelsior resumed their racing activities and gained the interest of many younger buyers (100,000 machines sold in 1919, with high export numbers), while the more conservative Harley-Davidson management concentrated on the utility market and began a strong advertising campaign to exploit the potential. Harley-Davidson grew from strength-to-strength, and during the Spring of 1919, export agencies were established in Australasia and Europe and Scandinavia.

Excelsior purchased the manufacturing rights to the Henderson Four in 1917, but despite their V-twin competition successes, the Chicago factory discontinued all further motorcycle output in the Autumn of 1931. Hendee, after various management changes and new financial investors, recovered some of their former market position, and became a major US military and police supplier under the Indian name, until their final demise in the 1950s. While Harley-Davidson and their international dealer network continued to provide well made motorcycles, that were easy to use and maintain, to military and police procurement groups in the USA and worldwide.

CHAPTER TWO

Interwar Years 1919-38

I GERMAN STRATEGY . . .

Following WW1, and side-stepping the conditions laid down in the Treaty of Versailles, Germany in the Nazi era developed military equipment under various guises. For example, commercial manufacturers were encouraged to develop 'experimental' vehicles, some examples of which appeared during military manoeuvres in the 1930s. During these preparations Germany assembled a vast reserve of military equipment, recognizing that the motorcycle offers remarkable flexibility for light and inexpensive go-anywhere messenger, passenger and general liaison transport. By 1937, Germany had one million motorcycles in military colours (Britain and France each had about 600,000). Creating larger civilian reserves of machines and mechanically experienced men, motorcycle units were organised by the Army, State Police, and private clubs alike, and their characteristics studied to determine all possible military potential.

While unable to match the carrying capacity of a car or truck, and without protection for the engine or rider in poor weather, the German High Command decided such deficiencies were more than compensated for in other ways. The small size of the motorcycle enabled easier camouflage, greater manoeuvrability and made it possible to bring troops closer to the front line. The light weight and narrow tread of the motorcycle enabled it to travel over almost any ground, and its greater speed and agility made possible the splitting of troops into smaller groups; making them less vulnerable to hostile fire from the ground or air.

The major problem with any motorcycle convoy was the considerable length of the column. With an average speed of between 30 and 60 km/h for the motorcycles and only 20 and 30 km/h for a convoy of cars and trucks, it was decided that the best measure of effectiveness was the time it required for an entire convoy to pass any given point, rather than its actual length. Whenever it became necessary to employ a swift and highly mobile force, or when required to operate under conditions where the situation or terrain was not well known, the motorcycle was seen as the best form of transport. German military advisors considered any future war would centre upon speed and there would not be the time to prepare obstacles, trenches, wire entanglements, minefields and firing positions; which the motorcycle would not realistically be expected to overcome.

Motorcycle strategy. Frontal attacks were to be carried by the traditional infantry, brought to the front line in large numbers by car and truck, and then reinforced with tanks and artillery. With greater mobility and being less vulnerable from ground or air attacks, motorcycles would then be brought into action through the gaps created

during the first attack. Operating in close liaison with tanks, motorcycle units were trained to then widen the breach and move against hostile reserves. With a particular interest in the cross-country capability of the motorcycle, motorcycles were also attached to transport reserves, senior commanders, and used for general despatch and reconnaissance duties.

With an acute shortage of horses during the 1920s, and high cost for fodder and bedding, by 1937, the German Army did not maintain a single cavalry division; having only one brigade of three regiments in East Prussia. A representative of the German War Office at this time stated "Our decision in this matter is a clear cut one. We are accepting the principle of mechanisation in total". At first, the majority of military motor-cycles were standard production models, but by the late 1930s, a number of manufacturers introduced features to meet military requirements. Throughout the 1920s the majority of these were purchased from NSU, Victoria, and Wanderer, but within a decade this situation changed, and the factories of BMW, DKW, TWN, and Zün-dapp became leading suppliers.

Victoria

Founded in Nuremburg by Max Frankenburger and Max Offenstein in 1886, the Victoria bicycle factory introduced their first motorcycle some 13 years later; with a single-cylinder proprietary engine. Similar machines continued to be pro-duced until 1920, when the works introduced a new heavyweight model, with a horizontally opposed twin-cylinder BMW engine. Unlike the now familiar transverse layout, these early 493cc (68 x 68mm) sv unit were mounted in line with the frame. Designed by Martin Stolle and desig-nated the M2B15, the same 6.5hp engine was supplied to Bison, SBD, SMW, and other smaller Austrian and German factories of the early 1920s. Known as the Victoria KR-I, the model had the outward appearance of the British Douglas; with an exposed external flywheel, belt final drive, 2-speed gearbox, parallelogram front forks and a rigid rear wheel. Further features included foot boards, deep mudguards, high handlebars, and block brakes on the rear wheel.

In 1923, BMW began their own motorcycle production, but Victoria engaged the services of Stolle, and his co-worker Max Fritz; and a new series of ohv engines were introduced. The units were to be manufactured by the Wilhelm Sedl-bauer Works in Munich, but the factory could not cope with demand, and Victoria AG bought the business and moved the production equip-ment to Nuremburg. With the new 499cc (70.5 x 64mm) ohv engine, but retaining the belt final drive and 2-speed gearbox. The Victoria KR-II remained very similar, but in 1924, the KR-III adopted a 3-speed gearbox, and later versions had a chain final drive. The ohv gear was now fully enclosed and the engine could offer 12hp at 2600rpm. The rear wheel had an internal expanding drum brake.

By the mid 1920s, Victoria AG had some 2500 employees, and with an annual output of 150,000 machines, the factory became a major supplier to the German Army. Stolle left the works in 1925, but the KR series remained in production for a number of years; between 1927–32, the Victoria KR-VI (p 186) was supplied in large numbers, providing solo and sidecar military service. The KR-VI had an enlarged 598cc version of the ohv

Right: **1936-1937 Victoria KR-9, an unusual middleweight model with fully enclosed engine and chain final drive, a mixture of tubular and pressed steel design. Note the combined leg shields and running boards, and hand pump mounted on front forks.** *(Sven-Olof Persson)*

engine, with a 3-speed gearbox, chain drive, and internal expanding drum brake front and rear. Military conversion was largely restricted to additional panniers, full lighting, horn, and service library.

The Victoria KR-VI also provided the basis for an experimental military model with two smaller rear wheels in tandem. The two rear wheels were chain-drive with a caterpillar track to increase multi-terrain capabilities and carry two passengers at a time. The KR-VI in-line three-wheeler, however, remained a prototype only, along with a number of similar prototypes produced by different companies worldwide.

The KR-VI was superseded by the completely revised KR-6 (p 186), and between 1933–38, the new model was supplied to the German Army. With a fully enclosed external flywheel, 4-speed gearbox, shorter wheelbase, higher ground clearance, saddle fuel tank, and increased output from 16 to 18hp at 3800rpm, a number of the KR-6 machines remained in use throughout World War 2. During the same period, between 1936–37, a smaller number of the Victoria KR-9s were also supplied. The in-line opposed twin-cylinder engine had been re-designed as a 498cc parallel twin-cylinder unit mounted with a forward incline.

The *Wehrmacht* (1935–45) was particularly interested in the fully enclosed chain final drive and enclosed engine side panels (with leg shields and foot boards). Like many contemporary German manufacturers, Victoria adopted a pressed-steel and tubular frame for the KR-9; with pressed-steel parallelogram front forks and a rigid rear wheel, inverted handlebar levers and fully enclosed control cables.

During the war, however, Victoria concentrated production onto the KR35WH model; a more conventional 'sports lightweight' machine with a vertical single cylinder 350cc ohv engine. For the *Wehrmacht* the exhaust system was mounted low, a tool-box was set into the fuel tank, a pillion saddle mounted on the rear mudguard, and a pair of leather panniers adopted. Alongside the DKW RT125 and NZ350, the KR35WH was one of the few German motorcycles to remain in production until the end of the war (see chapter 3).

BMW

Following the rapid expansion of the German Air Force, BMW *Bayerische Motoren Werke GmbH* came into existence on 29 July 1917; developing and producing a range of outstanding aircraft engines. But in accordance with the Treaty of Versailles, BMW had to abandon interest in aircraft development. Materials originally intended for aircraft engines were diverted into agricultural

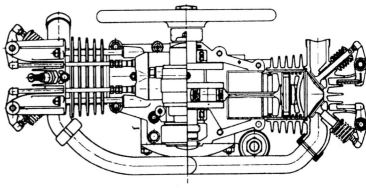

Above: **1927-32 Victoria KR-VI engine detail, presenting the units fully exposed flywheel, valve springs, and push-rods.** *(Sven-Olof Persson)*

designs, tool boxes, and even office equipment. After many months, BMW returned to engine production, with a new design from chief designer Max Fritz for heavy trucks, buses and boats, and in 1920, the works began to experiment with their first motorcycle. This lightweight had a Kurier 148cc 2-stroke engine and belt final drive. Sold under the name of Klink, the machine was not a success, and discontinued.

The next year, BMW designer Martin Stolle developed a 494cc (68 x 68mm) sv engine; an in-line flat 2-cylinder unit for either chain or belt final drive. Sold as a proprietary unit, in 1922, the design was used by BMW to power the Helios motorcycle. Although the complete machine was assembled at the Munich works, the Helios was not a BMW design, and once again it was not a very good motorcycle. Max Fritz, however, realised the design had some potential, and when his work was finally unveiled at the Paris Show in 1923, the foundation of many years of BMW motorcycle success had been established. Designated the R32, the engine had been remounted across the cycle frame, with a unit construction 3-speed gearbox and shaft final-drive; a layout to which BMW remained singularly faithful for some 60 years, when the factory finally diversified with the introduction of the flat-4 K series. By the early 1990s, however, the boxer engine was back, albeit completely re-engineered with 4-valve cylinder heads and electronic fuel injection.

While the R32 could not provide the performance of many of its contemporaries, it had a rugged reliability seldom associated with motorcycles, and it was only a few years before BMW became a major supplier to the German Army. Max Fritz returned to aircraft production in 1924 (when Treaty restriction were lifted), and the next year Rudolf Schleicher introduced the R37, with an ohv version that could produce 16hp; nearly double that of the K32. Various lightweights followed and within four years BMW had assembled its 25,000th motorcycle.

Retaining the basic R32 design (a triangulated tubular frame with leaf sprung front forks), in 1928, the first 750cc BMW model R62 (p 184), and smaller version 500cc (78 x 63mm) R52

were introduced. Providing solo and sidecar duties alike, these were the first BMW motorcycles to be supplied for military service. The following year, these machines were replaced by the BMW R11; with the first pressed steel cycle frame design in the world. While adopting the R62 engine and gearbox, between 1929–34, a total of five different R11 models were purchased by the *Reichswehr*, for despatch, reconnaissance, and personnel transportation.

By the late 1920s, the Great Depression had hit BMW, and in 1931 the factory introduced the R2; a commuter lightweight with a vertical single-cylinder 198cc (63 x 64mm) ohv engine. The similar, but larger R4 appeared in 1932, with a 398cc (78 x 84mm) ohv engine, and between 1932–36, the larger lightweights were also supplied to the *Reichswehr*. By 1933, the year Hitler came to political power, BMW had almost recovered from the financial crisis, and within 2 years the R11 was replaced by the R12 (p 185); the most successful BMW motorcycle of the inter-war years, with a total of 36,000 built before 1938.

While not the first motorcycle with telescopic front forks, it was the first production model to incorporate hydraulic damping. The R12 retained the pressed-steel frame and overall performance of the R11, but was also the first BMW motorcycle to have a 4-speed gearbox and interchangeable wheels. Purchased by the German post-office, police, and armed forces, the public service R12 continued to be built until 1941.

In 1938, BMW assembled their 100,000th motorcycle, and the 745cc R71, and smaller version 600cc (70 x 78mm) R61 models were introduced; the last BMW motorcycles to adopt a sv design. With the re-introduction of the tubular cycle frame, these machines were equipped with telescopic front forks and a plunger-type rear suspension. Both models had twin carburettors as standard (optional for the R12). Limited numbers were immediately procured by the *Reichswehr*, for both solo and sidecar use, alongside the ageing R12 until 1941. The BMW sv models remained popular military machines until the introduction of the purpose-built military R75 model in 1941 (see chapter three).

To replace the R4 lightweight, the R35 appeared in 1937; and was also prepared in military finish. While retaining the earlier pressed-steel frame and rigid rear wheel, the machine had undamped telescopic front forks. The machine was too heavy for the 340cc, 72 x 84mm ohv engine to support, and with the additional weight of military accessories (pillion saddle and leather panniers), the R35 was generally disliked in military service.

Zündapp

An amalgamation of three factories during World War 1, *Zünder und Apparatebau GmbH* shortened to Zündapp, was founded in Nuremburg in September 1917 to produce fuses for artillery shells. With the return of peace-time production the company did not have the expertise to prepare for the commercial market, and in 1919, Zündapp became part of the Dr. Fritz Neumeyer empire; which included cable and radio, tractors and rolling stock.

Neumeyer provided Zündapp with the financial support to take a new direction, and in the autumn of 1921, the Nuremburg factory built its first motorcycle. Designated the Z22, the first

machine had a single-cylinder 211cc three port two-stroke engine, produced by the British Levis factory. Providing 2¼hp to the rear wheel via a belt final-drive, this simple machine proved popular, and by October 1922, 1000 had been assembled. Within two years Zündapp introduced assembly-line production, and had built more than 10,000 machines with engines of their own design. From 1926, Zündapp began to establish a nationwide dealer network, and with sales continuing to rise, a total of 16,877 Zündapp motorcycles were sold in 1928. That year the four congested Zündapp factories moved into a single purpose-built manufacturing base at Nuremburg-Schweinau, and in just seven years Zündapp moved from obscurity to a leading German motorcycle force.

In April 1929, Zündapp set a new monthly record of more than 4000 machines, and then the great depression hit Germany. With more than 5½ million Germans unemployed, Zündapp could no longer maintain such production; only 300 machines were assembled during December that year. For the following four years Zündapp faced an impossible position, but the company was able to design new models.

By 1933, the German economy had made a strong recovery, and Zündapp introduced the 'K' series; the K400 (398cc), K500 (498cc), K600 (598cc) models with sv boxer twin-cylinder engines, and the K800 (791cc), with a sv boxer 4-cylinder unit (pp 186-87). These designs were all mounted transversely over a pressed-steel frame, with pressed steel parallelogram front forks. Transmission ran via an unusual, but successful, chain and sprocket 4-speed gearbox, with an exposed shaft final drive to a rigid rear wheel. The models, designed by Richard Kuchen, proved both robust and reliable, and were used in large numbers by the German post office, police and military.

A new small capacity 2-stroke model also appeared that year. Designated the K200, the machine had a vertical single-cylinder 198cc engine, also mounted within a pressed steel frame and parallelogram front forks, and a shaft final-drive. Far too heavy for the engine output, the K200 was discontinued the following year, and the factory introduced the DB200 in 1935. Based upon the DB175 of 1933, the lightweight had a more traditional tubular frame, with pressed-steel front forks, and chain final-drive. The popular DB200 remained in production until 1940 (re-introduced in 1947–51), and was used by the *Wehrmacht* during 'Blitzkrieg'. Military modifications came down to a pair of leather pannier bags and livery.

Zündapp sales continued to rise, and in 1937, the Nuremburg-Schweinau factory was enlarged with a second complex. The following year the company became officially known as the Zündapp Werke GmbH, but as Hitler and the Nazi Party prepared the country for World War 2, military requirements governed Zündapp output and German industry in general. With limitations on raw materials, engineering production was dominated by military demands, but Zündapp introduced several more motorcycles before the hostilities of September 1939, including the KS600 (p 187), an ohv version of the earlier K600. The factory continued to produce motorcycles throughout World War 2.

NSU, DKW & Triumph

These three well established motorcycle companies manufactured models continuously with varying success well into and beyond the war years. The DKW NZ350 and NZ500 2-strokes followed the company's well-known preference for 2-stroke engines for both vehicle and motorcycle use (p 184). NSU pursued their policy of ohv high-performance 4-strokes, the 251OS and 601OSL being produced in quantity.

Of unusual technical interest was the Triumph BD250W of 1938 (p 186), which was manufactured until 1945. With a split-single 2-stroke engine it was probably unique as the only non-prototype machine with a rotary valve. Austrian Puch machines of the same period also used the split-single arrangement, as did the mid-fifties British EMC with twin pistons on a Y-shaped connecting rod. (See also Puch.)

Austria

In the period running-up to 1938, Austria was of course under German influence and control, so much of the country's motorcycle production destined for military service found its way into the *Wehrmacht*. Technically, several models were of note: the 1936 Puch type 800 V-four of 800cc mounted transversely in a combined press-steel and tubular frame (p 182).

Following in 1937 and '38 were two split-single 2-strokes, also from Puch, the earlier model of 200cc and the later of 350cc. An unusual twin-piston arrangement with a Y-shaped connecting rod, which gave improved gas-flow characteristics. The British EMC of the early '50s was designed by a Dr. Ehrlich, no doubt responsible for, or influential upon, the two Puch 2-stroke models. All three models had another unusual feature, the rear-wheel hub-located clutch.

II EASTERN EUROPE . . .

By the end of the First World War, established trading agreements worldwide had been broken; for some four years production had centred upon

P5472

war supplies and capital investments abroad had been sold, abandoned or lost. The United States, parts of the British Empire, Japan, and some South American countries began a rapid programme of industrial expansion to meet domestic military demands. With the return of peacetime production many world markets changed location; newly independent countries introduced new tariff barriers. Eastern Europe began to trade more freely, while Russia, in the grip of the Bolshevik Revolution, became more isolated. The United States began to trade directly with South America and the Far East, while Japan established commercial links with North and South America, and many factories in Australasia, Europe and India. Western Europe remained one of the largest industrial markets in the world, but could no longer be considered the centre of worldwide industrial development.

Without domestic manufacturing, Russia had imported vast quantities of military equipment to maintain its war effort, and by the time the Tsar was compelled to abdicate on 17th March 1917, the old regime faced financial ruin and total collapse. The provisional liberal leaders, under Prince Luov, declared the country a republic, and wanted to establish a democracy, but sharing common ground with the Allies, proclaimed their intention to continue the war against Germany. The Bolsheviks were in exile, but Lenin prepared a four point programme; land for the peasants, food for the starving, power to the Soviets, and peace with Germany. The next month the German government offered the Bolshevik leaders a safe passage from Switzerland to Russia through Germany in a sealed train, and in return Trotsky signed a peace agreement with German High Command at Brest-Litovsk in March 1918.

Many foreign armed forces were sent in opposition to the Bolsheviks. Expeditionary troops from America, Britain, and France were sent to North Russia, while American and Japanese troops were sent to Siberia, and a larger force of Austrian soldiers (ex-prisoners known as the Czech Legion) were involved in the Russo-Finnish and Russo-Polish wars; the last of these foreign contingents did not leave Russia until late 1922. It is against this background and that of Stalin's Five-Year Plans, from 1928 to 1950, that the development of the motorcycle in the eastern bloc must be understood.

Motorcycles were ridden in Russia as early as 1894, but these machines were imported by individuals or speculative dealers. Two- and three-wheeled vehicles from America and Europe became increasingly popular, until 1913, when steps to produce the first Russian-built motorcycle began. With bought-in components from the Swiss proprietary engine works of Moto-Reve, and Latvian bicycle factory Alexander Leytner & Co, a lightweight machine was to be assembled at Dukes factory in Moscow. With the outbreak of World War 1 this project was halted; it was not until after the Socialist Revolution, and following civil war, that plans for a domestic motorcycle industry returned.

In 1924, under the direction of P. L. L'vov, a group of engineers in Moscow introduced a motorcycle known as the Soyuz (Union). Fitted with plunger-type rear suspension, this machine had a 500cc (80 x 100mm) single cylinder ohv engine. Front suspension was provided by a leaf-sprung trailing-link fork, and transmission ran through a 3-speed hand-change gearbox and exposed chain drive. Further advanced features included a saddle-type fuel tank, rear drum brake, and handlebar-end control levers. Manufacture began the following year, but the factory then decided upon a change of policy, and the Soyuz was discontinued.

Forged-Steel Design

Four years later, a second team of designers was set up at the Izhevsk Steel Plant, in Ustinov, under the direction of P. V. Mozharov. That year the new group designed, manufactured, and tested five new motorcycles; known as the Izh-1, Izh-2, Izh-3, Izh-4, and Izh-5. The first two had a V-twin engine of 1200cc, mounted across a forged-steel frame of massive proportions. The unit-construction engine and 3-speed gearbox provided some 24hp and top speed of about 65km/h. Gear-change was by hand, the final drive by exposed shaft, and the wheels were interchangeable. No rear suspension, but the front forks had a leading-link leaf-sprung design.

The frame was of such large proportions, the lower members were also used as the exhaust system. This lumbering giant was often used with a sidecar attached, which may well have been the best way to control the machine; with a wheelbase of 1400mm and wheels of 27 x 4". At that time it was not possible to start full production at Izhevsk (probably just as well) and these machines also were discontinued.

DKW influence. The Mozharov design group moved to Leningrad, where they concentrated on various 2-stroke lightweights. The first batch of 25 were assembled in September 1930, and after trials the model went into full production the next month. Designated the L-300, this simple 300cc 2-stroke became the first mass-produced motorcycle in the Soviet Union. The machine was a mixture of forged-steel and tubular construction, with girder-type front forks and a rigid rear wheel: similar to many DKW designs of the period. Producing 6hp at 3000rpm and a top speed of 75km/h/46mph, transmission ran through a 3-speed separate unit with hand-change gearbox, and exposed chain final drive.

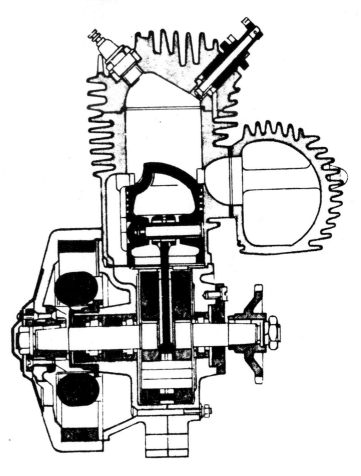

Also in 1930, a further team of engineers known as the Ukremto Enterprise assembled a similar lightweight; designated KhMZ-1M. This machine had a single-cylinder sv engine with a displacement of 347cc and a power output of 9hp. But by May 1931, only six of these machines had been assembled, before the project was abandoned.

A special committee for motorcycle engineering was set up at the Heavy Engineering People's Commissariat the next year, and this team organised a further enterprise in 1933. The test workshops of the Izhevsk Steel Plant became known as the Izhevsk Motorcycle Works, and in a short time the proven L-300 model began to be produced in quantity; eventually re-named the Izh-7. With an ever-growing reputation, the machine

Right: **1933-40 L-300.** The test workshops of the Izhevsk Steel Plant became known as the Izhevsk Motorcycle Works in 1933, and within a short period the L-300 became a major success. *(Frank Nyklicek)*

Below right: **1933-40 L-300,** later known as the Izh-7. The model was widely deployed by the Red Army for solo despatch and general liaison duties during the Second World War. *(Jacek Gorski)*

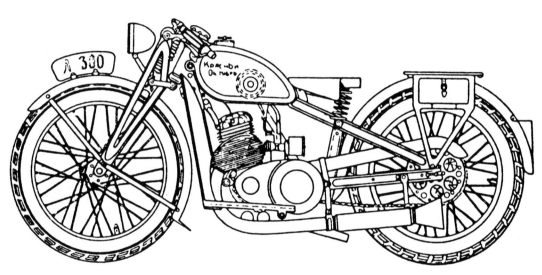

Below: **1935-36 PMZ A750,** originally known as the NATI A750, and produced at the Izhevsk Steel Works. After tests and modifications the model was transferred to the Podolsky factory. *(Frank Nyklicek)*

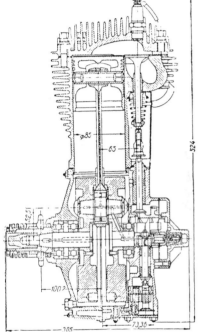

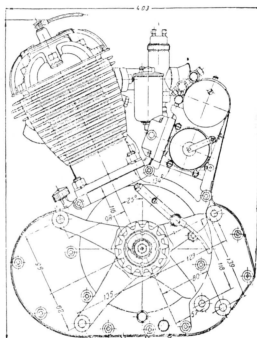

Left: **TIM-AM600. The first Soviet motorcycle to adopt a tubular cycle frame, the military version was often equipped with a machine-gun upon the handlebars; a solo attack vehicle.** *(Jacek Gorski)*

Centre left: **1936-42 TIM-AM600 engine detail. Following contemporary British design, a forward sloping single-cylinder side valve unit, with a separate three-speed gearbox.** *(Jacek Gorski)*

Bottom left: **1936-42 TIZ AM600, a popular middleweight deployed by the Red Army, providing solo despatch, reconnaissance, and armed attack units; a machine-gun was mounted on the handlebars.** *(Frank Nyklicek)*

was soon in great demand, and as recently as 1995 the factory received letters from happy Izh-7 owners.

During this period, a heavyweight motorcycle with a sidecar was being designed by the automotive industry's technical institute, the Scientific Research Car and Tractor Institute, later to be superseded by the Central Red Labour Banner Scientific Research Automobile and Vehicle Institute. In 1933, four of these NATI-A750 motorcycles were also assembled at the Izhevsk factory to a design provided by the Institute, but after tests and minor modifications final production was transferred to the Podolsky works. Redesignated the PMZ-A750, the machine had a V-twin 750cc engine and 4-speed hand-change gearbox, mounted in-line with a pressed-steel frame, with leaf-sprung, trailing-link front forks and rigid rear wheel (p 189).

The first Soviet motorcycle to adopt a tubular frame, the TIZ-AM600 of the Tagnarog factory was introduced in 1935. Very similar to

contemporary western design, this middle-weight had a forward-sloping single-cylinder 600cc (85 x 108mm) sv engine and separate unit 4-speed gearbox with hand-change. Equipped with girder-type front forks and a rigid rear wheel, the AM600 quickly became known as a robust and reliable performer, and remained in production until 1943.

Military Potential

With only limited roads suitable for motor vehicles, the traditional cavalry had been maintained in reduced numbers, to be deployed with a growing number of motorised units and artillery. Motorcycles became known as the 'Wheeled Cavalry', and with such a limited domestic industry, all Soviet motorcycle factories supplied machines at some time, based upon the L-300 (Izh-7), PMZ-A750, and TIM-AM600 models (p 189).

Other 2-strokes, similar to the L-300, were the Izh-8 and the Izh-9. Both had a single-cylinder 293cc (74 x 68mm) unit, with an external flywheel. The engine had a twin-ported exhaust system, and gave 9hp at 4000rpm, offering a top speed of about 90 km/h/60mph. These machines were seen as suitable for the Red Army and were used as lightweight despatch models throughout World War 2.

The Izh-12 was introduced in 1941, with a single-cylinder two-stroke 346cc (72 x 85mm) engine, able to produce 13.5hp and a top speed of 105km/h/65mph. Within days of its introduction, however, all motorcycle production ceased at the Izhevsk Works, and not for the first time the factory had to produce weapons. Too late for

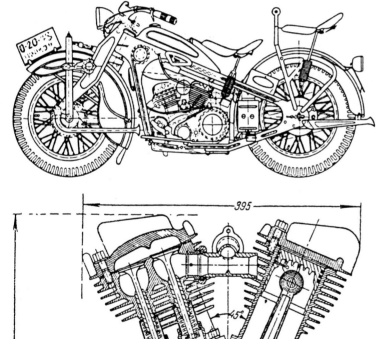

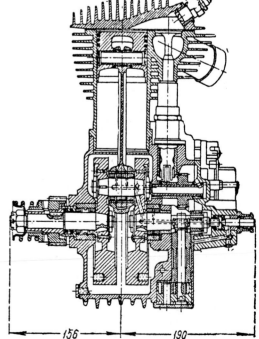

military duties, the Izh-12 was re-introduced after the war as the Izh-49; with a revised frame, telescopic front forks and a plunger-type rear suspension. The most widely used Soviet military motor-cycle was the flat-twin sidecar outfit designated the M-72, which was based on the BMW R71, built under licence at the Iskra Zavad plant in Moscow from 1939. It remained in production throughout the war (see chapter three).

Poland

Some years earlier, chief engineer B. Fuksievich, of the *PZInz; Panstwowych Zakladow Inzynierii* (State Engineering Enterprise) in Warsaw, received instructions to produce a heavyweight motorcycle and sidecar outfit for the Polish Army; to be based upon the Harley-Davidson frame, and Indian engine and transmission. In reality, the project entailed little more than detailed measurement of the two machines, with only minor modifications.

Produced by the *Centraine Warsztaty Samochodowe* (Central Cars Workshop) and designated the CWS M55 series S-0, the first 50 machines were introduced 1928/29 (the first motorcycles to be mass produced by the state industry), but during trials various defects were found.

The project was reconsidered, however, and an experienced engineer Stanislav Malendovich, was appointed to analyse the parts prone to failure. Many engine and transmission changes were made, and in 1931, the CWS M55 series S-III was introduced.

The model offered both improved performance and a stronger frame, and was immediately purchased by the Polish Army. Although manufactured by CWS, the S-III adopted a number of imported parts; tyres, electrical components, carburettor, speedometer and bearings. Proving reliable, the Polish Army obtained the entire production, with several machines supplied to each armoured battalion.

Within a few months, however, an improved replacement was being prepared, known as the CWS M-III (p 188). Full output began the next year with few changes, and some 4000 machines were produced before the country fell to the *Wehrmacht*.

The new machine had the outward appearance of its predecessor, but with modifications a significant increase in power output was available from the same cubic capacity.

Probably influenced by the success of a new touring machine, the Sokol (Falcon) 600 RT/211, the CWS M-III adopted the commercial name of Sokol 1000 M-III and a few machines found their way onto the civilian market. The CWS M-III or Sokol 1000 M-III was exclusively for sidecar use. The sidecar wheel brake was coupled with the motorcycle rear wheel. A limited number of later machines also had a sidecar wheel drive. Produced for military transport reconnaissance duties, the M-III was also used for armaments transportation, and as a mobile machine-gun vehicle.

In addition to the purpose-built M-III, the Polish Army procured a number of domestic commercial motorcycles; Sokol 600 RT/211 (from 1936), MOJ 130 (from 1937), Sokol 200 M411 (from 1938), and a number of 2-stroke lightweights from domestic manufacturers Niemen, Perkun, Podkowa, SHL, Tornedo, WPN and Zuch (p 188); all of which had a single-cylinder 98cc (Villiers) unit.

Supplied in limited numbers, the larger Sokol machines were deployed for solo/sidecar despatch, convoy control, and military police duties, while the remainder provided short distance messenger services.

Below: **A restored CWS MIII (Falcon 1000). A mixture of Harley-Davidson and Indian influence, this machine was produced for the Polish military, police and postal service. Eventually some 4000 were assembled between 1934-39.** (Jacek Gorski)

Bottom: **A restored Sokol 600RT M211, later known as the Falcon 600, the second motorcycle (after the CWS MIII) of the Polish Army interwar.** (Jacek Gorski)

Czechoslovakia

(Czech & Slovak Republics from 1.1.93)

In October 1918, Bohemia, Moravia and Slovakia, united to form Czechoslovakia; long since an industrialised region. It is generally accepted the Nesselsdorfer Works assembled their first horseless carriage in 1897, and the Laurin & Klement (see under Austria – Chapter 1) company produced their first motorcycle in 1899. Even earlier motor vehicles have been discovered, but these were not commercially produced. The L & K factory provided the foundation for the AZNP works, from which Skoda production became famous. In 1923, the Nesselsdorfer Works provided the original assembly line for the Tatra truck business; the backbone of domestic and armed forces vehicle manufacture.

(In keeping with this engineering tradition, the National Technical Museum, Prague, held an exhibition for the centenary of the motor car in 1986 and, following its success, the more remarkable 'Motorcycles of Prague' exhibition the next year.) It is believed that around 120 motorcycle manufacturers have appeared in Czechoslovakia. While many remained unknown outside Prague, others, such as Praga, Jawa, and Walter, gained both national and international fame.

The newly formed Czechoslovakia armed forces procured a wide range of domestic commercial motorcycles, for solo despatch and general liaison, with a limited number of sidecar models. The majority were CZ (175cc:1934, 250cc:1936, & 350cc:1938), and Jawa (350cc SV:1934 & 175cc:1937), but military motorcycles were also supplied by Itar (744cc:1921), BD (500cc:1926), Praga (500cc:1928) (p 183), and Ogar (250cc:1937). Czechoslovak military motorisation remained very limited throughout the inter-war years; only 1238 motorcycles were available for active service in 1939. Under Nazi occupation, however, all military equipment was confiscated, and a motorisation programme was ordered; including the CZ 175cc & 350cc Jawa 175cc, 250cc, & 350cc, and Ogar 250cc motorcycle models for the *Wehrmacht* and Axis armed forces.

CZ

With the disintegration of the Austro-Hungarian Empire, the *CZ; Ceska Zbrojovka* (Czech Arms Factory), Strakonice, was founded to equip the Czechoslovak military. The company established an excellent reputation, also for armaments. By 1929, CZ had bought a bicycle workshop in Kralupy nad Vltavou and another in Jince-Cenkov. Within four years the first CZ motorcycle was assembled and exhibited at the Prague Design Fair in 1933; a 98cc single-cylinder 2-stroke model, with front fork suspension. Apart from the engine bearings and magneto, the entire machine had been built at Strakonice.

The next year a 175cc model (p 183) was ready for production. This machine had a unit construction single cylinder 2-stroke engine and a 3-speed gearbox, mounted in a pressed-steel duplex cradle frame. In 1936 the CZ 250cc was introduced. With a very similar appearance to the smaller 175cc, both models remained in simultaneous

Right: **1935-37 CZ 175. A popular model within the Czechoslovak Army, widely deployed for lightweight despatch and general liaison. Minimal military conversion included an overall coat of service livery. Under Nazi rule the machine was also produced for the *Wehrmacht* and their partners.**
(*Frank Nyklicek*)

production until 1939. Shortly before the war a 350cc model was introduced, as well as an unusual 500cc twin-cylinder 2-stroke model.

Jawa

While CZ was developing a utility lightweight motorcycle, Frantisek Janecek, a young entrepreneurial engineer of considerable success, also considered motorcycle production. By the late 1920s, such manufacturers as Cechie, Itar, Orion and Walter, and above all Praga and Premier, produced both popular and advanced machines. During the latter inter-war years, however, without adequate finance, the majority of Czechoslovak

Above: **1938 CZ 500cc. Procured in limited numbers by the Czechoslovak Army, a number were also pressed into service by the** *Wehrmacht.* *(Frank Nyklicek)*

Left: **Official factory photograph of 1935-37 CZ 175, a standard production model procured by the Czechoslovak Army.** *(Frank Nyklicek)*

Bottom left: **1935 CZ 175. This detailed view of restored model clearly shows the simplicity of the unit construction design, and twin port cylinder head.** *(Frank Nyklicek)*

Moto Jawa 175 ccm pro zábavu a povolání za Kč 4650:-
Zbrojovka ING. F. JANEČEK Praha-Nusle II.

factories could not meet a production run of a few thousand and motorcycles were largely imported from Britain and America. Janecek decided to face this situation with a domestic machine, based upon a well proven model, and eventually bought a licence for the Wanderer 500 ohv motorcycle from Germany (see Chapter 1).

For many years Wanderer continued to develop their V-twin 4-stroke series, but in 1927, a new 500cc (84 x 90mm) single-cylinder ohv model was introduced to widen their market. However, at a time when Wanderer faced a financial loss to cover guarantee repairs, Janecek showed an interest in a licence for the new 500cc model. The German business wanted to make a complete break from two-wheel transport, and sold the Prague company the licence and plant and parts for all their motorcycles.

In Prague a new trademark was proposed, and the Jawa name appeared for the first time; the first two letters of the names Janecek and Wanderer. For the home customers the name had a foreign feel, as the letter W does not exist in Czec. While it is possible the new model also underwent military trials, Janecek quickly realised the model was a commercial failure and it was discontinued in 1931 with a total of 1016 built. Following numerous changes the model gained some popularity, but the heavy and costly machine was introduced at a time of worldwide economic depression, and the Janecek dream of mass production was postponed.

In 1931, the third year of Jawa motorcycles, the company's profit from armament sales was double that for their motorcycles, but after a number of prototypes, Jawa returned to the motorcycle market with a lightweight 175cc 2-stroke design. The machine had a single cylinder Villiers (57 x 67mm) unit with a flywheel magneto and deflector piston crown. An immediate success, the model remained in production until 1946, with minor changes each year, and eventually 27,535 were built.

This model, more than any other, began to redress Czechoslovak domestic sales. To maintain their 1932 production, Britain supplied the engine, gearbox, wheel hubs, brakes, magneto, headlamp, carburettor, and chain, but by 1933, many of these components were also produced by Jawa. The engine was built under licence, and only the magneto, carburettor, and drive chain continued to be imported. For the first time, Jawa motorcycle profits exceeded armaments. The Czechoslovak motorcycle industry was hit hard by the Economic Depression, and many factories collapsed at this time, but Jawa continued to cut their unit costs, the 175cc (p 183) was introduced in 1932, and in 1934, a new 350cc model was added with a vertical single-cylinder

350cc (70 x 90mm) sv engine and hand-change 3-speed gearbox, mounted in a pressed steel frame.

By 1935, the 350cc sv model was also available with an ohv conversion. Jawa dominated the domestic market, but continued to develop new machines. Shortly before the war, Jawa introduced the Duplex-Block; a single-cylinder 2-stroke 250cc (68 x 68mm) based upon the existing 250cc model, but the engine was modified so the gearbox, while remaining a separate unit, was integral with the engine. Limited numbers were supplied for military service, but as the final model before the war, the Duplex-Block provided the foundation for Jawa post-war production, and the international acclaim that was to follow (see Chapter 4).

Ogar

Manufactured by Machek & Company, Prague, the first Ogar motorcycle was not assembled until 1934, but gained public interest immediately. At this time the Jawa 175 was the most common motorcycle in the country; the only major rival to the larger and more expensive 350cc and 500cc machines. With a single cylinder 2-stroke 250cc (68 x 68mm) engine, the Ogar was the country's first 250cc motorcycle produced in quantity. It was able to provide more performance than the smaller Jawa, at a similar price.

The small factory was tooled up for a substantial production run, which reduced the cost of individual parts, and a number of features were adopted to keep working components to a minimum. A 2-speed gearbox was set within a unit construction crankcase and lubricated by the same oil and petrol mixture required by the 2-stroke engine. The design had constant mesh gearing with a sliding claw gear-change device and a 4-plate clutch on the end of the crankshaft. This unusual arrangement demanded that the rider had to remember to leave the engine in gear from previous use and, with the clutch held in, the kick-start was brought into action. Such a sequence must have caused a few accidents, with the rear wheel spinning before the unwary rider was correctly seated.

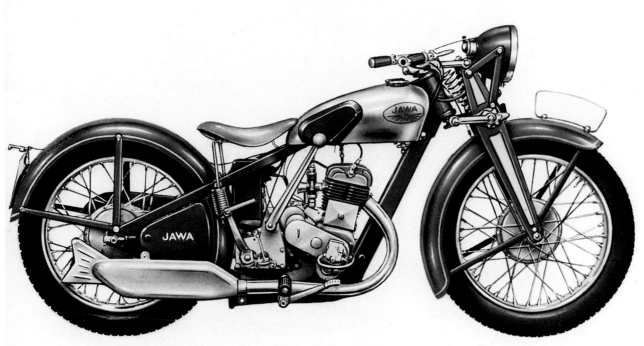

Right: **Autfit AS, Prague, clearly presenting their military involvement during the late 1930s; a silhouette of an Ogar 4 against the outline of a Czechoslovak Tankette.** *(Frank Nyklicek)*

Below: **1937 Ogar 4 in an original factory drawing. Widely deployed by the Czechoslovak Army, it was also produced under German rule during the War. Note side-mounted carburettor and mixture of tubular cycle frame and pressed steel front forks.** *(Frank Nyklicek)*

Jako by dovedl šplhat, tak le˙ce překonává každé stoupání a prokazuje svoji spolehlivost v nejtěžš.m teré˛u. Jeho rychlost jest obdivuhodná – spotřeba nepatrná. I při vytrvalostních jízdách skýtá nejvyšší pohodlí. Svoji elegancí a vyspě-lou výpravou jest chloubou svého majitele a přece není drahý. Síla, spolehlivost, krása a vytrvalost čini ho motocyklem náročných jezdců.

Kdo chce jezdit dobře, jezdi na Ogaru, symbolu mládí!

Ogar

AUTFIT A. S. PRAHA XII, ŘÍMSKÁ 20

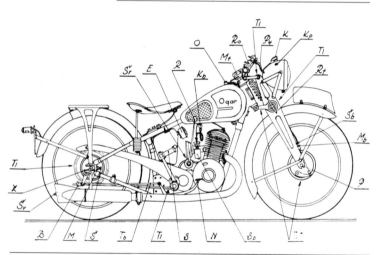

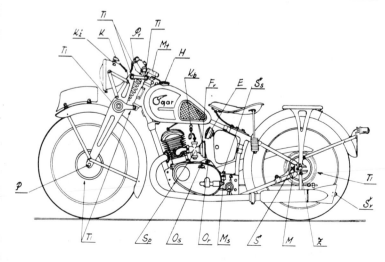

The Ogar, however, proved a success, and an improved model was ready the following year. Whilst the original standard 2-speed model remained in production, the new machine, with a 4-speed box, was described as Model 4. The two machines had basically the same engine; the Model 4 had the refinement of highly polished twin ports, producing an increase from 6 to 7.5hp at 4000rpm. Additional changes included the adoption of a foot gear-change and the option of a high level exhaust system.

Both CZ and Jawa responded to the Ogar challenge, and a number of 250cc models were introduced in the years before the war. Although a new class for Czechoslovakia, the 250cc was found ideal for the location and period, and it was largely the 250cc class that established CZ, Jawa, and Ogar as the major domestic manufacturers. With a workforce of only 120, the works did well to produce 1000 machines a year. Ogar machines were also bought by the Czechoslovak Army and remained in production for the *Wehrmacht*. Under German occupation the Machek works was ordered to abandon all commercial work in favour of military motocycles and bicycles. But a small, brave team continued development work in secret and an improved model was ready for production by mid 1945, weeks after the German withdrawal.

The new Ogar had telescopic front forks; perhaps copied from the BMW machines of the Wehrmacht. The engine remained a single cylinder 2-stroke twin port design, but the new machine had a flat top piston and revised carburettor mounting. With extensive internal polishing a maximum speed of 100km/h could be obtained. Like many Czechoslovak factories of the inter-war years, however, the small Machek factory was nationalised in 1948, and effectively closed down. CZ and Jawa were chosen to represent the Czechoslovak motorcycle industry, and part of the Ogar works was taken over by Jawa and the rest by CZ. The original building in the Strasnice, Prague, became a Jawa research and development office.

Praga

While CZ and Jawa gained an international reputation, most domestic industry remained little known outside the country; but few products could compare with the hand crafted Praga BD model. Originally known as the BD, then as the Praga BD and finally as just Praga, this succession of names punctuated the career of a single man; a name which featured in more Czechoslovak motorcycle histories than any other, Jaroslav Frantisek Koch. In 1919, Koch founded his first business, the AVIA Aircraft Works. During these early years, Koch designed his first motorcycle, a

350cc single, shortly followed by a 500cc model.
Both remained at the prototype stage until AVIA
was bought out by the Skoda Works, and Koch
moved to the Breitfeld & Danek business in
Prague. BD, as the firm became known, introduced the BD model in 1927.

Unlike many East European motorcycles of
the period, all structural reinforcement was kept
to a minimum; which emphasised the proportions of the power unit. The vertical single-
cylinder 499cc (84 x 90mm) ohc engine was
mounted in a tubular frame. Transmission comprised a 3-speed gearbox, a multi-plate clutch and
exposed chain final drive. This advanced and
continually improved design gained a reputation
as a reliable workhorse until 1938 and was procured by the Czech Army in limited numbers.

Itar & Walter

Originally a gear manufacturer, the Walter company introduced a new single-cylinder 500cc sv
model in 1926 followed by a more advanced
motorcycle; with a transverse mounted V-twin
750cc (75 x 85mm) ohv engine, and unit construction 3-speed gearbox. The factory also built
cars and aircraft engines, motorcycle production
ending in 1928.

Left: **1928 Praga
500 ohc, virtually
identical to the BD
500, a luxury
despatch model
procured by the
Czechoslovak
Army.** *(Frank
Nyklicek)*

Below: **1928 Praga
BD 500. A restored
example of this
advanced machine,
one of the first
double overhead
camshaft (dohc)
engines ever
produced.** *(Frank
Nyklicek)*

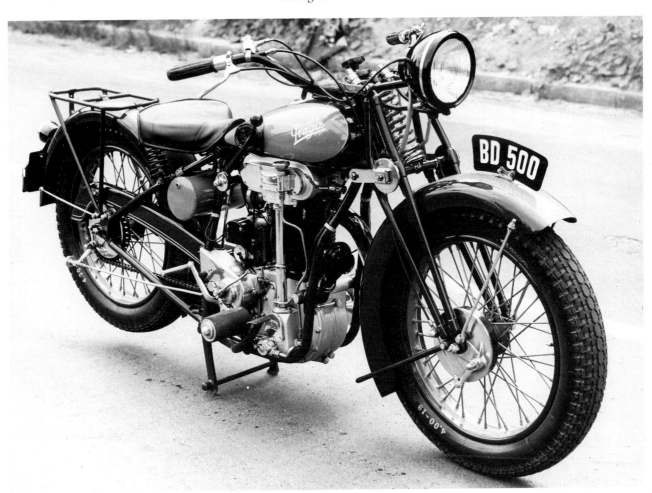

Above: **1928 Praga BD 500, engine viewed from the right, a robust design of outstanding reliability.** *(Miroslav Sochor)*

Right: **1928 Praga BD 500, engine viewed from the left, presenting a fully enclosed alloy primary chain case. Note the gear change control at the rear of the crankcase.** *(Miroslav Sochor)*

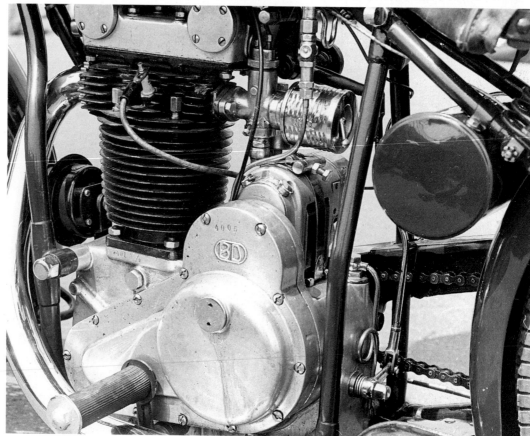

In 1917, while at the original Walter factory, the designer Josef Zubaty also prepared a 2-cylinder motorcycle with a 700cc (74 x 80mm) sv engine mounted in-line with a separate unit 3-speed gearbox and exposed chain final drive. The tubular frame had girder-type front forks and a rigid rear end, and both wheels featured block brakes upon dummy rims. The machine, however, was never produced by the Walter concern, but sold to the J. Janatka factory, and between 1920–24, produced under the trade name of Itar. In 1923, the engine capacity was increased to 750cc (77 x 80mm), and remained in production until 1929.

Both the Walter and Itar machines were manufactured in limited quantities, until replaced by the previously described Czech lightweights, with production going to the military for solo, sidecar, despatch and military police duties.

Left: **1926 BD 500 ohc. One of the few four-stroke motorcycles adopted by the Czechoslovak Army, later replaced by the Praga 500. Under Nazi rule CKD/ Praga tracked vehicles were produced for the** *Wehrmacht* **and their partners.** *(Frank Nyklicek)*

Centre left: **1922-27 Walter 750 ohv; available as type A with 3hp and type B with 4hp V-twin engine, and unit construction three-speed gearbox. Limited numbers of both were procured by the newly formed Czechoslovak Army.** *(Frank Nyklicek)*

Bottom left: **Walter 750 V-twin engine detail, clearly showing the in-line power train through the unit.** *(Frank Nyklicek)*

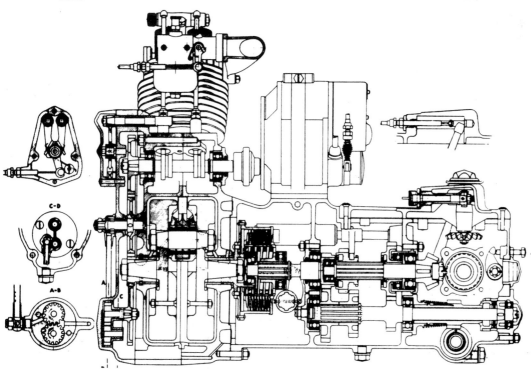

Right: **The Moto Guzzi GT17, prepared as a solo assault vehicle.** *(Moto Guzzi)*

Below right: **An official factory photograph of the Moto Guzzi GT17 fully armoured; the ideal solo sniper machine? Note the fully exposed flywheel beside the marksman's foot.** *(Moto Guzzi)*

III: FALSE EXPECTATIONS . . .

Limitations

For some years, a number of military 'experts' throughout the world ignored the agility of the motorcycle, and considered the machine an ideal foundation for a less expensive assault or combat vehicle, and a number of fully armoured machines were produced, complete with machine-gun or small cannon. The Italian government, and most governments at the time, were not fully aware of military motorcycle possibilities and limitations, and requested a number of such mobile sniper or combat machines. Solo and sidecar machines were equipped with arms and armour shields; machine-guns, small cannons, anti-aircraft weapons, and various tripods carried horizontal alongside the rider, mounted on the handlebars, or the nose of the sidecar. No matter how impractical these machines look now, the lure of cheap, mobile armour was irresistible.

With or without armour shields, many solo machines offered a revised seating position (removable or tilting saddle), to provide the rider/gunner with a lower firing position. A machine-gun carried on the handlebars could be detached (often with tripod) as required, or fired from the handlebars once the motorcycle had stopped moving. Dependent upon duties, Italian military equipment included various extra tool boxes, leg shields, rear carrier rack or pillion saddle (with collapsible pillion handlebars), reinforced or revised cycle parts, controls, and wheels, cross-country tyres, and wider section mudguards, and with additional arms and armour, solo machines lost most of their original manoeuvrability. Such machines, however, continued to be prepared until the early 1940s, with a smaller number of armoured sidecar outfits and arms carrying tricycles.

Italy

It may be surprising in view of Italy's motorcycle achievements in World War 1 that their industry was allowed to decline, until the Mussolini regime reorganized design, development and production. Along the way, motorised tricycles were manufactured and used right up to the sixties, primarily as lightweight arms carriers.

Indeed throughout the 1920s, Italian military motorisation relied upon machines originally designed during World War 1, but from the early 1930s, Benelli, Gilera and Moto Guzzi became the principal military motorcycle suppliers; machines were also supplied by Bianchi (p 187), Frera, Garelli, MAS, and Sertum (p 188). Moto Guzzi, however, quickly established the wider range of purpose-built military models, and became a popular choice in the African War of the mid 1930s, both solo or with sidecar.

Moto Guzzi

This company supplied their first military order in 1928; a batch of 245 modified GT models, which provided the basis for the purpose-built military model GT17 9p 188). Introduced in 1932, the GT17 had a 499cc exhaust-over-inlet valve engine, with a 3-speed hand change gearbox and exposed chain final drive. The horizontal single cylinder engine with a large exposed flywheel on the left side, was mounted within a pressed steel and tubular frame, with girder-type front forks and a helical sprung rear sub-frame assembly.

Produced as a solo or pillion model, the rear suspension could be adjusted to suit; the rear footrests were connected by levers to adjust the preload on the rear suspension, the springs mounted horizontally beneath the engine and gearbox, as an integral part of the frame. Although the wheels, brakes, footboards, and

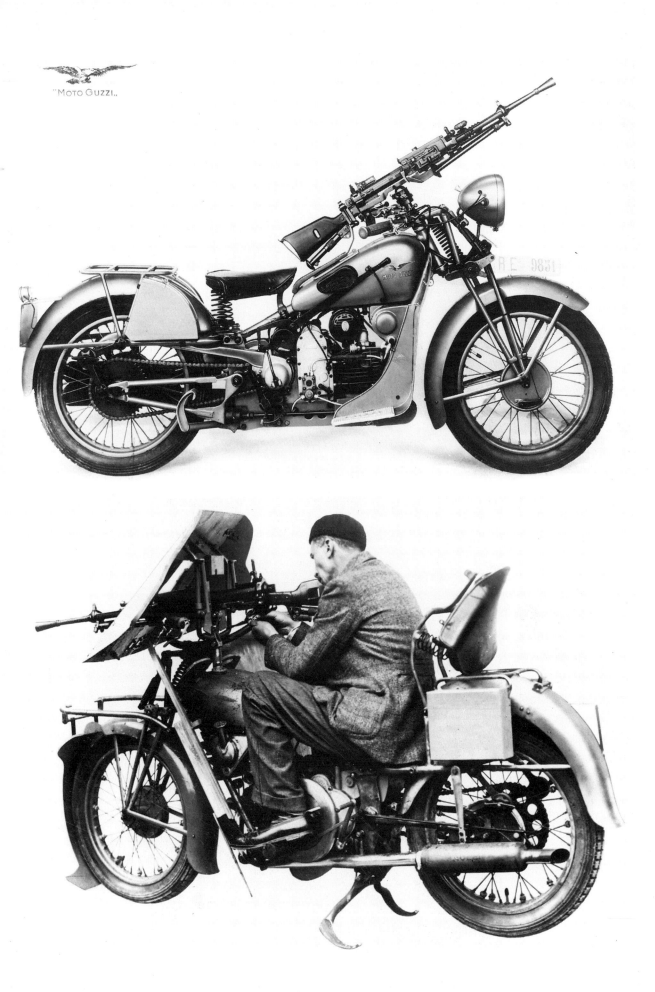

"Moto Guzzi"

legshields followed the layout of the civilian model, the gearbox had closer ratios. The fuel tank was also shorter and more rounded on the two seater model, as the riders' saddle was moved further forward. Prepared to meet all possibilities, with or without a machine-gun on the handle-bars, additional arms carrying facilities, various tool boxes and carrier racks, etc, the GT17 was finished in a number of colours to suit the range of operations; a total of 4810 were manufactured between 1932–39, and many remained in service throughout World War 2.

Based upon the technical developments and practical experience of the GT17, Moto Guzzi introduced a new military model in 1938. Designated the GT20, the engine was up-rated with overhead valves and connected to a 4-speed gearbox. A new frame increased ground clearance for off-road duties. The front fork legs could be removed independently for faster repair work, and the wheels were interchangeable and could be fitted with cross-country tyres. For easier engine repairs, the oil tank was remounted behind the headstock, with a filler cap through the fuel tank. Within a few months, however, the GT20 was superseded, with only 248 built before the Alce model was introduced in 1939.

The Italian armed forces acquired very few foreign vehicles during the inter-war years, mainly American and British built trucks, but relied entirely upon the domestic industry for their military motorcycle requirements. While the Moto Guzzi GT17 maintained a principal position, a wide and established range of machines was supplied in limited numbers throughout the 1930s, often providing a foundation for future models during World War 2 and later years (eg. Benelli 4T NM 220, Gilera LTE 500, etc).

Generally derived from commercial models, the majority of these machines successfully offered front and rear suspension, robust and reliable performance, leg shields and foot boards, and a diverse range of touring accessories suitable for military modification. With a capacity between 175cc and 500cc, they were all single-cylinder (horizontal or vertical) machines, with an exposed chain final drive; prepared for solo despatch, reconnaissance, convoy control, and general police duties (see chapter three).

Denmark

With varying degrees of success, between 1898 and 1954, some 40 different manufacturers produced motorcycles in Denmark; but the Company of Fisker & Nielsen and their Nimbus motorcycle became synonymous with Danish public service (Army, Police & Post Office). From a small rented workshop of Copenhagen, Peder Fisker began producing electric motors in 1905. Within a few months, H. M. Nielsen, the works foreman, went into partnership with Fisker, and the Fisker & Nielsen firm was founded. During 1910, domestic electrical equipment and electric were developed, and during World War 1, Fisker turned his attention to motorcycle design, and the Nimbus motorcycle was introduced in 1918.

Strongly influenced by FN of Belgium (see Chapter 1), the Nimbus had a vertical in-line 4-cylinder engine with four independent cast-iron cylinders mounted on an alloy crank-case, and an enclosed shaft final drive. The pressed-steel frame had front and rear suspension with leading-link front forks and helical-sprung rear forks attached to the unit construction gearbox. Early production machines (1919–27), known as 'Stovepipe' models, after their unique cylindrical fuel tank (from the headstock to saddle downtube), became very popular after regular road-race success; nearly always used with a sidecar and ridden by P. A. Fisker.

Hand books and sales literature were printed in Danish, English, German, and Czech, and demand quickly exceeded production. In 1924 however, the Danish government announced a new 'Sales Tax' on motorcycles, and Nimbus machines were finally discontinued in 1927, after some 1285 had been built.

P. A. Fisker, however, did not forsake Nimbus, and in partnership with his son, Anders, a new 4-cylinder Nimbus began to take shape in

Above: **1932-36 Moto Guzzi 32. A general load military tricycle, widely deployed by the Italian Army. Based upon the GT17, both models remained in service until replaced by the Alce and Trialce respectively.** (*Moto Guzzi*)

1932. This machine went into production in 1934 (p 183), and with only minor changes, continued to be manufactured until 1960, by which date a total of 12,715 had been produced. The new machine was quite different, with the cylinders cast as a single block, mounted within a triangulated pressed steel frame with telescopic front forks and rigid rear wheel. With its 4 cylinders and 750cc capacity (with, unusually, exposed valves) the machine was ideal for sidecar work, and from the first months, the Nimbus was available with a lower sidecar gearing.

Between 1934 and 1950, a total of 5 sidecar models was introduced, providing variation for private and public use. During this period, major changes included a new carburettor, larger drum brakes, improved front forks, revised shaft drive, higher compression ratio, and an improved exhaust system.

Military Service

Danish military motorisation did not include a motorcycle programme until after World War 1. The first machines were Ellehams acquired in 1912–14, followed in 1916 by a Harley-Davidson and an Indian (ambulance sidecar outfit). It was not until 1920 that motorcycle trials began to take place, and the following year two Nimbus 'Stovepipe' models were procured for military service. While the Danish produced motorcycle became standard equipment for many years it was thought that the simplicity of imported single and 2-cylinder models would be more suitable for military use, and a number of military officials were pleased when Nimbus production ceased in 1927. BSA, BMW, Douglas, Norton, and others quickly found their way into the Danish Army.

In 1932, however, the Danish Army introduced a programme for full motorisation, and news of a second Nimbus model (1934) was well received within military circles. For the next two years, extensive trials of Harley-Davidson (1200cc) and Nimbus (750cc) sidecar machines were undertaken. The Harley-Davidson could offer some speed on a surfaced road, but the Nimbus was found easier to start and far easier to control. The Harley-Davidson outfit was almost impossible for two men to push out of off-road difficulty, while it was often possible to recover the Nimbus.

A second military trial took place in the Autumn of 1939, when about 150 machines were tested, including AJS, Ariel, BSA, BMW, Harley-Davidson, Matchless, Royal Enfield, Zündapp, and others, but once again the Danish military decided that the Nimbus provided the most suitable qualities for their requirements.

With a production target of 1000 machines a year, Nimbus motorcycles were prepared in batches of 50 at a time; the Army, Police & Post Office often taking 30 at a time, while the remainder were usually sold off through a network of dealers. The Nimbus remained a limited production model, but Fisker & Nielsen promoted the machine worldwide; from Argentina to China. The Chinese Army took a delivery in 1937 and the Yugoslav Air Force ordered 100 Nimbus machines in 1941, but when the machines arrived in German-occupied Yugoslavia, the *Wehrmacht* commandeered and took them to Norway.

Used solo or with a sidecar attached (ambulance, personnel carrier, flat-bed with machine-gun or light cannon), the Nimbus remained the major motorcycle in the Danish Army until 1967–68, when eventually replaced by the BSA B40; the ubiquitous NATO model. Military and civilian departments continued to maintain their Nimbus motorcycles until 1980 and Fisker & Nielsen continued to produce most essential parts to keep these machines in operation.

Sweden

Aktiebolaget Landsverk, of Landskrona, designed and produced a wide range of armoured military vehicles, for domestic overseas customers and during the early 1930s, a motorcycle and sidecar combination. While not quantity produced, the Harley-Davidson/Landsverk L210 was a typical example of a 'motorcycle tank' assembled during the inter-war years. Designed to provide an armoured mobile machine-gun/cannon position, at minimum cost, the L210 was better than many similar machines, but still could not compete with the majority of conventional four- and six-wheeled or caterpillar tracked military machines. The L210 was not taken up by the Swedish Army, but ten were adopted by the Danish and Mexican military.

Husqvarna

With the exception of the Suecia 500 Armee of 1937–40, Husqvarna Vapenfabriks AB, supplied all the motorcycles used by the Swedish Army during the inter-war years; all V-twin sv machines of either 990cc (79 x 101mm) or 550cc (65 x 83mm) capacity, mounted in a duplex cradle frame, with girder-type front forks and rigid rear wheel. Transmission ran through a separate 3-speed gearbox, with hand-change and exposed chain final drive. The kick-start was an integral part of the gearbox,

with a foot-operated clutch. Later machines adopted full chain drive, balanced light-alloy pistons, drum brakes all-round (earlier machines were without a front wheel brake), and more traditional single sprung girder-type front forks.

In 1922, Husqvarna introduced the model 500 (990cc V-twin) sidecar machine to supersede the military Husqvarna 145A of 1916, and, modified for the civilian market, the machine remained in production until 1936, when the factory discontinued all further heavyweight motorcycle production (p 189). Well received within the Commercial market, Husqvarna was quick to realise the advantage of producing sidecars, and the factory maintained at least one sidecar model in the annual brochure until 1936. The 990cc V-twin continued to develop, with model nomenclature as follows: model 600 in 1926, model 610 in 1929 and the model 120 in 1932.

Between 1926–27, Husqvarna also supplied the Swedish Army with a smaller number of the lighter model 180 (550cc V-twin), for solo despatch, escort and reconnaissance duties. With a similar outward appearance to the Husqvarna 550cc model of World War 1, the machine retained one-piece sv cylinder castings, and the front wheel still lacked any means of braking. A twist-grip throttle, however, was offered as an alternative to the traditional throttle lever. Military conversion for both models consisted of service livery and full lighting.

Right: **Introduced in 1922, the Husqvarna model 500 (990cc V-twin) sidecar machine was produced to supersede the military Husqvarna 145A of 1916. Modified for the civilian market, the machine remained in production until 1936, when the factory began to concentrate on smaller two-stroke.** *(Husqvarna)*

Suecia

Founded in 1928, Suecia Verken Motor AB, of Orelljunga, quickly gained an excellent competitive reputation. Following contemporary British style, with a variety of proprietary engine and gearbox units, the first Suecia motorcycles had British single-cylinder Blackburn engines of 350cc, 500cc, and 600cc, with a British 3-speed Sturmey-Archer gearbox, tubular rigid frame, girder-type front forks and drum brakes. Designated 'Sport' models with an ohv engine and 'Tourist' with a sv layout, by the mid 1930s, the Blackburn engines were subsequently replaced by British JAP or Swiss MAG units, and the Sturmey-Archer gearbox with a British 4-speed Burman design.

Suecia production ceased with the declaration of World War 2, but during the 3-year production period from 1937–40, some 5000 500 type Armee models were supplied to the Swedish Army. Based on the 500 'Tourist', the machine had a MAG 496cc engine and Burman 4-speed gearbox; for solo or with a purpose-built military sidecar. Well built and with a reliable performance, many of these machines remained in service during World War 2.

France

Principal changes during the inter-war years concentrated on a reduction in the number of cavalry regiments and the elimination of cyclist battalions, deployment of the *Dragons Portées* (dismounted cavalrymen transported by trucks), and the introduction of various motorised units. There had been 89 French cavalry regiments in World War 1, but by 1933, this number had dropped to 44. In 1914, the French cavalry was trained and deployed for mounted action only, but from 1918 it gained in fire power due to the acquisition of motorised vehicles. The cavalry was no longer expected to perform combat duties. By 1933 the decline of the remaining cavalry regiments at the expense of armoured vehicles had gained momentum and motorcycles began to be employed in increasing numbers.

With a particular interest in multi-terrain or cross-country vehicles, the full potential of French military motorisation was thoroughly studied throughout the 1920–30s; a wide range of machines tried and tested, often on secret manoeuvres. No foreign officers were attached to French regiments with any vehicles, and no foreign officers at the *Ecole de Guerre* (Army School) were permitted to attend any conferences or exercises on motorisation. The effectiveness of these measures is anybody's guess . . .

Prototypes

In 1936, the Mercier factory introduced a motorcycle with a single driven tracked bogie at the front, and a single tyred wheel at the rear. The rider sat behind a large curved armour shield, with two slots for forward viewing, and a cutaway for vertical movement of the front bogie. With a weight of 160kg, a single-cylinder 350cc JAP engine provided a top speed of about 60km/h/37mph. Two years later, the factory prepared a 'motorcycle tank', with a single rubber track running around the full length of the armoured body, with a steering/stabilizer wheel mounted each side. A single-cylinder 500cc Chaise engine drove the track via a rear sprocket. These two machines were prototypes, but the works of Gnome Rhône, Monet-Goyon, Rene-Gillet, Terrot, etc, successfully supplied numerous traditional motorcycles and sidecar combinations for military service.

In the Autumn of 1933, General Boucherie, commanding the French 1st Cavalry Division had stated, "A large part of the cavalry will have to remain on a horse basis, as the horse ensures sufficiently mobility in many cases and even over certain terrain is preferable to the machine." Military motorisation, however, slowly increased, and large numbers of 1935–40 French vehicles (including some American trucks) were pressed into German service in World War 2. Orders were placed with French manufacturers to supply

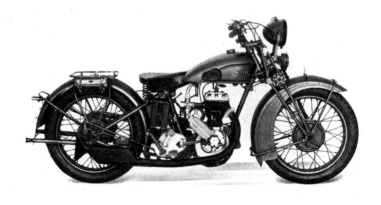

Below: **1937-40 Suecia 500 Armetyp; based upon the 500 Tourist, many of these machines remained in service during the Second World War, but the m/42 remained in the principal Swedish military motorcycle of the war.** *(Sven-Olof Persson)*

Bottom: **1937-40 Suecia 500 Armetyp; prepared solo or with a purpose-built military sidecar, attached to the left, the bodywork was mounted on a pair of semi-elliptic springs.** *(Sven-Olof Persson)*

Above **A detachment of French soldiers upon commercially produced (note civilian fuel tank) Rene Gillet G1's of pre-war years. Improvised black-out masks on the head lights.** *(ECPA)*

Right: **French soldiers equipped with Terrot VAAT sidecar outfits. More improvised black-out shields.** *(ECPA)*

Below: **Another detachment of French troops riding Terrot VAAT sidecar outfits.** *(ECPA)*

the *Wehrmacht*, and widely deployed across Europe and Russia. Many motorcycles remained in active service post-war.

General Production

From the mid 1920s, Rene-Gillet, of Paris, became a principal supplier, with their G type Armee model prepared for solo or sidecar service with the *Dragons Portées*; sidecars included a fully enclosed communications unit, various machine-gun mountings, and as a stretcher carrying ambulance. The 750cc (70 x 97.7mm) sv engine was mounted in-line with a tubular frame and 3-speed gearbox with girder-type trailing-link front forks and a rigid rear wheel. While the model continued to develop, a 4-speed gearbox introduced in 1939, these specifications remained basically unchanged until the early 1950s; widely used by the French Army and police throughout.

From numerous *Velomoteur* lightweights, to purpose-built sidecar outfits, *Motocyclettes*, the French military ordered from a wide range of domestic manufacturers. The principal machines (pp 183–4) used during the 1930s included the middleweight single-cylinder Gnome Rhône D5A (500cc ohv in 1938), Motobecane S5C (500cc ohv in 1934), and Terrot RDA (500cc sv in 1938), and heavyweight twin cylinder Gnome Rhône AX2 (800cc Boxer sv in 1938–40) which replaced the Monet-Goyon L5A1, Gnome Rhône 750 Armee (750cc V-twin ohv: 1938–40), Rene-Gillet type G1 (750cc V-twin in 1937–40), and Terrot VAAT (750cc V-twins in 1934). Largely derived from manufacturers' own civilian models, French military modifications included reinforced parts, cross-country tyres, governed top speed, spare wheel (sidecar models), leg shields, pillion saddle or rear carrier rack, and service livery. The majority of larger French military motorcycles were prepared with a sidecar, but a number of smaller, middleweight, and some heavyweight solo machines were ordered with additional tool boxes, canvas pannier bags, reinforced side stand, etc.

With the exception of the Gnome Rhône models, these machines all had a tubular frame, with girder-type front forks and chain drive to a rigid rear wheel. From the early 1930s, however, a number of Gnome Rhône models featured a pressed-steel cycle frame and front fork, a unit construction engine and gearbox and a shaft final drive. Very similar in appearance to the German Zündapp machines, these robust designs were found well suited to military requirements. Based upon the sv flat-twin type V2 model, the purpose-built military Gnome Rhône AX2 had a capacity increase from 500cc (68 x 68mm) to 800cc, and the 4-speed gearbox featured a reverse ratio. The shaft final drive was equipped with a

cross-shaft to the sidecar wheel, which could be disengaged on later models. The 750 Armee had an ohv flat-twin of 750cc (80 x 72mm), and was without a sidecar wheel drive. Both models were pressed into service for the *Wehrmacht*, who reportedly maintained their production during World War 2.

Belgium

FN motorcycles (Fabrique Nationale des Armes de Guerre SA), of Herstal, established an outstanding military reputation from the turn of the century, and during World War 1, but in common with most European armed forces, Belgian military motorisation did not really start until the 1930s. Meanwhile, the majority of Belgian motor vehicle manufacturers closed down during the early inter-war years, and by the time the army began a full-scale motorisation programme in 1936, more than 100 motorcycle factories had

Above: **French despatch riders with a Gnome Rhône XA sidecar outfit.** *(ECPA)*

Top: **1931 Gnome Rhône V2 prepared for French military service. Superseded by the purpose-built 750 Armee and AX2, the V2 provided the basis for later Gnome Rhône military models. The similar CV2, over-head valve version, was also prepared for the French Army.** *(DGA)*

Right: **Late 1930s, Gnome Rhône AX2 sidecar outfit, prepared for multi-terrain service within the French Army. As the Gnome Rhône 750 Armee, without a sidecar wheel drive, both models were later adopted by the *Wehrmacht* during World War 2.** *(ECPA)*

Centre right: **Official factory photograph presenting the Gnome Rhône V2 and sidecar machine-gun. Note the multi-purpose mounting and barrel holder upon the sidecar nose.** *(DGA)*

Above: **In final military trim, the Gnome Rhône V2 sidecar outfit, demonstrating the machine-gun in action. Note the leg shields have been removed.** *(DGA)*

disappeared. Motorcycles of both commercial and military design, however, were supplied in some quantity by FN, Gillet-Herstal and Sarolea; from solo lightweights to purpose-built sidecar combinations, and many of these machines were exported to South America, Europe, and the Middle East. Manufacturing plants were commandeered by the *Wehrmacht* during the years of German occupation.

Advanced Specifications: From 1937, Belgian sidecar outfits offered excellent military potential, with sidecar wheel drive as required, high/low ratio and reverse gearbox, high ground clearance and exhaust system, additional filters on the carburettors, and interchangeable wheels with cross-country tyres. A range of sidecars were produced with or without armour shields or machine-gun mountings, wireless communications, spares storage and spare wheel. These machines, with particular reference to the FN type 12 (p 182), Gillet-Herstal 750, and Sarolea type H) were reportedly kept in production by the *Wehrmacht* during World War 2, and influenced the German BMW and Zündapp military machines of the early 1940s.

The FN type 12 and Sarolea type H were very similar in general design; both had a sv flat-twin (FN: 992cc, Sarolea: 978cc), with a unit construction hand-change gearbox, and shaft drive to the rear and sidecar wheels. The M12 had 4-speeds, while the type H only 3-speeds, but both machines had a reverse and high/low ratio change; giving eight- or six-forward speeds and two reverse ratios. These unit construction designs were mounted within a tubular duplex cradle frame, with girder-type front forks and a rigid rear wheel.

Both models had the exhaust system mounted between the machine and sidecar, the single silencer held high alongside the rear wheel. Further military features included a pillion saddle on the rear mudguard, mud flaps, front and rear crash bars, sump guard, and FN/Browning machine-gun on the sidecar. The machines were limited production models, with a total of 1090 M12's built between 1937–39, exported to Greece, Iran, and elsewhere, while only 300 of the type H were supplied to the Belgian Army. The Belgian forces also procured single cylinder 350cc, 500cc, and 600cc FN and Sarolea models.

The Gillet-Herstal 750 was quite different; a vertical twin-cylinder two-stroke engine of 728cc (76 x 80mm), driving the rear and sidecar wheels through a 4-speed foot-change gearbox (with reverse) by chain, with shaft-drive to the sidecar wheel. This unit construction engine and gearbox was mounted within a tubular duplex cradle frame, with girder-type front forks and a rigid

Above: **An outstanding design, the FN M12 was also exported to Greece, Iran, and South America, and is generally thought to have inspired the later military outfits of BMW and Zündapp.** *(FN Herstal)*

Left: **Gnome Rhône V2 multi-terrain model,´presenting the flexibility of the machine-gun mounting; anti-aircraft position.** *(DGA)*

rear wheel. As the FN and Sarolea, further military features included a high mounted exhaust system, huge cross-country tyres and interchangeable wheels, and a pillion saddle on the rear mudguard. A modified version with a smaller sidecar was supplied to the Belgian Police and once again both models were widely used by the *Wehrmacht*.

Based upon the FN type 12, between 1939–40, FN also produced the Tricar; a multi-purpose three-wheeler which could carry a load of some 600kg/1,323lb or a team of five, including the driver. The front half remained as the standard motorcycle, similar to many Italian military tricycles, with a shaft drive to a pair of disc rear wheels. Dependent upon use, some machines had a disc front wheel as well. Various platforms were prepared for personnel, ammunition transport, and an anti-aircraft machine-gun. With a ground clearance of 225mm, the machine also had some off-road ability.

Far left: **1937-39 FN M12, a purpose-built multi-terrain military motorcycle outfit, a total of 1090 deployed by the Belgian Army, but from 1940, extensively used by the *Wehrmacht*.** *(FN Herstal)*

Left: **FN M12 outfits and Belgian soldiers on parade. Note the unique helmets of the Belgian motorcycle troops.** *(FN Herstal)*

IV: ONCE AND FUTURE ALLIES . . .

Great Britain

British military motorisation began in 1903, with the formation of No. 77 Mechanical Transport (MT) Company ASC, which acquired the traction engines of the Royal Engineers, based at Chatham, Kent. With however, a growing confidence in the internal combustion engine, the development of British military transport became the responsibility of the War Office Mechanical Transport Committee, and by 1914 nearly 900 standardised vehicles were available for military service. Throughout World War 1 the use of motorised vehicles rapidly expanded, and in 1920, the War Office MT Advisory Board replaced the pre-war MT Committee, and the RASC MT School, Aldershot took responsibility for trials and development of military motorised vehicles. The RASC retained this position until 1928, when these tasks were transferred to the Master General of the Ordnance's department, and the Advisory Board became part of the Mechanical Warfare Board (later known as the Mechanical Board).

In 1919, with a mixture of financial caution and optimism for a period of international peace, the British Government issued the 'Ten Year Rule' for defence spending, which stated "It should be assumed for framing revised estimates that the British Empire will not be engaged in any great war during the next ten years", and the British Army entered a period of continual

Left: **A line-up of Venezuelian soldiers in 1936, equipped with armoured FN M86 military sidecar outfits. These machines were also supplied to Argentina, China, and the Middle East.** *(FN Herstal)*

Far left: **1936 FN M86 military solo. Standard production model procured by the Belgian Army, also used with various sidecar types, eg ammunition carrier, wireless, machine-gun, etc.** *(FN Herstal)*

reduction and mechanical stagnation. Between 1923 and 1932, British Army spending was reduced each year; while the Navy had an annual average of £13 million, and the newly formed RAF (an amalgamation of the RFC and RNAS) had £7 million, the Army had an allocation of only £2 million.

At the start of World War 1, the combined strength of the Regular Army, Reserves, and Territorial Forces was 733,514, but by 1918, there were more than 1,750,000 British troops on the Western Front alone. During 1922, in accordance with the 'Ten Year Rule', 22 infantry battalions and 8 cavalry regiments were disbanded, and between 1922 and 1926, the Territorial Army was reduced from 216,041 to 184,161. With a combination of low pay and poor living conditions, between 1923 and 1932, the total strength of the Regular Army fell from 231,000 to 207,000.

Manoeuvres

Throughout the interwar years, British Forces underwent various trials and experiments (strategy and tactics of units or individual motorised machines), but with only limited funds, the British Army lost its leading position for motorisation. In 1931, the Secretary of State for War stated, "Mechanisation is being carried on with due caution. When a type can be fixed and its efficiency thoroughly proved, then it will be time to build up a stock. Until the War Office is convinced that horses can be dispensed with absolutely, the cavalry will remain as it is."

While the value of motorisation had been well proven, the extent and type of vehicles to be procured was still a matter of trial; in 1933, there were 136 infantry battalions, 18 horsed cavalry regiments, but only four tank battalions, and two regiments of armoured cars. To provide communications between army units, the Royal Corps of Signals was formed in 1920, and during World War 2, the Corps expanded from 541 officers and 9837 other ranks, to 8518 officers and 142,472 other ranks. The Corps, however, had been unable to keep pace with the new wireless technology, and remained largely dependent on foot and vehicle communications. While a limited number of wireless sets provided the main command links, most administration and general liaison duties fell upon the Signal Corps motorcycle despatch rider; the 'Don R' and his solo machine.

In spite of non-cooperation from various official departments, the British Army tried and tested a wide range of vehicles during the 1920s. At this time the 6x4 cross-country truck became popular, and a number of motorcycles were modified to provide a similar tandem-drive two rear wheels. Alternative front suspensions and the

option of tyres or tracked rear wheels were tested. Following extensive trials by the RASC, similar to those in France and Germany, these more complicated machines were not found to offer any major advantage, and did not go into full production.

An example prepared by Triumph can be seen at the Museum of Army Transport, Beverley. The even more extraordinary multi-terrain British 'Roadless' model was also tested at this time; a 2¾hp Douglas flat-twin engine powered a single undulating endless rubber track, with a steering post, single saddle, and the power unit mounted above. This unique machine could achieve some 20 mph over a grassed field, but was far too precarious to tackle much more and also remained a prototype.

Procurement

For additional mobility, however, a growing number of solo motorcycles and sidecar outfits were widely deployed for command and liaison duties; at battalion level the Colonel was issued with a civilian car, but platoon and troop commanders were expected to learn to ride a motorcycle for active service conditions. A number of machines were retained from World War 1, but a limited number of motorcycles were purchased to maintain this service. Major models included the Triumph model P (500cc sv in 1926) and Triumph 'Silent Scout' (500cc sv in 1933). P & M produced a revised version of their military 'Sloper' of 1914–18 (500cc ohv in 1926), and Douglas prepared a military model based upon the flat-twin B-29 (350cc sv in 1929). With little direction or overall requirements agreed upon, British military motorisation remained very restricted throughout the inter-war years, but the basic simplicity of the single-cylinder sv model became standardised, and the P & M and Douglas models did not receive any major orders.

Triumph

The utility Triumph model P was priced as the cheapest British 500cc model ever produced. By taking various short-cuts in design (operating the side valves direct in the cylinder head, and fitting an asbestos rope brake) and planning an initial production run of 20,000, the model P could be sold at just £42-17s-6d! At this unbeatable low price, less than the materials alone for many, the machine quickly became the best selling 500cc (84 x 89mm) in Britain, and forced more than half of the small production British manufacturers out of business.

By May 1925, output was set at the previously unattainable figure of 1000 machines a week, and later that year, an improved version was introduced with a drum front wheel brake and valve

guides. Sales continued to rise, and the model P-II was ordered by the British Army for solo despatch and general liaison duties. With a 3-speed gearbox and exposed chain final drive, the model also provided the basis for the single track three-wheeler (tandem-drive) prototype tested by the RASC in Aldershot.

Looking for customers wherever possible, after the financial crisis of 1930, BSA set a new sloping engine theme. Within a year most British manufacturers adopted a sloping cylinder to counter the BSA challenge, and Triumph introduced the Silent Scout, with a sloping single-cylinder twin port 500cc (84 x 89mm) sv engine. Further new features included a saddle fuel tank (first adopted by Triumph in 1929), a semi-enclosed engine and 3-speed hand change gearbox, an access panel for tappet adjustment, larger front and rear drum brakes, and standard-type girder front forks; setting new standards for commercial production. By 1933, a number of these machines had been supplied for British military and police.

BSA

By the early 1930s, the War Office decided to re-equip the Army with a new design of motorcycle; an ohv model to provide solo despatch and general liaison duties. BSA was quick to produce a robust and reliable machine, and after a 10,000 mile test, an order was placed in 1932. The model had a 500cc (63 x 80mm) V-twin engine, with a 4-speed gearbox and chain final drive (p 187). BSA's first dry sump design, a separate oil tank was mounted beneath the solo saddle. Heavy girder-type front forks and wheels were adopted from BSA single cylinder sv models, and the tubular frame had a heavy forged steel backbone, but the new military model was lighter than many single-cylinder 500s of the period.

BSA had listed the model as "Possessing that characteristic peculiar to medium twins – flexibility so wide that whilst the speed man will be delighted by its maximum performance, the medium weight sidecar enthusiast will find it equally satisfactory. The new twin is amazingly docile and extremely economical." With a top speed of 80mph, 130kp/h, however, the public service customers decided the machine was no faster than single-cylinder alternatives, and not well suited to sidecar work.

By 1934, a civilian version was introduced as the J34-11, with a positive footstop gearbox; a double ratchet-and-pawl mechanism was housed within a triangular box above the kick-start. The following year this configuration was replaced by a single gearbox unit, but general sales remained low, and the machine only managed a third year as the J35-12 before it was discontinued. By 1938 however, BSA had prepared their far less complicated single-cylinder 500cc sv model M20 (p 187) for both solo and sidecar military service; machines that were very widely ordered in Britain, Eire, Netherlands and Sweden, and deployed throughout World War 2.

United States

From the turn of the century, the USA became the traditional home for the enduring large capacity V-twin engine. European factories (AJS, Husqvarna, Motosacoche, Matchless, Royal Enfield, Rene-Gillet, etc), produced large twin-cylinder machines, but these were primarily for sidecar or commercial use. The higher performance British machines of Brough Superior and Vincent-HRD were luxury models, and were sold in limited numbers only.

Unlike the majority of European models, American motorcycles featured a hand gear-change with a foot-operated clutch; this arrangement enabled a far heavier clutch (often needing 50-60ft/lbs torque) for the larger V-twin engines, in contrast to the lighter European system with Bowden-type cables. The hand gear-change also offered a positive control that was easy to adjust. While lacking the manoeuvrability of many European designs, the American heavyweights provided the robust reliability essential for the many unmade roads. With dealers located far and wide it was important that machines could be maintained with the very minimum of factory assistance; qualities found ideal for police and military service.

After World War 1, the US Marine Corps acquired a large number of surplus military motorcycles, and for a short period it was reported that every recruit would be issued with a motorcycle upon their graduation. The US armed forces however, were not exempt from the financial crisis developing worldwide, and in direct response to the limitations placed by the Assistant Secretary of the Navy, on the 27th June 1921, Major General Commandant John Lejeune USMC issued the following order:

1. After July 1, 1921, the operation and maintenance of motor-propelled passenger carrying vehicles, including motorcycles and sidecars, will be discontinued at all posts, stations, and offices of the Marine Corps within the continental limits of the United States, except where the operation is specifically authorised by the Major General Commandant on this or later date.

2. All automobiles, motorcycles and sidecars on hand and not authorised to be operated, as stated above, will be carefully inspected and those not deemed worth storage for repair at a later date, will be surveyed for sale at auction. Those considered to be worth retention will be placed in storage, if Government storage is available, otherwise they will be transferred to the nearest depot, and the Quartermaster advised when shipment has been made. All motor vehicles laid-up and placed in storage pursuant to this order will be slushed-down, jacked-up, protected from weather and dirt, and every precaution taken to prevent deterioration while in store.

3. The above instructions do not refer to ambulances, the operation of which may be continued.

4. The restriction in the operation of passenger-carrying motor-vehicles is made necessary by the limitation placed by the Congress on the amount that may be expended for the operation, maintenance and repair of such vehicles.

While in reduced numbers, American military motorcycles, Harley-Davidson and Indian, continued to provide active service throughout the World. Under the command of Brigadier General Smedley Butler, US Marines of the 3rd Brigade were stationed in China in 1927, with solo motorcycles performing police duties and escorting tanks. These machines were Harley-Davidson 74-JD models of 1926 (first introduced in 1922 and remained basically unchanged until 1929); limited military modifications were largely restricted to white wall tyres, for ceremonial duties, and an insignia on the tool box.

US Motorcycle Marines were also stationed in Nicaragua in 1926, providing protection for Americans and other foreigners in the country. Once again, Harley-Davidson motorcycles were adopted to perform these police duties, and officers of the 2nd Brigade served as instructors and unit commanders in the Guardia Nacional until January 1933.

Motorcycles, however, were not particularly well supported within the US Marine Corps, and in December 1928, First Lieutenant Vernon Megee, USMC, wrote on the subject of 'Motor Transportation for Expeditionary Units' in the *Marine Corps Gazette*, "Given the proper care the modern motorcycle is as reliable and durable as a good automobile, but they will not stand up under service conditions. The machines now in use are far more powerful than is necessary for solo work; they are in fact dangerous in the hands of any but an expert rider. Several serious accidents have occurred in the 3rd Brigade (in China) due to the use of these heavy machines in traffic." The Lieutenant strongly recommended the limited use of smaller, less powerful motorcycles for expeditionary forces, stating, "The water cooled engine of the car is superior to the air-cooled motorcycle engine for hard cross country travelling and for slow running behind an infantry column."

In February 1929, the Marine Corps Table of Organisation and Equipment listed the following motor transport vehicles for a Detached Regiment: nine bicycles, five motorcycles with sidecars, one light repair truck, one ambulance, 25 passenger or cross country cars, two other cross country cars, two one-ton trucks, and 24 two-ton trucks or tractors.

January the following year, Lieutenant Colonel Walter Hill, USMC, wrote a memorandum to

Above: **1923 Indian Chief, providing a basis for many years public service; a restored example owned by Miroslav Sochor in Vrbno nad Lesy, Czechoslovakia.** (Miroslav Sochor)

the Director, Division of Operations and Training, including, "It is believed that the cross country car can successfully take the place of the motorcycle. It possesses all the advantages of the motorcycle, and furthermore is more efficient in negotiating areas impracticable for the motorcycle. It can be used for distant reconnaissance, and is better suited than the motorcycle for use as a 'Flying Patrol'. The motorcycle, on the other hand is very liable to crash, and its radius of activity is confined strictly to fairly good roads." In February, Captain Kenneth Inman, USMC Headquarters, sent a memorandum to the Quartermaster including, "Cross country cars should, to some extent, replace motorcycles; for message running at the base motorcycles still have their place. They should, however, be very much restricted on some of the units."

General Decline

The US Army deployed far more machines than the Marine Corps, but followed a very similar pattern of procurement, while on a far larger scale. Motorcycles in general did not reach the height of popularity as their European counterparts, and this attitude was mirrored in US military policy. American motorcycle registrations fell and rose during the inter-war period (more than 165,000 in 1929, falling to 96,401 in 1935, and rising to 126,233 in 1939), but as the population in America had increased by one third since 1930, these figures illustrated a general decline in motorcycle interest. Car and truck registrations tripled during the same period. While Harley-Davidson continued to export half of their pro-

duction, to many Americans the motorcycle was associated with law enforcement duties only. By 1925, the majority of American city and county police departments were using solo motorcycles to enforce the speed limits, and in many areas these were the only motorcycles to be seen.

By mid 1932, however, the economic crisis worldwide had reached disastrous proportions in America; one third of the workforce, between 13 and 15 million, were unemployed, one third of the railways were bankrupt, 5000 banks had failed, and countless factories faced an impossible position. During this period, it has been alleged that Walter Davidson offered to sell to any domestic police department any number of the new 74-VL model (replacement to the 74-JD) at the cost price of $195.00, in exchange for their existing machine, irrespective of condition, mileage, or manufacturer. The deal was to be handled through the factory, without any reference to existing dealers, who would lose the sales commission in return for service and maintenance on machines sold. Such tactics infringed the dealer franchise contracts, and many hundreds of non Harley-Davidson machines were destroyed – again, allegedly – needlessly in this way.

While Walter Davidson is said to have been amazed at the hostile reaction to this offer he is reported to have withdrawn the idea after only a few months. But many Americans have named this single action as having caused the widest gap between the two major American factories; adding perhaps to the decline of the US motorcycle industry.

Above: **A detail view of Miroslav Sochor's 1923 Indian Chief. Note the cylinder head bracing bracket from beneath the fuel tank.** *(Miroslav Sochor)*

Harley-Davidson

With only very limited modifications between civilian and military machines, the Harley-Davidson factory changed little to return to peace-time production after World War 1; even the olive green military finish was maintained. Introduced in 1922, the first Harley-Davidson 74 cu.in./ 1200cc (86.97 x 101.60mm) model remained virtually unchanged until 1929; the 45° V-twin inlet-over-exhaust valve engine mounted within a seamless steel loop cycle frame, with helical sprung trailing link front fork suspension. Transmission comprised an enclosed primary chain, multi-plate dry clutch, hand-change 3-speed countershaft gearbox and exposed chain to the rigid rear wheel. A pedal on the right footboard operated the rear wheel internal expanding drum brake (no front wheel brake), with an external contracting band, upon the same drum, available as an optional extra. While the inlet-valve pushrod remained fully exposed, the throttle control cables were neatly hidden within the handlebars. Further new features included a revised lighting and ignition system, with a gear-drive to the dynamo and car type distributor mounted behind the rear cylinder.

74-JD. This model had been prepared in direct response to the 4-cylinder Henderson, which had started to take sales from the H-D 61 cu.in./ 1000cc model; a series continually developed since 1907, and procured for military service during World War 1. An immediate success from 1924, aluminium pistons were introduced, offering more power with less chance of seizing. A teardrop fuel tank and balloon tyres were adopted in 1926, and throttle controlled oil pressure and a front-wheel drum brake became standard in 1928. Standard equipment also included a 6 volt dynamo and battery, headlight, tail-light, horn, and oil-pressure warning light.

Machines intended for sidecar use had a lower compression ratio; the spacer plate between the cylinders and crankcase extending engine life. One of the finest machines produced by the Milwaukee works, only the high cost prevented the model dominating domestic sales.

During 1933, a total of only 7418 US motorcycles were produced; 5689 Harley-Davidson and 1657 Indian, with some 800 dealer outlets for each factory. The two manufacturers sold about the same number domestically, with the additional Harley-Davidson machines exported, generally for police/military service, to South America and Japan, with a smaller number to Germany, Netherlands, Spain, and Scandinavia. Limited numbers were also supplied to the motorised units of Chiang Kai-shek's 8th Route Army (74-VL machines with left-hand sidecar). American motorcycles were also used in the Spanish Civil War; Harley-Davidson had dealers in Madrid, Seville, and Barcelona, and machines already in military service were used by both sides. With however, the involvement of Communist Russia and Nazi Germany, American factories tried to conceal their involvement in this conflict.

74-VL. In July 1929, this model was introduced to replace the 74-JD; proclaimed 'The greatest achievement in motorcycle history', in reality the new model proved a poor design, just two months before the American stock market collapsed. While no single specification was proven incorrect, the VL had been badly developed and required almost immediate attention. To the factory's credit, the first 1326 machines were recalled and rebuilt with a revised engine, silencer, and frame.

Once these problems had been corrected, however, the VL evolved into a reliable machine and remained in production until 1940; providing solo and sidecar police and military service worldwide, and the basis for the 74-UA, procured by the US armed forces during World War 2, and the Sankyo/Rikuo model of the Japanese Imperial Army (see Chapter 3 and p 188). From the start the machine had also had its good points, and quickly became popular within public service departments, maintaining Harley-Davidson's reputation throughout the World.

With side-by-side valves, both push-rods were fully enclosed, and with a revised plunger-type crankcase oil drain and cam-gear case, the VL engine leaked far less oil over machine and rider. An extra heavy duplex primary chain was introduced, and with modified valve springs and pistons, the engine offered an output increase of some 15% over the JD series.

Further new features included a high-frequency horn, an improved 22-amp battery, and sealed ignition coil. The wheels could be quickly removed and were interchangeable, including the sidecar, and featured full balloon 27 x 4.00in. tyres. The frame, while heavier than before, gave an even lower riding position, and the saddle fuel tank held 4 US gallons of fuel and a gallon of oil. While highlighted with a vermilion strip, the finish remained olive green until 1932, when Harley-Davidson finally introduced a multi-coloured model range: the standard V, high-comp VL, and without the use of aluminium pistons, the sidecar-geared VS and VC.

Indian

Generally accepted as the best all-round American motorcycle of the period, the Indian 101 Scout was first introduced in April 1928, and went into full production in March the following year. A mixture of innovation and traditional design, the machine was an immediate success; with a night-shift working, within a few months output reached more than 75 machines a day.

Based upon the original model of 1920, new features included a revised engine, gearbox and frame. While the original front forks were retained, the wheelbase was lengthened and the saddle height lowered; requiring a smaller, rounder fuel tank. An internal expanding drum brake became standard on the front wheel. A combination of light weight and high performance, the 101 Scout offered excellent acceleration, with a maximum speed of some 75mph. The machine's greatest qualities, however, centred upon outstanding handling and stability; appealing to the novice and experienced rider alike.

With their lack of vibration and greater acceleration, the 4-cylinder Henderson (1911–31) and Indian (1927–42) models were popular police machines in the larger cities of Chicago, San Francisco, New York, etc, while the less expensive V-twin models of Harley-Davidson and Indian were widely deployed in most other parts of the country. Following an aggressive sales campaign, by the late 1930s, Harley-Davidson had become the recognised leaders in this market, with an impressive two-to-one lead over their Indian rivals. For some years, Harley-Davidson dealers with political influence had ensured suitable specifications were written into local government requirements.

In 1932, the smaller 'Scout' Pony 30.50cu.in./500cc V-twin sv model was introduced. Intended as an economical utility model, the machine was based upon the 37cu.in. Scout of 1920, with reduced capacity, larger carburettor and dry-sump lubrication system. Further new features included a clutch lever on the right handlebar and front-wheel brake lever on the left. With a shorter wheelbase, girder-type front forks replacing the traditional leaf-sprung Indian design, a low weight enabled a surprisingly good speed, and the machine quickly gained a sports reputation. The similar, but larger, 45cu.in./750cc Motoplane was also introduced that year.

Later known as the 'Junior' Scout, the lightweight model provided the basis for the military model Indian 640 of 1940, with the 30.50cu.in. engine mounted within the frame of the larger Sport Scout. From the mid 1930s, the Sport Scout also adopted the more common girder type parallelogram front forks and dry sump lubrication. Although the 30.50cu.in. 640 machines were deployed by the British during World War 2, interested in the fuel economy of the smaller model, the larger 45cu.in. Sport Scout became the more powerful military model Indian 741, preferred by the US forces. Both machines featured milder tuning, lower compression ratio, and restricted breathing for increased engine life, with the addition of a larger air filter for dusty conditions. Further military modifications included a heavy duty rear carry rack, a pair of large panniers and racks for extra fuel containers.

To end this chapter, Condor motorcycles should be mentioned, as used by the Swiss Army for many years, with MAG engines, particularly Models 641 and 752, (p 189).

CHAPTER THREE

Second World War 1939-45

I: GERMANY RE-ARMS . . .

As Nazi Germany prepared for war, a vast range of vehicles were procured for military service, but with very little standardisation, apart from load classification, this vast unmanageable fleet had to be reduced for any effective duty. Under the control of one Col. Oberst. von Schell, later promoted to General, the more expensive and sophisticated machines were abandoned as too complex to maintain, and increased production centred upon the more basic models. While many existing vehicles of the *Reichswehr*, up to 1935, were kept in use, new machines became increasingly basic and easier to manufacture and repair. With reference to motorcycles alone, more than 150 different models was reduced to 30, from nine factories. In addition, 41 smaller manufacturers were instructed to produce two autocycle models, of an agreed design and in numbers as required.

The greatest rationalisation was made with electrical and mechanical accessories and component by selecting just one, or a greatly reduced number of each. With the declaration of war, from the lightweight despatch model to the heavyweight outfit, the *Wehrmacht*, 1935–45, had procured motorcycles of every size and configuration, but the Schell Programme greatly simplified both models and parts deployed. Divided into three categories, the lightweight under 350cc (DKW RT125, Phänomen AHOJ, pp 191–2, NSU 251OS, TRW BD250 etc) the middleweight under 500cc (BMW R4, BMW R35, DKW NZ350, Victoria KR35WH, etc), and the heavyweight over 500cc (BMW R12, NSU 601 OSL, Zündapp K500, K800 and KS600, etc), these machines were basically all standard production models, with service livery and a pair of leather bags. With, however, the introduction of the lightweight four-wheel drive vehicle, the German military motorcycle was almost replaced, and for the final few months of the war all production was restricted to the DKW RT125 and NZ350 models alone.

Kradschützen (Motorcycle troops)

As ever larger numbers of people bought motorcycles and became experienced in both riding and maintenance, many civilian motor-sport organisations required their members to train on military equipment, preparing a huge army in waiting. The motorcycle was seen to provide both inexpensive and rapid transportation of men and arms and by the time war was declared, German military opinion dictated that all other ranks should travel by motorcycle or truck, while officers had the use of cars. Recognised as an appropriate replacement for the horse, in addition to general transport, motorcycles were widely

Left: **1940 Puch GS350, a pre-war model produced for German use.** *(Hadtorteneti Intezet es Muzeum)*

deployed for despatch or supplied to sharpshooters. Motorcycle despatch riders replaced both the horse and bicycle and motorcycle sharpshooters took the place of the cavalry. The military police also obtained motorcycles for escort, convoy control and border patrol.

Considered to be elite troops, motorcycle units frequently proved their worth at the front, but their equipment was not always reliable. As early as the Polish campaign, and the invasion of France, many military experts began to doubt the suitability of these modified commercial machines. The much greater demands of the Russian front further demonstrated their shortcomings; lightweights were completely worn-out within a few days and heavier models would only last weeks. With opportunities for service behind the front lines, riders were able to increase the

machines' operational value, but many models were found to be unable to withstand the rigors of active service.

While despatch riders continued to provide a service wherever possible, many machines were discarded for a smaller number of purpose-built models. Motorcycles had been modified from general production and requisitioned from private owners, but German factory output was reduced from some 200,000 in 1938 to only 33,000 by 1944. Many motorcycle units were transferred to lightweight four-wheel drive vehicles, heavy trucks or light armoured cars, while the sharpshooters were gradually moved into the Panzer Group and became tank gunners. During this period of specialisation German factories manufactured some of the most complex military models ever produced, such as the BMW R75 and

Above: **1942 M-72 sidecar outfit, a close copy of the BMW R71, widely deployed by the Red Army until 1959, when eventually superseded by the further developed K-750. Produced in vast numbers, the model provided solo and sidecar military service throughout the Soviet Union and Eastern Europe.** *(Frank Nyklicek)*

Right: **Two Hungarian soldiers upon a Puch GS350. Under Nazi control a number of Austrian and Czechoslovak factories were used to meet German and Axis military requirements.** *(Hadtorteneti Intezet es Muzeum)*

Far right: **Hungarian despatch rider (note padded black leather AFV helmet) upon a pre-war CZ 175; a popular lightweight in Eastern Europe.** *(Hadtorteneti Intezet es Muzeum)*

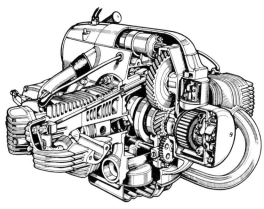

the Zündapp K5750 (p 192), but eventually the simple single-cylinder, two-stroke proved to be more successful, leaving heavier demands to four or more wheels.

BMW and Zündapp

Originally intended for service in the *Afrika Korps*, the BMW R75 and Zündapp KS750 models were first introduced in the autumn of 1940, but these heavyweight sidecar outfits were soon deployed in more rigorous operations. Designed for towing light-guns in the paratroop regiments, it was found the towbar weight lifted the front wheel, and while this problem could not be corrected, the machines fulfilled expecta-

tions for multi-terrain duties. The Belgian and French military had adopted similar motorcycle outfits during the late 1930s (FN M12, Gillet-Herstal 750 and Sarolea 1000, and Rene-Gillet G1 and Gnome Rhône AX2, and the manufacturers, with Ford and General Motors and others,

Above: **German despatch rider and Zündapp K500W in action. Note the WH (Wehrmacht) on number plate.** *(Zündapp)*

Left: **Zündapp K800 engine; horizontal transverse four-cylinder design. With distributor and single coil ignition under the forward cover.** *(Zündapp)*

Top left: **Zündapp KS600 engine, transverse boxer overhead valve design. Note the cross-cut helical gear train.** *(Zündapp)*

Opposite, below: **Hungarian soldiers manhandle a CWS-MIII outfit, captured during the German invasion of Poland. Note the sidecar body is mounted upon leaf springs.** *(Hadtorteneti Intezet es Muzeum)*

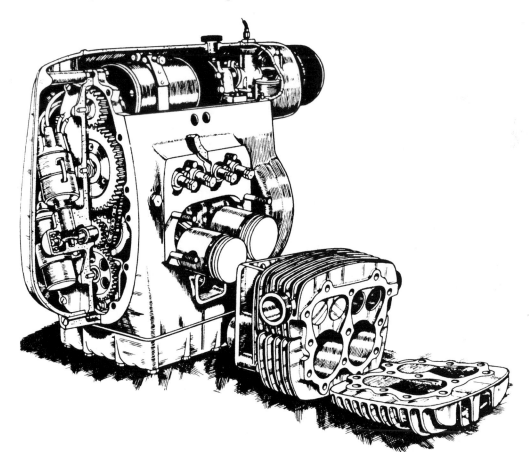

were forced to supply the *Wehrmacht* throughout the war years. Reportedly, it was these Belgian and French models that provided the basis for the later BMW and Zündapp designs.

With such features as sidecar wheel drive, four-speed and reverse gearbox, some with high-low ratio, and lockable differential on BMW, high-level exhaust system, fully protected air filters, hydraulic brakes and suspension, wide-section cross-country tyres and interchangeable wheels with a spare mounted on the sidecar, these machines achieved outstanding service, with which few other vehicles could compare. As described earlier in Chapter 2, the BMW featured a tubular duplex cradle frame and the Zündapp had a pressed-steel frame and front fork design. Both engines provided 26hp, modest by today's standards, to the rear wheel via an exposed shaft drive, with a transfer shaft to the sidecar wheel, with hydraulic brakes on the two driven wheels and a mechanical one on the front. With low ratio gears on the BMW and a single crawler gear on the Zündapp, the two machines had an ability to travel almost anywhere, until lightweight four-wheel vehicles were developed and successfully provided the all purpose solution.

Neither model had rear suspension, both with a helical sprung saddle and pillion mounted upon the carrier rack The single seat sidecar was of strictly functional design and carried ammunition, spares and a radio, two petrol cans and a full tank of fuel gave the machines a range of some 800 km. The sidecar was also used to mount a machine-gun, but behind the front lines was

Above: **A typical German despatch park; Zündapp outfits prepared and awaiting final delivery.** *(Zündapp)*

Right: **1933-1940 Zündapp K500W, a standard production model widely deployed by both *Reichswehr* and *Wehrmacht*.** *(Zündapp)*

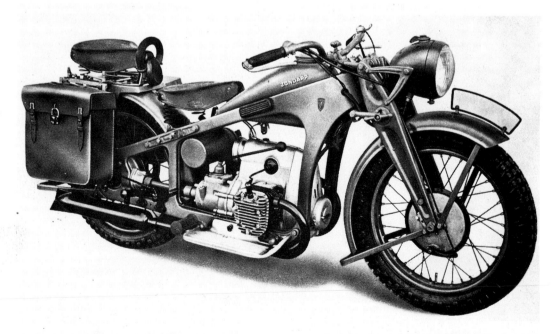

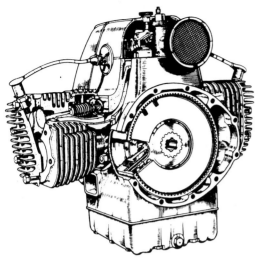

more often seen with a convoy light. By 1943, both models modified their exhaust system, with a high mounted single silencer and heat exchanger, providing ducted warm air over the rider's feet and hands, and into the sidecar, helping to combat the extreme cold of the Russian Front.

In skilled hands these outfits could provide an excellent means of rapid transportation, for three soldiers and equipment. Without thorough training, however, the machines could prove a liability; a further reason for the eventual demise of these costly vehicles. Widely used from North Africa to Eastern Europe, a total of 16,510 BMW R75s and 18,635 Zündapp KS750s were manufactured before both were discontinued in 1944, but with an additional 450 Zündapps built after the war.

Left: **The clutch side of the Zündapp K500 engine.** *(Zündapp)*

Below left: **Zündapp KS750W sidecar wheel drive.** *(Zündapp)*

Below: **1933-1938 Zündapp K800W remained popular throughout World War 2.** *(Zündapp)*

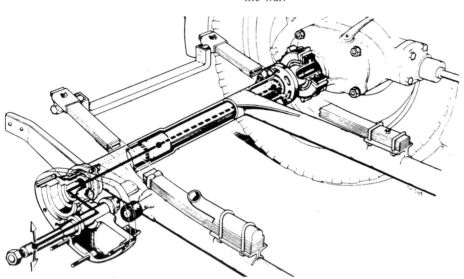

The BMW R12 and its later derivative the R71 was a further model that won a special popularity within the *Wehrmacht*, not only solo, but with a sidecar attached. While the civilian customer could purchase a 20hp version with twin carburettors, the military version was restricted to an 18hp single carburettor engine. With a robust design, the military R12 frequently distinguished itself with astonishing pulling-power, and relatively generous load carrying capacity. Produced between 1935 and 1938, the model introduced the BMW 'maintenance free' telescopic front forks. While not the first motorcycle to have a telescopic design, it was the first to adopt hydraulic damping in series production. It was also built under licence in Russia, where it remained in production until 1956.

Together with BMW's flat-twins, Zündapp's similar machines proved their equal worth. In particular, the K800 flat-four was a surprisingly sophisticated machine with car-type clutch and gearchange.

It was the only four-cylinder motorcycle used by the *Wehrmacht* apart from a small quantity of Puch 800 flat-fours and remained in production until the early forties, at which time some 5000 were in service. The Puch flat-four was discontinued under the Schell programme after 550 had been built. Puch however, maintained output for the *Wehrmacht* and other Axis forces, with their split-single two-stroke models 125-T, 250-S4 and 350-GS, until 1942, when the factory in Graz was heavily bombed and put out of action.

Left: **1936 Bianchi 498cc type 500M; widely used by the Italian Army in both Italy and North Africa, the 500M remained in service throughout the Second World War for despatch and liaison duties. Note the advanced plunger-type rear suspension.** *(Museo Storico della Motorizzazione Militare)*

Below: **1957 Moto Guzzi 350cc Airone; solo lightweight adopted by the Italian Army for solo despatch and pillion service. The high ground clearance is an Italian factory trademark.** *(Museo Storico della Motorizzazione Militare)*

Above: **1973 Moto Guzzi 850cc T3; a standard production model adopted by police departments worldwide. This machine has been prepared to meet the requirements of the Italian military police (***Carabinieri***). Like BMW, the Italian factory began to offer a wide range of various accessories for both military and police service.** *(Moto Guzzi)*

Right: **1981 Moto Guzzi 350cc V35-II; the smallest version of the V-twin series production. This machine is one from a delivery order for the former Yugoslav Army.** *(Moto Guzzi)*

Above: **1940 Zündapp 750cc KS750; a specialised military motorcycle and sidecar, the KS750 was widely used in Europe and North Africa throughout the Second World War. Often used with a trailer the machine provided a multi-terrain vehicle for 3 soldiers and all their equipment.** *(François-Marie Dumas)*

Left: **1939 Zündapp 597cc KS600W & Steib sidecar; primarily adopted with a sidecar for military service, more than 18,000 were produced between 1938 and 1941. Note the pressed steel front fork suspension.** *(Andrew Morland)*

Above: **1941 BMW 746cc R75;** widely deployed across Europe and North Africa this military combination has been prepared for desert service, with a large carburettor sand filter. *(François-Marie Dumas)*

Right: **1970 Hercules K125Bw;** a multi-terrain lightweight developed to replace the ageing Maico M250/B. Some 15,000 were delivered for military service before a revised version was introduced in 1981 with telescopic front forks. *(Hercules-Werke)*

Left: **Designed for multi-terrain military service, the Zündapp KS750W sidecar outfit, with a sidecar wheel drive, ratio change and reverse gearbox. A total of 18,635 of these outstanding machines were eventually produced between 1940-44, with a further 450 post-war.** (Zündapp)

Below: **Drawing of the Zündapp K800 engine, a rare military flat-four.** (Zündapp)

Below left: **Zündapp K800W sidecar outfit in North Africa; the only four cylinder motorcycle procured by the German armed forces.** (Zündapp)

Additional machines

Any list of German military motorcycles deployed in World War 2 should also include the NSU 601-OSL. This more traditional model featured a vertical single-cylinder 562cc (85 x 99mm) ohv engine (see Chapter 2). Smaller lightweight two-strokes produced by Ardie were also widely used. In particular the 125cc and 200cc VF125 and RBZ200 models proved popular (p 191). Under Nazi rule, Czechoslovak industry also remained in production during the war, deployed to provide new machines or repairs. As in Austria, the *Wehrmacht* took control of armament manufacture and seized a wide range of vehicles, before particular models (including cars, trucks and motorcycles) were chosen for continued production. The Ogar 250cc, CZ 175 and 350cc, and Jawa 175, 250 and 350cc models had been selected by the Czechoslovak Army (see Chapter 2), and were employed by the *Wehrmacht*. These basically commercial lightweights remained in production for most of the war, while these factories also maintained various German built military vehicles.

As previously mentioned, another machine widely used by the *Wehrmacht* was the 250cc split-single two-stroke Puch 250-S4 (p 190).

II: ITALIAN DIVERSITY . . .

Historically, Italy's motorcycle industry had an ability to meet military requirements. Very few machines were employed during the 1920s, but as in Germany, Italy began a massive re-armament programme during the following ten years. In October 1935, Italian troops invaded Ethiopia,

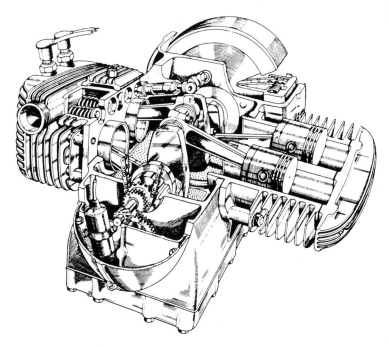

Right: **BMW R75s, heavily camouflaged, and Hungarian mobile troops.**
(Hadtorteneti Intezet es Muzeum)

Below right: **Hungarian troops advance; Don Front, 1942.**
(Hadtorteneti Intezet es Muzeum)

Below: **Hungarian despatch rider upon a Zündapp DB200W; single cylinder two-stroke lightweight widely deployed by German and Axis armed forces.**
(Hadtorteneti Intezet es Muzeum)

and between 1936-39, Italy took part in the Spanish Civil War. In April 1939, Italy overran Albania, and the following year, Italy entered World War 2 in Libya. Italy's Fascist government however, collapsed in 1943, and Germany took control of large parts of the country until the end of the war. Existing military equipment was taken over by the *Wehrmacht*, and Italian factories remained in production for the Germans.

Throughout the 1930s, a diverse range of motorcycles (Benelli, Bianchi, Gilera, Moto Guzzi, Sertum etc) were adopted by the Italian Army (see Chapter 2). Italian solo models were often used with a pillion saddle, providing both despatch and troop carrying duties and with a sidecar attached, a third soldier, and all his

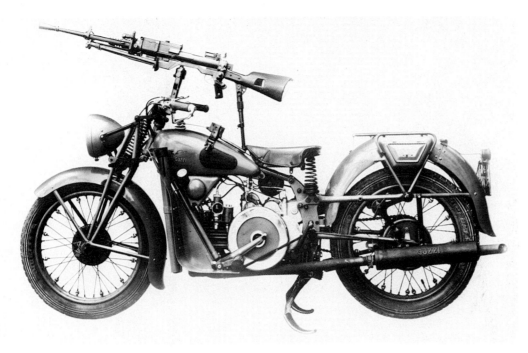

Left: **1940 Moto Guzzi GTS, a pre-production military Alce model, complete with a machine-gun mounted upon the fuel tank, leaving the handlebars to move freely.** *(Moto Guzzi)*

Below: **Official factory drawing of the Moto Guzzi Alce model, introduced to replace the GT17 of the inter-war years. Widely adopted by the Italian Army, a total of 6390 solo Alce's (in addition to 669 machines with a sidecar) were assembled between 1939 and 1945.** *(Moto Guzzi)*

equipment, could be carried, or a mobile machine-gun position provided. Solo machines were also supplied with machine-gun mountings on the handlebars, or equipped with support brackets to carry weapons into combat. Both solo and sidecar models were also available with either semi or fully enclosed armoured shields, to give some protection for an assault vehicle or mobile sniper position. Similar designs were also prepared by FN, Rene-Gillet and Harley-Davidson.

Moto Guzzi

The Moto Guzzi Alce was introduced in 1939, and quickly became a very popular military machine (p 194). While keeping the wheelbase as short as possible, the Alce offered a remarkable

ground clearance. This was largely due to the traditional horizontal single-cylinder engine, with its familiar exposed flywheel. Breathing through a 26mm Dell'Orto carburettor, with a steel-wool air filter, the 500cc (88 x 82mm) unit produced 13hp at a low 3800rpm. Following its forerunners GT17 and GT20 models (see Chapter 2), the Alce featured an exhaust-over-inlet valve design, with an unusual single-port exhaust and twin silencer system, mounted high on the left side. Transmission ran through helical primary gears, a four-speed gearbox and exposed chain final drive. Engine-oil was stored within the tubular frame, with a filler cap through the fuel tank, which also had a gear indicator mounting.

Italian motorcycles generally adopted a mixture

Right: **Moto Guzzi Alce sidecar outfit, with minimal military equipment, to provide transport for Italian Army officers.** *(Moto Guzzi)*

Centre right: **1940 Moto Guzzi Alce, prepared for machine gun and tripod transport, one of numerous variations adopted by the military model.** *(Moto Guzzi)*

Below right: **1940-46 Moto Guzzi Airone, a 250cc lightweight, for solo despatch and general liaison. The model featured overhead valves for improved performance. Note the pressed steel front forks.** *(Moto Guzzi)*

of pressings and forged and tubular steel. As with many Italian machines, girder type front forks and a friction damped rear sub-frame provided front and rear suspension, able to cope with most off-road requirements. The wheels were interchangeable, and could be removed without disturbing either the brakes or rear-wheel drive. The Moto Guzzi sidecar was a very basic pressed-steel construction with a spare wheel and fly screen, and it had third wheel suspension. The Alce remained in service throughout the war, prepared for either on- or off-road conditions, and a version was also produced with ski attachments to maintain all-year-round duties. Many Alce machines were also equipped with a novel peg device to enable the machine to be parked upon a steep hill.

Well respected by the Italian Army, and opponents that captured working examples, 6390 solo and 669 sidecars were supplied between 1939 and 1945. The Alce V, later known as the Superalce, was introduced in 1946. After a period of 25 years of excellent service, the opposed valve engine was finally replaced with an ohv design, 18.5hp at 4300rpm. The four-speed gearbox adopted a foot-change, and with very few further modifications, the military Superalce remained in production until 1957. A smaller 250cc Moto Guzzi was also supplied until 1946. Known as the Airone (p 194), it was widely used.

The Alce sidecar outfit was only ever considered a transitional machine by Moto Guzzi. Between 1942 and '43, Moto Guzzi worked on a sidecar model, with large section tyres, and a third-wheel drive. The traditional horizontal 500cc engine featured overhead valves, some four years ahead of the Superalce. Prepared for off-road use only, there was no differential, with the two driven wheels locked to improve traction. Designated the Trialce (p 194), the model remained a prototype; following the heavy losses of the Italian Army in Russia and Africa.

The Trialce name, however, was eventually adopted for a military model; based upon the three-wheeled commercial light carrier Moto Guzzi had produced since 1928. From the front wheel to the saddle the model was a standard motorcycle, but the remainder extended to provide a load carrying platform. An exposed chain provided power to the two rear wheels, with an aluminium casting upon the axle, containing a reduction gear, recoil stop and the differential. The vehicle was used in various forms, to transport stores, troops and arms, or as a heavy machine-gun position complete with protection shield. From 1941–42, Moto Guzzi produced the 500U Unificato for heavier military duties, with a traditionally horizontal 17.8hp 500cc ohv power unit, driving the rear two wheels via a three-speed gearbox and exposed chain.

Gilera

Similar tricycles to the Moto Guzzi machines were also produced by Gilera, 500 & 600cc sv, and 600cc ohv, offering drop sides, canvas top and fully-tipping models throughout the war. In addition, the larger model Gilera Mercurio (p 194) was built for heavier service. The Mercurio had a vertical single cylinder 500cc ohv engine, providing 20hp through a four-speed and reverse gearbox, and shaft final drive. With a carrying capacity of some 1500kg, the Gilera Mercurio, remained in production until 1963 for both civilian and military use.

Above: **1942 Moto Guzzi Trialce, based upon the GT17 tricycle, the folding frame (horizontally hinged in the centre) Trialce was introduced as a multi-purpose military load carrier;** *the* **mobile gun design.** *(Moto Guzzi)*

Designated the VL Marte, Gilera also produced a military sidecar outfit in 1942, complete with a sidecar wheel drive. Based upon the LTE model of 1936 (see Chapter 2), the Marte had a single cylinder 500cc sv engine, and four-speed gearbox, but the transmission had been revised to shaft drive for military use. While perhaps an unsophisticated compromise, Gilera alone had remarkably been able to provide full suspension to all three wheels, and include a sidecar wheel drive.

Moto Benelli

A Benelli won the 1939 250cc TT, and with ever growing demands from the Italian Army, the 250cc (67 x 70mm) and 500cc (85 x 87mm) ohc sports models were prepared for active duty, alongside the more traditional Benelli VLM-500 military machine. The VLM-500 had a vertical single cylinder 500cc (85 x 87mm) sv engine, mounted within a single downtube cycle frame, with a four-speed gearbox and exposed chain final drive. The engine provided 11hp at 4200rpm, and with a good ground clearance, this well balanced model gave reliable solo/pillion service throughout the war.

The Benelli ohc engine featured a forward inclined single-cylinder, with exposed valve springs and a twin-port head. Widely used for solo/pillion despatch, reconnaissance and general liaison, the 500cc model also provided the front half of the Benelli military tricycle (p 194).

In typical Italian style, the 500cc ohc model was available with a platform body mounted above two rear wheels and became the basis for a 47mm anti-tank gun. The Benelli tricycle was eventually superseded by the larger and stronger Gilera Mercurio and Moto Guzzi 500U models.

Folding Airborne Motorcycle

In 1942, the Societa Volugrafo, Turin, prepared a special fold-away lightweight motorcycle, designed for the Italian airborne troops. This unique model, with a wheelbase of only 900mm/35½ inches, had a single-cylinder 125cc two-stroke engine, with a unit construction two-speed gearbox and clutch, mounted within a rigid box frame. A reduction gear provided a dual range, giving speeds of 20 and 40mph in high, 32 and 64km/h, dropping to 7 and 15mph, 11 and 24km/h in low. The lower frame tubes also acted

as the exhaust system. Both wheels were discs with split rims with mechanical hub brakes, and were often used in pairs to double the tyre width, which enabled the machine to stand alone.

The engine was tucked away for added protection, and with the removal of a locating pin, the handlebars could be folded back for a parachute container. Equipped with telescopic front forks, an exposed chain final drive, a kick-start and full lighting, overall dimensions were variable depending on the model, but the machine remained light enough to carry. These advanced machines were not extensively used; but perhaps laid the foundation for the successful Italian post-war scooter.

III: UNPREPARED BRITAIN . . .

When Britain declared war on Germany in September 1939, the country was ill-prepared to offer any full military offensive. The Army could only provide four divisions as an Expeditionary Force in Europe, six infantry and one armoured division in the Middle East, a field division and brigade in India, and two brigades in Malaya. Many years of neglect left the British unable to face the modern forces of Germany and British industry was not ready to make up the deficit. The Royal Navy and Royal Air Force had successfully started rearmament programmes in 1935–36, replacing older equipment and increasing arms wherever possible, but the Army remained quite old-fashioned in both organisation and equipment.

While innovations followed, the majority of British military motorcycles were basically pre-war civilian models throughout the war. The more robust machines, with a proven history of enduring design, were prepared for active service; with the addition of extra tool boxes, a pair of standard issue canvas pannier bags, a rear carrier rack, and masked lighting. Few British machines adopted a pillion saddle, but were equipped with a rubber pad on the rear mudguard, for the limited occasions when not used as a solo mount. With the removal of kneegrips, rubbers for the handlebar and footrests, all chromium plating, and other non-essentials, the machines were given a coat of khaki paint. Depending on individual manufacturers, further modifications included engine sump guards, reprofiled mudguards and reinforced side and centre/rear stand.

Barely suited to military use, major models included the Ariel W/NG (p 192), BSA M20, Matchless G3 & G3L, Norton 16H & Big Four, Royal Enfield WD/C & WD/CO, Triumph 3SW & 3HW, and Velocette MAF (p 193). Intended primarily for surfaced roads, these machines provided solo despatch, reconnaissance, convoy control and military police duties, while the BSA M20 and Norton 16H were also used with a sidecar attached, offering personal transport. The Norton Big Four sidecar outfit was adapted for multi-terrain service. From 1942, the light James ML and Royal Enfield WD/RE models were also prepared for use by the airborne troops, to be dropped by parachute in special crates, while the Excelsior Welbike was packed into its own cylindrical container for parachute use.

Various smaller models were also supplied in limited numbers for solo duties in the Home Guard, training, and general despatch, such as the Ariel W/NG, BSA C10 & C11, and Royal Enfield D/D. In addition, various experimental models of different capacities and performance were produced to meet military requirements; the BSA B30, Cotton/JAP 500cc and Royal Enfield WD/G & WD/J2 were all used in limited numbers. Late in 1939, a batch of some 100 Ariel W/VA machines were built from surplus stock, and within six months, Triumph completed a French order for the 5SW, a larger version of the 3SW, and these two models were also both deployed by the British.

When France fell to the *Wehrmacht* in 1940, a number of ex-French contract machines were redirected in this way. To add to this confusion, in addition to British manufacturers, the British & Commonwealth armed forces also used American motorcycles; Harley-Davidson and Indian models in solo and sidecar versions. The British Army had an almost impossible task to maintain and repair this diverse range of machines, of every possible size, configuration and complexity, and with very few interchangeable or common parts. The War Office began to take stock and eventually more ideal specifications were prepared, but very few of these proposed machines would be introduced during the war years.

Norton

Throughout the war, the Norton Big Four outfit remained the only British military model to offer a sidecar wheel-drive, a feature widely used by European multi-terrain machines (p 193). Based upon the well established civilian model, modifications provided the Norton with a shaft running directly from the rear wheel, and a simple dog-clutch engaged by a left-hand lever when the additional drive was required. To accommodate this development, the frame and rear forks were enlarged for the extra bearings. All three wheels were interchangeable, with 4in. cross-country tyres for increased traction, and a spare carried on the back of the sidecar.

The sidecar was a simple construction, with a single seat, stowage box at the rear, and a large

Above: **An early Matchless G3 (girder type front forks), the basis for the later Matchless G3L (telescopic front forks) – perhaps the most popular British military motorcycle of World War 2. The G3 formed the foundation for many years of post-war military production.** *(David Ansell)*

specifications, AMC prepared the 250cc Matchless G2D as a replacement for the G3, and in early 1940, two prototypes were sent to Farnborough for military trials. The Army however, decided the model had insufficient torque at low speeds, and the 350cc engine was specified as the minimum capacity for general use, leaving the 250cc, and smaller, for training, home defence and special duties. \

In keeping with the G3LS's renowned military heritage, for a further 20 years or more, it and the larger 500cc (83 x 93mm) version G80CS, and their AJS equivalents, the 16MS and 18CS models, continued to provide public service worldwide. Apart from the fore and aft position of the magneto, each side of the vertical cylinder respectively, AJS and Matchless post-war machines were virtually identical. With either on or off road specifications, AMC models successfully replaced many of the wartime machines.

Triumph

The entire stock of completed machines was purchased from the Triumph works in 1939, but as military requirements became more apparent the War Office restricted their interest to the 350cc (70 x 89mm) sv model 3SW. Originally designed in 1932, these robust single-cylinder machines were used by the British armed forces, providing reliable, if not exciting output. Early in 1940, the 3SW was joined by the French ordered 5SW. Apart from two extra teeth on both the engine and gearbox sprockets, to handle the 5SW's 500cc performance, the two models were virtually identical. The extra capacity came from an 84mm bore, but with a common 89mm stroke. The single downtube frame was bolted together, with a duplex cradle beneath the engine. Transmission was entirely by chain, via four-speed foot change gearbox.

With the declaration of war, the War Office prepared specifications for a single military motorcycle, to be assembled as required by any available factory. To meet this demand, Triumph prepared a 350cc ohv twin-cylinder model. Originally intended to replace the single cylinder Triumph Tiger 80, the new model was only weeks away from its civilian market, when the re-designated 3TW, with heavier flywheels, and a smaller carburettor, was found most suitable. The

as the exhaust system. Both wheels were discs with split rims with mechanical hub brakes, and were often used in pairs to double the tyre width, which enabled the machine to stand alone.

The engine was tucked away for added protection, and with the removal of a locating pin, the handlebars could be folded back for a parachute container. Equipped with telescopic front forks, an exposed chain final drive, a kick-start and full lighting, overall dimensions were variable depending on the model, but the machine remained light enough to carry. These advanced machines were not extensively used; but perhaps laid the foundation for the successful Italian post-war scooter.

III: UNPREPARED BRITAIN . . .

When Britain declared war on Germany in September 1939, the country was ill-prepared to offer any full military offensive. The Army could only provide four divisions as an Expeditionary Force in Europe, six infantry and one armoured division in the Middle East, a field division and brigade in India, and two brigades in Malaya. Many years of neglect left the British unable to face the modern forces of Germany and British industry was not ready to make up the deficit. The Royal Navy and Royal Air Force had successfully started rearmament programmes in 1935–36, replacing older equipment and increasing arms wherever possible, but the Army remained quite old-fashioned in both organisation and equipment.

While innovations followed, the majority of British military motorcycles were basically pre-war civilian models throughout the war. The more robust machines, with a proven history of enduring design, were prepared for active service; with the addition of extra tool boxes, a pair of standard issue canvas pannier bags, a rear carrier rack, and masked lighting. Few British machines adopted a pillion saddle, but were equipped with a rubber pad on the rear mudguard, for the limited occasions when not used as a solo mount. With the removal of kneegrips, rubbers for the handlebar and footrests, all chromium plating, and other non-essentials, the machines were given a coat of khaki paint. Depending on individual manufacturers, further modifications included engine sump guards, reprofiled mudguards and reinforced side and centre/rear stand.

Barely suited to military use, major models included the Ariel W/NG (p 192), BSA M20, Matchless G3 & G3L, Norton 16H & Big Four, Royal Enfield WD/C & WD/CO, Triumph 3SW & 3HW, and Velocette MAF (p 193). Intended primarily for surfaced roads, these machines provided solo despatch, reconnaissance, convoy control and military police duties, while the BSA M20 and Norton 16H were also used with a sidecar attached, offering personal transport. The Norton Big Four sidecar outfit was adapted for multi-terrain service. From 1942, the light James ML and Royal Enfield WD/RE models were also prepared for use by the airborne troops, to be dropped by parachute in special crates, while the Excelsior Welbike was packed into its own cylindrical container for parachute use.

Various smaller models were also supplied in limited numbers for solo duties in the Home Guard, training, and general despatch, such as the Ariel W/NG, BSA C10 & C11, and Royal Enfield D/D. In addition, various experimental models of different capacities and performance were produced to meet military requirements; the BSA B30, Cotton/JAP 500cc and Royal Enfield WD/G & WD/J2 were all used in limited numbers. Late in 1939, a batch of some 100 Ariel W/VA machines were built from surplus stock, and within six months, Triumph completed a French order for the 5SW, a larger version of the 3SW, and these two models were also both deployed by the British.

When France fell to the *Wehrmacht* in 1940, a number of ex-French contract machines were redirected in this way. To add to this confusion, in addition to British manufacturers, the British & Commonwealth armed forces also used American motorcycles; Harley-Davidson and Indian models in solo and sidecar versions. The British Army had an almost impossible task to maintain and repair this diverse range of machines, of every possible size, configuration and complexity, and with very few interchangeable or common parts. The War Office began to take stock and eventually more ideal specifications were prepared, but very few of these proposed machines would be introduced during the war years.

Norton

Throughout the war, the Norton Big Four outfit remained the only British military model to offer a sidecar wheel-drive, a feature widely used by European multi-terrain machines (p 193). Based upon the well established civilian model, modifications provided the Norton with a shaft running directly from the rear wheel, and a simple dog-clutch engaged by a left-hand lever when the additional drive was required. To accommodate this development, the frame and rear forks were enlarged for the extra bearings. All three wheels were interchangeable, with 4in. cross-country tyres for increased traction, and a spare carried on the back of the sidecar.

The sidecar was a simple construction, with a single seat, stowage box at the rear, and a large

Right: **Norton Big Four**; based upon the trials model of the late 1930s, a total of 4737 (under nine contracts) were eventually produced. Note the girder-type front forks base through the larger mudguard. *(IWM)*

Below: **Norton** supplied 100,000 motorcycles during World War 2, the most numerous model being the 16H. Deployed both solo or with a sidecar attached, the 16H was supplied to British and Allied armed forces worldwide. *(David Ansell)*

protective front panel. For manhandling, handles were positioned at the front and rear. A pillion saddle was mounted on a pair of tubes extended to form a handle at the rear, while a forward mudguard stay was modified to offer a front lifting position. Extra wide and high clearance mudguards reduced mud clogging.

Several thousand of these outfits were produced and widely used for reconnaissance and personal transportation in most campaigns. Fittings for a swivel mounted machine-gun were available, or the entire sidecar body could be replaced for a platform carrying a mortar and tripod, and two boxes of ammunition. The engine, however, a vertical single-cylinder 633cc (82 x 120mm) sv design of the 1920s, could not offer the pulling power required for a multi-terrain vehicle, and after several improved versions, the War Office requested a replacement in 1942.

Widely deployed throughout Europe, North Africa and the Far East, of over 100,000 Nortons produced during World War 2 the 16H was built in the greatest number. As the BSA M20 and Matchless G3L, the Norton 16H was extensively used by the British Commonwealth armed forces providing a major contribution, alongside the American models of Harley-Davidson and Indian. A traditional British design, the 16H was a smaller version of the Big Four. A vertical single-cylinder 500cc (79 x 100mm) sv engine was mounted within a single downtube frame, with girder type front forks and a well-sprung saddle offering the only, limited, suspension. In most respects the machine was better suited to military duties than many, with sufficient speed, adequate brakes, and a higher ground clearance than others.

The engine had a good reputation for reliability, and shortcomings in the gearbox and rear-wheel mountings were often overlooked. From modifications to the air filter for desert duty to retractable ski fittings, the 16H was assembled for most climatic conditions. As the war continued, the speedometer was moved from its central position above the forks, to a bracket on the left, to stop the cable from becoming trapped. Handlebar rubber grips were replaced by webbing, and the footrests became metal tubes, with a disc at the end to stop the rider's foot from sliding off. Finished in various colours, depending upon destination, most machines were rebuilt at least once in their service life, often with some changes from their original specification.

AMC (Associated Motor Cycles)

AMC prepared a replacement for the Norton Big Four. Known as the Sunbeam 1000 (AMC had acquired Sunbeam in 1936, and sold the concern to BSA in 1943); while the sidecar remained as that of the Big Four, the new model featured the powerful Matchless V-twin 990cc (85.5 x 85.5mm) ohv engine. Transmission ran through a four-speed gearbox, with a supplementary unit which offered either forward or reverse (four forward and four reverse speeds!), and an exposed chain final drive, which in turn could drive the sidecar wheel in the same manner as the Norton. The gearing, however, limited the powerful machine to less than 50mph, as the design centred upon great pulling power for off-road service.

With an excellent ground clearance, the engine was mounted within a tubular frame, with a pair of heavyweight AMC Teledraulic front forks and a rigid rear wheel. A single carburettor was positioned between the cylinders, and the two exhaust pipes ran into a single silencer, mounted high on the right. Following military trials, the War Office placed an order for the Sunbeam 1000. By which time AMC was totally committed to the Matchless G3L, and the contract was passed to the Standard car factory.

The USA however, declared war in 1942, and with the introduction of the four-wheel drive Jeep, the Sunbeam 1000 order was never fulfilled. Although a good sidecar outfit could surpass the Jeep in many ways, far greater power-to-weight ratio, much smaller turning circle, etc, in unskilled hands three wheels were often proven dangerous, and the War Office decided to replace their combinations with the safer Jeep. The Army also knew how disastrous it was to leave the sidecar wheel drive engaged when returning to the surfaced road. Neither the Norton Big Four nor Sunbeam 1000 was equipped with a differential, and could easily maintain a straight line with the handlebars at full lock. For this reason, the sidecar drive-shaft was deleted from both models before they reached the civilian market after the war.

AMC focused their military production on the vertical single-cylinder 350cc (69 x 93mm) ohv Matchless G3 and G3L models (p 193), providing one of the most popular British despatch models of the war; between 1941 and 1945, more than 63,000 G3Ls were built. The G3 underwent its first military trials in 1933, and was highly commended, but as testing continued faults began to appear. A further series of trials was undertaken in 1936, and the first batch of 110 was delivered. Limited orders followed until 1940, when the G3 appeared in its final military format. The hair-pin valve springs were replaced with AJS coil-springs (AMC had acquired AJS in 1932), and the original duplex cradle frame was replaced by a single downtube design. The G3 model remained in production until 1942; the final batch assembled with AMC Teledraulic front forks to replace the original girder type suspension.

Developed to meet some new War Office

Above: **An early Matchless G3 (girder type front forks), the basis for the later Matchless G3L (telescopic front forks) – perhaps the most popular British military motorcycle of World War 2. The G3 formed the foundation for many years of post-war military production.** *(David Ansell)*

specifications, AMC prepared the 250cc Matchless G2D as a replacement for the G3, and in early 1940, two prototypes were sent to Farnborough for military trials. The Army however, decided the model had insufficient torque at low speeds, and the 350cc engine was specified as the minimum capacity for general use, leaving the 250cc, and smaller, for training, home defence and special duties. \

In keeping with the G3LS's renowned military heritage, for a further 20 years or more, it and the larger 500cc (83 x 93mm) version G80CS, and their AJS equivalents, the 16MS and 18CS models, continued to provide public service worldwide. Apart from the fore and aft position of the magneto, each side of the vertical cylinder respectively, AJS and Matchless post-war machines were virtually identical. With either on or off road specifications, AMC models successfully replaced many of the wartime machines.

Triumph

The entire stock of completed machines was purchased from the Triumph works in 1939, but as military requirements became more apparent the War Office restricted their interest to the 350cc (70 x 89mm) sv model 3SW. Originally designed in 1932, these robust single-cylinder machines were used by the British armed forces, providing reliable, if not exciting output. Early in 1940, the 3SW was joined by the French ordered 5SW. Apart from two extra teeth on both the engine and gearbox sprockets, to handle the 5SW's 500cc performance, the two models were virtually identical. The extra capacity came from an 84mm bore, but with a common 89mm stroke. The single downtube frame was bolted together, with a duplex cradle beneath the engine. Transmission was entirely by chain, via four-speed foot change gearbox.

With the declaration of war, the War Office prepared specifications for a single military motorcycle, to be assembled as required by any available factory. To meet this demand, Triumph prepared a 350cc ohv twin-cylinder model. Originally intended to replace the single cylinder Triumph Tiger 80, the new model was only weeks away from its civilian market, when the re-designated 3TW, with heavier flywheels, and a smaller carburettor, was found most suitable. The

Left: **Late 1942, motorcycles (largely Triumphs) awaiting repair at the NT Force Division Ordnance Workshop, Adelaide River, NT Australia.** *(AWM neg no 027659)*

Opposite, above **Norton 16H prepared for military service by the Norwegian Army; skis were widely used in this way by Scandinavian troops during World War 2.** *(Norwegian Embassy)*

Below: **Triumph Model 3SW engine detail.** *(David Ansell, owned by P Couchman)*

Above: **1940 BSA 500cc M20; a British despatch rider providing a message for a pigeon carrier, often a vital link with many forward positions. With only limited military conversion, the M20 offered outstanding service in many parts of the world.**
(Mick Woollett)

was revived in 1944, and eventually became the post-war military Triumph TRW (see Chapter 4).

BSA

During 1938, BSA supplied more than 3000 motorcycles to the British Army, and with the declaration of war a further 690 were requisitioned, and an order for some 8000 placed. Britain however, was not alone in wanting British motorcycles for the armed forces, and BSA's overseas customers included Eire, India, Netherlands, Sweden and South Africa. The Dutch Government, which had changed their allegiance from BMW to BSA the previous year, placed some of the largest foreign orders; during the two years before Nazi occupation, BSA supplied the Dutch Army with more than 1750 of the M13 (600cc) and G14 (1000cc) models.

With the collapse of France, BSA increased their weekly 500 machines output, until a figure of 1000 per week was achieved, in a bid to recover the lost equipment, which included every motorcycle in the British Expeditionary Force. BSA eventually produced 126,334 of the 425,000 motorcycles supplied to the British forces by British factories during World War 2; a fact well remembered for many years, though the BSA sales slogan 'One in four was a BSA'.

A change of priorities in 1937 replaced the BSA 500cc V-twin ohv military model for the simplicity of a single-cylinder sv design, and following trials at Farnborough, the War Office placed a large order for the BSA M20. With the addition of some B30s for training use (p 192), and a limited number of C10 and C11 models for home base duties, the majority of BSA military motorcycles were M20s. As the Norton 16H, the BSA M20 was extensively used worldwide, with a similar general design (see specification tables) the two machines offered robust and reliable performance, for both on and off road service.

Early in the war, when the War Office requested ideas for a new military model, BSA, as Triumph had done, presented a lightweight model. Based on the civilian 350cc B30 ohv machine, initial trials proved successful and an order for 10,000 placed, but as problems with spares and maintenance for two quite different BSA models were realised, the order was quickly changed to another contract for the M20. With the bombing of Coventry and Birmingham, all further plans for the new lightweight were abandoned, and factories began to concentrate maximum output upon existing machines. For many post-war years the BSA M20 remained in service with many armed forces, eventually replaced in Australia and Great Britain by the BSA B40 during the mid 1960s (see Chapter 4).

Triumph Works, however, was bombed in November 1940, and the idea for a single military model was abandoned, and the 3TW discontinued.

Triumph moved into temporary buildings in Warwick, and finally moved into a new factory at Meriden, but this was not operational until 1942. The year before, Triumph re-introduced the sv model 3SW, alongside the ohv version 3HW (p 193). Once again, the two machines were very similar in outward appearance, adopting common parts wherever possible. The 3HW was largely used by the Royal Navy, while the 3SW adopted by the WRNS.

Alongside the single-cylinder production, Triumph continued to develop a twin-cylinder military model, and in 1942, the 5TW made its first appearance. The engine retained the traditional Triumph 500cc (63 x 80mm) configuration, but with a sv operation. With minor modifications, a camshaft lay in front of the lay vertical cylinders, providing lift to all four valves. With a shortage of aluminium, the cylinders were in a single cast-iron block, surmounted by a one-piece cast-iron head. Apart from telescopic front forks, the 5TW followed traditional Triumph design. The prototype, however, did not go into production, but

Royal Enfield

The majority of Royal Enfield military motorcycles were based upon their pre-war 350cc (70 x 90mm) sv and ohv machines, the C and CO models respectively. Supplied from 1940, the WD/C (p 193) was gradually replaced by the WD/CO, which eventually became the main model supplied; between 1942 and 1944, a total of 29,037 WD/COs were supplied for solo despatch and home base liaison, with at least 2820 supplied to the RAF. Various changes to frame design were introduced as production continued, but the engine remained as the original version. A third frame variant replaced the top rear tubes with either a pressed steel design or used standard tubes, bent and with flattened ends, because of wartime shortages.

Royal Enfield also supplied about 1000 of their 250cc model D/D for training, a limited number of the 350cc model G and 500cc model J for general despatch and in direct response to War Office specifications, the Redditch factory experimented with a large capacity V-twin model, with a sidecar wheel-drive, to replace the Norton Big Four. This model never proceeded beyond the prototype stage.

Flying Flea, Clockwork Mouse & Welbike

Perhaps, however, Royal Enfield was best known

Top: **BSA M20, prepared either solo or with a sidecar, of the 126,334 BSA's supplied during World War 2, this was the most numerous model.** *(David Ansell, owned by Peter Allen)*

Above and left: **Royal Enfield WD/CO, a single-cylinder 350cc ohv model, procured in number by the British and Allied armed forces.** *(David Ansell)*

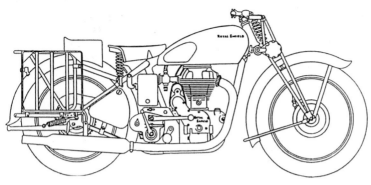

Above: **Official factory drawing of the Royal Enfield WD/CO model. Based upon pre-war standard production, military conversion was largely limited to an overall coat of service livery and a pair of canvas panniers.**
(Sven-Olof Persson)

for its 125cc lightweight, affectionately known as the Flying Flea by the Red Berets. Nearly 8000 of these two-stroke machines were prepared for the British Army's Airborne Division. Apart from a small increase in capacity, the RE125 was based on the DKW RT98.

Originally produced during the immediate pre-war years, the RE125 was re-introduced in 1942, when the military potential for a lightweight motorcycle for airborne troops was realised. In common with the James ML (p 192), known as the Clockwork Mouse, these lightweights were dropped by parachute, in purpose-built crates, from Horsa and other gliders, to give mobility to the landing forces. The two models remained in production until 1944, with a total of 6040 James MLs built for military use. Specifications required foldaway footrests and handlebars for parachute use, but the machines were also carried on the back of tanks, and effectively used to direct men and materials on numerous beach landings.

In addition, from late 1942, the Excelsior Welbike was also supplied to the airborne troops, designed to be packed within its own cylindrical container (p 192). With a Villiers 98cc single-cylinder, two-stroke engine, mounted horizontally, very small wheels (12½ x 2¼in.), folding handlebars and seat pillar, the overall dimensions could be reduced from some 52 x 22 x 31in. with a wheelbase of 39½in. to just 51 x 12 x 15in. Directly driving the rear wheel, through a dry-plate clutch and exposed chain, and mechanical brake on the rear wheel only, the weight was below 70lb, 31½kg. By the end of the war, a total of 3840 of these collapsible parascooters was produced, a forerunner of the Brockhouse Corgi, a modified post-war civilian version.

Final Request

Until 1944, virtually all British military motorcycles had been civilian machines, with minor modifications to meet particular service requirements, and then the Ministry of Supply prepared an outline for a purpose-built solo model. Specifications called for a top speed of 60-70mph/97-

114km/h, a consumption of 80mpg/28km/l at 30mph/48km/h, a weight of under 300lb/136kg, and a braking distance of less than 35ft/10.8m from 30mph/48km/h. The machine was to have a ground clearance of at least 6 inches (150mm), should be inaudible from half a mile, and use a sv engine with totally enclosed transmission. The BSA M20 and Norton 16H were both some 100lb heavier, 1½ inches lower in ground clearance, and had an exposed chain final drive.

The factories of BSA, Douglas, Royal Enfield and Triumph all prepared prototypes to these specifications, but before the authorities could make any final decisions, the war in Europe had virtually ended. Finally in a changed form, the Triumph (TRW) was adopted for military service in 1948, and although the BSA and Douglas models (Douglas 3 machines) took part in the Scottish Six Days Trial in 1948, the other three prototypes were not developed further.

The four prototypes all featured twin-cylinder sv engine, mounted within a duplex cradle frame, with a rigid rear wheel and some form of forward suspension, but from there the similarity ended. The Douglas (DV60) adopted a short-stroke flat-twin engine, while the others all featured vertical parallel-twin units. For simplicity and ease of maintenance, all four adopted a single carburettor, and fully enclosed chain final drive. The Douglas had a single flat silencer mounted beneath the gearbox, without any loss in ground clearance, the other three had a siamese exhaust system, with a single more conventional silencer mounted on the right. The Royal Enfield cylinder head was inclined backwards, with a forward-facing carburettor, to protect the spark plug from water or mud thrown up by the front wheel. The BSA and Triumph machines were based upon the A7 and Speed Twin models respectively, but with a side-valve operation and basic utilitarian conversion.

The BSA 500cc/62 x 82mm adopted telescopic front forks, the Douglas 600cc/74 x 70mm a leading link design (Douglas Radiadraulic, with hydraulic damping), the Royal Enfield 350cc/52 x 82mm traditional girder-type forks, and the Triumph 500cc/63 x 80mm also had a pair of telescopics. The Douglas, the least conventional of the group, also had a fully sprung seat pillar, that offered more than three inches vertical travel, while the Royal Enfield had a fat 4.50 x 17in rear tyre to offer some additional comfort to the rigid rear end. All four machines had magneto ignition, and foot-change 3-speeds BSA & Douglas, 4-speeds Royal Enfield & Triumph, and a kick start. While the minimum 6in. ground clearance was achieved by all, only the Triumph (TRW), with fairly extensive use of light alloy, cylinder head, barrel, primary chaincase, etc, met

Left: **A line-up of the US Armoured Division equipped with Harley-Davidson WLA's. Note scabbard upon the front forks to hold the sub-machine gun. Harley-Davidson supplied tens of thousands of motorcycles during World War 2, the majority were WLA's for solo despatch, reconnaissance, and military police duties.** (Harley-Davidson)

Below left: **Fully loaded Harley-Davidson WLA under test.** (Harley-Davidson)

the 300lb required; BSA: 361lb, Douglas: 360lb, Royal Enfield: 340lb, and Triumph: 280lb.

Unlike World War 1, when Douglas provided a major contribution to the motorcycles selected by both British and Allied armed forces, the Bristol factory was largely engaged with work for the Ministry of Aircraft Production. The DV60 remained the only military Douglas motorcycle of the period, and with various financial and production difficulties, the concern did not produce any further motorcycles for military consideration.

IV: AMERICAN MODELS . . .

During the summer of 1939, President Roosevelt announced American industry should be made ready to assist the Allies, in the supply of military equipment. The ever growing menace of the German U-boat attacks brought sympathy for the European cause, and before the end of the year, both the Harley-Davidson and Indian motorcycle factories had accepted contracts to supply military machines to the Allied Forces. Indian had already had an order to supply the French Army with 5000 Chief sidecar outfits, and with the bombing of the Triumph factory, the two American works each received a contract to supply 500 solo machines to Great Britain.

In March 1941, America set up the Lend-Lease programme and under this scheme the US eventually supplied more than 42 billion dollars worth of equipment to 44 countries. Great Britain and the Soviet Union received the vast majority of these materials; the USSR receiving more than 400,000 trucks, tanks, cars and motorcycles.

Before Lend-Lease, large numbers of commercial-type vehicles were supplied directly from the American automotive industry to Great Britain, France, China, and other countries. In addition, large orders placed by the French were re-directed to Great Britain and Russia, when France fell to the *Wehrmacht*.

Servi-Cycle

Little more than a powered bicycle the Servi-Cycle (p 196) was produced by Simplex, New Orleans, for the USAF. The machine also proved useful for the American airborne troops, with a total of 654 delivered between 1942–43, with an improved version supplied during the early 1950s. Changing little for some 20 years, this simple, but effective design, offered basic push-start transport

The Husky 16M71 engine was mounted under the saddle, fan cooled, with a flywheel magneto, centrifugal clutch, 2-speed gearbox and exposed chain drive for the tiny wheel. The wheels were shod with fat 6.00 x 6in. tyres.

Cushman, well known as manufacturers of golf-course three-wheelers, also supplied their sidecar models 32 and 34 between 1943–44, to the US Army and Navy. The company also supplied more than 600 of its model 39 Package Car tricycle during this period. The same Husky engine and transmission was used to power this model, but with two wheels at the front, supporting a large covered box load of 386lb/175kg, and a single rear wheel drive. These vehicles provided the same service as the sidecar type.

Harley-Davidson

From one extreme to the other, in both size of machine and scale of production, Harley-Davidson produced the majority of motorcycles used by the American military during World War 2. The Milwaukee factory produced more than 88,000 machines for armed forces worldwide (exact numbers are difficult to ascertain), selected by all branches of the US forces. Under either Government order or Lend Lease, substantial numbers were supplied to Canada, China, Great Britain, Russia and South Africa.

Following the Coventry bombing, the British War Office placed the first military order with Harley-Davidson during the war, and the WLA model was supplied (p 195). For Canadian forces, the designation was WLC. A design dating from the late 1920s, the narrow angle 750cc V-twin sv engine was mounted within a rigid frame, with a steel pressing to give protection to both engine and gearbox. This fitting was in a channel section for extra strength, and extended rearward to protect the silencer and exposed rear chain. The front forks were traditional H-D leading links design.

The well established engine breathed through a single carburettor; and had coil-ignition. The left foot controlled the clutch, which could be disengaged, for the rider to use both feet to support the machine as required. A right-hand clutch lever was later fitted.

From 1940–41, motorcycles of the US Armoured Division were equipped with a leather scabbard for a Thompson sub-machine gun or rifle; held vertical to the right front fork leg, and an auxiliary box was mounted on the left leg. Earlier WLA machines had a left hand throttle twistgrip, with the front brake lever, leaving the rider's right hand free to use a pistol or the sub-machine gun while moving, an idea which subsequently proved impractical. While among the most numerous military motorcycles of the war, the WLA weighed some 540lb/245kg, and could

Above: **Solo rider of the US Armoured Division upon a Harley-Davidson WLA, with holstered machine gun, and ammunition box upon the front forks. The Canadian version WLC did not adopt these features, and often replaced the rear carrier rack for a pillion saddle.** *(Harley-Davidson)*

over short distances and weighed less than 165lb. An unusual 125cc, two-stroke, engine powered the rear wheel, via variable-ratio pulleys and two V-belts, with the final belt drive providing a combined tension control and clutch. The drive pulleys expanded or contracted their diameters for varying the ratio. Produced in light alloy, the sleeved cylinder and head were cast as one, with two spark plugs and a flywheel magneto. The design included foot-boards, front crash bar, parachute rings and rear pintle hook.

Cushman

As the parascooter gained interest, Cushman Motor Works, part of the Johnson-Evinrude concern of Nebraska, introduced a lightweight model in 1944, developed for airborne use. Designated the Cushman model 53 Autoglide (p 195), by the end of the war 4734 had been manufactured. Equipped with a pintle hook and parachute rings, at 255lb/116kg the Cushman was heavier than the Servi-Cycle, but with a 244cc sv engine offered a more rapid dispersal for landing troops.

Left: **1921 Walter 750cc; standard models adopted in limited numbers by the newly-formed Czechoslovak Army, with V-twin engine across the frame.** *(Frank Nyklicek)*

Below: **1942 Monark m/42 OHV; prepared for Swedish forces. 3,000 machines were supplied during the War, and many remained in active service until the mid 1960s.** *(Harry Ljungdahl)*

POLEN
JUNAK 350

Top left: **1936 Sokol 600cc RT M211;** a standard production model adopted by the Polish Army. The vast majority of Polish military vehicles were destroyed during the first German invasion. *(Jacek Gorski)*

Left: **1960 Junak 350cc M10;** a reliable standard product, the model was adopted by the Polish Army during the early 1960s. The Junak factory of Stettin, a former German town, assembled the only four-stroke motorcycles of post-war Poland. *(François-Marie Dumas)*

Above: **1953 Condor A581;** specialised military model produced for the Swiss armed forces. Note the unique Swiss auxiliary light on the front mudguard and machine gun brackets. *(David Ansell)*

Left: **1961 Tempo 175 Militar;** standard production model adopted by the Norwegian Army. One of the very few motorcycles produced in Norway, military conversion meant a rear carrier rack, canvas panniers, headlamp protection and service livery. *(Gunnar Schroder)*

1937 FN 992cc M12 SM; specialised military motorcycle and sidecar designed and produced for the Belgian armed forces, from 1940 widely adopted by the German Army. A multi-terrain vehicle with outstanding performance, the machine established many of the standards for BMW and Zündapp to follow. Note the wrap-around engine protection bars, high level exhaust system and carburettor sand filter. *(François-Marie Dumas)*

Right: **1956 Nimbus 750cc Military model;** rugged and reliable, produced with only minor changes between 1937 and 1956. Cylindrical metal tool box on the rear mudguard.

Below: **1934 Puch 200;** a lightweight solo machine with an unusual split single cylinder two-stroke engine, widely deployed by the Austrian Army pre-war, and later adopted by the German Army. Very limited military conversion: a pair of leather pannier bags and service livery. *Wehrmacht* number plate. *(Both François-Marie Dumas)*

Above: **1936 Terrot 500cc type RDA; a typical French model of the mid 1930s, the RDA was adopted by the French Army for solo despatch duties. Several other Terrot models were also procured, eg, HDA (350cc sv), RGMA (500cc ohv) and VATT (750cc V-twin sv). Some elegant French lines upon the push-rod plate and engine casing.**

Left: **1951 Gillet-Herstal 500cc Estatette AB; standard production model adopted by the Belgian armed forces throughout the 1950s. An unusual rear suspension design.**
(Both François-Marie Dumas)

111

Above: **1939 Gnome Rhône 804cc type AX2;** for the French Army, the AX2 continued to be assembled from 1936 until 1940, when re-deployed by the German forces. Shaft drive to the rear wheel and cross shaft for sidecar drive. *(François-Marie Dumas)*

Right: **1978 Suzuki GS400-GP;** a standard production model procured by the Australian armed forces and deployed for solo despatch, escort and military police duties. These machines have been prepared for GP (General Purpose) duties. *(Victoria Barracks)*

Above: **1937 Sankyo 1196cc type 97;** a Japanese copy of the American V-twin design, the machine became an important workhorse for the Imperial Japanese Army, deployed either solo or with a sidecar (left-hand). This machine has a high level exhaust system for multi-terrain duties, but the model was also used for escort and more general road service. *(IWM)*

Left: **Harley-Davidson WLA, engine;** note the military air-filter upon the carburettor for desert conditions. *(David Ansell, owned by Gary Howard)*

not offer the agility of many European machines. With only 4in./102mm ground clearance the machine was unsuited for most off-road service, but it did have an ability to withstand many road miles in the most arduous conditions.

Like many Allied military models, the majority of machines procured by the US forces were originally civilian designs, with various accessories and coat of service livery. Large capacity engines, however, developed for the American market, provided a mixture of pulling power and reliability unknown in Europe. Comprehensively prepared with wind-screen, crash bars, ammunition boxes, armament fittings and radio equipment, American machines began to gain a wider international interest, within commercial, military and Government organisations. American military procedure included throwing down motorcycles when the enemy was close, and the WLA was often carried horizontally by the Armoured Division tanks, 540 motorcycles to each division, but neither action caused problems for these robust machines.

The WLA was generally used solo, but after many thousands had been sent to the Red Army, in 1944, Harley-Davidson prepared a prototype with a sidecar for the Russian front. This was basically a WLA model, with leg shields and a handlebar screen, and a single seater sidecar, with a matching screen and interchangeable spare wheel. Known as the WSR, the model did not go into full production. The WLA, however, remained in production until the early 1950s, supplied under contract as some of the last American military motorcycles.

Harley-Davidson supplied various military sidecar outfits during the war, but these heavyweights remained in restricted production only. The UA, 1200cc and ELA (p 195), 1000cc V-twin sv models ('A' for Army) were prepared with a handlebar windscreen, crash bars, and rear carrier rack. The sidecar was a single seater with an interchangeable spare wheel, and a pillion saddle fitted as standard. The sidecar and pillion saddle were both known to be removed during operations, and various armament fittings added where available. Outfits were procured in very limited numbers.

It is reported that only 670 Harley-Davidson UA models were supplied to the US Army between 1939–41, 1597 to British forces in South Africa, and a similar number of the lighter ELA model were supplied to the US Navy for shore patrol and coast guard duties. The US Marine Corps deployed 125 machines between 1941 and 1946; the majority of these were UA machines, some solo, and a smaller number of Indian Scout and Chief models. These limited numbers, however, found their way around the world for general despatch, convoy escort, military police and personnel transportation.

Harley-Davidson Flat-Twins. In addition to numerous other military projects, Harley-Davidson developed the XA model (p 195). Based upon the robust machines of BMW and Zündapp, so successfully used by the Germans in North Africa and elsewhere, the US Army Procurement Authorities wanted a similar machine, and in late 1941, sent specifications to Harley-Davidson and Indian. H-D measured a captured BMW R12, and prepared a 750cc model, with a flat-twin engine and shaft-drive. Like the German original, the gearbox had four speeds, with a foot-change, and additional right-hand lever and transverse kick-start. The sv engine had a pair of carburettors and a single air-filter mounted on top of the gearbox housing, which in turn bolted onto the rear of the crankcase. The unit construction was mounted within a tubular cradle frame, with plunger-type rear suspension, and standard H-D leading link front forks, but with a hydraulic damping unit on the right leg.

Wherever possible all other details remained in common with the WLA. Standard footboards were adopted, with the addition of footrests behind, heat shields to protect the rider's boots from the cylinder fins, front and rear crash bars, a rear carrier rack, additional masked lighting and high level mudguards. A limited number were prepared with solid disc wheels for desert terrain, and in 1942, a sidecar version, known as the XS, was introduced with a sidecar wheel-drive and wide-section tyres.

Before full production however, America transferred military activities to the Pacific theatre, and the four-wheel drive Jeep came into its own and the XA project was abandoned in 1943, with about 1000 machines built. Interestingly, H-D supplied a number of XA engines to Willys for an intended lightweight mini-Jeep for airborne assault, but the project was never developed.

Indian

An Indian military model, also based upon German multi-terrain machines, took a quite different form. Designated the Model 841 (p 196), this machine featured a 90° V-twin set across a tubular duplex cradle frame, with girder-type front

Above: **20/21st June 1942, riders of the 1st Australian Armoured Divisional Provost Company on Harley-Davidson WLA's, during a review of the Armoured Division by the Commanders in Chief, Allied Land Forces, General Sir Thomas Blamey, Puckapunyal, Australia.** *(AWM neg no 25503)*

forks, hydraulically damp and plunger-type rear suspension. The 750cc sv engine ran through a four-speed unit construction gearbox, with foot-change, a single dry-plate clutch, and exposed shaft final-drive. The detuned engine, required by the authorities, only offered a top speed of some 70mph/113km/h, but the model was easy to handle and pleasing to ride, and received a lot of interest; with promise of a civilian version to follow.

A total of 1056 were built before the production contract was terminated, and apart from a few on service trials, the factory retained most in storage. The 841 was not re-introduced during post-war years, but as with the Harley-Davidson XA, many were civilianised, sold as surplus at the established price of $500.00, and remain within various collections. Coincidentally, the Italian factory of Moto Guzzi introduced virtually the same design some 30 years later, with a more powerful ohv

engine, that was widely accepted as ideal for military and police service; the V7 (see Chapter 5).

From early 1940, Indian was fully occupied with the military Chief and sidecar model, designated the 340B (p 196). The factory had received an order of 5000 for the French Army, the contract being completed in March, and some 2200 were loaded onto the Swedish freighter SS *Hanseatic Star*, but at the height of the U-boat campaign, the ship was presumed lost with all hands. Some 1500 were supplied to the US Army, and under the Defense Aid act, and later Lend Lease, Allied military, in particular British and Commonwealth forces, also received limited numbers. The 340B had a V-twin 1200cc sv engine mounted within a tubular duplex frame, with traditional leaf-sprung front forks, and a plunger type rear suspension. Transmission ran through a chain primary drive and multi-plate clutch, enclosed within an alloy case, and a three-

carrier provided fittings for a pair of large leather saddle bags. Military accessories included additional masked lighting, handlebar mounted windscreen, front crash bars, leg shields, and a larger air filter for sandy conditions.

The 640A was proven a robust and reliable design, but with a restricted output and weight of 450lb/204kg, a more powerful 750cc version was introduced shortly after. Very similar in general appearance, the larger model was designated the 640B (p 196), and following trials orders for both were placed. Widely used by American and Allied forces, these machines remained in production throughout 1942 (finally known as the 741A 500cc and the 741B 750cc), providing solo despatch, reconnaissance and military police duties, until the Indian works began to concentrate research on the 841 prototype.

An American sidecar outfit of the 1940s could weigh more than 850lb, or about 1000lb when fully loaded with military equipment, but lacking sidecar wheel-drive or sufficient ground clearance, any machine that left a surfaced road for any distance often demanded extensive repairs. In the Spring of 1940, following training manoeuvres of some 4000 miles, the 6th Cavalry Regiment of Louisiana and Georgia needed to completely rebuild the engines for more than half their 81 machines.

With this experience, the US War Dept. prepared the specifications which eventually led to the Harley-Davidson XA and Indian 841 models, but with the introduction of the ubiquitous Jeep, the US military cancelled all outstanding motorcycle contracts.

Japanese Copies

Some three years before the American military Jeep was introduced, the Japanese built a four-wheel drive multi-terrain vehicle. Designed by Morikichi Sakurai, an employee of the Harley-Davidson Motorcycle Sales Company of Japan, five prototypes were assembled, each powered by a Harley-Davidson V-twin 1200cc sv engine. These machines were tested and approved by the Japanese Imperial Army, and Sakurai was decorated by his government for this design, but the project was later abandoned, as the Japanese military marched into Manchuria.

The Japanese Imperial Army had shown an interest in Harley-Davidson motorcycles as early as 1912, when a model was imported for evaluation, and within four years a Japanese factory had acquired the distribution rights of the American machines in Japan. Indian motorcycles were also tested, but the Harley-Davidson was preferred by the Japanese Army, and by the late 1920s, the VL

speed gearbox with exposed chain to the rear wheel. The very basic single seat sidecar (without screen or door) was also leaf-sprung, and could be equipped with a spare wheel, but did not have a sidecar wheel-drive.

Off-Road Designs. At the request of the US War Department, Indian also prepared a number of smaller solo models, and designated the 640A, a 500cc machine was first introduced, based on the standard Sport and Junior Scout. With milder tuning, lower compression ratio and restricted breathing for longer service life, the 641A adopted the Chief gearbox for additional reliability and rationalisation. The front forks were extended some 1½in./38mm, and with the seat stays extended, almost 5in./127mm of ground clearance was made possible. With generous wheel clearance and wide section mudguards, mud clogging was reduced, and a heavy duty rear

Above: **An abandoned Sankyo type 97 sidecar outfit, following the recapture of the Dutch Barracks at Balikapapan, Netherlands Borneo, by the Australian and Royal Netherlands Indies armed forces.** *(AWM neg no 305117)*

Right: **September 1942, a damaged Kurogane military tricycle, following the Japanese invasion of Milne Bay, Papua.** *(AWM neg no 26625)*

Far right: **Exploded drawing of the M72 engine.** *(Jacek Gorski)*

1200cc sv V-twin model had become the standard motorcycle for military service, while the national police were equipped with Indian machines. In 1929, Harley-Davidson granted manufacturing rights to the Sankyo Pharmaceutical Company (the Japanese concern behind the H-D Motorcycle Sales Company in Japan), and a new factory known as the Shinagawa Works was built in Tokyo. As the first complete motorcycle manufacturing works in Japan, the factory could be seen as the forerunner of the successful Japanese motorcycle industry to follow.

The Shinagawa Works did not assemble their first complete machine until 1935, and Harley-Davidson continued to export to Japan until this time, but with a growing awareness of Japanese military intentions, and diverse difficulties with Sankyo, Harley-Davidson decided to terminate all agreements with the Japanese company. From 1937, Sankyo introduced an H-D copy known as the Rikuo (King of the Road), and a military version was prepared. Designated the Sankyo type 97, by the end of World War 2, some 18,000 had been adopted by the Japanese military, both solo or with a sidecar attached.

The Sankyo 97 remained basically as the Harley-Davidson 1200cc model VL, but a three-speed and reverse gearbox was adopted for sidecar use, and a 750cc version prepared for solo use. As for the Harley-Davidson, the V-twin sv engine was mounted within a tubular frame, with

leading link front forks. The transmission remained chain drive, but when a sidecar was fitted, on the left, a third wheel drive could be driven via a shaft from the rear sprocket. With rubber universal couplings at each end, a dog clutch could disengage the shaft drive as required. The single seat sidecar was leaf sprung, often equipped with a light machine gun, and with excellent ground clearance and high mounted exhaust system, the outfit could often out-run the much heavier Jeep along the mud tracks of the Pacific islands.

In addition to the Sankyo 97, the Japanese

Army and Navy purchased various motor-tricycles. These vehicles, known as 'Sanrinsha', were very similar in outward appearance to a number of Italian models of the same period, with the front half of a motorcycle and platform body mounted above a pair of rear wheels (p 195).

During the late 1930s, the Nippon Nainenki Seiko Company, later known as the Tokyo Kurogane Motor Company was a major supplier of military tricycles and light four-wheeled vehicles. The Kurogane Type 1 featured a V-twin sv engine within a pressed steel frame, with a larger section rear sub-frame to support different passenger and general load carriers, from cargo box to water carrier. The 750cc unit provided power to the rear wheels via a three-speed and reverse gearbox, and shaft drive to the rear axle. Pressed steel parallelogram front forks offered forward suspension, with the additional help of 4.75 x 18in. tyres upon interchangeable disc wheels, and a leaf-sprung rear platform.

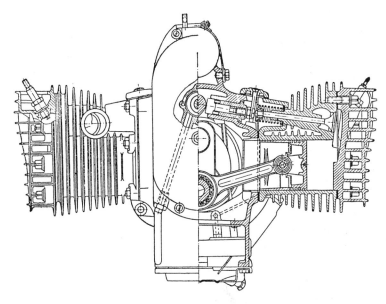

V: FRANCE, BELGIUM & USSR . . .

The specifications of several major French, Belgian and Russian motorcycles and tricycles are given in the data tables. Many French and Belgian models were commandeered by the *Wehrmacht* and also continued to be used by civilian authorities. It is believed that some models were deployed by the Belgian and French military authorities in their respective colonial territories.

Both the Russian models detailed in the specifications were extensively used, particularly the M-72, based on the BMW R71. This machine was developed as the K-750 and continued in military service until the mid 1950s.

Above: **Cross section drawing of the M72 engine. Note the extra finning upon the cylinder heads to reduce heat from the side valve design.** *(Jacek Gorski)*

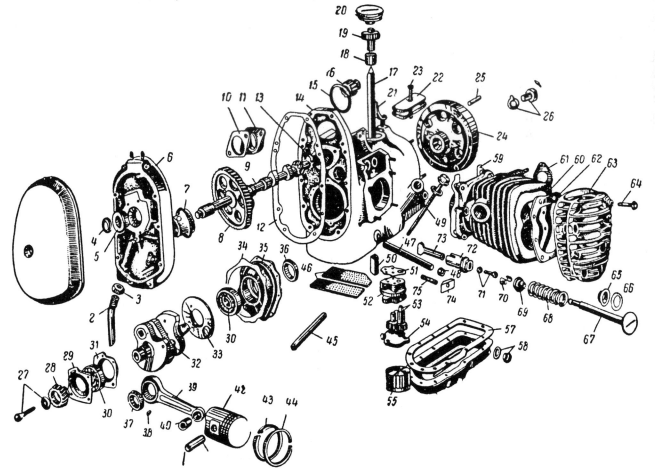

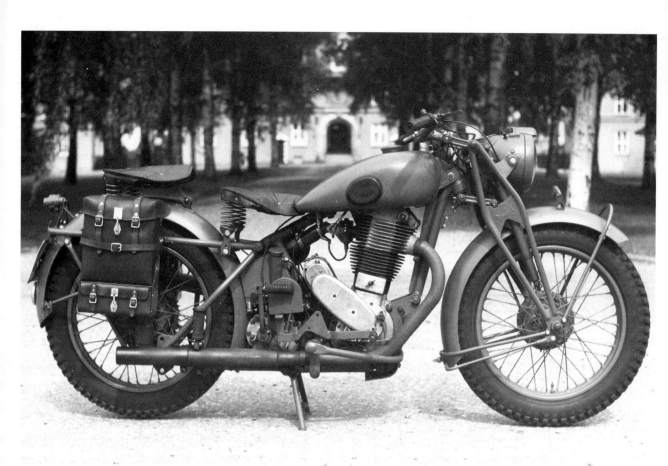

Above: **m42/TV** (ohv version); based upon a pre-war Husqvarna design, and produced by Albin (engine) and Monark (frame), the major military motorcycle of the Swedish army during World War 2. *(Harry Ljungdahl)*

Right: **m42/TV** engine detail. Note the spare spark plug holder, horizontal split primary chain case, hand pump, and combined foot rest and protection bar. *(Harry Ljungdahl)*

VI: NEUTRALS . . .

In conclusion, while not directly involved, the motorcycle industry of neutral Sweden and Switzerland did not remain inactive during the war. With Sweden, lying as it did between German occupied Norway and Russian occupied Finland, the greatest diplomacy was required to keep the Swedish military from hostilities. Like many other countries, the Swedish Army procured various civilian motorcycles, DKW 350cc and 500cc models in particular, but as others found, commercial machines were often unable to withstand active service. The Swedish force had the additional problem of insufficient spares, when not procuring from domestic manufacturers.

By the late 1930s, the Swedish motorcycle industry had virtually collapsed; the well known Husqvarna works totally committed to the production of rifles, pistols, and other armaments for the Swedish Army. Smaller factories (Ebe, Esse, Monark, NV, Rex, Suecia) had reduced their output in the face of increased imports, largely from Germany and Great Britain, and were unable adequately to support the Swedish armed forces.

During the first months of the war, the

Above: **m42/TV left side; a mixture of unique and traditional design, it looks right and lived up to its looks in terms of ruggedness and serviceability.** (*Harry Ljungdahl*)

Left: **m42/TV purpose-built pannier frame. The unique plunger type rear suspension can also be clearly seen.** (*Harry Ljungdahl*)

Swedish Procurement Office prepared specifications for a German style flat-twin model, but without any similar machine readily available from domestic production, the authorities decided to concentrate upon the simplicity of a single-cylinder design. The Husqvarna 500cc 112SV and 112TV models, with sv and ohv engines respectively, were chosen as suitable for military conversion. Designated the Army motorcycle m/42 (p 195), these 1935 machines, with some history of both on- and off-road success, were assembled cooperatively between several companies.

Major differences between the two models centred upon the frame; the sv version had a rigid rear wheel, the ohv model adopted an unusual plunger-type design. Both machines had conventional girder-type front forks, but the ohv model was also equipped with a pair of vertical rear suspension units. The exhaust system was finished in black. A small additional fuel tank was carried on the rear frame, with built-in pump, to carry better quality fuel for cold start.

Providing a well balanced model for solo despatch and general liaison, eventually more than 3000 m/42s were manufactured, and remained in

active service until the mid 1960s, when finally superseded by the Husqvarna MC-256A.

Sidecar Design. The Swedish military, however, remained interested in a more sophisticated sidecar outfit, and in 1942, the NV (Nymans Verkstader) factory in Uppsala began to develop a multi-terrain prototype. The model had a narrow angle V-twin engine, mounted in-line with the frame; a mixture of pressed steel and tubular construction, with telescopic front forks and a rigid rear wheel. To reduce costs wherever possible, the top half of two m/42 ohv engines provided the 1000cc capacity, modified to breathe through a single carburettor between the two cylinders. The exhaust pipes ran to the right, and were mounted above the rear wheel axle.

Two levers mounted on the left side of the fuel tank, controlled six forward and a reverse speed, with the gearbox mounted in-line with the shaft final drive. Offset and extended rearwards, the gearbox lined up with the rear bevel-box, driving the rear wheel and a cross-shaft to the sidecar wheel. The interchangeable wheels had steel

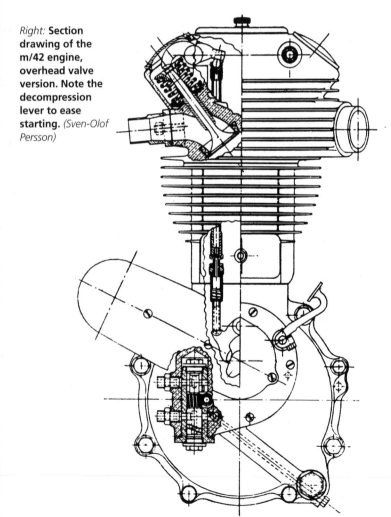

Right: **Section drawing of the m/42 engine, overhead valve version. Note the decompression lever to ease starting.** *(Sven-Olof Persson)*

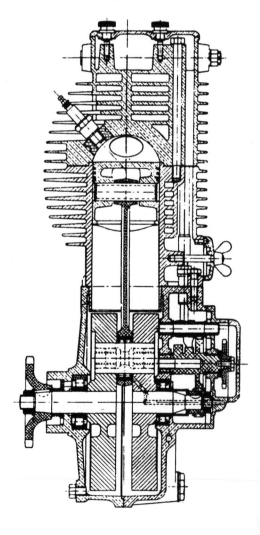

Left: **1943 NV 990cc military outfit; a purpose-built multi-terrain sidecar machine for the Swedish Army. A pair of m42/TV cylinders and heads upon a common crankcase, with a shaft drive to the rear and sidecar wheels.** *(Harry Ljungdahl)*

Below: **Designed for sidecar use only, the NV 990cc presenting the off-set transmission between engine and rear wheel.** *(Harry Ljungdahl)*

rims, short spokes and huge hydraulic drum brakes, with large section cross-country tyres. A pair of well sprung saddles gave further comfort. The sidecar was a large basic sheet metal design, with ample storage behind the single seat, and a spare wheel mounted on the back.

The NV 1000cc was however, produced in very limited numbers, and with the introduction of the four-wheel drive Jeep, like many similar machines worldwide, the NV project was abandoned.

From the late 1930s, the Suecia works in Orelljunga supplied a military motorcycle to the Swedish Army; a standard production model with a single cylinder MAG 500cc sv engine (see Chapter 2), and this model was deployed during the war. The Swedish Army, however, did not procure any further domestic machines and the m/42 remained the major model throughout the war years.

Switzerland

With the declaration of war the Swiss military was fully mobilised, and within two weeks, all able-bodied civilians were enrolled for military service or some form of defence work. For many years, with very few exceptions, the Swiss armed forces had relied upon various commercial vehicles, but as procurement groups worldwide found, many models were found unsuitable for modern warfare.

During the interwar years, the domestic motorcycle factories Condor, MAG (Moto-sacoche) and Universal supplied the majority of Swiss Army machines, and many of these remained in active service during the war; generally large capacity V-twin sv models, providing both solo and sidecar service.

As the war continued, a series of new military motorcycles was requested, and in 1943, the Universal Works introduced the A-680 and A-1000 (A for Army) models. These machines featured a narrow angle V-twin sv engine, of 676cc and 990cc respectively, mounted in a tubular frame, with pressed steel parallelogram front forks. A single carburettor was positioned between the cylinders, with the exhaust pipes running to the right and a large flat silencer mounted above the rigid rear forks. Transmission ran through a multi-plate clutch and four-speed Burman gearbox, with hand-change.

Designed for either solo or sidecar service, the Universal machines remained in active use throughout the rest of the war, providing despatch, reconnaissance, convoy control, and military police duties. The sidecar was a moulded panel design, held within a wrap-around tubular frame, with a spare wheel mounted on the nose. To help recover the outfit, lifting handles were positioned both sides of each wheel and over the rear mudguard. Additional military accessories included fittings for a sub-machine gun on the sidecar, and heavy cross-country tyres. The sidecar outfit was also used with an anti-aircraft gun mounted upon a two-wheeled trailer. With the return of peace-time production, the Universal A-680 and A-1000 models were superseded by the Condor A-580 solo and A-750 sidecar models.

CHAPTER FOUR

Postwar Production 1946-66

I: WARSAW PACT . . .

Technically and militarily, the Warsaw Pact was divided into virtually two levels, with the relatively modern vehicles and arms supplied to the northern forces of East Germany, Czechoslovakia and Poland, while the southern forces of Bulgaria, Hungary and Romania were equipped with older equipment. Even so, these 'second-string' armies were not to be taken lightly, with some 775,000 troops between them, rivalling the US Army's 781,000.

Under Communist control, post-war Eastern Europe was of course subjected to ever greater conformity. By the early 1950s, the majority of smaller private factories had been incorporated into a nationalisation programme or closed down altogether.

State-run manufacturing was imposed upon each country's industry. At the cost of many established names, with historical links from the turn of the century, the extremely diverse motorcycle industry of Eastern Europe was reduced to a fraction of its former self. Soviet-bloc military motorcycles centred upon three factories; MZ (East Germany), Jawa (Czechoslovakia), and Dneiper (Russia).

While standardisation was achieved, without sufficient funds for further development, the factories proved increasingly less able to compete with the more affluent West.

East Germany

In 1945, the pre-war DKW factory, Zschopau, became part of Soviet-controlled East Germany. For some years all production centred upon a few mechanical consumer goods, followed by stationary engines, and finally, renamed *VEB Motorradwerke Zschopau* in 1950, the works resumed motorcycle production under state control. With all the facilities of DKW, the Zschopau factory introduced the IFA RT 125, a close copy of the war-time model, so widely deployed for military service. No previous lightweight had inspired such confidence, to be eventually copied worldwide; BSA (Great Britain), Harley-Davidson (United States), Izh (Soviet Union), and many more.

MZ

Until 1953, all further development was undertaken with the very minimum financial support, and then the East German government realised the political potential of a national race team. The factory was granted aid from the State Committee for Physical Culture and Sport, and officially recognised as an independent organisation, with the now well known MZ initials as their trademark. That year the RT 125 featured an improved engine, mounted within a modified frame, with telescopic front forks and plunger-type rear suspension.

From 1954, Zschopau machines also adopted their traditional fully enclosed rear chain drive; a pair of rubber gaiters for the upper and lower chain run.

MZ models retained plunger rear suspension until the mid 1950s, when the ES series was introduced, with a swinging arm layout for both front and rear wheels; this arrangement remained another unique MZ feature for some years. The Zschopau designers were not afraid to face new problems, and when the Wankel rotary engine was introduced in 1960, as an alternative to the reciprocating piston design, MZ gave the concept close consideration.

Within three years, MZ had prepared and tested the world's first motorcycle with a rotary engine, mounted in a modified ES 250 frame. Designated the kkm 350, the engine offered a cylinder capacity of 3 x 175cc, with a top speed of some 140 km/h. Following a second prototype in 1965, MZ decided that the model was not commercially viable, and the works returned to their single-cylinder two-stroke machines.

Although an MZ race team was successfully established for both on and off-road events, with various twin-cylinder designs, these machines

Motor je vzornou ukázkou konstruktérského umění. Je kompaktní, jednoduchý, účelně uspořádaný, snadno rozebiratelný, tvar aerodynamický.

Left: **The Jawa 350cc twin-cylinder engine of 1949; an outstanding design of advanced specifications. Note the sleek lines and simplicity of construction.** (Frank Nyklicek)

Below: **1948 Hungarian parade; a mixture of former *Wehrmacht* BMW R71s and Zündapp KS600s, with a mixture of single seat sidecars, prepared to meet post-war Hungarian military requirements.** (Hadtorteneti Intezet es Muzeum)

Right: **Still produced in the 1970s MZ ES 250/2 military model prepared for the East German armed forces, with upswept single silencer and single pannier bag.**
(Motorrad-Museum)

Below: **1969 MZ ES 250 single-cylinder two-stroke engine and unit construction four-speed gearbox; a mixture of DKW tradition and MZ development.**
(Motorrad-Museum)

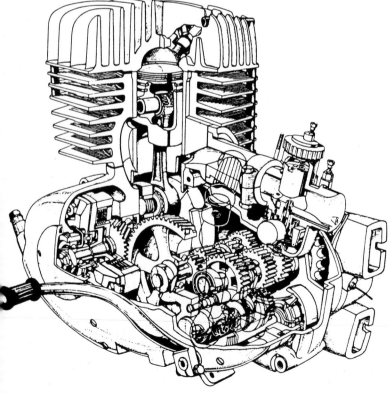

were assembled in very limited numbers, and were not for general sale. In 1953, MZ also introduced the BK 350, with a 343cc (58 x 65mm) flat-twin 2-stroke design, with transmission through a 4-speed gearbox and a shaft final-drive. Produced as a standard road model, the BK 350 took part in off-road trials with a sidecar attached, but unlike any MZ before or since, the model did not remain in production for very long.

From the mid 1950s, the East German Army procured the MZ ES 250/1, and revised ES 250/2 models until the mid 1970s, for solo despatch, general liaison and border patrol. The single-cylinder 243cc (65 x 69mm) engine was rubber mounted in a tubular frame with the unusual swinging arm suspension front and rear; the handlebars passing through the pressed steel headlamp shell. The model also featured fully enclosed pressed steel side panels. A fully sprung sidecar was also available for military use.

EMW. During the closing stages of the war, the BMW factory in Munich, was almost destroyed by Allied bombing. With defeat in sight, on 11th April 1945, Hitler ordered all remaining facilities destroyed. This order was ignored however, to be followed by acquisition orders, from the Deputy Commander of the US garrison in Munich, to dismantle the factory, with anything usable to be sent to Detroit. Under such circumstances, a lot was lost, but staff managed to have all remaining car and motorcycle equipment moved to the old BMW/Dixi factory at Eisenach. The Dixi factory, however, was found to be in Russian controlled East Germany after 1945.

Nevertheless, an immediate start was made upon the EMW R35, with vertical single-cylin-

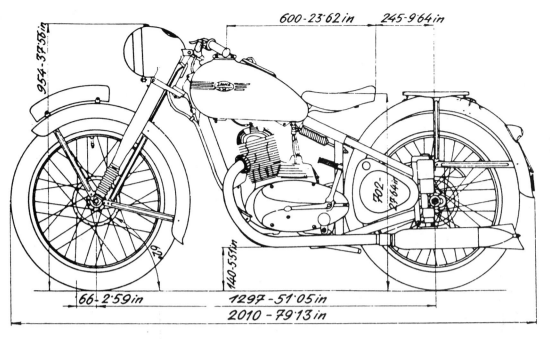

600 – 23·62 in 245 – 9·64 in

954 – 37·56 in

702 – 27·64 in

66 – 2·59 in 1297 – 51·05 in 140 – 5·55 in 2010 – 79·13 in

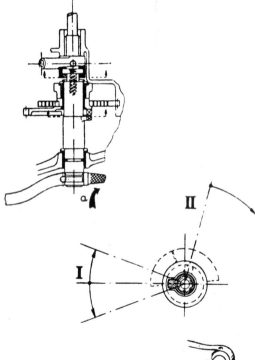

a

I II

der 340cc ohv engine, with 4-speed gearbox and exposed shaft final drive. The machine was quickly adopted by the East German Army. With the performance of a machine some 20 years earlier, MZ were able to provide a welcome replacement during the mid 1950s, with the ES series offering an all-round improvement.

Until 1948, the Munich factory of BMW was reduced to making pots and pans, with motorcycle production then being strictly limited to utilitarian lightweights. While the Eisenach Works, in addition to the EMW R35, provided the Russians with the basis of the Ural motorcycle; basically a BMW R66 engine in the frame of the later R67 and R52 series. From the early 1930s, Russian motorcycles had been largely limited to European and American copies, and the BMW equipment and designs made a major contribution to Russian production.

Czechoslovakia

Six months before the war, the *Wehrmacht* moved into Czechoslovakia, and reorganised the country's

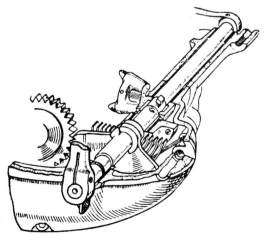

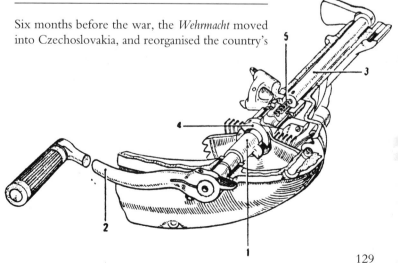

5

3

4

2

1

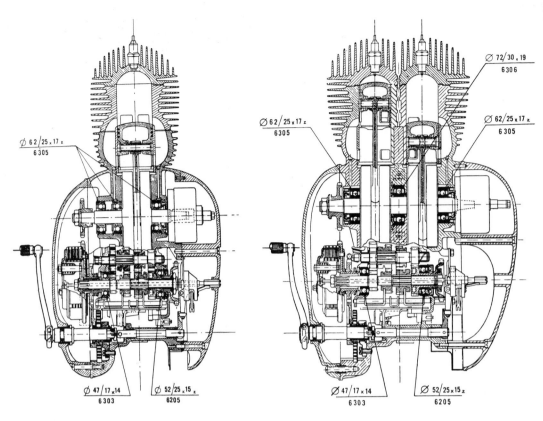

Right: **Section drawings of Jawa Perak 250 and 350cc two-stroke engines. Clearly, the same thinking behind the single- and twin-cylinder designs.** *(Frank Nyklicek)*

Below: **1963 Jawa 350 Kyvacka under test; equipped with ski attachments the model was widely deployed by the Finnish and Swedish armed forces throughout the 1960s.** *(Miroslav Sochor)*

automotive industry. The motorcycle factories of Autfit, CZ and Jawa were commandeered to repair and produce new machines. Jawa was ordered to scrap tons of components, but was able to hide away sufficient parts to build some 8500 post-war motorcycles and 700 cars. The factory's servicing workshop was taken over to repair BMW and DKW motorcycles, but the company secretly planned for peace-time production. By 1945, Jawa had drawings ready for single- and twin-cylinder, two- and four-stroke design, in 125cc, 175cc, 250cc and 350cc capacities, with both chain and shaft final-drive, as well as a diverse range of lightweight powered vehicles.

In September 1946, the Jawa Perak (Springer) made its debut at the Paris Salon, where it won a gold medal. The spring rear suspension, patented front forks and foot change 4-speed gearbox put the company ahead of the competition. By then, both the advanced 250cc and 350cc models had been developed, which gained widespread international recognition for Jawa. Later, the Jawa 350cc twin (p 198), and a limited number of the smaller 250cc models, became standardized military machines with the Czechoslovak Army, widely deployed both solo or with a sidecar attached, and with a two-wheeled light trailer. The machine also appeared prepared for airborne troops. As the machines continued to develop, Jawa supplied both Soviet-bloc Western and neutral armed forces, notably Sweden & Finland, with a number of different versions.

USSR

In 1938, the 750cc/78 x 78mm engine of the BMW R12 was adopted by the R71, the final BMW to adopt a side-valve layout. The next year under licence, the R71 was also produced by the Russians and the entire factory was

moved to the Urals in 1941, where the R71 became the M72; the leading Soviet military motorcycle during World War 2, and until the mid 1950s. Virtually unchanged throughout this period, the M72 (p 202) was mainly used with a sidecar, with a spare wheel and different panniers and machine-gun mountings. The engine and cycle parts retained much of the German design.

Widely used for multi-terrain service in most climatic conditions, the Russian model did not have a sidecar wheel-drive or inter-connected brakes, but remained in continuous production until 1954, when replaced by the M72K (1954–60), M72H (1956–59), and M72M (1956–60) variants, (with minor changes to the mudguards, fuel tank, brakes and air filter), and eventually superseded with the introduction of the K750 (1959–63) and K750M (1963–77) models, adopting a swinging arm rear suspension, leading link front forks and increased engine output. Demonstrating the strength of the original German design, the K750 then provided the basis for the Dnieper MT12 military model introduced in 1977 (see Chapter 5).

II: NATO . . .

On 4th April 1949, the North Atlantic Treaty was signed in Washington DC, by the 12 founder members; Belgium, Canada, Denmark, France, Great Britain, Iceland, Italy, Luxembourg, Netherlands, Norway, Portugal and the United States. Greece and Turkey joined NATO on 18th February 1952, West Germany on 9th May 1955, and Spain on 30th May 1982.

The Treaty was established primarily to maintain peace in Europe by preventing or repelling any Soviet-bloc aggression. Numerous military vehicles, including motorcycles, were prepared to achieve some level of standardisation within NATO countries, but with their largely independent manufacturing organisations, this generally proved unsuccessful and was usually abandoned! Although military equipment could be exported with relative ease between NATO countries, most immediate post-war motorcycle production was supplied for domestic service. Few restrictions were placed upon personnel transportation and the most sales-orientated companies inevitably eventually began to export worldwide.

Top: **1956-1959 M-72H, a Soviet development of the BMW R71. This model features leading-link front forks and revised rear mudguard mounting.** *(Frank Nyklicek)*

Above: **1946-1951 Izh-350, a single-cylinder two-stroke middleweight procured by the Red Army.** *(Frank Nyklicek)*

Left: **1951 Gillet Herstal 400, a single-cylinder SV model adopted by the Belgian Army (also supplied with a 500cc engine), for solo despatch and general liaison. Note the unusual position of the rear suspension unit.** *(Musee Royal de l'Armee et d'Histoire Militaire)*

Above: **Australian military police riders upon Harley-Davidson WLA's escort the Rt Hon Viscount Dunrossil, KCMG, MC, QC, Governor General of Australia, at Victoria Barracks, Sidney, Australia, on 14 May 1960.**
(Victoria Barracks)

American Policy

With the end of the European conflict in sight, the American military transferred their activities to the Pacific Theatre, and the US government cancelled all outstanding motorcycle contracts. By the Spring of 1944, the US Army announced 4600 motorcycles (1900 Indian, 2700 Harley-Davidson) were that surplus and would be sold to the public. By August, a further 3500 machines were sold through the same channels.

The US Army continued to reduce their motorcycle fleet, and during the Summer of 1945, a further 15,000 WLAs and 6000 Indians 741s were placed on the market, both at the government retail price of $450. The limited edition shaft-drive Harley-Davidson XA and Indian 841 models, were released to the public for $500 shortly afterwards.

The remarkable war-time production of Harley-Davidson and Indian had been eliminated from American active service; the small number of remaining machines mainly deployed for military police duties. Having assembled such large numbers, many remained within numerous armed forces worldwide: including Australia, Belgium, Canada, Great Britain, the Netherlands and South Africa. Many more were civilianised and re-sold by dealers and with sufficient spares, both government and private machines could be satisfactorily maintained. It is not unusual today to meet an ancient WLA in the hands of a French farmer on the lanes of Normandy.

Indian

In spite of wartime production feats, Indian made a net loss of $617,890, and on 25th October 1945, it was announced that Ralph Rogers, a young industrialist, had acquired a little more than 30% of the business. It was also revealed that the Atlas Corporation had secured a 20% holding. Under Rogers' control, the Indian company began to revise their domestic sales, and update their production equipment. Rogers had noticed the impact British and other European motorcycles were having on the American market. Generally found to be of good quality, lighter in weight and with reliable performance, these imports were far easier to ride – particularly in the city – than the traditional far larger American machines. The hand controlled clutch and foot operated gearbox also became a major attraction.

Closely following contemporary European machines, a project by a company not previously involved in motorcycles, Torque Engineering, offered basically two designs; a vertical single-cylinder machine designated the 149, and a twin version known as the 249. The single-cylinder engine had a capacity of 213cc, and the twin, a double-sized version, 426cc. These engines had an ohv layout, separate unit 4-speed gearbox, and exposed chain final drive. Both machines adopted the same cycle frame, with a single downtube, and cradle support beneath the engine. The two machines featured telescopic front forks; the 249 with a plunger-type rear suspension, while the

149 had a rigid rear wheel (with plunger rear units as an option). The overall dimensions and riding position were often criticised as too restricted by the average American rider, but it was this size to power ratio that interested the US military. Following trials in the late 1940s, a limited number of the 148 model, a sv version of the single-cylinder design, was acquired with parachute attachment rings by the US airborne troops (p 202). A similar number of the Indian 149 was also procured in 1953, modified for the same duty. These became the final Indian motorcycles to be used for American military service.

Harley-Davidson

In 1950, US armed forces adopted the final production Harley-Davidson WLA models, as well as the model G tricycle (p 202), known as Servicar, for military police duties, and in 1963, a further 418 Harley-Davidson Sport models were designated the military XLA and supplied for shore patrol duties. The company also supplied KH and FL to the armies of the Netherlands and Belgium. With however, the exception of limited lightweights (Cushman) for internal postal use,

and special airborne USAF machines (Simplex), the US Forces did not place any further major motorcycle contracts (US Forces began experimenting with multi-terrain lightweights in the mid 1970s – see Chapter 5), and Harley-Davidson began to concentrate public service sales onto civilian police departments.

III: BRITISH DOMINATION . . .

Large numbers of British motorcycles from the factories of BSA, Matchless, Norton, and Triumph and smaller numbers from Ariel, Royal Enfield and Velocette, remained in active service worldwide, before they were gradually phased out and replaced during the late 1950s and early 1960s. A major difference, compared with the USA was that in 1945, the British Forces still had more than 250,000 motorcycles in their possession, and although many were sold as ex-WD, a large number remained on duty.

Maintaining a demand for two-wheeled transport, a variety of new motorcycles were adopted by the British military to replace the ageing war

Below: **French despatch rider of the early 1950s on a Harley-Davidson WLA of World War 2. Note the larger carburettor filter and leather pannier bags.** *(ECPA)*

Right and below right: **1951 FN M13 military model; a single-cylinder 450cc side valve model widely deployed by the Belgian armed forces. An unusual rubber sprung front fork suspension design.** *(FN Herstal)*

Above: **Belgian paratroops and FN M13s in the Belgian Congo (raid upon Brussels-Kamina) in 1953.** *(FN Herstal)*

Opposite: **1969 BSA B40 of the Australian Army; a single-cylinder 350cc engine mounted within a 250cc frame. A reliable model that remained in service until the late 1970s.** *(Victoria Barracks)*

This page: **1969 BSA B40**, a successful off-road model with a single-cylinder 350cc ohv engine, was widely procured (Australia, Great Britain, Netherlands, etc), for solo multi-terrain despatch, or could be equipped with a police escort conversion (frame mounted fairing).
(David Ansell)

models. From a 99cc two-stroke lightweight, James J10 Comet (p 190), adopted by the RAF/Air Ministry for internal post, to a 500cc twin-cylinder sv model, Triumph TRW, for solo despatch and military police duties, a diverse range of machines were procured by the British armed forces. The Douglas/Vespa 125cc and 150cc, and Triumph Tina scooters were used by the Royal Navy, for short distance despatch duties. In the late 1960s, the BSA B40, a successful off-road model with a single-cylinder 350cc ohv engine, provided multi-terrain solo despatch, or could be equipped with a police escort conversion (frame mounted fairings).

Having gained an international reputation during the war, British factories won orders from Armed Forces worldwide, and during the immediate post-war years the British motorcycle industry began to dominate both military and police sales throughout the world. It would be well nigh impossible to list all exports, but by the late 1950s and early 1960s, AJS & Matchless, BSA, and Triumph had become major suppliers in most parts of the Western World.

In 1963, the Netherlands Army was supplied with 1100 Triumph 3TAs; modified for military use with a solo saddle and siamese exhaust system. These machines were eventually discarded and offered for public sale in the mid 1980s. The Triumph TRW was supplied to a number of overseas forces, in particular to Canada and Pakistan. From the late 1940s, BSA exported machines worldwide; in 1947 the B31 and M20 to the Netherlands, and B33 to Swedish armed forces. In 1957, the B33 was replaced in Sweden

by the Triumph TR5 Trophy. During the late 1960s, the BSA B40 was procured by the Australian Army; the 350cc engine mounted in a modified 250cc frame. The AMC factories of AJS and Matchless, under the same roof at the Plumstead Works, South London, were also able to maintain military contracts worldwide for a number of years post-wars AMC military models centred upon the Matchless G3L (p 199) and later G3LS, rear swinging-arm version, single-cylinder 350cc ohv models, and the larger AJS 18CS and Matchless G80CS 500cc ohv machines; supplied to the Netherlands, Sweden, and South Africa.

Triumph

In 1944, the Ministry of Supply prepared a list of basic requirements for the ideal military motorcycle, and BSA, Douglas, Royal Enfield, and Triumph submitted suitable prototypes, but the war in Europe came to an end before any contract was placed; see Chapter 3. In July 1946, the four prototypes were put on display at an exhibition of military vehicles; but two years later Triumph introduced the TRW model, to meet the post-war demands of the British Army. While retaining the original 500cc sv twin cylinder engine, to reduce costs, Triumph adopted standard production parts wherever possible. Based upon the TR5 Trophy off-road model, including the telescopic front forks and rigid rear wheel, 4-speed gearbox and wheels, the machine weighed some 340lb (154kg), some 60lb/27kg heavier than the war-time model, although the original fully enclosed rear chain drive had been discarded. The result was a robust looking machine, with an off-road capability, but an engine output of less than 17hp. While not in the Tiger class for performance, the machine was found acceptable for a number of years.

A similar second version, the Mk-II, was introduced in 1953, by which time the magneto had been replaced with a coil ignition and an alternator, like the Speed Twin, and the overall weight was reduced by about 20lb. The TRW handled well, with adequate acceleration and a top speed of 74mph. The brakes were good, and some comfort was provided with a fat 4in rear tyre. Although only supplied in limited numbers to the British Army, further contracts from both the RAF and RN, and overseas, maintained TRW production into the early 1960s. The TRW continued to be deployed in Britain until 1969, when the Royal Corps of Signals replaced their machines with a detuned military version of the Triumph Tiger 100 (p 200).

IV: NEW MODELS . . .

With the exception of such makers as Jawa, which maintained a secret design programme during the years of German occupation, the majority of manufacturers re-introduced their more popular pre-war machines to meet post-war demands. Pre-war components were also produced to return ex-WD machines to civilian specifications. Eventually, factories were able to look closer at the technical lessons gained during the war, but with a world shortage of both raw materials and fuel, all further development

Right: **1963 Jawa 350 Kyvacka of the Finnish Defence Forces. Note the braced handlebars and additional rear carry rack.** *(Finnish Defence Forces)*

Opposite: **Factory literature presenting the 1955 DWK RT-175-VS and RT-200-VS; lightweight models procured by the newly established West German armed forces.** *(Hercules)*

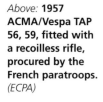

centred upon smaller machines. With a substantial increase in both output and reliability, these machines became a major influence upon motorcycle design and within a decade, a former production 500cc model could have been replaced by the abilities of a new 200cc model, or less.

Among the larger machines, Ariel, BSA, Norton, Panther, Royal Enfield and Triumph were popular, while the smaller machines of AJS, BSA, Triumph and Velocette were proving even more successful. For flexibility and ease of maintenance, and initial low cost, the sv engine continued to be improved, but the ohv operation had become standard for the majority of new machines. During the 1930s, the 750-1200cc V-twin had been essential for any major factory, providing the low torque required for a long distance touring model or sidecar machine, but the new generation of smaller, more powerful engines made the V-twin largely redundant.

With only Harley-Davidson, Indian and Vincent remaining faithful to the V-twin concept, the layout was generally dropped from post-war production, until Moto Guzzi and Ducati re-introduced the configuration during the late 1960s and early 1970s respectively. However, with the introduction of the vertical twin-cylinder engine, Triumph gained military contracts. Vertical twin cylinder models followed from AJS, BSA (p 199), Matchless and Norton, and these machines were purchased by military and police departments worldwide, but for the majority of cautious government authorities, the vertical single-cylinder machine reigned supreme for some years.

BMW Revived

In accordance with the Four Powers Agreement, BMW was proscribed from any motorcycle production until 1948, and then limited to basic utilitarian single cylinder lightweights. Within a year, a makeshift workshop had been established, and more than 9000 of the single-cylinder R24 had been built, a derivative of the R4 (1932–38) which saw military service, and its later variants. As the D-Mark gained an international value, the factory was given permission to extend its operations, and within a few years the more traditional flat-twin engine was re-introduced. Naturally, initial production closely followed a pre-war model, the R51/2, introduced in 1950, was a variant of the 1938 design.

Flat-Twins

From the mid 1950s, BMW became actively involved in the development and production of general police motorcycles. This on-going programme successfully provided a range of machines for military police duties worldwide; becoming a major alternative to the established single-cylinder design. The BMW R51 had been used by the German traffic police during the late 1930s, and with its proven reputation, the post-war R51/2 variant became an excellent foundation for public service machines (p 198).

Having re-established their pre-war reputation, the later R50 and R60 models laid the foundation for post-war BMW and many years of public service production. The R50 remained in production until 1969, by when 32,000 had been assembled. Initial military police orders were placed by Austria, France and Netherlands, to provide solo escort, pursuit, and general liaison duties. These machines were equipped with a handlebar mounted fairing, leg shields, crash bars, additional lights, and a two-way radio, offering, alongside Harley-Davidson, two basic concepts of military motorcycle for post-war service: the multi-terrain lightweight and then purpose-built heavyweight.

Lightweights

BMW single-cyl... tradition for military ...4 and R35 models we... *Reichswehr* and the *W*... utility finish. The R24, BMWs first post-war design was a mixture of pre-war development, with post-war modifications. While keeping the utilitarian appearance, with its bolted together frame and auxiliary gear-change lever the R24 provided the success required to revive the BMW name. Cleaner external lines and a 4-speed gearbox replaced the earlier 3-speed design. The R24 was only produced in 1949, but a total of 12,007 were built before the R25 was introduced the following year. As the larger twin-cylinder models, permitted for production the same year, the R25 had a new tubular frame with telescopic front forks and plunger rear suspension.

Although under-powered, production continued to rise, with a total of 23,405 R25s built in 1950, 38,651 R25/2s in 1951–53, and 47,700 R25/3s in 1953–55. With such advanced features as light-alloy wheel rims, central brakes in light-alloy hubs, new telescopic front forks with greater travel, and additional control for hydraulic damping, the R25/3 set even higher standards for the BMW lightweights.

With the introduction of the R26 1955–60 and R27 1960–67 (the last in the series), adopting Earles front forks and swinging-arm rear suspension as the twin-cylinder models, BMW continued to develop their single-cylinder machines until the late 1960s. The engine retained its original 247cc capacity, but output increased to 18hp. The BMW lightweight, however, had become too heavy and too expensive for the 250cc market.

As the West German economy recovered, domestic production was utilised by the occupation forces. In addition to *Bundesgrenzschutz* West German Border Police, a number of BMW lightweights were employed for occupation duties. After the formation of the *Bundeswehr* Federal Army in 1956, many 'occupation' machines were taken over by the new service, some remaining in use until the early 1970s. Early export orders were also placed by the military police of Austria, France and the Netherlands, widely superseded by the more traditional BMW flat-twin.

Also at the lightweight end of Germany military motorcycle deployment in the '60s was the Maico M250/B, a fairly conventional two-stroke. (The Triumph 250 split-single two-stroke preceded the Maico and had been in service for several years – see Chapter 3.) Another famous name from pre-war days supplied for military service up to 1958 was the DKW 175cc two-stroke.

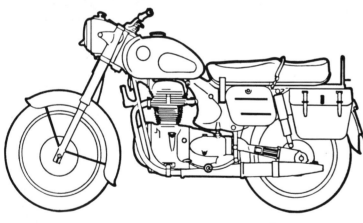

Swiss Boxer

BMW was not the only factory with the distinction of supplying a flat-twin for military/police service. The Swiss Condor, Russian Dnieper and French Ratier, are post-war examples. The Universal A-680 and A-1000 models of the Swiss Army, both sv V-twin machines, were replaced during the late 1940s, with the introduction of the Condor A-580 (p 201) solo and A-750 side-car machines. The Condor heavyweights had sv flat-twin engines, mounted transversely in a tubular duplex cradle frame, with pressed steel parallelogram front forks (similar to the Zündapp KS750) and a rigid rear wheel.

In the German style of the 1930s, all electrics, controls, and carburettor were under covers; air vents positioned on both sides and the front casing. The siamese exhaust system had a large flat silencer, mounted alongside the rear wheel. Transmission ran through a 4-speed gearbox, with high/low ratio change (8 speeds), and exposed shaft final-drive, providing multi-terrain despatch and reconnaissance or standard road escort and general police duties from a single model. The machines were re-introduced in 1951, with telescopic front forks and plunger rear suspension.

Following the procurement of different 4 x 4 military vehicles, the Condor heavyweights were eventually replaced during the mid 1960s, with the development of the Condor A-250. Like armed forces worldwide, the Swiss Army abandoned the heavyweight design for a new generation, more powerful, lightweight. After a trial period of 3 years with about 100 prototypes, the smaller and more manoeuvrable A-250 was officially adopted in 1965. While the model retained a shaft final-drive, the engine had a vertical single-cylinder with an ohv layout. A 4-speed unit

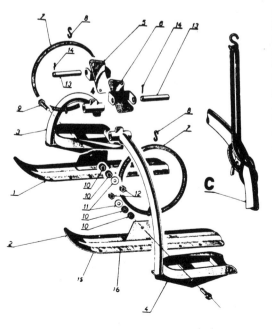

Ny sensationsmodell
av Sveriges segerrikaste motorcykel

NV:s tekniska fulländning avspeglas i den ständigt växande segerraden. Erfarenheterna från tävlingsbanorna kommer vardagsförarna till godo i bättre och säkrare konstruktioner. Vill Ni slippa köra "med skiftnyckeln mellan tänderna" välj NV — Sveriges säkraste och segerrikaste motorcykel.

NV 36
'Army Sixdays'
250 cc

250 cc DKW-motor — 11,5 hk vid 4.500 varv — Max. fart 100—110 km/tim. — 0,26 liter/mil — Bakhjulsfjädring med hydraulisk dämpning — Helkapslad kedja — Fullnav fram och bak — Specialkonstruerad dubbelsadel — Inbyggt stöldlås — Tjänstevikt 144 kg.

Gör som tävlingsförarna vinn på att välja Sveriges segerrikaste motorcykel

NYMANS   UPPSALA

Far left: **1963 Jawa 350 Kyvacka in Finland** *(Finnish Defence Forces)*

Left: **NV (Nymans Verkstader) advert presenting the trial model of 1953; designated the MC-262, some 300 were procured by the Swedish Army the following year. Fully enclosed chain final drive.** *(Sven-Olof Persson)*

Centre left: **Scandinavian Jawa 350 Kyvacka military model. The additional hand gear change enabled the rider to keep both feet upon the skis as required.** *(Miroslav Sochor)*

Far left: **1948, despatch rider of the Finnish Defence Forces, upon a post-war Ariel 500cc ohv model, prepared for military service. Note the crankcase protection plate.** *(Finnish Defence Forces)*

Left: **Jawa 250/350cc ski attachments; produced by the Swedish Fleron factory for military service in Finland and Sweden. Note the independently sprung arms.** *(Frank Nyklicek)*

construction gearbox offered a top speed of some 100km/h/62mph, and with a 14 litre fuel tank a radius of action of about 375km/233 miles was available. Developed for solo despatch and general liaison, the machine was still equipped with a dual seat and fittings to hold two rifles.

Finland & Sweden

While the Finns had been in their snowy element during the Winter War of 1939–40, the opposing Red Army had little experience as ski troops, and

Above: **1967 Jawa type 579/03 prepared for the Swedish Army; a single-cylinder 250cc two-stroke model with twin-port cylinder head. Based upon the moto-cross 579/02, military features included the provision for ski use; note the mounting bracket at the base of front down-tube and hand-change gear lever.** *(Frank Nyklicek)*

Far left: **A Norton 16H and post-war Norwegian despatch rider.** *(Norwegian Embassy)*

Bottom pictures and left: **1961-1966 Tempo 175 Militar, one of 650 standard production models delivered to the Norwegian armed forces. Military equipment was generally restricted to a folding rear carry rack, a pair of canvas panniers, deeply valanced mudguards (mud flaps front and rear), a protective guard around headlamp, fuel tank top document holder, ski attachments, and overall service livery.** *(Norsk Tempoklubb)*

Right: **Section drawing of the single-cylinder 1953 Gilera Saturno 500cc ohv engine. Unit construction gearbox and geared primary drive.** *(Moto Gilera)*

Far right: **Lubrication drawing of the single-cylinder 1956 Gilera GT-175 ohv engine. Fully enclosed pushrod design.** *(Moto Gilera)*

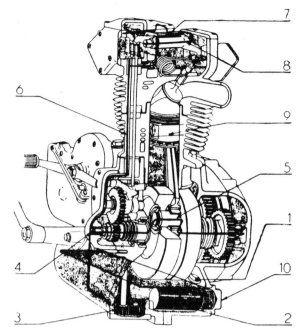
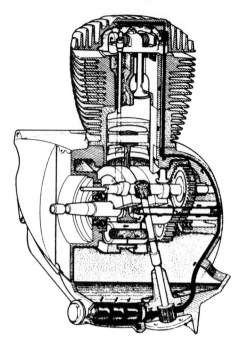

Centre right: **1953 Gilera Saturno 500cc, a standard production model modified for Italian military and police service. Limited changes centred upon an overall coat of service livery and pillion saddle.** *(Museo Storico della Motorizzazione Militare)*

Below right: **1956 Gilera 175GT, a standard model procured by the Italian Army, for solo despatch and general liaison. The Moto Morini 175 and MV 175 models were procured for similar Italian military service during this period.** *(Museo Storico della Motorizzazione Militare)*

prepared a number of motorised sledge vehicles to compensate, but only succeeded following heavy losses. The Russians also built a motorcycle with a short, broad ski in front of the forward wheel to trample down the snow. Although greater stability could be gained with a sidecar attached, mounted upon a sledge runner, unusually skilful riding was demanded at all times, and the project was shortly abandoned. With however, a history of winter competition on two wheels, both Russian and Scandinavian troops deployed conventional motorcycles providing solo and sidecar service in some of the most difficult climates possible for both rider and machine.

Motorcycles have been modified for use on snow since the turn of the century, but such machines were not successfully available as commercial models until the late 1950s. Different ski and caterpillar attachments had been available in limited numbers for some years, but in 1958, the Swedish military adapted a series of Matchless G80s with ski attachments built domestically. Within a few years, the Swedish and Finnish Armies adapted the Jawa 350cc with the ski conversion. When assigning a conscript in the Finnish Forces, any civilian occupation or skill is taken into consideration as far as possible, and the success of this doctrine can be clearly demonstrated by the riders of these machines. Climatic conditions have made many demands upon troops and vehicles, but few could equal the skill required to handle a motorcycle with ski outriggers.

Jawa introduced a pair of machines developed for use on snow and ice; a single-cylinder 250cc, 65 x 75mm and twin-cylinder 350cc 58 x 65mm model, equipped with a pair of Swedish-made skids. The steel skids were fitted to outrigger arms of steel tubing, with horizontal hinges, and as the riders replaced their feet on the pegs, giant elastic bands lifted each arm independently.

Means were employed to maintain the motorcycles as vertical as possible by limiting the movement of the outrigger arms.

On approaching any ice, snow or deep mud, the rider moved his feet from the foot-pegs onto the foot-boards (mounted upon the upper surface of the skids), and pressed down until in contact with the ground surface. Stability was maintained and the machine was then steered by the front wheel in the usual manner. To maintain this position, with both feet firmly on the skids, the 4-speed gearbox could be hand-changed by an additional lever mounted on the right side of the fuel tank, and a second right-hand lever operated the rear brake. As many post-war Jawa models, these machines were also equipped with a semi-automatic clutch, that only required the clutch lever for a standing start, and the final transmission was fully enclosed.

After military trials in Sweden, with BSA and Husqvarna and their own Monark models, the Jawa 350 Special was ordered by the Swedish Army in 1963; to provide multi-terrain duties throughout the year. Designated the Jawa type 554/05, it remained in active service in Sweden until the late 1960s, when superseded by the Husqvarna 256A in 1967.

Alongside the Jawa 350cc Special, the Swedish Army ordered the Monark MC-356A (p 201); with the same Jawa 350cc twin-cylinder two-stroke engine. The major difference was that the Monark had a tubular frame of their own design, with Earles-type front fork suspension and high level mudguards. In 1967–68 1100 Husqvarna MC-256A single cylinder 250cc two strokes were supplied to the Swedish Army. They remained in service until 1980, when superseded by the MC-258A.

Above: **1961 Bianchi MT61 (Motociclo Tattico 1961); tactical motorcycle introduced and adopted by the Italian Army in 1961. A single-cylinder lightweight 320cc ohv model, prepared for multi-terrain service, with upswept exhaust system and pillion grab rail.** *(Museo Storico della Motorizzazione Militare)*

Norway

The Norwegian Armed Forces did not deploy many motorcycles before World War 2, but after 1945, acquired a number of war-surplus machines for solo despatch. The majority of these were of British origin, modified with ski attachments, for all year service. Many remained in active use for more than 20 years; Ariel W/NG remained in strength until 1959, and a number of BSA M20s and Norton 16Hs were used until 1965. In addition, during the early 1960s, the Jonas Øglaend A.s. factory in Sandnes, supplied a number of motorcycles for active duty.

The company supplied a total of 650 (1961–62: 25, 1964–65: 115, 1965–66: 510) of the Tempo Taifun Militar model to the Norwegian Army.

Right: **1956 Puch 250-SG, a multi-terrain lightweight, prepared for the Austrian Army, with fully enclosed chain final drive.** *(Steyr-Daimler-Puch)*

Centre right: **1957 Moto Guzzi 350cc military prototype, based upon the Lodola trials 175cc model, the machine did not go into series production. Note the Earles-type front forks.** *(Moto Guzzi)*

Below right: **1946-1957 Moto Guzzi 500 Superalce, a direct replacement for the military Alce of World War 2. Prepared solo or with a sidecar attached, the machine was never sold commercially. Major new features included over-head valves, and a foot-change gearbox.** *(Moto Guzzi)*

Left and bottom:
1967-1970 Moto Guzzi V7 Polizia. Originally prepared for Italian police service, the model was later procured by the Italian Army and used for military and police service abroad. A robust and reliable design, the model established a new series of V-twin models for the Italian factory. The machine shown was prepared for the Ghana Army in 1970. *(Moto Guzzi)*

Below: **1959 Puch 175MCH, standard production lightweight procured by the Austrian Army for short distance service. Military equipment centred upon a pillion saddle and pannier bags.** *(Steyr-Daimler-Puch)*

The Tempo Taifun Militar (p 201) was a standard road model, with a single-cylinder Sachs 175cc two-stroke engine, 4-speed unit construction gearbox and fully enclosed chain final drive. Having a top speed of some 95km/h/60mph and a radius of action of some 300km/186 miles. The machine had a single downtube frame, with telescopic front forks and swinging arm rear suspension. Military accessories were of a fairly standard nature such as a folding rear carrier rack and a pair of canvas panniers.

co from Spain. These companies supplied the majority of immediate post-war (1945–65) military motorcycles worldwide. With a few exceptions, these machines followed similar specifications, but as Japanese innovations continued, many of the older works could not compete with the mass production techniques or technology of Japan. A new era for the military motorcycle had begun.

V: THE NEW GENERATION . . .

In the years up to 1966, Japanese industry was establishing new areas of expertise to replace the old factories devastated or seized as reparations. Only towards the end of this period did Japanese motorcycles begin to appear, including some under military colours.

While Japanese industry slowly gained an international reputation, Western military demands were largely met by domestic production. With the addition of the American works of Harley-Davidson, the majority of European countries outside the Communist-bloc, maintained an independent motorcycle output that provided machines for military service. The works of Puch (p 197); FN (p 197); Gillet-Herstal and Sarolea; Nimbus (DK); Gnome Rhône, Peugeot and Terrot (p 198); BSA, Norton and Triumph; Moto Guzzi (p 200); Gilera and Bianchi; Husqvarna and Monark; Condor; BMW, DKW and Maico and Sanglas and Bulta-

CHAPTER FIVE

Contemporary Design

From the mid 1960s, military motorcycles fell into two basic categories, the multi-terrain lightweight despatch model or heavier road machine for escort and general police duties. Outside these groups a number of mopeds and scooters were used in limited numbers for internal despatch and parcel deliveries. Similar machines for airborne troops were largely discontinued. Numerous commercially produced models were ear-marked as suitable and available if required.

The military sidecar outfit had been largely replaced by the Land Rover 4x4 and similar vehicles. The early Jeep was still used in the Soviet Union and Communist-bloc; a reflection of the shortcomings of the state-run industry, more than any military requirement. During the mid 1970s, the Russian-built Dnieper MT12 was introduced to supersede the K750. Designed for sidecar use only, the M12 had a 4-speed and reverse gearbox, with a differential that could supply in the ratio of two thirds to the rear wheel, and one third to the sidecar wheel. A lock could also be engaged to provide equal power to the two drive wheels on steep hills. While a long way from its origins of the 1930s, the German design could be clearly seen beneath detail changes and a revised frame, and the engine retained its sv layout and 750cc capacity.

The once mighty British motorcycle industry had (practically) come to an end; some of the final military machines were supplied in 1978, when a limited number of Triumph Tridents were supplied to the Saudi Arabian Army. A victim of their own size, military V-twin Harley-Davidson machines had also been widely replaced by the early 1970s; the Belgian Army adopted the model FLH in 1967, the final military service for this marque in Europe. (Though H-D sales to US Police departments are still vigorously pursued.)

Public service procurement groups turned their attention to BMW, Moto Guzzi, and the Japanese Four; Honda, Suzuki, Yamaha and Kawasaki. Following Harley-Davidson, the companies of BMW and Moto Guzzi both offered a comprehensive range of equipment for military or police service, without becoming overweight, while the Japanese machines were generally equipped with specified domestic accessories as and when required.

I: ITALIAN ALTERNATIVE . . .

From the late 1960s, Moto Guzzi, well known for their horizontal single-cylinder machines, become a major alternative to BMW. With the introduction of their 3x3 military tricycle in 1960, the foundation for a new series of V-twin motorcycles was established, and became a strong influence upon military and police requirements. Moto Guzzi had produced motorcycles for the Italian Forces since 1932, but the new twin-cylinder machines gained the factory a wider international acceptance.

Above: **1966 Triumph T20WD, single-cylinder lightweight multi-terrain model, procured by the French Army; military equipment meant a pair of leather panniers.** *(ECPA)*

Left: **1973 Condor A350 military model, prepared for the Swiss Army, to replace the A250 of the late 1950s. A total of 3004 were eventually supplied for solo despatch and general liaison duties. The machine-gun mountings have been retained each side of the front downtubes.** *(Condor)*

Right: **1966 Moto Guzzi 500 Falcone Polizia, widely deployed by Italian military and police departments alike. The external flywheel continues to be retained.** *(Moto Guzzi)*

Below right: **1968-1969 Moto Guzzi 160 Stornello, a standard production lightweight procured by the Italian Army,.** *(Moto Guzzi)*

Opposite: **1960-1963 Moto Guzzi 3x3 Mulo Meccanico, a purpose-built military tricycle prepared for the Italian Alpine troops; the V-twin engine becoming the basis for the V7 and a new series of machines.** *(Moto Guzzi)*

Military Tricycle

Known as the *Mulo Meccanico*, Mechanical Mule, the 3x3 military tricycle had a V-twin engine, with shaft-drive to all three wheels. By mounting the power unit and gearbox transversely, the drive could be carried fore and aft with the minimum loss of power. Although the cylinders were air-cooled they were partly shrouded by the body steelwork, and it was necessary to force air over the cylinder fins, by a centrifugal fan at the front of the engine shaft, drawing in air through a filter and delivering it through ducts to the cylinders.

Between 1960–63, some 200 Mechanical Mules were supplied to the Italian Army's Alpine Regiment, for use in mountainous territory.

Engine capacity was 745cc (80 x 75mm), but as torque more than performance was the aim, a modest 20hp met the military requirement. In normal use the two main rear wheels ran on rubber tyres, but for cross-country travel a caterpillar track could be fitted over these wheels and a pair of smaller auxiliary rear wheels. For increased traction over any tricky or boggy ground, behind each main wheel a small skeleton wheel could be lowered to ground level as required.

Integral with the engine the gearbox provided six forward speeds and one reverse, with a differential dividing the torque in the proportions of one-fifth to the front wheel and four-fifths to the rear two wheels. From the gearbox, a shaft ran forward between the V-twin cylinders, to a bevel

box at the base of the steering head, then downward by a shaft housed within the single telescopic front fork leg to a spiral-bevel and crown-wheel on the front wheel spindle. There was no single rear axle, instead, a cross-shaft and bevels behind the gearbox took the power to each wheel through individual drive-shafts in the two rear wheel support arms.

The V7 Model

The Italian military approached Moto Guzzi once again during the late 1960s; this time for a large capacity motorcycle for escort and patrol duties. The V-twin engine and shaft drive of the Mechanical Mule was resurrected, and with a revised gearbox and power output to suit, the outcome was the 1967 V7 model, and derivatives, for which Moto Guzzi was to become so well known (p 205).

Quick to secure an outstanding reputation for robust and reliable design, the V7 was sold worldwide, and became the principal model for the Italian Army, highway patrol, military and municipal police, and Presidential Guard. A low centre of gravity provided excellent stability, and with a speed as low as 3mph possible without clutch assistance, the machine was ideal for solo patrol and escort duties alike. A revised gearbox ratio was available later for sidecar use; adopted by the Netherlands Police.

Above: **1970-1976 Moto Guzzi Nuovo Falcone Militare, a direct replacement of the original Falcone model, new features included a fully enclosed flywheel, and more generally excepted rear suspension. Widely deployed by Italian military and police, and supplied abroad, the model shown was prepared for the Yugoslav Army in 1971/72.** *(Moto Guzzi)*

Following the V7, Moto Guzzi developed a new single-cylinder model in 1967, for lighter military and police duties. Based upon the earlier Falcone, the machine retained the traditional horizontal cylinder layout of 500cc (88 x 82mm), but greatly revised and in a new duplex cradle frame. The New Falcone, so called, was first presented at the Milan Show in 1969, and went into full production the following year. Immediately specified by the Police and Army, the new model was also exported to Africa and to the former Yugoslavia. The new model, however, suffered from various technical problems and was eventually discontinued in 1976; the final horizontal single cylinder machine from Moto Guzzi.

The 850T3 Model

Two further Moto Guzzi V-twin models, V7 Ambassador and V850GT were supplied in limited numbers to the Italian military/police, before the second major V-twin machine was widely procured for public service; the Moto Guzzi 850T3. Engine capacity increased from 704cc to 844cc, compression ratio increased from 7.2 to 9.5:1, and a 5-speed gearbox was introduced. Further new features included hydraulic disc brakes front and rear, a revised frame increased the wheelbase from 1445mm to 1470mm and a triplex chain primary drive replaced the original gear train.

Introduced in 1973, the Moto Guzzi 850T3 remained in production until 1979, and while maintaining the factory's V-twin reputation worldwide, military and police production con-

tinued to expand. Moto Guzzi introduced their integral braking system in 1975, and the 850T3 was equipped with this feature the same year. This was a hydraulically operated triple-disc system, with twin front discs and a single disc. This system provided pressure on the rear disc and one front disc by operating the foot pedal. By removing the responsibility for the rider to coordinate hand and foot pressures, the system was designed to automatically produce the correct amount of power for maximum braking efficiency.

The V1000 Convert

Virtually identical in outward appearance to the 850T3, and with the same military/police accessories available, the Moto Guzzi V1000 Convert was also introduced in 1975, and became the company's largest capacity model. As with BMW Moto Guzzi prepared a wide range of public service/military equipment, and these were all interchangeable within the largest model range.

The engine capacity increased from 844cc to 948cc, but the principal new feature of the V-1000 Convert was the introduction of a Sachs hydraulic torque converter, providing a semi-automatic transmission system. The gear change pedal remained in position, but was only used to change the high and low speed ratio; in and around town or on the open road respectively.

Further new features included an oil radiator, and a second rear wheel brake operated when the side-stand was in use. The sidestand also had an automatic cut-off switch for the engine, and a warning light to indicate when in use. Simultaneous flashing hazard lights could be used during an emergency stop. To accommodate this additional equipment and radio requirements, the electrical output was increased to 350W. Although not ordered by the Italian Army, the V1000 Convert was supplied for public service worldwide. In 1978, the manual version G5 model was also produced.

Lightweights

Moto Guzzi continued to develop their original design, and in 1977, the V-twin range was further extended with the introduction of the V35 and V50 models. While adopting many of the established features of the larger models, these machines had 346cc (66 x 50.6mm) and 490cc (74 x 57mm) V-twin engines, mounted within a revised, smaller cycle frame. An immediate success, the lightweights provided the foundation for a second series of V-twin machines, supplied for military/police service worldwide and available with an extensive range of accessories. With a similar range of optional accessories, scaled down to suit, Moto Guzzi prepared machines from 350cc to 1000cc throughout the 1970s and 80s, equipped to meet public service requirements at

home, but also in America, Britain, Africa, Yugoslavia and the Netherlands.

II: GERMAN DESIGN . . .

From the mid 1960s (the *Bundeswehr* Federal Army of West Germany), purchased a number of lightweight machines for multi-terrain despatch, reconnaissance and convoy control. While impossible to forget the intolerable conditions experienced by the *Kradschutzen* (Motorcycle troops) in Russia during World War 2, it was generally accepted that any future crisis could not compare with the Eastern Front.

The first *Bundeswehr* motorcycles, a variety of commercial machines, included a number of BMW 250cc models; utilitarian transport for the austere post-war period. These machines were dropped from production in 1967, but a number remained in active service until the early 1980s, within the Federal Frontier Force.

Further machines included the DKW RT175VS and TWN BDG250SL models (see Chapter 4), of the mid 1950s, but remaining virtually standard road machines, they were often found incapable of withstanding the demands of military duty. With a change of policy, it was decided to order from manufacturers with a history of off-road competition success, and between 1960–66, the Maico M250B (see Chapter 4) was supplied as the first multi-terrain lightweight of the Bundeswehr. An outstanding mixture of standard road and cross-country design,

Above and left: **French troops of the early 1970s deploy the vertical single-cylinder BMW R25/3 lightweight of some 20 years earlier; military modifications are more or less restricted to an overall coat of service livery.** *(ECPA)*

some 10,000 machines were supplied to the West German Forces, and often European Forces, and remained in active service for a decade.

Hercules

The *Bundeswehr* eventually replaced the Maico M250/B, (B for *Bundeswehr*) in 1971, with the Hercules K125BW (p 204), another off-road lightweight prepared for military use. The Maico,

however had established such a high reputation- that for many, the lighter weight of the Hercules was the only advantage of the new model. Unlike the Maico, the exposed chain final drive, open battery mounting, and unprotected Bowden control cables of the Hercules were all details that received military criticism. The higher-revving engine (both were 2-strokes), 5-speed gearbox and louder noise level were also considered unsuitable by the Army at this time.

Largely unable to meet the incompatible demands of the military authorities, the Hercules K125BW was a compromise; as are many motorcycles procured by armed forces. The Nuremburg factory, however, produced a general purpose multi-terrain machine, essentially a detuned, heavier version of their successful Enduro model, that quickly proved both popular and reliable in service. The low cost, less than 2000 DM per machine (civilian version was offered at 2650 DM), was an important factor, but with a seemingly indestructible Sachs engine, the K125BW remained in active service in a number of armed forces throughout the 1970s. Widely deployed for despatch, reconnaissance and general liaison, the small size and light weight was emphasised by the company in an attempt to supply airborne troops, but such experiments remained largely non-operational.

With service livery, braced handlebars, headlamp and engine crash bars, dual seat and rear carry rack, either high- or low-level exhaust system, the model remained virtually unchanged

until 1981, when the original Earles-type front forks were replaced by a telescopic design. By the mid-1980s, more than 15,000 of the Hercules K125BW had been supplied for military service worldwide.

Maico

During the mid 1970s, the Maico company gained a further contract to supply the *Bundeswehr*

with a multi-terrain lightweight. Designated the M250/M (p 204) the new military motorcycle was based upon their successful off-road 250cc model. Procured alongside the Hercules K175BW, the two machines were equipped with similar military accessories, while the Maico was able to provide a greater flexibility from a larger power unit. Based on their World Championship model, the single-cylinder piston-ported 2-stroke engine and 5-speed gearbox, was mounted within a trials frame with high ground clearance and longer travel front forks. While not supplied in the quantity of the Maico M250/B of the 1960s, several thousand M250/Ms were used by the West German military and police departments, and additional armed forces worldwide.

By the early 1980s however, both Hercules and Maico were in financial difficulties. While Hercules remained in production with the support of Sachs, after several years of uncertainty, Maico was sold to Laurence Merkle in the summer of 1987. Hercules production was relegated to ultra-lightweights of under 100cc, and the Maico name remained within motocross events alone. The factories survived, not as originally founded, but saved in a country that could only support a single large volume manufacturer, of large capacity motorcycles.

BMW Heavyweights

Armed Forces throughout the World continued to procure large numbers of BMW flat-twins, and from the later in-line horizontal flat-three/four-cylinder K Series, to maintain their motorcycle fleets. Prepared for solo despatch, escort, convoy control and military police duties, BMW continued to develop their range of accessories to meet new requirements (in later years to include clothing and helmets).

Widely deployed across Western Europe, these machines were used on standard roads, but from the late 1980s, a range of multi-terrain BMW models became available for military service.

In 1988, the Danish Material Command procured the off-road BMW R65GS (p 204), for multi-terrain duties; a 27hp version for general purpose, and a 48hp machine for escort and military police duties. A well balanced design, with good all-round performance, 50 of these machines were also selected by the Netherlands Army. From the mid 1960s, the majority of off-road military motorcycles had been single-cylinder 2-stroke models, but the GS series successfully established the four-stroke BMW twin as a dual-purpose machine.

BMW Boxer

Throughout the pre- and post-war years, and into the 1980s, the flat-twins of BMW remained a major provider for public service duties. Well known for their reliability, lasting design and performance to match, BMW gained an unrivalled international reputation; with few models not selected by some police or military authority. From the early 1980s, BMW public service machines centred upon the R45, R65, R80, and

Below: **1988 BMW R65GS, a standard production trial model procured by the Danish Army, to replace Yamaha DT250MX. Limited military equipment restricted to a pair of leather panniers.** *(Danish Army)*

157

Far right: **Honda CB250K4 of the late 1960s, as supplied to the French Army for solo despatch work; replaced by the later Honda CB250G5.** *(ECPA)*

R100 models for standard roads, and R65GS and R80GS models for multi-terrain duties. To meet the most demanding requirements, BMW offered a comprehensive range of special equipment and accessories, that could prepare both machine and rider for virtually any task envisaged. In addition, all machines could be supplied in a range of colours, with special paintwork schemes available upon request.

The majority of BMW optional extras were interchangeable within the factory public service production. Factory developed and fitted, BMW were the initial supplier and could provide any parts servicing required, within the general maintenance schedule of the complete machine. Prepared to the same standards as the motorcycle, accessories were developed wherever a demand could be met, for example self-levelling rear suspension for larger models, twin disc braking for smaller models, alternating horns, identification lights (flashing red or blue), siren, revolving beacon light (flashing red, blue, or yellow), power socket, extra battery mounting for smaller models, a choice of handlebars, wheels, mudguards, protection bars for the engine or panniers, mounting plate for radio equipment, fuel tank stowage compartment, solo seat, plastic or leather panniers and different frame mounted fairings or handlebar windscreens.

Wind-tested Fairings. BMW introduced the first full-fairing for a standard production road motorcycle in 1976. Developed with the use of a wind tunnel, a technical support initiated by BMW, the fairing was specifically designed to improve the machines' public service; reducing

rider effort and fatigue for either fast or continuous riding. With the support of their large range of accessories, by the early 1980s, more than 80 countries were using BMW motorcycles for police/military duties; an outstanding level of confidence in BMW design and engineering.

Since the first BMW motorcycle in 1923, the factory had remained continuously faithful to the flat-twin engine layout, but in October 1983, this situation changed. Just three months before a special rally to celebrate 60 years of BMW motorcycle production, a flat-four cylinder design was introduced. After seven years experimentation, and different three and four cylinder prototypes, ranging from 800cc to 1300cc, a four-cylinder 1000cc model was prepared with a three-cylinder 750cc to follow. Designated the K Series, BMW finally accepted a major break with tradition. Further models followed and by the mid 1980s, BMW offered a record number of 14 machines; a mixture of traditional twins and new multi-cylinder series, in touring, sports and off-road trim.

BMW K Series

Both radical in terms of what a conservative public would expect and a practical solution for a new engine layout, the K Series brought a new dimension to BMW motorcycles. By placing the crankshaft, gearbox, and transmission in a straight line, with the cylinder block placed horizontally, a functional design was produced as an integral part of the frame; while maintaining the BMW tradition for a low centre of gravity and shaft-drive to the rear wheel. The layout was also sufficiently different to have various patents, which upheld BMW's exclusive reputation, at a time

Right: **1981, BMW R80 TIC & R100 TIC.** *(BMW)*

when many manufacturers were inclined to produce machines that looked very similar.

Designed in a modular fashion with many components in common, the two K models (three- and four-cylinder block) had a dohc engine, but for the first BMW production model, the power-unit was water-cooled and fuel-injected to improve reliability. With an all-alloy cylinder block, weight was kept to a minimum and against a background of ever stricter environmental control, both emissions and noise levels were low. A single-plate dry clutch and 5-speed gearbox bolted onto the back of the engine. The wheels were cast alloy, of 18in. diameter front and 17in. rear, with twin discs and single disc braking respectively. Rear suspension was a monolever design, very similar to that first seen on the R80GS in 1980, while a pair of heavy duty telescopic front forks provided the forward suspension.

Following unprecedented publicity, it was widely accepted the original K100 fell between two specifications, neither a total touring model nor an all-out racer. With a weight of only 473lb, claimed to be the lowest for any machine of this class, handling and speed was good on most road conditions, without offering competition performance. In January 1984, the K100RS was introduced with a sports fairing that completely changed the machine's appearance. Without technical changes, the RS style was universally accepted worldwide and the K Series' success assured.

In the summer of 1984, the fully-faired K100RT (p 202) was introduced, and with the support of BMW optional accessories, a new generation of public service motorcycles became available. With an advanced all-weather and high-speed fairing, many armed forces began to either adopt BMWs for the first time, or replaced their flat-twins with the new K Series. While the 750cc version became available from early 1985, the 1000cc model remained the more frequently specified for police/military service.

III: THE JAPANESE FOUR . . .

From the mid 1950s, the Japanese motorcycle industry emerged as a major influence upon international design; setting new standards in engineering, reliability and performance. The Japanese invasion of Europe and North America revived motorcycle sales overall, but as interest continued to grow, Japanese production increased and larger models were introduced. Few other countries could equal the Japanese for speed of development, or design innovation, and as established motorcycle names of the West

declined in popularity, Japanese names became increasingly recognised.

There had been many motorcycle factories in Japan, but as sales continued to increase, production centred upon the now famous four; Honda, Suzuki, Yamaha and later Kawasaki. At first following a European style of general design, but as reputations were established a diversity of specifications and performance began to be introduced; eventually offering every possible capacity and configuration, to meet all requirements.

As Japanese motorcycles became known worldwide, a growing number of procurement agencies turned to the four marques to provide machines for military/police service. With the addition of locally available touring equipment (fairing or screen, panniers, crash bars, rear carry rack, etc) and two-way radio, Japanese machines were deployed for military duties with varying degrees of success, from the cold of Scandinavia to the heat of Australia and South Africa.

Above **1980 Yamaha DT250MX, a standard production motocross model modified for multi-terrain service in the Danish Army. The conversion comprised an enlarged fuel tank, canvas pannier bag, and all-over service livery.** *(Army Technical Service)*

Europe

As one of the first European military forces to procure from Japan, the French Army was equipped with a limited number of the Honda CB250K1 in 1969, for solo despatch, escort, and military police service. This machine had a vertical-twin 250cc (56 x 50.6mm ohc engine, with a 5-speed unit construction gearbox and exposed chain final drive. The model was replaced in 1976, with the further developed CB250G5 model, with the introduction of a 6-speed gearbox and hydraulic disc front brake. Both machines were equipped with a pair of leather panniers, front crash bars and service livery and deployed until the end of the decade.

In 1980, the Danish Material Command procured a number of Yamaha DT250MX machines, for multi-terrain despatch and general reconnaissance service. Following some 10 years of off-road competition, a clear resemblance could be seen between the DT250MX and Yamaha's world-beating works motocross machine. With more than adequate performance for either on or off-road use, and equipped with fittings to suit, the model was considered suitable for military conversion.

The single-cylinder 250cc two-stroke engine and 5-speed gearbox was mounted in a race developed frame; heavy duty front forks with increased travel and mono-shock rear suspension for longer and slower action to give improved traction over rough ground. Military conversion centred upon the fuel tank; the upper surface was replaced with a bulbous hump that increased fuel capacity from eight to 12 litres. Further military accessories included a rear carry rack and a canvas pannier bag mounted on the left-side (the high level exhaust system prohibited the use of a right-hand pannier).

For more general road service, despatch and escort, the Danish military police were also equipped with the Honda CB400N in 1982, and the two Japanese machines remained in active use until the mid 1980s, when replaced by the BMW R65GS and BMW K100RT respectively. The CB400N was a further development of the CB400T (p 205) used by the South African Defence Force from 1978.

The CB400N and CB400T models both had a vertical-twin 395cc ohc engine, with a 5-speed gearbox and exposed chain final drive, mounted within a tubular frame with telescopic front forks and conventional swinging arm rear suspension. The power units featured three valves per cylinder and capactive discharge ignition; providing a smooth and economical performance at all engine speeds.

For many years Finland has virtually maintained a defence force of individuals, almost an enormous Home Guard, and in this way a wide range of Japanese motorcycles have been regularly deployed in snow and ice. With very limited military conversion, except with the use of skis, these machines were used as and when required; privately owned by the particular rider/soldier. These were generally single-cylinder 250cc two-stroke lightweights, able to provide multi-terrain despatch, reconnaissance, and general liaison duties.

Australia

Designated the GP for general purpose or MP for military police, the Suzuki GS400 was purchased by the Australian Army in 1978, to replace the ageing fleet of BSA B40s. The GP model had a pair of leather panniers, crash bars and handlebar mounted windscreen, while the MP model had an additional syren, public address system, auxiliary patrol lights, and a two-way radio on a rear rack.

Below right: **A privately owned Honda CB350 (virtually identical to the smaller CB250), leased by the Finnish Defence Forces, for the duration of a field exercise and ridden by the owner, a conscript or reservist. POL-maintenance is arranged through the military unit. This picture shows a Finnish lieutenant and his motorcycle despatch rider.** *(Finnish Defence Forces)*

Below: **1982 Honda CB400N procured by the Danish Army, military equipment consisted of an overall service livery and a pair of panniers.** *(Danish Army)*

Top: **1942 Harley-Davidson 750cc WLA; the split fuel and oil (right side) tank design, a Milwaukee feature that continued to be adopted for many years post-war. Hand gear-change mounted upon the left side of the tank.** (Andrew Morland)

Above: **1942 Harley-Davidson 750cc XA; an American copy of German ingenuity, a boxer twin mounted across the H-D frame. While 1,000 of these machines were assembled the model remained a prototype. Indian also produced a thousand shaft drive machines sharing a similar fate.** (Andrew Morland)

Top: **1942 Harley-Davidson 750cc WLA & sidecar; originally the US Army intended 8 solo motorcycles and 3 sidecar outfits as part of a reconnaissance squadron to lead armoured divisions. Restored by members of the UK HD45 Owners Club, as part of the 2nd Armoured Division. Sidecar is not original.** (Garry Stuart)

Above: **The high number of WLAs in civilian hands today is a tribute to the robustness of the original design. Claudia Perry's 1942 machine is painted in the scheme of one used in the UK.** (Garry Stuart)

Right: **1942 Harley-Davidson 750cc WLA in the rain at a British Harley-Davidson rally. This machine is fully equipped with all the kit a US soldier would have carried. Note the dual lighting on the rear mudguard for black-out situations.** (Garry Stuart)

Above: **1942 Harley-Davidson 750cc WLC (prepared to Canadian specifications); a restored machine assembled by Alan Dark, a member of the British Military Vehicle Trust of Swansea, South Wales, from a number of boxes of parts. The machine has been prepared as a US Army model and is regularly ridden to military vehicle meetings.** *(Garry Stuart)*

Top right: **WLA and WLC models differed in details, including lights. These are Canadian.** (Garry Stuart)

Right: **1941 Indian 500cc 741A; military version of pre-war Scout, produced 1941-44 for Lend-Lease.** (Garry Stuart)

Top left & bottom left: **1942 Harley-Davidson 750cc XA; military prototype equipped with various standard US Army parts, including front fork rifle scabbard, ammunition box, rear carrier rack, and front and rear crash bars.** *(Garry Stuart)*

Centre left: **1942 Indian 500cc 741A;** the Indian factory of Springfield, Massachusetts, remained the major competitor for Harley-Davidson throughout the 1930s, and provided equal numbers for military service during the Second World War. The pre-war Scout and Chief models provided the basis for the majority of these machines. *(Roland Brown)*

Above: **1942 Harley-Davidson 750cc XA;** Peter Maas of Helmond, Holland, found this machine in a number of boxes at an autojumble, and painstakingly rebuilt it with parts from several countries. He regularly rides the machine at different shows and at one event was presented with a trophy by Willie G. Davidson, grandson of one of the company's founders. *(Garry Stuart)*

Right: **1944 Cushman 53 Autoglide; designed to be dropped by parachute. A mixture of pressed steel, and both box and tubular section parts; a total of 4,734 of these machines were produced and adopted by US forces.**

Below: **Tony Silvey's 1917 Excelsior 7-10hp; a standard model procured in limited numbers by the American forces during the First World War. Leaf sprung front fork suspension. Maintained in its original finish.** *(Tony Silvey)*

This page: **1979 Suzuki GS400, a standard production model procured by the Australian Army, to replace the ageing BSA B40. A wide range of accessories were adopted to provide multi-terrain despatch, reconnaissance, and military police service; designated GP for general purpose or MP for military police. The GP model had a pair of leather panniers, crash bars and handlebar mounted windscreen, the MP model an additional siren, public address system, patrol lights, and a two-way radio.** *(Australian Army)*

Since its first motorcycle in 1952, Suzuki remained faithful to the two-stroke layout until the mid 1970s, when the factory introduced a series of four-stroke models. The 400cc commuter model was a strongly contested category, for which Suzuki successfully introduced the GS400 in 1977. Beyond any comparison with the BSA B40 from some 20 years before, the Suzuki became the first of various Japanese motorcycles in Australian military service.

The Australian mobility requirements for vehicles procured by the armed forces were defined within the following categories:

A: Mobility Category 1 (MC1). Capable of sustained operation cross-country, with an accepted reduction in road performance.

B: Mobility Category 2 (MC2). Capable of sustained operation on roads and tracks with sufficient cross-country capability to effect deployment and reach weapon sites.

C: Mobility Category 3 (MC3). Capable of sustained operation on roads and tracks with sufficient cross-country capability to reach echelons, distribution points, or work sites.

D: Mobility Category 4 (MC4). Primarily for use on formed roads, with a limited capability to operate on tracks and off-road capacity sufficient to seek cover from attack or make detours.

By the mid 1980s, the majority of Japanese motorcycles had achieved high standards of performance and reliability and the Australian

military restricted their choice to four-stroke machines, with single- or twin-cylinder design.

The Suzuki GR650, 139 units, was specified for MC4 service in 1985, and the smaller Suzuki DR250S, 170 units, was specified for MC2 the same year. Twin- and single-cylinder models respectively, with dry weights of 184 and 127kg each, military service was undertaken with the minimum of conversion. Both machines had a 5-speed gearbox and exposed chain drive transmission, with an output of 40.5hp at 7000rpm and 15.5hp at 8000rpm respectively.

The larger model was re-introduced in 1990, as the GR650AF (122 units) for MC4 service with the military police. Standard accessories included a three-quarter white fairing and a pair of white panniers, with a revolving blue lamp on a telescopic stand. These machines were supplemented in 1992, with the purchase of the lightweight Honda XR250RM, 24 units and the larger Yamaha XT600EA, 351 units. Both machines were for off-road competition and considered ideal for MC2 service.

Limitations

Throughout the 1970s and 1980s, armed forces worldwide, including Japan, continued to specify Japanese motorcycles for military/police service. Produced to high specifications, many standard factory machines offered performance well beyond public service requirements, which brought new limitations. While sophistication raised general standards, a growing number of commercial models became too refined and complex for practical modifications; the machines were designed with too little tolerance.

While the Australian military and other forces operating in similar climatic areas expanded their Japanese fleet, many European and Scandinavian Forces replaced these machines, as unsuitable to withstand the everyday abuse of military duty. With electrical, mechanical, and transmission components left relatively unprotected from the weather, or with just insufficient strength of design, Japanese machines were widely withdrawn. A number of smaller manufacturers successfully produced motorcycles for domestic military use; prepared to meet local requirements, with basic operation and maintenance procedures. As an example, in late 1995, MoD consultants Dr Stuart McGuigan and John Crocker revealed a prototype Diesel Enfield based on the famed 1940s-designed Bullet 500. Tests are expected to confirm a top speed of 75mph and miserly 15mpg economy. A production version of the Diesel Enfield could replace the British Army's 350cc Armstrongs early next century.

IV: BRITISH PRODUCTION . . .

Continuous British motorcycle production for the army and other forces since the early years of the century came to an end with the BSA B40WD (p 205). This final BSA marks a sad landmark in British military motorcycle history, although the Company assembled the Canadian-designed Bombardier (p203).

During the late 1970s, military motorcycles began to centre upon the multi-terrain lightweight; generally with a single-cylinder two-stroke engine, for ease of operation and general maintenance. Often the result of many years of off-road competition, such machines were expected to remain in service for between 10 and 15 years. While, at first, designed for a particular local or national requirement, having established a reputation, many of these machines were widely exported.

Armstrong

Armstrong Motorcycles of Bolton, England, made motorcycling history in 1985, becoming the first British factory to be awarded a major defence contract since the British industry had collapsed more than a decade earlier. The Armstrong contract eventually provided some 2300 machines for the British Army and a further 500 to the Jordanian and 100 to Canadian Armies; at the same time, a revised military policy introduced a programme for all British officers to receive motorcycle training.

The Armstrong MT500 (p 205) was not an adaptation from any previous design, but had been the result of some two years continuous research and development to produce a robust and reliable military machine. Working to precise Ministry specifications, Armstrong had won the contract from 16 other contenders, including the 'Japanese Four', following a series of demanding trials carried out by Army representatives and by a civilian consultancy.

The Armstrong factory, an automotive division of Armstrong Equipment plc, had achieved notable success during the early 1980s, with their CM36 road-race and CMT320 trials machines. The latter providing Armstrong with the British Trials Cup in 1983 and 1984; the first time in 20 years that a British machine had won the trials for two successive years. This was an experience that certainly helped Armstrong successfully fulfil all the multi-terrain military requirements. With a single-cylinder Rotax 500cc ohc engine, the MT500 also marked a return to the four-stroke engine in the British Army, replacing the Bombardier 250cc two-stroke model of the previous seven years.

Bombardier

A division of Bombardier Inc, the world's largest snowmobile manufacturers, began production of the Can-Am motorcycle in 1973. Within a short time the Valcourt factory in Canada had prepared an excellent range of trials/motocross machines. A standard road model was also designed, but this project failed to get off the ground. The Austrian Rotax factory provided the power unit for these lightweights. Joseph-Armand Bombardier, the company founder, first approached Rotax in 1962 for a suitable engine for his snowmobile, officially registered the Ski-Doo in 1959. Since then, Rotax has provided Bombardier with various engines for a wide range of vehicles, developed to travel over land, water and snow.

In line with contemporary thought, Bombardier prepared a multi-terrain motorcycle for military service. Promoted as sturdy, agile and versatile, the Bombardier military model was offered with four engine capacities, but only the 250cc model was produced. All of Rotax origin, the 125cc, 175cc, 250cc (p 203), and 370cc engines were single-cylinder two-stroke designs, with a rotary valve, except the 370cc which had a piston port and reed valve. Virtually identical in outward appearance, the engine was mounted within a double-loop frame, with the engine oil carried in the tapered backbone single spine. The two smaller models were planned to have a 6-speed gearbox, while the larger two had the power for only five.

In 1969, Canadian Forces Headquarters decided their existing motorcycle fleet based on Triumph T100s supplied in 1957, was both excessive and costly to store, and a policy was made to dispose of all machines with more than 500 miles on the speedometer. As a result, by 1973, a total of 140 motorcycles was held at Canadian central storage.

With however, the introduction of the Bombardier military 250cc model, the Canadian reduction policy was revised, and in 1978, the two-stroke lightweight became the first motorcycle to be procured by the Canadian Forces for more than 20 years. By 1981, there were 72 Bombardier machines in active Canadian service, with five held in storage.

The British Army placed an order for the Bombardier 250cc model in 1979, with the Belgian Army and US Marines following in 1981 and 1982 respectively. The British contract was eventually assembled by BSA, at their Coventry factory, where a total of 872 machines were produced. British built components included the fuel tank, wheels, tyres, lights and panniers. With a growing interest in off-road competition models, BSA produced the Canadian lightweight Can-Am motorcycles until 1987.

V: AMERICAN PROGRAMME . . .

After 1945, motorcycles continued to be withdrawn from the US Forces, until 1957, when

Above: **1985 Armstrong MT500, following some two years development, the first British motorcycle to gain a major defence contract for more than a decade. The Armstrong contract eventually provided some 2300 machines for the British Army, with a further 500 to the Jordanian and 100 to the Canadian Army. The machine shown has been prepared for the British Army (36 Eng Regt, Maidstone, Kent). Note the twin port exhaust system of the single-cylinder Rotax two-stroke engine.** *(David Ansell)*

Right: **1979 Bombardier 250 (Belgian version) lightweight, procured by various armed forces for multi-terrain despatch and reconnaissance; eventually becoming recognised as the NATO model and adopted by the US Army.** *(Forces Armees)*

they were officially taken off the US tables of organisation and equipment. Apart from very limited attempts to use trial machines, neither the Korean nor Vietnam wars saw any use of American military motorcycles. By the late 1970s however, with rising costs of fuel and a concern for unprotected radio communications, the new generation of multi-terrain lightweights rekindled US military interest in the motorcycle. Heavy volume radio traffic was found often to delay important, though low priority, messages, that a despatch rider could more safely deliver.

Following initial agreements for testing and standards to be achieved, four lightweight motorcycles were procured early in 1977, for detailed evaluation by the 5th Marine Amphibious Brigade (MAB), Camp Pendleton, California. After a period of 100 days, and more than 5000 miles riding, Brig. Gen. Moore, Commanding General of the Brigade, was very pleased with the results, and the machines underwent further tests in the combined forces exercise 'Brave Shield XVI', during the summer that year. The 7th MAB were also encouraged by the results, and prepared an evaluation programme of their own, with similar machines during the same exercise at Twentynine Palms.

That year, various off-road motorcycles were also acquired by the Marines on the East Coast for similar manoeuvres, and in August 1977, the Fleet Marine Force began its own tests in Norfolk, Virginia. Eventually, from March to August

1981, the Marine Corps Development and Education Command at Quantico, Virginia, concentrated their attention on three machines considered most suitable, and after some 1800 miles of multi-terrain trials, in January 1982, the Bombardier 250cc military model was selected to re-establish the US Marine despatch rider. With a weight of less than 300lb, the US Army also experimented with the machine and various parachute designs, but these investigations remained largely inconclusive. Once again, however, the motorcycle had become an integral part of US military communications, widely accepted as an essential requirement to maintain an effective service.

Although no longer part of the American military scene, Harley-Davidson motorcycles were being supplied to the armed services of Belgium and the Netherlands, and elsewhere, up to 1967. In particular, the model FLH, a classic 1200cc machine bucking the general trend of highly manoeuvrable lighter weight machines.

VI: SCANDINAVIAN INDEPENDENCE . . .

Finland had a very small motorcycle industry, largely restricted to two-stroke lightweight machines, generally with Puch, Villiers or DKW engines; produced during the 1950–1960s under the names of Helkama, Juitper, Pyrkija, Tunturi and Vasama.

The Winha K-340, however, was different. A combination of advanced technology and many years of snow travel experience, this multi-terrain motorcycle was designed to provide all-year mobility from a single power unit. At first with a single-cylinder Sachs SA-340-R engine from Germany, and then a twin-cylinder Kohler 340-2AX unit from Canada (both were two-stroke designs producing 33hp and 30hp respectively), were specified to produce a motorcycle and snow-scooter partnership. Early development began in 1974, and within two years the Polar Metal Plast factory of Rovaniemi had assembled various examples of the two different forms of transport to use the single engine.

A single caterpillar track propelled the snow-scooter over snow and ice during the winter, and the same engine, the Kohler 340-2AX, (eventually chosen) could be re-mounted within a duplex cradle frame, to provide the power for a cross-country motorcycle for the summer months. With the majority of mechanical/electrical components readily available in the most inaccessible parts of the country the Winha also became a reliable work-horse for the reindeer herding Lapps of Northern Finland.

A belt primary drive ran over a pair of expanding and contracting pulley wheels, producing a stepless range of gears that could provide speeds from 3–100km/h. This automatic transmission proved ideal for cross-country use, with steady, flexible and self adjusting traction to meet all requirements, letting the rider concentrate on the changing terrain. The engine was air-cooled (heated air ducted to rider/driver), and designed to run in all positions, even upside down; a crankshaft pulley could also power such external equipment as a generator, water pump or chain saw. The service application possibilities were almost limitless and while the motorcycle had an ungainly appearance, it offered a robust agility exceeding standard production models.

Registered by the authorities in 1976, a number of Winha motorcycles were procured by the Finnish Defence Force when serial production began the following year. For various political reasons however, the full potential of the Winha was never realised. To protect the very fragile eco-system, the Finnish Government banned all off-road motorcycles in Lapland, and the Polar Metal Plast factory went out of business as a result in 1978. While only a small number of Winha K-340 motorcycles were produced, many continued to provide reliable military service well into the 1980s.

Hägglund/Sweden

In 1970, the Swedish Materials Administration requested motorcycles with automatic transmission. Although existing military machines were acceptable, the Swedish Army prepared a list of requirements for a more specialised replacement. The new model had to be easier to handle, with significant improvements in general reliability, yet cheaper to repair and maintain. It was to have a maximum speed of at least 100km/h/62mph, should handle well both on- and off-road, and

Above: **1994 Armstrong MT500; a specialised model designed and produced by CCM-Armstrong, of Bolton, England, for solo multi-terrain military service. First procured by the British Army in 1984, this particular machine has been equipped with various additional load carrying features, and is currently in service for former Yugoslavia. The machine also has revised front and rear brakes.**
(Sgt Callum Davey, 32 Engr Regt)

Above and above right: **Winha Automatic during trials with the Finnish Defence Forces, demonstrating multi-terrain ability throughout the year.** *(Finnish Defence Forces)*

Right: **1967 Husqvarna MC256A, a single-cylinder 250cc two-stroke model, procured by the Swedish Army, for multi-terrain despatch and general liaison duties., with ski brackets at the base of the front down tube.** *(Husqvarna)*

the transmission should be fully automatic.

This schedule of requirements was sent to the Swedish factories of Husqvarna, Monark-Crescent and Hägglund, with a request that prototypes were to be available for evaluation the following year. While Husqvarna and Monark-Crescent were established names within the Swedish motorcycle industry, since 1957, Hägglund had produced all the light armoured vehicles ordered by the Swedish Forces.

A motorcycle for Hägglund was something different, but in 1972, their first prototype, designated the XM-72, was undergoing Swedish military trials. The power unit was a Sachs 300cc (73 x 70mm) single-cylinder two-stroke snow-scooter engine, capable of 26hp at 5500rpm, with a pull-cord start on the right of the crankcase. Suspended beneath a box-section frame of steel plate, transmission ran through an infinitely variable automatic unit, based upon the DAF design for light car use.

The unique Hägglund frame, a box-section design with the steering head welded to one end and the rear mudguard mounted on the other, housed some 15 litres of fuel, four litres of oil and a substantial air filter. Both wheels were of pressed-steel construction mounted on stub axles

and front suspension was a single leading arm, half an Earles-type fork, while the rear wheel was held by a single trailing arm; which also housed the final drive shaft. Hydraulic disc brakes were installed front and rear, and to maintain maximum ground clearance, the exhaust system was mounted high and tucked well-in on the left.

While all three factories submitted machines for testing, Husqvarna and Monark-Crescent were far from any production stage, but when tenders were eventually sought, both Husqvarna and Hägglund felt able to bid for the contract. With the latter being successful.

During 1973, the Hägglund model greatly changed, and emerged as the XM-74 (p 206) the next year. The new machine gained 50mm in wheelbase and was 19kg heavier. The Sachs 300cc engine was replaced by a Rotax 350cc single-cylinder two-stroke engine which, while of increased capacity, developed some 2hp less than the Sachs. In compensation, peak power was reached at 5300rpm, but with improved low-rev torque. The frame provided an increase in both fuel and oil capacities and the single leading arm front suspension was replaced by Ceriani telescopic front forks. The pressed-steel wheels now had an eight-spoke design, and drum brakes

project to be transferred, and by September the Swedish Material Command agreed, on the understanding that Husqvarna could complete the contract quickly and at no extra cost.

Hägglund had original and advanced ideas, but were unable to match Husqvarna's – HVA – years of production experience. HVA prepared an off-road competition model from their military prototype, and were able immediately to deliver five test machines to the Swedish Army. The Husqvarna model had a more conventional layout, with a single-cylinder 250cc two-stroke engine, mounted within a tubular frame with telescopic front forks and trailing fork rear suspension. Transmission ran through an enclosed primary gear train, and 4-speed unit construction gearbox, with an automatically engaged centrifugal design and exposed chain final drive. The

Above: **Final Hägglunds XM74, prepared to Swedish military specifications, with a DAF Variomatic automatic transmission and shaft final drive (within a single rear arm suspension), eventually replaced by the Husqvarna MC258A.** *(AB Hägglund & Söner)*

Right: **1980 Husqvarna MC258A military model; final outcome of some 10 years development, the first 1000 were supplied in the Spring of 1980, with a further 2000 the following year – expected service life until 1999.** *(Husqvarna)*

replaced the original hydraulic disc units, to improve performance for multi-terrain service or during adverse weather conditions. Further new features included a folding kick-start to replace the pull-cord, and a decompressor valve in the cylinder head.

During troop tests, however, difficulties arose with the Hägglund/DAF belt primary drive, and in spring 1976, Hägglund approached Husqvarna for a possible source of alternative transmission. This eventually led to a proposal for the entire

production model remained for public sale, and a revised machine was prepared for military service. Designated the MC-258A-MT, the first 1000 were supplied in Spring 1980, with a further 2000 the year later; expected service life until 1999.

From the turn of the century, Sweden remained faithful to the military motorcycle; with an unbroken history of continuous use of two-wheeled transport. While not an ideal climate for all year service, with the development of ski

Left: **1979 Peugeot SX8 lightweight, prepared for the French armed forces, for solo despatch and general liaison duties.** *(ECPA)*

Below: **1969 Puch 250MCH, a standard production model procured by the Austrian Army. Note the extra long side stand hinged from beneath the dual seat.** *(Steyr-Daimler-Puch)*

attachments, the motorcycle became an essential part of the Swedish Armed Forces. During the 1990s, in addition to standard procurement, the Swedish Army had a number of volunteer auxiliary organisations, including a Motor Cycle Corps. While limited in numbers, the Swedish military motorcycle offered rapid transportation where few other vehicles could travel.

Two-stroke dominance

Other European countries continued military motorcycle production for several years, ranging from the ultra lightweight Peugeot SX8 AR 80cc (p 203), to developments in Austria, East Germany and Czechoslovakia of well-tried lightweight two-strokes. Notably the MZ ES250/2A (p 204), the Puch MCM 250, which retained the split-single two-stroke configuration (See previous Chapters) and the Jawa 350 Military 634-5-16, with a 350cc two-stroke twin.

Switzerland had previously developed large capacity flat-twins, but in 1973 the Condor

Engineering Company followed the general European trend with the A350 (p 206), fitted with a Ducati-designed ohc single-cylinder engine. And Spain, a country mentioned rarely in this book, developed a Bultaco machine for military service. Increasingly well-known in competition circles at the time, the Bultaco MOD224 (p 206) used an over-square two-stroke engine of 240cc, also available in a 350cc version.

Technical Specifications

CHAPTER ONE

Early Years – 1900–18

The following specifications are for 25 of the best known motorcycles in the years up to 1918, described in Chapter 1. Each is cross referenced to the text and listed alphabetically by country.

Austria
Puch R1 1914 *p 17*
Puch R2 1914 *p 17*

Belgium
FN Models 3½/4hp 1906/7 *p 28*
FN Model 2¾hp 1912 *p 28*

France
Peugeot 2½hp 1914 *p 27*
Terrot 2hp 1912 *p 27*

Germany
NSU 2¾hp 1904 *p 13*
NSU 3hp 1913 *p 14*
NSU 7½hp 1915 *p 14*
Wanderer 3hp 1908 *p 14*

Great Britain
BSA Model H 1915 *p 24*
Clyno 5-6hp 1915 *p 21*
Douglas 2¾hp 1914 *p 20*
P & M 3½hp 1914 *p 21*
Rudge Whitworth 3½hp
   Multi 1914 *p 24*
Scott 3¾hp 1912 *p 19*
Sunbeam 4hp FMM 1916 *p 25*
Triumph Model H 1915 *p 20*

Italy
Bianchi Type A 1914 *p 28*
Frera Model S 1916 *p 28*

Netherlands
Eysink Model 3½hp 1914 *p 28*

Sweden
Husqvarna Model 145 1916 *p 30*

USA
Excelsior Model 7-10hp 1917 *p 32*
Harley-Davidson 7-9hp 1917 *p 32*
Indian Powerplus 1917 *p 32*

NB. Discrepancies between model Nos expressed in horsepower and the value expressed in the specifications, are due to differing formulae used to calculate power.

AUSTRIA

MODEL **PUCH TYPE R1 1914**

Manufacturer	Johann Puch AG, Graz
Military Service	Standard production model works modified for military service, adopted by Austro-Hungarian armed forces in 1914, for solo lightweight despatch and general liaison.

ENGINE & TRANSMISSION
Type	Puch, air-cooled vertical sv single-cylinder
Capacity	254cc 68 x 70mm
Comp. ratio	5 : 1
Output	2 hp nom
Starting	auxiliary cycle pedals
Carburettor	single jet
Electrics	6v, Bosch magneto
Clutch	without clutch
Gearbox	single-speed
Final	exposed V-belt

FRAME & WHEELS
Type	tubular construction, single downtube design
Front forks	without suspension front or rear, a basically cycle frame
Rear forks	design with heavy duty front forks
Brakes	external contracting belt upon rear wheel hub
Tyre size	26 x 1.75″ front and rear, road pattern

DIMENSIONS
Wheelbase	1300mm	(51.1″)
Dry weight	52 kg	(114 lb)
Performance	50 km/h	(31 mph)
	overall length 2000mm (78.7″)	

MILITARY EQUIP. full acetylene lighting, leather saddle bag, and all over service livery

MODEL **PUCH TYPE R2 1914**

Military Service	Standard production model works modified for military service, adopted by Austro-Hungarian armed forces in 1914, for solo lightweight despatch and general liaison.

ENGINE & TRANSMISSION
Type	Puch, vertical sv single-cylinder
Capacity	308cc 68 x 85mm
Comp. ratio	5 : 1
Output	2.5 hp nom
Starting	auxiliary cycle pedals
Carburettor	single jet
Electrics	6v, Bosch magneto
Clutch	without clutch
Gearbox	single-speed, 2-speed later
Final	exposed V-belt

FRAME & WHEELS
Type	tubular construction, single downtube design
Front forks	without suspension (plunger design later developed)
Rear forks	without suspension
Brakes	external contracting belt upon rear wheel hub
Tyre size	26 x 2″ front and rear, road pattern

DIMENSIONS
Wheelbase	1300mm	(51.1″)
Dry weight	58 kg	(127 lb)
Performance	65 km/h	(40 mph)
overall length	2000mm	(78.7″)

MILITARY EQUIP. full acetylene lighting, leather saddle bag and all over service livery.

BELGIUM

MODEL **FN 3.5/4 hp 1906/7**

Manufacturer	Fabrique Nationale SA, Herstal
Military Service	Standard production model works modified for military service, used by Belgian armed forces for general despatch and liaison. A design that continued to be developed until 1925† and widely procured, eg, Russian, Swiss, French, Australian, etc.

ENGINE
Type	FN, vertical in-line 4-cylinder, inlet-over-exhaust valves
Capacity	412cc 48 x 57mm
Comp. ratio	5 : 1
Output	3.5 hp at 1800 rpm/4.0 hp at 2000 rpm
Starting	auxiliary cycle pedals
Carburettor	single FN spray type
Electrics	6v, Simms & Bosch magneto
Clutch	multi-plate, dry
Gearbox	single-speed (2-speed in 1908)
Final	enclosed shaft

†The FN 4-cylinder range comprised four basic models, of which the 412cc 3.5/4 hp model is specified above. The other three models were: 362cc 3 hp 1-speed 1904. 493cc 5 hp 1 & 2-speed 1908/10, and 747cc 7 hp 4-speed 1915.

FRAME & WHEELS
Type	tubular construction, duplex cradle design
Front forks	telescopic parallelogram, helical sprung, frictin damped
Rear forks	without suspension
Brakes	internal expanding (foot) and external contracting (hand) rear drum only
Tyre size	26 x 2.5″ front and rear, road pattern

DIMENSIONS
Wheelbase		
Dry weight	75 kg	(165 lb)
Performance	65 km/h	(40 mph)
	7 litre fuel tank, 2 litres of oil (1.5 gal imp)	

MILITARY EQUIP. full acetylene lighting, rear carry rack, all over service livery.

Brief specification 1904-1915, of Belgian model FN Four; widely procured by a number of European (Belgian, German, Russian, Swiss, etc) armed forces during pre-war years.

Model	1904	1906/7	1908	1910	1915
Capacity	362cc	412cc	493cc	493cc	747cc
Bore & Stroke	45 x 57mm	48 x 57mm	52.5 x 57mm	52.5 x 57mm	52 x 88mm
Output	3 hp at 1800 rpm	4 hp at 2000 rpm	5 hp at 2000 rpm	5 hp at 2000 rpm	7 hp at 2000 rpm
No. of Gears	None	None	None	2	3
Aux. pedals	Yes	Yes	Yes	None	None
No. of brakes	1	1	1	2	2
Tyre size	2.00 x 26"	2.00 x 26"	2.5 x 26"	3.00 x 26"	3.00 x 26"
Weight	95 kg	95 kg	100 kg	100 kg	128 kg
Max speed	45 km/h	45 km/h	75 km/h	75 km/h	90 km/h

Brakes were internal expanding and external contracting upon the same rear wheel drum.

MODEL	FN 2.75 hp 1912
Military Service	Standard production model works modified for military service, adopted by Belgian Army for general despatch and liaison and widely used by Allied forces.

ENGINE & TRANSMISSION
Type	FN, vertical single-cylinder, inlet-over-exhaust valve
Capacity	285cc 65 x 86mm
Comp. ratio	5 : 1
Output	2.75 hp
Starting	auxiliary cycle pedals
Carburettor	single FN
Electrics	6v, Simms & Bosch magneto
Clutch	single-plate, dry
Gearbox	rh change, 2-speed
Final	exposed shaft

FRAME & WHEELS
Type	tubular construction, duplex cradle design
Front forks	girder parallelogram, telescopic hydraulic damping
Rear forks	without suspension
Brakes	internal expanding (foot) and external contracting (hand) rear drum only
Tyre size	26 x 2.00" front and rear, road pattern

DIMENSIONS
Wheelbase		
Dry weight	54.5 kg	(120 lb)
Performance	56 km/h	(35 mph)

MILITARY EQUIP. full acetylene lighting, rear carry rack, all over service livery.

FRANCE

MODEL	PEUGEOT 2½ hp 1914
Manufacturer	Cycles Peugeot, Paris
Military Service	Standard production model works modified for military service, adopted by French armed forces in 1914, for solo despatch and general liaison.

ENGINE & TRANSMISSION
Type	Peugeot, V-twin, inlet-over-exhaust valves
Capacity	380cc 55 x 80mm
Comp. ratio	5 : 1
Output	2.5 hp nom
Starting	auxiliary cycle pedals
Carburettor	single Claudel
Electric	6v, Bosch magneto
Clutch	without clutch
Gearbox	single-speed
Final	exposed V-belt, with tension pulley

FRAME & WHEELS
Type	tubular construction, single downtube design
Front forks	telescopic plunger within headstock, helical sprung, friction damped
Rear forks	without suspension
Brakes	two block brakes upon rear wheel belt rim
Tyre size	650 x 50mm front and rear, road pattern

DIMENSIONS
Wheelbase		
Dry weight		
Performance	55 km/h	(35 mph)

MILITARY EQUIP. full acetylene lighting, rear carry rack with saddle bag, bulb horn, and all over service livery.

MODEL	TERROT 2 hp 1912
Manufacturer	Ets. Terrot, Dijon
Military Service	Standard production model works modified for military service, adopted by French armed forces for general despatch and liaison. The first of many Terrot motorcycles to be procured by French military, until the factory ceased production during the early 1960s.

ENGINE & TRANSMISSION
Type	Zedel forward-inclined single-cylinder, inlet-over-exhaust valve
Capacity	317cc 67 x 90mm
Comp. ratio	5 : 1
Output	2 hp nom
Starting	auxiliary cycle pedals
Carburettor	single Terrot

Electrics	6v, Bosch magneto
Clutch	without clutch
Gearbox	single-speed
Final	exposed V-belt

FRAME & WHEELS
Type	tubular construction, single downtube design
Front forks	telescopic plunger within headstock, helical sprung
Rear forks	without suspension
Brakes	block brake upon rear wheel belt rim, and caliper upon rear wheel rim
Tyre size	600 x 55mm front and rear, road pattern

DIMENSIONS
Wheelbase		
Dry weight		
Performance	70 km/h	(43 mph)

MILITARY EQUIP. full acetylene lighting, rear carrier rack, bulb horn, all over service livery.

GERMANY

MODEL	NSU 2¾hp 1904
Manufacturer	Neckarsulmer Fahrradwerke AG, Neckarsulm
Military Service	Standard production model works modified for military service, adopted by the German Army for solo despatch duties. The first eleven procured following the Kaisermanövern in 1904; the start of a long tradition of NSU motorcycles.

ENGINE & TRANSMISSION
Type	NSU, vertical single-cylinder, inlet-over-exhaust valves
Capacity	375cc 80 x 75mm
Comp. ratio	4.25 : 1
Output	2.75 hp at 2000 rpm
Starting	Auxiliary cycle pedals
Carburettor	single NSU (auto drip)
Clutch	without clutch
Gearbox	single-speed
Final	exposed leather belt

FRAME & WHEELS
Type	tubular construction, single downtube design
Front forks	without front or rear suspension
Rear forks	
Brakes	external contracting band upon front wheel hub
Tyre size	28 x 2.5" front and rear, road pattern

DIMENSIONS
Wheelbase		
Dry weight	50 kg	(110 lb)
Performance	55 km/h	(34 mph)

MILITARY EQUIP. rear carrier rack and overall coat of service livery (Emperor Grey).

MODEL	NSU 3 hp 1913
Military service	Standard production model works modified for military service, adopted by the German Army for solo despatch duties.

ENGINE & TRANSMISSION
Type	NSU, V-twin, inlet-over-exhaust valves
Capacity	396cc 58 x 75mm
Comp. ratio	4.4 : 1
Output	4.8 hp at 2200 rpm
Carburettor	single
Electrics	6v, Bosch magneto
Clutch	multi-plate, dry
Gearbox	single-speed
Final	exposed V-belt

FRAME & WHEELS
Type	tubular construction, single downtube design
Front forks	leading link, single helical sprung, friction damped
Rear forks	helical sprung rear sub-frame
Brakes	block brake upon rear wheel belt rim
Tyre size	26 x 2.5" front and rear, road pattern

DIMENSIONS
Wheelbase		
Dry weight	75 kg	(165 lb)
Performance	80 km/h	(49 miles)

MILITARY EQUIP. rear carrier rack and overall coat of service livery (Emperor Grey)

MODEL	NSU 7½hp 1915
Military Service	Standard production model works modified for military service, adopted by the German Army for sidecar service; with a removable machine gun mount. Widely used throughout the war.

ENGINE & TRANSMISSION
Type	NSU, V-twin, inlet-over-exhaust valves
Capacity	995cc 80 x 90mm
Comp. ratio	4.2 : 1
Output	12 hp at 2500 rpm
Starting	right foot kick start
Carburettor	single
Electrics	6v, Bosch magneto
Clutch	multi-plate, wet, foot operated
Gearbox	hand-change, 3-speed
Final	exposed chain

FRAME & WHEELS
Type	tubular construction, single downtube design
Front forks	leading link, single helical sprung, friction damped
Rear forks	helical sprung rear sub-frame
Brakes	internal expanding rear drum
Tyre size	26 x 2.5" front and rear, road pattern

DIMENSIONS
Wheelbase		
Dry weight	130 kg	(286 lb) solo
Performance	100 km/h	(62 mph) solo

MILITARY EQUIP. rear carrier rack and overall coat of service livery (Emperor Grey) and platform-type sidecar to carry a machine gun tripod into action.

MODEL	WANDERER 3 hp 1908
Manufacturer	Wanderer-Werke, Winklhofer & Jäenicke AG, Schonau, Chemnitz
Military Service	Standard production model widely procured for solo military despatch and general police duties (Austria, Germany, Russia, Switzerland, etc). A later version remained in production throughout World War 1 for German armed forces.

ENGINE & TRANSMISSION
Type	Wanderer, V-twin, sv
Capacity	408cc 65 x 76mm 45°
Comp. ratio	5 : 1
Output	3 hp at 2000 rpm
Starting	auxiliary cycle pedals
Carburettor	single semi-automatic
Electrics	6v, Bosch magneto
Clutch	without clutch
Gearbox	single-speed
Final	exposed leather belt

FRAME & WHEELS
Type	tubular construction, single downtube
Front forks	trailing link, helical sprung, friction damped
Rear forks	double helical sprung rear sub frame
Brakes	internal expanding (foot) and external contracting (hand) rear drum
Tyre size	26 x 2.5" front and rear, road pattern

DIMENSIONS
Wheelbase		
Dry weight	67 kg	(148 lb)
Performance	70 km/h	(43 mph) max.

MILITARY EQUIP. full acetylene lighting, rear carrier rack, all over service livery.

GREAT BRITAIN

MODEL	BSA H 1915
Manufacturer	BSA Cycles Ltd, Birmingham
Military Service	Standard production model works modified for military service, adopted by British armed forces for solo despatch and general liaison. Widely used, by 1918 armistice a total of 1088 BSAs were in British military possession, a mixture 3.5, 4 and 4.25 hp models from 1912-17 period.

ENGINE & TRANSMISSION
Type	BSA, vertical sv single-cylinder
Capacity	556cc 85 x 98mm
Comp. ratio	5 : 1
Output	4.25 hp nom
Starting	right foot kick start
Carburettor	single: BSA variable jet
Electrics	6v
Clutch	multi-plate, wet
Gearbox	foot-change, 2-speed rear wheel hub
Final	enclosed chain

FRAME & WHEELS
Type	tubular construction, single downtube
Front forks	cantilever, helical sprung, friction damped
Rear forks	without suspension
Brakes	block brakes upon dummy rims front and rear
Tyre size	26 x 2.5" front and rear, road pattern

DIMENSIONS
Wheelbase		
Dry weight	260 lb	(118 kg)
Performance	50 mph	(80 km/h)
	1⅓ imp gal fuel tank	

GEAR RATIO
(Overall)
I	= 11.8 : 1	
II	= 8.7 : 1	
III	= 5.5 : 1	

MILITARY EQUIP. full acetylene lighting, rear carrier rack, and all over service livery.

MODEL — CLYNO 5-6 hp 1915

Manufacturer	Clyno Engineering Company, Wolverhampton
Military service	Standard production model works modified for military sidecar service, adopted by Motor Machine Gun Corps and Allied Armed forces. By Armistice a total of 1792 in British service. A further 1500 model 8 hp (JAP engine) also built for Russian Army.

ENGINE & TRANSMISSION

Type	Clyno, V-twin sv
Capacity	744cc 76 x 82mm
Comp. ratio	5 : 1
Output	5-6 hp nom
Starting	right foot kick start
Carburettor	single – Brown & Barlow
Electrics	6v
Clutch	multi-plate, wet
Gearbox	hand-change, 3-speed
Final	enclosed chain

FRAME & WHEELS

Type	tubular construction single downtube
Front forks	girder pivoted design, helical sprung, friction damped
Rear forks	without suspension
Brakes	caliper front and drum rear brake
Tyre size	26 x 3.5" front and rear, road pattern

DIMENSIONS

Wheelbase		
Dry weight	299 lb	(136 kg) solo
Performance	50 mph	(80 km/h) solo

MILITARY EQUIP. full acetylene lighting, rear carry rack, sidecar mounted machine gun or ammunition boxes and spare wheel, and all over service livery.

MODEL — DOUGLAS 2.75 hp 1914

Manufacturer	Douglas Motors Ltd, Kingswood, Bristol
Military Service	Standard production model works modified for military service, adopted by British and Allied armed forces throughout Great War, for general despatch and liaison. By 1918, a total of 13,477 of the 2.75 hp models and 4816 of the 4 hp combinations were in service.

ENGINE & TRANSMISSION

Type	Douglas, in-line sv flat-twin
Capacity	348cc 60.8 x 60mm
Comp. ratio	4 : 1
Output	6.5 hp at 3600 rpm
Starting	right foot kick start
Carburettor	single Amac
Electrics	6v, magneto ignition
Clutch	single plate, dry operation
Gearbox	hand-change, 2-speed, later 3-speed
Final	exposed V-belt

FRAME & WHEELS

Type	tubular construction, duplex cradle design
Front forks	girder parallelogram, helical sprung, friction damped
Rear forks	without suspension
Brakes	calliper front and block brake upon rear wheel belt rim
Tyre size	

DIMENSIONS

Wheelbase		
Dry weight	172 lb	(78 kg)
Performance	47 mph	(75 km/h)

MILITARY EQUIP. Full acetylene lighting, rear carry rack with spares/tool box, additional smaller leather bags, leg shields, bulb horn, and all over service livery. (Standardised British WD requirements).

MODEL — P & M 3.5 hp 1914

Manufacturer	Phelon & Moore Ltd, Cleckheaton
Military Service	Standard production model works modified for military service, adopted by British armed forces (mainly RFC), for solo/sidecar despatch, personnel carrier and general liaison. By 1918 armistice a total of 3883 machines and P & M sidecars in British service.

ENGINE & TRANSMISSION

Type	P & M, forward-inclined sv single-cylinder
Capacity	495cc 84.1 x 88.9mm
Comp. ratio	5 : 1
Output	3.5 hp nom
Starting	kick start
Carburettor	single Brown & Barlow
Electrics	6v, Bosch magneto
Clutch	multi-plate, wet
Gearbox	hand-change, 2 primary chains for 2-speeds
Final	enclosed chain

FRAME & WHEELS

Type	tubular construction, integral engine support design
Front forks	girder parallelogram, helical sprung, friction damped
Rear forks	without suspension
Brakes	calliper front brake and contracting band upon rear wheel hub
Tyre size	26 x 2.25" front and rear, road pattern

DIMENSIONS

Wheelbase	54.0" (1372mm), Ground Clearance: 9.0" (229mm)
Dry weight	210 lb (95 kg) solo

Performance	47 mph	(75 km/h) solo

1.5 gal imp fuel tank (6.8 litre)

GEAR RATIO (Overall)

4.8 : 1 & 8.4 : 1 solo
5.4 : 1 & 9.3 : 1 w/sidecar

MILITARY EQUIP. full acetylene lighting, rear carry rack, bulb horn and all over service livery.

MODEL — RUDGE WHITWORTH 3½ hp Multi 1914

Manufacturer	Rudge Whitworth Ltd, Coventry
Military Service	Standard production model works modified for military service, adopted by allied forces (Belgium, Italy, Russia, etc) with a limited number also used by British Army and Admiralty.

ENGINE & TRANSMISSION

Type	Rudge Whitworth, vertical single-cylinder, inlet-over-exhaust valves
Capacity	499cc 85 x 88mm
Comp. ratio	
Output	3.5 hp nom
Starting	hand lever
Carburettor	single Senspray
Electrics	6v, CAV magneto
Clutch	exposed multi-plate, hand-controlled
Gearbox	none, hand adjustable engine and rear-wheel pulley
Final	exposed rubber-canvas belt

FRAME & WHEELS

Type	tubular construction, single downtube design
Front forks	girder parallelogram, friction damped
Rear forks	without suspension
Brakes	calliper front brake and block brake upon belt wheel rim
Tyre size	650 x 65mm front and rear, road pattern

DIMENSIONS

Wheelbase	55.0"	(1397mm)
Dry weight	214 lb	(97 kg)
Performance	40 mph	(64 km/h)

(2 gallon tank)

GEAR RATIO
multi-variable between 7 : 1 and 3.5 : 1

MILITARY EQUIP. full acetylene lighting, rear carry rack and all over service livery.

MODEL — SCOTT MODEL 3¾ hp 1912

Manufacturer	Scott Engineering Co. Ltd, Bradford
Military Service	Standard production model, works modified for military service; with a machine gun mounted upon the handlebars. Remained experimental only, but provided the basis for the Scott gun carrier outfit of 1914.

ENGINE & TRANSMISSION

Type	Scott, water-cooled 2-cylinder, 2-stroke
Capacity	486cc 70 x 63.5mm
Comp. ratio	
Output	3.75 hp nom
Starting	right foot kick start
Carburettor	single Binks
Electrics	6v, Thompson-Bennett magento
Primary	semi-exposed double chain, 2 ratios
Clutch	multi-plate
Gearbox	none, foot-change primary drive selector
Final	exposed chain

FRAME & WHEELS

Type	tubular triangulated open design
Front forks	telescopic, single helical sprung, without damping
Rear forks	without rear suspension
Brakes	caliper brakes front and rear
Tyre size	2½ x 26" front and rear, road pattern

DIMENSIONS

Wheelbase	51.0"	(1296mm)
Dry weight	220 lb	(100 kg)
Performance	55 mph	(35 km/h) max.

2½ imp. gal. fuel (11.4 lt)

MILITARY EQUIP. Laird Menteyne machine gun mounted upon handlebar, front and rear centre stands to keep machine stable while gun is used, and ammunition box upon rear carrier rack.

MODEL — SUNBEAM 4 hp FMM 1916

Manufacturer	Sunbeam Cycles Ltd, Wolverhampton
Military Service	Standard production model works modified for the French armed forces, less than a 1000 built for solo despatch and sidecar military duties. Continued to be supplied until 1918.

ENGINE & TRANSMISSION

Type	Sunbeam, vertical sv single-cylinder
Capacity	545cc 85 x 96mm
Comp. ratio	5 : 1
Output	4 hp nom
Starting	right foot kick start
Carburettor	single Brown & Barlow
Electrics	6v
Clutch	multi-plate, wet
Gearbox	hand-change, 3-speed
Final	exposed V-belt

FRAME & WHEELS

Type	tubular construction, single downtube
Front forks	Sunbeam-Druid flexi forks, helical sprung, friction damped
Rear forks	without rear suspension
Brakes	internal expanding front drum, block brake upon belt rim
Type size	650 x 65mm front and rear, road pattern

DIMENSIONS

Wheelbase		
Dry weight		
Performance	40 mph	(64 km/h) max

GEAR RATIO (Overall)

I	= 12.67 : 1	
II	= 7.4 : 1	
III	= 4.3 : 1	

MILITARY EQUIP. full acetylene lighting, rear carrier rack or pillion pad, and all over service livery.

MODEL — TRIUMPH H 1915

Manufacturer	Triumph Engineering Co. Ltd, Coventry
Military Service	Standard production model works modified for military service, adopted by British armed forces for solo/sidecar despatch and general liaison. The model that gave Triumph the 'Trusty' nickname, by the armistice a total of 17,998 machines (306 sidecars) remained in active service.

ENGINE & TRANSMISSION

Type	Triumph, vertical sv single-cylinder
Capacity	550cc 85 x 97mm
Comp. ratio	5 : 1
Output	4 hp nom
Starting	right foot kick start
Carburettor	single – Triumph semi-automatic
Electrics	6v, magneto ignition
Clutch	multi-plate, wet
Gearbox	hand-change, 3-speed, Sturmey-Archer
Final	exposed V-belt

FRAME & WHEELS

Type	tubular construction, single downtube design
Front forks	cantilever, helical sprung, friction damped
Rear forks	without suspension
Brakes	caliper front and block upon rear wheel belt rim
Tyre size	26 x 2.5" front and rear, road pattern

DIMENSIONS

Wheelbase		
Dry weight	200 lb	(91 kg) solo
Performance	45 mph	(72 km/h)

1.5 gal Imp fuel tank (6.8 litre)

GEAR RATIO

I	= 13.5 : 1	
II	= 8.2 : 1	
III	= 5 : 1	

MILITARY EQUIP. full acetylene lighting, rear carry rack with spare/tool box, additional smaller leather bags, bulb horn, and all over service livery (Standardised British WD requirements).

ITALY

MODEL — BIANCHI Type A 1914

Manufacturer	Edoardo Bianchi – Moto Meccanica SpA, Milan
Military Service	Standard production model works modified for military service, adapted by Italian armed forces in 1914 for solo despatch and general liaison, becoming one of the most numerous models used by the Italian military during World War 1.

ENGINE & TRANSMISSION

Type	Bianchi, vertical sv single cylinder
Capacity	499cc 85 x 88mm
Comp. ratio	5 : 1
Output	3.5 hp nom
Starting	right foot kick start
Carburettor	single Dell'Orto
Electrics	6v
Clutch	multi-plate, wet
Gearbox	single-speed
Final	exposed V-belt

FRAME & WHEELS

Type	tubular construction, single downtube design
Front forks	without suspension
Rear forks	without suspension
Brakes	block brake upon rear wheel belt rim
Tyre size	26 x 2.5" front and rear, road pattern

DIMENSIONS

Wheelbase		
Dry weight		
Performance	70 km/h	(43 mph)

MILITARY EQUIP. full acetylene lighting, rear carry rack, all over service livery

MODEL — FRERA TYPE S 1916

Manufacturer	SA Frere, Tradate
Military Service	Standard production model works modified for military service, used by Italian armed forces for solo despatch and general liaison. A larger 8/10 hp V-twin model was used for sidecar service.

ENGINE & TRANSMISSION

Type	Frera, vertical sv single-cylinder
Capacity	499cc 85 x 88mm
Comp. ratio	5 : 1
Output	4 hp nom

Starting | right foot kick start
Carburettor | single
Electrical | 6v, Bosch magneto
Clutch | multi-plate, wet
Gearbox | hand-change, 3-speed
Final | exposed V-belt

FRAME & WHEELS
Type | tubular construction, single downtube design
Front forks | girder parallelogram, helical sprung, friction damped
Rear forks | without suspension
Brakes | block brake upon rear wheel belt rim
Tyre size | 26 x 3.5" front and rear, road pattern

DIMENSIONS
Wheelbase |
Dry weight | 145 kg | (319 lb)
Performance | 45 km/h | (28 mph)

MILITARY EQUIP. full acetylene lighting, rear carry rack and all over service livery.

NETHERLANDS

MODEL | **EYSINK 3.5 hp 1914**

Manufacturer | Eysink NV, Amersfoort
Military Service | Standard production model works modified for military service, used by Dutch armed forces for solo despatch and general liaison. Pre-1914, 365cc and 425cc single-cylinder, and 774cc V-twin models were also used for military service.

ENGINE
Type | Eysink, vertical sv single-cylinder
Capacity | 408cc 74 x 95mm
Comp. ratio | 5 : 1
Output | 3.5 hp nom
Starting | right foot kick start
Carburettor | single Amac
Electrics | 6v, Bosch magneto
Clutch | multi-plate, wet
Gearbox | hand-change, 3-speed
Final | exposed V-belt

FRAME & WHEELS
Type | tubular construction, single downtube design
Front forks | girder parallelogram, leaf sprung, friction damped
Rear forks | without suspension
Brakes | caliper front and block brake upon belt rim
Tyre size | 26 x 3.5" front and rear, road pattern

DIMENSION
Wheelbase |
Dry weight |
Performance | 70 km/h | (43 mph)

MILITARY EQUIP. full acetylene lighting, rear carry rack, and heavy duty front forks and support legs for handlebar mounted machine gun and ammunition boxes, and all over service livery.

SWEDEN

MODEL | **HUSQVARNA 145 1916**

Manufacturer | Husqvarna Vapenfabriks AB, Husqvarna
Military Service | Standard production model works modified for military service, used by Swedish armed forces for solo/sidecar despatch and general liaison. 486 machines supplied, the first of many models the HVA works prepared for military service.

ENGINE & TRANSMISSION
Type | Moto-Reve, V-twin, inlet-over-exhaust valves
Capacity | 548cc 65 x 83mm
Comp. ratio | 5 : 1
Output | 4.25 hp nom
Starting | right foot kick start
Carburettor | single
Electrics | 6v, Bosch magneto
Clutch | multi-plate, wet
Gearbox | hand-change, 3-speed
Final | exposed chain

FRAME & WHEELS
Type | tubular construction, single downtube design
Front forks | girder parallelogram, helical sprung, friction damped
Rear forks | without suspension
Brakes | block brake upon dummy rear wheel rim
Tyre size | 26 x 2.5" front and rear, road pattern

DIMENSIONS
Wheelbase |
Dry weight | 118 kg | (260 lb) solo
Performance | 80 km/h | (50 mph) solo
| 9 litres fuel tank (2 gal imp)

GEAR RATIO | MILITARY EQUIP. full acetylene lighting, rear
(Overall) | carry rack, bulb horn, and all over service livery.
I | = 14.00 : 1
II | = 8.56 : 1
III | = 5.25 : 1

USA

MODEL | **EXCELSIOR 7-10 hp 1917**

Manufacturer | Excelsior Supply & Manufacture Co, Chicago
Military Service | Standard production model works modified for military service, adopted by US forces for solo/sidecar despatch, personnel carrier, reconnaissance, and general liaison. By Armistice a total of 2600 in service.

ENGINE & TRANSMISSION
Type | Excelsior, V-twin, inlet-over-exhaust valves
Capacity | 997cc 84.53 x 88.9mm
Comp. ratio | 5 : 1
Output | 7-10 hp nom
Starting | right foot kick start
Carburettor | single – Schebler type H
Electrics | 6v, Bosch magneto
Clutch | multi-plate, wet
Gearbox | hand-change, 3-speed
Final | exposed chain

FRAME & WHEELS
Type | tubular construction, single downtube design
Front forks | trailing link, leaf sprung, friction damped
Rear forks | without suspension
Brakes | internal expanding and external contracting rear drum brake
Tyre size | 28 x 3.00" front and rear, road pattern

DIMENSIONS
Wheelbase | 58.0" | (1475mm) solo
Dry weight | 350 lb | (159 kg) solo
Performance | 75 mph | (120 km/h) solo

MILITARY EQUIP. full acetylene lighting, rear carry rack, additional support members to cycle frame, horn, various commercial sidecar designs with spare wheel, and all over service livery.

MODEL | **HARLEY-DAVIDSON 7-9 hp 1917**

Manufacturer | Harley-Davidson Motor Co, Milwaukee
Military Service | Standard production model works modified for military service, for solo/sidecar despatch, personnel carrier, medical/general transport and reconnaissance. By Dec 1918 a total of 14,666 received from 26,487 ordered. (14,332 sidecars received)

ENGINE & TRANSMISSION
Type | H-D, V-twin, inlet-over-exhaust valves
Capacity | 987cc 84.1 x 88.9mm
Comp. ratio | 5 : 1
Output | 8.8 hp nom
Starting | right foot kick start
Carburettor | single – Wheeler & Schebler
Electrics | 6v, Bosch & Berling magneto
Clutch | multi-plate, wet
Gearbox | hand-change, 3-speed
Final | exposed chain

FRAME & WHEELS
Type | tubular construction, single downtube design
Front forks | leading link, helical sprung, friction damped
Rear forks | without suspension
Brakes | internal expanding and external contracting rear drum
Tyre size | 28 x 3.00" front and rear, road pattern

DIMENSIONS
Wheelbase | 59.5" | (1511mm) solo
Dry weight | 400 lb | (181 kg) solo
Performance | 75 mph | (120 km/h) solo

MILITARY EQUIP. full acetylene lighting, rear carry rack, horn, various sidecar mounted machine-gun fixings, spare wheel, and all over service livery.

MODEL | **INDIAN POWERPLUS 1917**

Manufacturer | Indian Motorcycle Co, Springfield
Military Service | Standard production model works modified for military service, for solo/sidecar despatch, personnel carrier, general liaison and medical support. By Dec. 1918 18,018 (16,804 sidecars) were delivered from 39,870 ordered.

ENGINE & TRANSMISSION
Type | Indian, V-twin sv
Capacity | 998cc 79.4 x 100.8mm
Comp. ratio | 5 : 1
Output | 15-18 hp nom
Starting | right foot kick start
Carburettor | single – Indian & Schebler automatic
Electrics | 6v, Splitdorf mag-dynamo
Clutch | multi-plate, wet
Gearbox | foot-change, 3-speed
Final | exposed chain

FRAME & WHEELS
Type | tubular construction, single downtube design
Front forks | trailing link, leaf sprung, friction damped
Rear forks | without suspension
Brakes | internal expanding and external contracting rear drum brake only
Tyre size | 28 x 3.00" front and rear, road pattern

DIMENSIONS
Wheelbase | 60.0" | (1524mm) solo
Dry weight | 368 lb | (167 kg) solo
Performance | 75 mph | (120 km/h) solo
| 2 gal US fuel tank (7.5 litre)

MILITARY EQUIP. full acetylene lighting, rear carry rack, horn, various sidecar mounted machine-gun fixings, spare wheel, and all over service library.

CHAPTER TWO

Interwar Years – 1919–38

The following specifications are for 55 of the best known motor-cycles in military service between the wars, and described in Chapter 2. Each model is cross referenced to the text.

Austria
Puch 800 1936 *p 43*
Puch 200 1937 *p 43*
Puch 350 GS 1938 *p 43*

Belgium
FN Military M86 1936 *p 69*
FN M 12SM 1937 *p 69*
Gillet 750 1938 *p 69*
Sarolea S6 1937 *p 69*

Czechoslovakia
BD/Praga 500cc 1927 *p 50*
CZ 175cc 1935 *p 50*
Jawa 175 1937 *p 52*

Denmark
Nimbus 750 1934 *p 60*

France
Gnome Rhône D5A 1938 *p 67*
Gnome Rhône AX2 1938 *p 67*
Gnome Rhône 750 Armee 1938 *p 67*
Monet-Goyon L5A1 1935 *p 67*
Rene Gillet G1 1937 *p 67*
Terrot VA 1934 *p 67*

Germany
BMW R62 1928 *p 41*
BMW R11 1929 *p 41*
BMW R12 1935 *p 42*
BMW R5 1936 *p 42*
BMW R35 1937 *p 42*
BMW R66 1938 *p 42*
BMW R71 1938 *p 42*
DKW NZ350 1938 *p 43*
DKW NZ500 1938 *p 43*
NSU 251OS 1938 *p 43*
NSU 601 OSL 1938 *p 43*
Triumph BD 250W 1938 *p 43*
Victoria KR VI 1927 *p 40*
Victoria KR6 1933 *p 41*
Victoria KR9 1936 *p 41*
Victoria KR35 WH 1938 *p 41*
Zündapp K500 1934 *p 43*
Zündapp DB200 1935 *p 43*
Zündapp K800 1934 *p 43*
Zündapp KS600W 1937 *p 43*

Great Britain
BSA Military 500cc 1932 *p 73*
BSA M20 1938 *p 73*
BSA Military G14 *p 73*

Italy
Bianchi 500M 1936 *p 58*
Gilera Military LTE 1936 *p 60*
Moto Guzzi GT17 1932 *p 58*
Moto Guzzi GTV 1934 *p 60*
Sertum 250MCM 1937 *p 58*

Japan
Sankyo Type 97 1937 *p 77*

Poland
CWS/Sokol Military M111 1934 *p 49*
Sokol 600 RT M211 1936 *p 49*
MOJ 130 1938 *p 49*

Sweden
Husqvarna 500A 1922 *p 62*
Suecia Arme-Type 1937 *p 63*

Switzerland
Condor 641 Armee 1927 *p 77*
Condor 752 Armee 1930 *p 77*

USSR
TIM AM600 1935 *p 48*
PMZ A750 1935 *p 48*

AUSTRIA

MODEL	PUCH 800 1936
Manufacturer	Steyr-Daimler-Puch AG, Graz, Austria
Military Service	Standard production model works modified for Austrian armed forces for solo/sidecar despatch, personnel carrier, reconnaissance and general liaison. Produced 550 between 1936-38.

ENGINE & TRANSMISSION

Type	Puch, transverse sv V-four
Capacity	792cc 60 x 70mm
Comp. ratio	5 : 1
Output	20 hp at 4000 rpm
Starting	right foot kick start
Carburettor	single Solex-Fallstrom 23mm Ø
Electrics	6v, 50/70 watt, coil ignition (Bosch W175T1)
Clutch	single-plate, dry, within rear-wheel hub
Gearbox	hand-change, 4-speed
Final	exposed chain

FRAME & WHEELS

Type	pressed steel and tubular construction, single downtube
Front forks	pressed steel parallelogram, helical sprung, friction damped
Rear forks	without suspension
Brakes	internal expanding drums, front and rear
Tyre size	4.00 x 19" front and rear, road pattern

DIMENSIONS

Overall length	2180mm	(85.8") solo
Overall width	830mm	(32.6") solo
Overall height	1050mm	(41.3") solo
Wheelbase	1430mm	(56.2") solo
Ground clearance	170mm	(6.6") solo
Seat height	680mm	(26.7") solo
Unladen weight	195 kg	(430 lb) solo
Fuel tank	17 litre	(3.7 gal Imp)
Performance	125 km/h max (78 mph) solo 6.2 litre/100 km	

GEAR RATIO

I	= 18.3 : 1	MILITARY EQUIP. rear carry rack or pillion saddle, often used with sidecar, of various commercial design.
II	= 10.0 : 1	
III	= 7.0 : 1	
IV	= 5.1 : 1	

MODEL	PUCH 200 1937
Military Service	Standard production model, works modified for Austrian armed forces, for solo despatch and general liaison duties. Also used by German military.

ENGINE & TRANSMISSION

Type	Puch, split-single cylinder 2-stroke
Capacity	198cc 2 x 45 x 62.8mm
Comp. ratio	5 : 1
Output	5.8 hp at 4000 rpm
Starting	right foot kick start
Carburettor	single, Puch 200
Electrics	6v, Bosch W 145 T1
Clutch	single-plate, dry
Gearbox	hand change, 3-speed
Final	exposed chain

FRAME & WHEELS

Type	pressed steel construction, single downtube
Front forks	pressed steel parallelogram, helical sprung, friction damped
Rear forks	without suspension
Brakes	internal expanding drum, front and rear
Tyre size	3.00 x 19" front and rear, road pattern

DIMENSIONS

Overall length	1980mm	(78.0")
Overall width	700mm	(28.0")
Overall height		
Wheelbase	1270mm	(50.0")
Ground clearance	150mm	(6.0")
Seat height	680mm	(26.8")
Unladen weight	102 kg	(225 lb)
Fuel tank	8.5 lt	(1.9 Imp gal)
Performance	78 km/h (48 mph) max (3.2 lt/100 km)	

GEAR RATIO

I	= 3.33 : 1	MILITARY EQUIP. rear carrier rack, masked lighting, hand pump, all over service livery.
II	= 1.67 : 1	
III	= 1.10 : 1	

MODEL	PUCH 350 GS 1938
Military Service	Standard production model works modified for Austrian armed forces in 1938, for solo multi-terrain despatch and general liaison. Also used by German military and other Axis forces.

ENGINE & TRANSMISSION

Type	Puch, split-single cylinder, twin-port two-stroke
Capacity	347cc 2 x 51.5 x 83.4mm
Comp. ratio	6 : 1
Output	12 hp at 4000 rpm
Starting	right foot kick start
Carburettor	single Puch
Electrics	6v, coil ignition
Clutch	single plate, dry, within rear-wheel hub
Gearbox	hand-change, 4-speed
Final	exposed chain

FRAME & WHEELS

Type	pressed steel and tubular construction, single downtube
Front forks	pressed steel parallelogram, helical sprung, friction damped
Rear forks	helical sprung plunger (often converted to rigid)
Brakes	internal expanding drums, front and rear
Tyre size	3.50 x 19" front and rear, cross country pattern

DIMENSIONS

Overall length	2160mm	(85.0")
Overall width	800mm	(31.4")
Overall height		
Wheelbase	1340mm	(52.7")
Ground clearance	150mm	(5.9")
Seat height	700mm	(27.5")
Unladen weight	166 kg	(366 lb)
Fuel tank	12.5 litre	(2.7 gal Imp)
Performance	110 km/h	(68 mph) max 3.5 litre/100 km

GEAR RATIO

I	= 13.19 : 1	MILITARY EQUIP. rear carry or pillion saddle, high level exhaust, all over service livery.
II	= 8.46 : 1	
III	= 5.98 : 1	
IV	= 4.32 : 1	

BELGIUM

MODEL	FN MILITARY M86 1936
Military Service	A standard production model works modified for Belgian armed forces in 1936, for solo/sidecar despatch, personnel carrier, reconnaissance and general liaison. Armoured sidecar version exported to Argentina, Chile, Bolivia & Venezuela.

ENGINE & TRANSMISSION

Type	FN, vertical ohv single-cylinder
Capacity	497cc 80 x 99mm
Comp. ratio	6.2 : 1
Output	22 hp at 4800 rpm
Starting	left foot kick start
Carburettor	single Amal 29
Electrics	6v, coil ignition
Clutch	multi-plate, wet
Gearbox	foot-change, 4-speed
Final	exposed chain

FRAME & WHEELS

Type	tubular construction, duplex cradle design
Front forks	girder parallelogram, helical sprung, friction damped
Rear forks	without suspension
Brakes	internal expanding drums, front and rear
Tyre size	3.25 x 20" front and rear, cross country pattern

DIMENSIONS

Overall length	2150mm	(84.6") solo
Overall width	720mm	(28.3") solo
Overall height		
Wheelbase	1380mm	(54.3") solo
Ground clearance	130mm	(5.1") solo
Seat height	720mm	(28.3") solo
Unladen weight	175 kg	(385 lb) solo
Fuel tank	15 litre	(3.3 gal Imp)
Performance	130 km/h max (80 mph) solo	

GEAR RATIO

I	= 9.0 : 1	MILITARY EQUIP. rear carry rack or pillion saddle, various machine gun mounted sidecar designs, with or without armour plating, spare wheel, all over service livery.
II	= 6.8 : 1	
III	= 5.2 : 1	
IV	= 4.3 : 1	

MODEL	FN M 12 SM 1937
Manufacturer	Fabrique Nationale SA, Herstal
Military Service	Specialised military model used by Belgian military for multi-terrain sidecar service. A total of 1090 built 1937-39 (exported* Iran & Greece) and widely used by German military. Belgian works of FN, Gillet & Sarolea reported to influence German BMW & Zündapp military outfits.

ENGINE & TRANSMISSION

Type	FN, transverse-opposed sv flat-twin
Capacity	992cc 90 x 78mm
Comp. ratio	5 : 1
Output	22 hp at 4000 rpm
Starting	left foot kick start
Carburettor	single Amal
Electrics	6v, 45/70 watt, coil ignition
Clutch	single plate, dry
Gearbox	hand-change, 4-speed & reverse with high/low ratios
Final	exposed shaft driving rear and sidecar wheel

FRAME & WHEELS

Type	tubular construction duplex cradle, bolt on rear sub-frame
Front forks	girder parallelogram, helical sprung, friction damped
Rear forks	without suspension
Brakes	internal expanding drums, 220mm diameter front and rear
Tyre size	12 x 45 all three wheels, heavy cross country pattern

DIMENSIONS

Overall length		
Overall width		
Overall height		
Wheelbase	1510mm	(59.4") w/sc
Ground clearance	200mm	(7.8") w/sc
Seat height		
Unladen weight	300 kg	(661 lb) w/sc
Fuel tank	19 litre	(4.1 gal Imp)
Performance	90 km/h max	(56 mph) w/sc
	190 km road, 150 km off road range	

GEAR RATIO

		MILITARY EQUIP. rear pillion saddle with knee
I	= 5.21 : 1	grips, high level exhaust, sand filter for carburettor,
II	= 2.30 : 1	various machine gun fittings and spare wheel for
III	= 1.43 : 1	sidecar, all over service livery.
IV	= 1.00 : 1	

MODEL   GILLET 750 1938

Manufacturer	Gillet SA, Herstal, Belgium
Military Service	Specialised military model prepared for multi-terrain heavy sidecar despatch, personnel carrier and liaison. Supplied to Belgian military 1938-40, subsequently widely used by *Wehrmacht*. A slightly different version (with smaller sidecar) was also used by Belgian police.

ENGINE & TRANSMISSION

Type	Gillet, vertical transverse-twin two-stroke
Capacity	728cc 76 x 80mm
Comp, ratio	5 : 1
Output	22 hp at 4000 rpm
Starting	left foot kick start
Carburettor	single Amal
Electrics	6v, 70 watt
Clutch	multi-plate, wet
Gearbox	foot-change, 4-speed & reverse
Final	exposed chain, with shaft drive to sidecar wheel

FRAME & WHEELS

Type	tubular construction, single downtube, duplex cradle design
Front forks	girder parallelogram, helical sprung, friction damped
Rear forks	without suspension
Brakes	internal expanding drums, front and rear
Tyre size	12 x 45" all three wheels, heavy cross country pattern

DIMENSIONS

Overall length	(Dimensions not available)	
Overall width		
Overall height		
Wheelbase	1500mm	(59.0") approx
Ground clearance		
Seat height		
Unladen weight	300 kg	(661 lb) w/sc
Fuel tank	18 litre	(4 gal Imp)
Performance	85 km/h max	(53 mph) max
	180/140 km range road/off road	

MILITARY EQUIP. rear carry rack or pillion saddle, crash bars and sump guard, spare wheel, high level exhaust system, and various fittings for either sidecar mounted machine gun, ammunition boxes, or ambulance service.

MODEL   SAROLEA S6 1937

Manufacturer	Sarolea SA, Herstal, Belgium
Military Service	Standard production model, works modified for military service by Belgium armed forces for solo despatch and general liaison; also used with sidecar for troop and equipment transportation. Belgian forces also employed a number of Sarolea 350cc machines for solo duties.

ENGINE & TRANSMISSION

Type	Sarolea, forward sloping ohv single-cylinder
Capacity	589cc 88 x 97mm
Comp, ratio	5.2 : 1
Output	25 hp at 4800 rpm
Starting	right foot kick start
Carburettor	single Amal 74/022
Electrics	6v, 35/45 watt
Clutch	multi-plate, wet
Gearbox	foot-change, 4-speed
Final	exposed chain

FRAME & WHEELS

Type	tubular construction, single downtube
Front forks	girder parallelogram, helical sprung, friction damped
Rear forks	without rear suspension
Brakes	internal expanding drum, front and rear
Tyre size	3.50 x 19" front and rear, road pattern

DIMENSIONS

Overall length	2130mm	(83.8")
Overall width	690mm	(27.2")
Overall height		
Wheelbase	1400mm	(55.1")
Ground clearance	140mm	(5.5")
Seat height	720mm	(28.3")
Unladen weight	165 kg	(364 lb)
Fuel tank	16 litre	(3.5 gal Imp)

Performance	125 km/h (78 mph) max
	(4.2 lt/100 km)

GEAR RATIO

		MILITARY EQUIP. rear carrier rack or pillion
I	= 11.0 : 1	saddle, high level exhaust system (option), masked
II	= 7.7 : 1	lighting, pannier bags and overall service livery.
III	= 5.5 : 1	Also used with single seat sidecar.
IV	= 4.6 : 1	

CZECHOSLOVAKIA

MODEL   BD/PRAGA 500cc 1927

Manufacturer	Breitfeld-Danek & Co, Prague
Military Service	Standard production model adopted by Czechoslovak military in 1927 for solo/sidecar despatch and general police duties. First produced as BD 500cc; from 1929 became Praga 500cc. Widely used until 1938 and in German occupation.

ENGINE & TRANSMISSION

Type	BD/Praga vertical ohc single-cylinder
Capacity	499cc 84 x 90mm
Comp, ratio	5 : 1
Output	15 hp at 4000 rpm
Starting	right foot kick start
Carburettor	single
Electrics	6v, Bosch magneto
Clutch	multi-plate, wet
Gearbox	hand-change, 3-speed
Final	exposed chain

FRAME & WHEELS

Type	tubular construction, duplex cradle design
Front forks	girder parallelogram, helical sprung, friction damped
Rear forks	without suspension
Brakes	internal expanding drums, front and rear
Tyre size	4.00 x 19" front and rear, road pattern

DIMENSIONS

Overall length		
Overall width		
Overall height		
Wheelbase	1440mm	(56.6")
Ground clearance	95mm	(3.7")
Seat height		
Unladen weight	170 kg	(374 lb)
Fuel tank		
Performance	105 km/h	(65 mph) max

MILITARY EQUIP. rear carry rack or pillion saddle, leather panniers, all over service livery.

MODEL   CZ 175cc 1935

Manufacturer	Ceska Zbrojovka, Strakonice
Military Service	Standard production model (1934-38) adopted by Czechoslovak military for lightweight solo despatch and general liaison. Widely used by German occupying forces.

ENGINE & TRANSMISSION

Type	CZ, vertical single-cylinder, twin port two-stroke
Capacity	172cc 60 x 61mm
Comp, ratio	5.6 : 1
Output	5.5 hp at 3800 rpm
Starting	right foot kick start
Carburettor	single Graetzin or Amal 200mm Ø
Electrics	6v, Bosch ignition
Clutch	multi-plate, wet
Gearbox	hand-change, 3-speed
Final	exposed chain

FRAME & WHEELS

Type	pressed steel duplex cradle design
Front forks	pressed steel parallelogram, helical sprung, friction damped
Rear forks	without suspension
Brakes	internal expanding drums, 150mm front and rear
Tyre size	3.00 x 19" front and rear, road pattern

DIMENSIONS

Overall length	2000mm	(78.7")
Overall width	770mm	(30.3")
Overall height		
Wheelbase	1300mm	(51.1")
Ground clearance		
Seat height	670mm	(26.3")
Unladen weight	97 kg	(213 lb)
Fuel tank	10.5 litre	(2.3 gal Imp)
Performance	80 km/h max	(50 mph)
	3.3 litre/100 km	

MILITARY EQUIP. rear carry rack, all over service livery.

MODEL   JAWA 175 1937

Manufacturer	Zbrojovka F. Janecek, Prague
Military Service	Standard production model works modified for Czechoslovak armed forces in 1937 for solo lightweight despatch and general liaison. Remained in production until 1945, for occupying German military

ENGINE & TRANSMISSION

Type	Jawa, vertical-single cylinder, two-stroke
Capacity	173cc (57.2 x 67mm)
Comp, ratio	6.2 : 1
Output	5.5 hp at 3750 rpm
Starting	right foot kick start
Carburettor	single Villiers
Electrics	6v, 25 watt

Clutch	multi-plate, dry
Gearbox	foot-change, 3-speed
Final	exposed chain

FRAME & WHEELS

Type	pressed steel duplex cradle design
Front forks	pressed steel parallelogram, helical sprung, friction damped
Rear forks	without suspension
Brakes	internal expanding drums, front and rear
Tyre size	3.00 x 19" front and rear, road pattern

DIMENSIONS

Overall length		
Overall width		
Overall height		
Wheelbase	1320mm	(51.9")
Ground clearance	120mm	(4.7")
Seat height		
Unladen weight	90 kg	(198 lb)
Fuel tank	10.5 litre	(2.3 gal Imp)
Performance	80 km/h max	(50 mph)
	3 to 3.5 litre/100 km	

GEAR RATIO

		MILITARY EQUIP. rear carry rack, leather
I	= 13.19 : 1	panniers, all over service livery.
II	= 8.46 : 1	
III	= 5.98 : 1	
IV	= 4.32 : 1	

DENMARK

MODEL   NIMBUS 750 1934

Manufacturer	A/S Fisker & Nielsen, Copenhagen
Military Service	Standard production model adopted for police, postal and military service, between 1934-58, with basically the same machine in production throughout. Danish military model used for solo/sidecar despatch, reconnaissance, mobile machine gun movement, ammunition carrier and ambulance.

ENGINE & TRANSMISSION

Type	Nimbus, vertical ohv in-line four cylinder
Capacity	746cc 60 x 66mm
Comp, ratio	5 : 1 (increased to 5.7 : 1)
Output	18 hp (increased to 22 hp)
Starting	left foot kick start
Carburettor	single
Electrics	6v, 70 watt
Clutch	single-plate, dry
Gearbox	foot-change, 3-speed
Final	exposed shaft

FRAME & WHEELS

Type	pressed steel construction, duplex cradle design
Front forks	telescopic, helical sprung
Rear forks	without suspension
Brakes	internal expanding drums, 180mm diameter front and rear
Tyre size	3.50 x 19" front and rear

DIMENSIONS

Overall length	2160mm	(85.0") solo
Overall width	780mm	(30.7") solo
Overall height	1050mm	(41.3") solo
Wheelbase	1410mm	(55.5") solo
Ground clearance	120mm	(4.7") solo
Seat height	710mm	(27.9") solo
Unladen weight	185 kg	(408 lb) solo
Fuel tank	12.5 litre	(2.7 gal Imp) solo
Performance	120 km/h	(74 mph) max solo

GEAR RATIO (Overall)

I	= 9.7 (11.9) : 1 (s/c)
II	= 6.1 (7.5) : 1 (s/c)
III	= 4.0 (4.9) : 1 (s/c)

MILITARY EQUIP. rear carry rack or pillion saddle, additional tool box, canvas panniers, and various fittings for either sidecar/platform mounted machine gun, ammunition carrier, or ambulance, and a spare wheel.

FRANCE

MODEL   GNOME RHÔNE D.5.A. 1938

Manufacturer	Societe des Moteurs, Gnome, Paris
Military Service	Standard production model works modified for French military for solo despatch, reconnaissance, and military police. Supplied between 1938-40.

ENGINE & TRANSMISSION

Type	Gnome Rhône, forward-inclined sv single-cylinder
Capacity	500cc 85 x 88mm
Comp, ratio	5 : 1
Output	
Starting	right foot kick start
Carburettor	single – Amal 6/001
Electrics	6v
Clutch	multi-plate, wet
Gearbox	hand-change, 4-speed
Final	exposed chain

FRAME & WHEELS

Type	pressed steel construction, duplex cradle design
Front forks	pressed steel parallelogram, helical sprung, friction damped
Rear forks	without suspension
Brakes	internal expanding drums, front and rear
Tyre size	3.5 x 26" front and rear, road pattern

DIMENSIONS

Overall length	2090mm	(82.2")
Overall width	750mm	(29.5")
Overall height	1150mm	(45.2")
Wheelbase	1370mm	(53.9")
Ground clearance	140mm	(5.5")
Seat height		
Unladen weight	180 kg	(397 lb)
Fuel tank	12 litre	(2.6 gal Imp)
Performance	100 km/h	(62 mph) max
	200 km range	

MILITARY EQUIP. rear carry rack and all over service livery.

MODEL   GNOME RHÔNE AX2 1938

Military Service   Specialised military model adopted by French armed forces, for multi-terrain, sidecar despatch, personnel carrier, reconnaissance and general liaison. Produced 1936-40, and widely used by German and Axis forces during years of occupation.

ENGINE & TRANSMISSION

Type	Gnome Rhône, transverse sv flat-twin
Capacity	804cc 80 x 80mm
Comp, ratio	5 : 1
Output	18.5 hp at 4000 rpm
Starting	left foot kick start
Carburettor	single Solex 30 FHOS
Electrics	6v, 60 watt, coil ignition
Clutch	single-plate, dry
Gearbox	hand-change, 4- & reverse-speed
Final	exposed shaft driving rear and sidecar wheel

FRAME & WHEELS

Type	pressed steel duplex cradle construction
Front forks	pressed steel parallelogram, friction damped, helical sprung
Rear forks	without suspension
Brakes	internal expanding drums, 220mm diameter front and rear
Tyre size	3.50 x 19" or 4.00 x 27" on all three wheels, heavy road pattern

DIMENSIONS

Overall length	2700mm	(106.2") w/sc
Overall width	1650mm	(64.9") w/sc
Overall height	1000mm	(39.3") w/sc
Wheelbase	1485mm	(58.4") w/sc
Ground clearance	180mm	(7.0") w/sc
Seat height		
Unladen weight	316 kg	(696 lb) w/sc
Fuel tank	15 litre	(3.4 gal Imp) w/sc
Performance	85 km/h max	(53 mph) w/sc
	180 km road, 130 km cross country range	

GEAR RATIO		MILITARY EQUIP. rear carry rack or pillion saddle, leg shields, high level exhaust, various machine fittings and spare wheel on sidecar, all over service livery.
I	= 5.21 : 1	
II	= 2.30 : 1	
III	= 1.43 : 1	
IV	= 1.00 : 1	
R	= 5.75 : 1	

MODEL   GNOME RHÔNE 750 ARMEE 1938

Military Service   Specialised military machine based upon standard production model type X, prepared for heavy sidecar despatch, personnel carrier, reconnaissance, and convoy control. Subsequently used by German armed forces.

ENGINE & TRANSMISSION

Type	Gnome Rhône, transverse ohv flat-twin
Capacity	750cc 80 x 72mm
Comp, ratio	5 : 1
Output	
Starting	left foot kick start
Carburettor	single Amal 26/185
Electrics	6v, 70 watt
Clutch	single-plate, dry
Gearbox	hand-change, 4-speed
Final	exposed shaft

FRAME & WHEELS

Type	pressed steel construction, duplex cradle design
Front forks	pressed steel parallelogram, helical sprung, friction damped
Rear forks	without suspension
Brakes	internal expanding drums, front and rear
Tyre size	3.5 x 26" front and rear, heavy cross country pattern

DIMENSIONS

Overall length	2200mm	(86.6")
Overall width	1680mm	(66.1")
Overall height	1130mm	(44.5")
Wheelbase	1450mm	(57.0")
Ground clearance		
Seat height		
Unladen weight	320 kg	(705 lb)
Fuel tank	20 litre	(4.4 gal Imp)
Performance	78 km/h	(48 mph)
	223 km range	

MILITARY EQUIP. rear carry rack or pillion saddle, leather panniers, high level exhaust system, leg shields, and various fittings for either sidecar mounted machine gun, ammunition, radio equipment, or ambulance service, and a spare wheel.

MODEL   MONET-GOYON L5A1 1935

Manufacturer	Monet & Goyon, Macon, Saone-et-Loire
Military Service	Standard production model (1935-36), adopted by French armed forces for sidecar despatch and personnel carrier duties; widely replaced by purpose built Gnome Rhône AX2 and 750 Armee military sidecar machines during late 1930s.

ENGINE & TRANSMISSION

Type	Monet-Goyon, vertical sv single-cylinder
Capacity	486 75 x 110mm
Comp, ratio	5 : 1
Output	12 hp at 4000 rpm
Starting	right foot kick start
Carburettor	single Amal
Electrics	6v, 45 watt, magneto ignition
Clutch	multi-plate, wet
Gearbox	foot-change, 4-speed
Final	exposed chain

FRAME & WHEELS

Type	tubular construction, single downtube
Front forks	girder parallelogram, helical sprung, friction damped
Rear forks	without suspension
Brakes	internal expanding drum front and rear
Tyre size	3.5 x 26" front and rear, road pattern

DIMENSIONS

Overall length	2250mm	(88.6")
Overall width	1760mm	(69.3")
Overall height	1020mm	(40.2")
Wheelbase	1150mm	(45.3")
Ground clearance		
Seat height		
Unladen weight	300 kg	(661 lb)
Fuel tank	15 litre	(3.3 gal Imp)
Performance	60 km/h	(38 mph) max
	60 km/h	(38 mph) max
	(10 lt/100 km)	

MILITARY EQUIP. rear carrier rack, single seat sidecar with spare wheel, and all-over service livery.

MODEL   RENE GILLET G.1 1937

Manufacturer	Rene Gillet, Paris
Military Service	Specialised military model prepared for sidecar despatch, reconnaissance and military police. French military standard sidecar model continuously developed between 1924-40, and re-introduced after the war.

ENGINE & TRANSMISSION

Type	Rene Gillet, V-twin sv
Capacity	750cc 70 x 97.7mm
Comp, ratio	5 : 1
Output	14.6 hp at 4000 rpm
Starting	right foot kick start
Carburettor	single Amac 5/211
Electrics	6v, 70 watt, magneto ignition
Clutch	multi-plate, wet
Gearbox	hand-change, 3-speed, (later 4)
Final	exposed chain

FRAME & WHEELS

Type	tubular construction, single downtube design
Front forks	girder leading link, helical sprung, friction damped
Rear forks	without suspension
Brakes	internal expanding drums, front and rear
Tyre size	4.00 x 27" front and rear, road pattern

DIMENSIONS

Overall length	2260mm	(88.9") w/sc
Overall width	1640mm	(64.5") w/sc
Overall height	1000mm	(39.3") w/sc
Wheelbase	1500mm	(59.0") w/sc
Ground clearance		
Seat height		
Unladen weight	254 kg	(560 lb) w/sc
Fuel tank	11 litre	(2.4 gal Imp)
Performance	65 km/h	(40 mph) max w/sc
	130 km range	

MILITARY EQUIP. rear carry rack or pillion saddle, leather panniers, sump guard, and various fittings for either sidecar mounted machine gun, ammunition, radio equipment, or ambulance service, and a spare wheel.

MODEL   TERROT VA 1934

Manufacturer	Ets. Terrot, Dijon, France
Military Service	Standard production model works modified for French armed forces in 1934, for solo (VATT model with sidecar) despatch, personnel carrier, reconnaissance, general liaison and military police.

ENGINE & TRANSMISSION

Type	Terrot, V-twin 50°, sv
Capacity	750cc 70 x 97mm
Comp, ratio	4.9 : 1
Output	
Starting	right foot kick start
Carburettor	single Amal 5/012
Electrics	6v, 45 watt
Clutch	multi-plate, wet
Gearbox	foot-change, 4-speed
Final	exposed chain

FRAME & WHEELS

Type	tubular construction, single downtube
Front forks	girder parallelogram, helical sprung, friction damped
Rear forks	without suspension
Brakes	internal expanding drums, half width, front and rear
Tyre size	4.00 x 27" front and rear, road pattern

DIMENSIONS

Overall length	2230mm	(87.7")
Overall width	900mm	(35.4")
Overall height	1050mm	(41.3")
Wheelbase	1480mm	(58.2")
Ground clearance	200mm	(7.8")
Seat height		
Unladen weight	130 kg	(286 lb)
Fuel tank	16 litre	(3.5 gal Imp)
Performance	90 km/h	(56 mph) max
	200 kms range	

GEAR RATIO		MILITARY EQUIP. rear carry rack or pillion saddle, leather panniers, spare wheel on sidecar, all over service livery.
I	= 2.78 : 1	
II	= 1.75 : 1	
III	= 1.25 : 1	
IV	= 1.00 : 1	

GERMANY

MODEL   BMW R62 1928

Manufacturer	Bayerische Motorenwerke AG, Munich
Military Service	Standard production model (1928-29), used by German military for solo/sidecar despatch, personnel carrier, reconnaissance and general liaison. Supplied and used alongside the very similar, but smaller engined, 500cc R52 (1928-29).

ENGINE & TRANSMISSION

Type	BMW, transverse sv flat-twin
Capacity	745cc 78 x 78mm
Comp, ratio	5.5 : 1
Output	18 hp at 3400 rpm
Starting	left foot kick start
Carburettor	single BMW
Electrics	6v, Bosch magneto
Clutch	single-plate, dry
Gearbox	hand-change, 3-speed
Final	exposed shaft

FRAME & WHEELS

Type	tubular construction, duplex cradle design
Front forks	trailing link, leaf sprung, friction damped
Rear forks	without suspension
Brakes	internal expanding drums, front and rear
Tyre size	3.25 x 26" front and rear

DIMENSIONS

Overall length	2100mm	(82.6") solo
Overall width	800mm	(31.4") solo
Overall height	950mm	(37.4") solo
Wheelbase	1400mm	(55.1") solo
Ground clearance	150mm	(5.9") solo
Seat height		
Unladen weight	155 kg	(341 lb) solo
Fuel tank	12.5 litre	(2.7 gal Imp)
Performance	115 km/h	(71.4 mph) max

GEAR RATIO		MILITARY EQUIP. rear carry rack or pillion saddle, leather panniers, various commercial sidecars, all over service livery, and black exhaust system.
I	= 2.58 : 1	
II	= 1.42 : 1	
III	= 1.00 : 1	

MODEL   BMW R11 1929

Military Service   Standard production model (1929-34), used by German armed forces for solo and sidecar despatch, escort, convoy control and personnel transport. Superseded by BMW R12 in 1935-41, with improved frame and output.

ENGINE & TRANSMISSION

Type	BMW, transverse sv flat-twin
Capacity	745cc 78 x 78mm
Comp, ratio	5.5 : 1
Output	18 hp at 3400 rpm
Starting	left foot kick start
Carburettor	single, SUM
Electrics	6v, 30 watt
Clutch	single-plate, dry operation
Gearbox	hand-change, 3-speed
Final	exposed shaft

FRAME & WHEELS

Type	pressed steel construction, duplex cradle star design
Front forks	trailing link, leaf sprung, friction damped
Rear forks	without suspension
Brakes	internal expanding drum, front and rear
Tyre size	3.50 x 26" front and rear, heavy road pattern

DIMENSIONS

Overall length	2100mm	(82.7")
Overall width	890mm	(35.0")
Overall height	950mm	(37.4")
Wheelbase	1380mm	(54.3")
Ground clearance	130mm	(5.1")
Seat height	700mm	(27.6")
Unladen weight	162 kg	(357 lb)
Fuel tank	14 lt	(3 Imp gal)
Performance	100 km/h	(62 mph) max
	(3.5 lt/100 km)	

GEAR RATIO		MILITARY EQUIP. rear carrier rack or pillion saddle, leather panniers, allover service livery and black exhaust (various commercial sidecars).
I	= 2.61 : 1	
II	= 1.43 : 1	
III	= 1.00 : 1	

MODEL — BMW R12 1935

Military Service	Standard production model (1935-41), used by German military for solo/sidecar despatch, personnel carrier, convoy escort and general liaison. Replaced R62 and superseded by revised tubular and plunger-framed, R71 (1938-41) and smaller 600cc (R61 (1938-41). All 3 widely used during World War 2.

ENGINE & TRANSMISSION

Type	BMW, transverse sv flat-twin
Capacity	745cc 78 x 78mm
Comp. ratio	5.1 : 1
Output	18 hp at 3500 rpm
Starting	left foot kick start
Carburettor	single – Sum
Electrics	6v, Bosch magneto, 45/70 watt
Clutch	single-plate, dry
Gearbox	hand-change, 4-speed
Final	exposed shaft

FRAME & WHEELS

Type	pressed steel construction, duplex cradle design
Front forks	telescopic, helical sprung, hydraulic damping
Rear forks	without suspension
Brakes	internal expanding drums, 200mm diameter front and rear
Tyre size	3.50 x 19″ front and rear, heavy road pattern

DIMENSIONS

Overall length	2100mm	(82.6″) solo
Overall width	900mm	(35.4″) solo
Overall height	940mm	(37.0″) solo
Wheelbase	1400mm	(55.1″) solo
Ground clearance	120mm	(4.7″) solo
Seat height	700mm	(27.5″)
Unladen weight	188 kg	(414 lb) solo
Fuel tank	14 litre	(3 gal Imp)
Performance	100 km/h (62 mph) solo 280 km range	

GEAR RATIO

I	= 3.18 : 1	MILITARY EQUIP. rear carry rack or pillion saddle, leather panniers, all over service livery and black exhaust system, with various commercial single seat sidecars and interchangeable spare wheel.
II	= 2.06 : 1	
III	= 1.42 : 1	
IV	= 1.09 : 1	

MODEL — BMW R5 1936

Manufacturer	
Military Service	Standard production model (1936-37), for German armed forces for solo despatch, escort, convoy control and military police duties. Limited production 2600, remained in service during World War 2.

ENGINE & TRANSMISSION

Type	BMW, transverse ohv flat-twin
Capacity	494cc 68 x 68mm
Comp. ratio	6.7 : 1
Output	24 hp at 5800 rpm
Starting	left foot kick start
Carburettor	two: Amal 5/423
Electrics	6v, 45/70 watt, Bosch RD
Clutch	single plate, dry
Gearbox	hand-change, 4-speed
Final	exposed shaft

FRAME & WHEELS

Type	tubular construction, duplex cradle design
Front forks	telescopic, helical sprung, hydraulic damping
Rear forks	without suspension
Brakes	internal expanding drum, front and rear, 200mm diameter
Tyre size	3.5 x 19″ front and rear, heavy road pattern

DIMENSIONS

Overall length	2130mm	(83.9″)
Overall width	800mm	(31.5″)
Overall height	950mm	(37.4″)
Wheelbase		
Ground clearance		
Seat height		
Unladen weight	165 kg	(365 lb)
Fuel tank	15 lt	(3.3 Imp gal)
Performance	135 km/h (84 mph) max (3.5 lt/100 km)	

GEAR RATIO

I	= 2.77 : 1	MILITARY EQUIP. rear carrier rack or pillion saddle, leather panniers, allover service livery, and black exhaust system.
II	= 1.75 : 1	
III	= 1.31 : 1	
IV	= 1.00 : 1	

MODEL — BMW R35 1937

Manufacturer	
Military Service	Standard production model (1937-40), used by German military for solo despatch and general liaison, superseding the similar BMW R4 (1932-36).

ENGINE & TRANSMISSION

Type	BMW, vertical ohv single-cylinder
Capacity	340cc 72 x 84mm
Comp. ratio	5.4 : 1
Output	14 hp at 4500 rpm
Starting	right foot kick start
Carburettor	single Sum
Electrics	6v, 45 watt
Clutch	single-plate, dry
Gearbox	hand-change, 4-speed
Final	exposed shaft

FRAME & WHEELS

Type	pressed steel duplex cradle design
Front forks	telescopic, helical sprung, without damping
Rear forks	without rear suspension
Brakes	internal expanding drums, 160mm diameter front and rear
Tyre size	3.50 xz 19″ front and rear, road pattern

DIMENSIONS

Overall length	2000mm	(78.7″)
Overall width	800mm	(31.4″)
Overall height	950mm	(37.4″)
Wheelbase	1300mm	(51.1″)
Ground clearance	130mm	(5.1″)
Seat height	710mm	(27.9″)
Unladen weight	165 kg	(363 lb)
Fuel tank	12 litre	(2.6 gal Imp)
Performance	100 km/h (62 mph) max (340 km range)	

GEAR RATIO

I	= 3.60 : 1	MILITARY EQUIP. rear carry rack, leather panniers, all over service livery and black exhaust system.
II	= 2.18 : 1	
III	= 1.35 : 1	
IV	= 1.00 : 1	

MODEL — BMW R66 1938

Manufacturer	
Military Service	Standard production model (1938-41), used by German armed forces for solo despatch and general liaison throughout the war in limited numbers, 2000, including military police.

ENGINE & TRANSMISSION

Type	BMW, transverse ohv flat-twin
Capacity	597cc 69.8 x 78mm
Comp. ratio	6.1 : 1
Output	30 hp at 5300 rpm
Starting	left foot kick start
Carburettor	twin Amal or Bing
Electrics	6v
Clutch	single-plate, dry
Gearbox	hand-change, 4-speed
Final	exposed shaft

FRAME & WHEELS

Type	tubular construction, duplex cradle design
Front forks	telescopic, helical sprung, hydraulic damping
Rear forks	plunger design, internal helical, without damping
Brakes	internal expanding drum, front and rear, 200mm diameter front
Tyre size	3.5 x 19″ front and rear, road pattern

DIMENSIONS

Overall length	2130mm	(83.6″)
Overall width	810mm	(31.9″)
Overall height		
Wheelbase	1400mm	(55.1″)
Ground clearance	130mm	(5.1″)
Seat height	720mm	(28.3″)
Unladen weight	187 kg	(412 lb)
Fuel tank	14 lt	(3 Imp gal)
Performance	140 km/h (87 mph) max (4.5 lt/100 km)	

GEAR RATIO

I	= 2.77 : 1	MILITARY EQUIP. rear carrier rack or pillion saddle, leather panniers, masked lighting, and allover service livery.
II	= 1.75 : 1	
III	= 1.31 : 1	
IV	= 1.00 : 1	

MODEL — BMW R71 1938

Manufacturer	
Military Service	Standard production model (1938-41), used by German armed forces for solo and sidecar despatch, escort, convoy control and personnel transport. 2000 total production, establishing requirement for purpose-built military BMW R75 model.

ENGINE & TRANSMISSION

Type	BMW, transverse sv flat-twin
Capacity	745cc 78 x 78mm
Comp. ratio	5.5 : 1
Output	22 hp at 4600 rpm
Starting	left foot kick start
Carburettor	twin Graetzin G24
Electrics	6v, Bosch W175 T 1
Clutch	single-plate, dry
Gearbox	hand-change, 4-speed
Final	exposed shaft

FRAME & WHEELS

Type	tubular construction, duplex cradle design
Front forks	telescopic, helical sprung, hydraulic damping
Rear forks	plunger design, internal helical, without damping
Brakes	internal expanding drum, front and rear, 200mm diameter
Tyre size	3.5 x 19″ front and rear, road pattern

DIMENSIONS

Overall length	2130mm	(83.6″)
Overall width	810mm	(31.9″)
Overall height		
Wheelbase	1400mm	(55.1″)
Ground clearance	130mm	(5.1″)
Seat height	720mm	(28.3″)
Unladen weight	187 kg	(412 lb)
Fuel tank	14 lt	(3 Imp gal)
Performance	125 km/h (78 mph) max (4 lt/100 km)	

MODEL — DKW NZ 350 1938

Manufacturer	Auto Union AG, Zschopau/Sachsen
Military Service	Standard production model adopted by *Wehrmacht* in 1938 for solo despatch and general liaison. Remained in production with very similar NZ 250 until 1940, when all DKW production centered upon RT 125 lightweight until 1945.

ENGINE & TRANSMISSION

Type	DKW, two-stroke forward-inclined single-cylinder
Capacity	346cc 72 x 85mm
Comp. ratio	5.75 : 1
Output	10.8 hp at 3250 rpm
Starting	left foot kick start
Carburettor	single – Amal, Bing or Graetzin
Electrics	6v, 75 watt, Bosch magneto
Clutch	multi-plate, wet
Gearbox	hand later foot-change, 4-speed
Final	exposed chain

FRAME & WHEELS

Type	pressed steel and tubular construction, single downtube design
Front forks	pressed steel parallelogram, helical sprung, friction damped
Rear forks	without suspension
Brakes	internal expanding drums, front and rear
Tyre size	3.25 x 19″ front and rear, road pattern

DIMENSIONS

Overall length	2110mm	(83.0″)
Overall width	770mm	(30.3″)
Overall height	925mm	(36.4″)
Wheelbase	1355mm	(53.3″)
Ground clearance	125mm	(4.9″)
Seat height	700mm	(27.5″)
Unladen weight	171 kg	(377 lb)
Fuel tank	14 litre	(3 gal Imp)
Performance	100 km/h (62 mph) max 350 km range	

GEAR RATIO

I	= 2.76 : 1	MILITARY EQUIP. rear carry rack or pillion saddle, leather panniers, and black exhaust system.
II	= 1.77 : 1	
III	= 1.30 : 1	
IV	= 1.00 : 1	

MODEL — DKW NZ 500 1938

Military Service	Standard production model, works modified for military use, for solo despatch, escort and military police. Widely used in limited numbers throughout the war.

ENGINE & TRANSMISSION

Type	DKW, two-stroke forward-inclined twin cylinder
Capacity	489cc 64 x 76mm
Comp. ratio	6 : 1
Output	18.5 hp at 4200 rpm
Starting	left foot kick start
Carburettor	single Amal WM 76/456
Electrics 6v	6v, Bosch W 175 T 1
Clutch	multi-plate, wet
Gearbox	hand-change, 4-speed
Final	exposed chain

FRAME & WHEELS

Type	pressed steel and tubular construction
Front forks	pressed steel parallelogram, helical sprung, friction damped
Rear forks	plunger design, helical sprung, without damping
Brakes	internal expanding drum, front and rear
Tyre size	3.50 x 19″ front and rear, road pattern

DIMENSIONS

Overall length	2200mm	(86.6″)
Overall width	730mm	(28.7″)
Overall height		
Wheelbase	1440mm	(56.7″)
Ground clearance	140mm	(5.5″)
Seat height	740mm	(29.1″)
Unladen weight	195 kg	(430 lb)
Fuel tank	14 lt	(3 Imp gal)
Performance	115 km/h (71 mph) max (4.5 lt/100 km)	

GEAR RATIO

(Overall)		MILITARY EQUIP. rear carrier rack or pillion saddle, leather panniers, masked lighting, hand pump, and allover service livery.
I	= 13.1 : 1	
II	= 7.9 : 1	
III	= 5.7 : 1	
IV	= 4.3 : 1	

MODEL — NSU 251 OS 1938

Manufacturer	Neckarsulmer Fahrzeugwerke AG, Neckarsulm
Military Service	Standard production model works modified for military service, for solo lightweight despatch and general liaison.

ENGINE & TRANSMISSION

Type	NSU, vertical ohv single-cylinder
Capacity	241cc 64 x 75mm
Comp. ratio	6.8 : 1
Output	10 hp at 4650 rpm
Starting	right foot kick start
Carburettor	single Amal or Graetzin
Electrics	6v, 45 watt

Clutch	multi-plate, wet
Gearbox	foot-change, 4-speed
Final	enclosed chain

FRAME & WHEELS

Type	tubular construction, single downtube design, integral engine
Front forks	girder parallelogram, helical sprung, friction damped
Rear forks	without suspension
Brakes	internal expanding drums, front and rear
Tyre size	3.00 x 19" front and rear, road pattern

DIMENSIONS

Overall length	2040mm	(80.3")
Overall width	780mm	(30.7")
Overall height	950mm	(37.4")
Wheelbase	1320mm	(51.9")
Ground clearance	120mm	(4.7")
Seat height	680mm	(26.7")
Unladen weight	144 kg	(317 lb)
Fuel tank	11.1 litre	(2.4 gal Imp)
Performance	92 km/h max	(57 mph)
	310 km range	

GEAR RATIO

I	= 3.57 : 1	MILITARY EQUIP. rear carry rack or pillion saddle, leather panniers, all over service livery and black exhaust system.
II	= 2.11 : 1	
III	= 1.37 : 1	
IV	= 1.00 : 1	

MODEL   NSU 601 OSL 1938

| Military Service | Standard production model works modified for military service, for solo/sidecar despatch, convoy escort personnel carrier an general liaison. |

ENGINE & TRANSMISSION

Type	NSU, vertical ohv single-cylinder, twin port
Capacity	562cc 85 x 99mm
Comp, ratio	6.5 : 1
Output	20 hp at 3800 rpm
Starting	right foot kick start
Carburettor	single – Amal
Electrics	6v, 45/70 watt, Bosch magneto
Clutch	multi-plate, wet
Gearbox	foot-change, 4-speed
Final	enclosed chain

FRAME & WHEELS

Type	tubular construction, single downtube design
Front forks	girder parallelogram, helical sprung, friction damped
Rear forks	without suspension
Brakes	internal expanding drums, front and rear
Tyre size	3.50 x 19" front, 4.00 x 19" rear, heavy road pattern

DIMENSIONS

Overall length	2180mm	(85.8") solo
Overall width	780mm	(30.7") solo
Overall height	950mm	(37.4") solo
Wheelbase	1420mm	(55.9") solo
Ground clearance	105mm	(4.1") solo
Seat height		
Unladen weight	185 kg	(408 lb) solo
Fuel tank	12 litre	(2.6 gal Imp)
Performance	100 km/h	(62 mph) max solo
	240 km range	

GEAR RATIO

I	= 2.66 : 1	MILITARY EQUIP. rear carry rack or pillion saddle, leather panniers, all over service livery and black exhaust system.
II	= 1.77 : 1	
III	= 1.20 : 1	
IV	= 1.00 : 1	

MODEL   TRIUMPH BD 250 W 1938

| Manufacturer | Triumph-Werke AG, Nuremburg, Germany |
| Military Service | Standard production model works modified for military service, for solo despatch and general liaison. Widely used throughout the war, and remained in production until 1945. |

ENGINE & TRANSMISSION

Type	TWN, forward-inclined, split single-cylinder, rotary valve
Capacity	248cc 2 x 45 x 78mm
Comp, ratio	5.5 : 1
Output	12 hp at 3850 rpm
Starting	left foot kick start
Carburettor	single – Bing
Electrics	6v
Clutch	multi-plate, wet
Gearbox	foot-change, 4-speed
Final	enclosed chain

FRAME & WHEELS

Type	pressed steel and tubular constriction, single downtube design
Front forks	pressed steel parallelogram, helical sprung, friction damped
Rear forks	without suspension
Brakes	internal expanding drums, front and rear
Tyre size	3.25 x 19" front and rear, road pattern

DIMENSIONS

Overall length	2050mm	(80.7")
Overall width	785mm	(30.9")
Overall height	975mm	(38.3")
Wheelbase	1300mm	(51.1")
Ground clearance	110mm	(4.3")
Seat height	720mm	(28.3")
Unladen weight	155 kg	(341 lb)
Fuel tank	11.3 litre	(2.5 gal Imp)
Performance	95 km/h	(59 mph) max
	370 km range	

GEAR RATIO

I	= 3.25 : 1	MILITARY EQUIP. rear carry rack or pillion saddle, leather panniers, desert air filter, black exhaust system.
II	= 1.80 : 1	
III	= 1.33 : 1	
IV	= 1.00 : 1	

MODEL   VICTORIA KR VI 1927

| Manufacturer | Victoria Werke AG, Nuremburg |
| Military Service | Standard production model works modified for military service by German armed forces for solo/sidecar despatch, personnel carrier, reconnaissance and general liaison. Produced 1927-32. Also the basis of a prototype with two rear wheels in tandem. |

ENGINE & TRANSMISSION

Type	Victoria, in-line ohv flat-twin
Capacity	596cc 77 x 64mm
Comp, ratio	5.2 : 1
Output	16 hp at 3800 rpm
Starting	left foot kick start
Carburettor	single Amal
Electrics	6v, Bosch magneto, 30 watt
Clutch	multi-plate, wet
Gearbox	hand-change, 3-speed
Final	exposed chain

FRAME & WHEELS

Type	tubular construction, duplex cradle
Front forks	girder parallelogram, helical sprung, friction damped
Rear forks	without suspension
Brakes	internal expanding drums, front and rear
Tyre size	3.00 x 26" front, 3.50 x 27" rear, road pattern

DIMENSIONS

Overall length	2315mm	(91.1") solo
Overall width	850mm	(33.4") solo
Overall height	1020mm	(40.1") solo
Wheelbase	1500mm	(59.0") solo
Ground clearance	120mm	(4.7") solo
Seat height		
Unladen weight	170 kg	(374 lb) solo
Fuel tank	12 litre	(2.6 gal imp)
Performance	95 km/h max	(59 mph) solo
	260 km solo range	

GEAR RATIO

I	= 2.48 : 1	MILITARY EQUIP. rear carry rack or pillion saddle, high exhaust system, all over service livery, and black exhaust system.
II	= 1.71 : 1	
III	= 1.00 : 1	

MODEL   VICTORIA KR6 1933

| Military Service | Standard production model, works modified for military service, and used for solo and sidecar despatch, reconnaissance and general liaison. Continued to be ordered until 1938 and limited numbers remained in service during World War 2. |

ENGINE & TRANSMISSION

Type	Victoria, in-line ohv flat-twin
Capacity	596cc 77 x 64mm
Comp, ratio	6.2 : 1
Output	20 hp at 4000 rpm
Starting	left foot kick start
Carburettor	single Graetzin
Electrics	6v, 30 watt
Clutch	multi-plate, wet
Gearbox	hand-change, 4-speed
Final	exposed chain

FRAME & WHEELS

Type	tubular construction, duplex cradle
Front forks	telescopic, helical sprung, without damping
Rear forks	without suspension
Brakes	internal expanding drum, front and rear
Tyre size	4.00 x 19" front and rear, heavy road pattern

DIMENSIONS

Overall length	2250mm	(88.6")
Overall width	940mm	(37.9")
Overall height	1120mm	(44.1")
Wheelbase	1480mm	(58.3")
Ground clearance	120mm	(4.7")
Seat height		
Unladen weight	160 kg	(353 lb)
Fuel tank	15 lt	(3.3 Imp gal)
Performance	100 km/h	(63 mph) max
		(5 lt/100 km)

GEAR RATIO

I	= 3.30 : 1	MILITARY EQUIP. rear carrier rack or pillion saddle, leather panniers, all over service livery and black exhaust system.
II	= 1.91 : 1	
III	= 1.39 : 1	
IV	= 1.00 : 1	

MODEL   VICTORIA KR9 1936

| Military Service | Standard production model used by *Reichswehr* & *Wehrmacht*, for solo and sidecar despatch, reconnaissance and general police duties. Limited numbers remained in service during World War 2. |

ENGINE & TRANSMISSION

Type	Victoria, in-line, sv, flat-twin cylinder
Capacity	498cc 60 x 88mm
Comp, ratio	5.9 : 1
Output	15 hp at 4600 rpm
Starting	left foot kick start

Carburettor	single Graetzin
Electrics	6v, 50 watt
Clutch	multi-plate, wet
Gearbox	hand-change, 4-speed
Final	enclosed chain

FRAME & WHEELS

Type	pressed steel and tubular construction
Front forks	pressed steel parallelogram, helical sprung, friction damped
Rear forks	without rear suspension
Brakes	internal expanding drum, front and rear
Tyre size	3.50 x 19" front and rear, road pattern

DIMENSIONS

Overall length	2130mm	(83.9")
Overall width	860mm	(33.9")
Overall height	920mm	(36.2")
Wheelbase	1380mm	(54.3")
Ground clearance	120mm	(4.7")
Seat height		
Unladen weight		
Fuel tank	10 lt	(2.2 Imp gal)
Performance	100 km/h	(62 mph) max
		(4.5 lt/100 km)

GEAR RATIO

I	= 3.30 : 1	MILITARY EQUIP. rear carrier rack or pillion saddle, leather panniers, (side panels and leg shields as standard model), and all over service livery.
II	= 2.19 : 1	
III	= 1.39 : 1	
IV	= 1.00 : 1	

MODEL   VICTORIA KR 35 WH 1938

| Manufacturer | |
| Military Service | Standard production model works modified for military service by German armed forces in 1938 onwards, for solo lightweight despatch and general liaison. |

ENGINE & TRANSMISSION

Type	Victoria, vertical ohv single-cylinder
Capacity	342cc 69 x 91.5mm twin port
Comp, ratio	6 : 1
Output	14 hp at 4000 rpm
Starting	left foot kick start
Carburettor	single Amal
Electrics	6v, 50 watt
Clutch	single-plate, dry
Gearbox	foot-change, 4-speed
Final	enclosed chain

FRAME & WHEELS

Type	tubular construction, single downtube
Front forks	girder parallelogram, helical sprung, friction damped
Rear forks	without suspension
Brakes	internal expanding drums, front and rear
Tyre size	3.25 x 19" front and rear, road pattern

DIMENSIONS

Overall length	2160mm	(85.0")
Overall width	780mm	(30.7")
Overall height	1000mm	(39.3")
Wheelbase	1400mm	(55.1")
Ground clearance	120mm	(4.7")
Seat height	740mm	(29.1")
Unladen weight	155 kg	(342 lb)
Fuel tank	14 litre	(3 gal Imp)
Performance	100 km/h	(62 mph) max
	400 km range	

GEAR RATIO

I	= 3.26 : 1	MILITARY EQUIP. rear carry rack or pillion saddle, leather panniers, all over service livery and black exhaust system.
II	= 1.81 : 1	
III	= 1.33 : 1	
IV	= 1.00 : 1	

MODEL   ZÜNDAPP K 500 1934

| Manufacturer | Zündapp Werke GmbH, Nuremburg |
| Military Service | Standard production model works modified for military service, by German armed forces, for solo despatch, reconnaissance and general liaison. Produced between 1934-39, and widely used 1939-45. |

ENGINE & TRANSMISSION

Type	Zündapp, transverse sv 2 cylinder, flat-twin
Capacity	498cc 69 x 66.6mm
Comp, ratio	5.8 : 1
Output	15 hp at 4500 rpm
Starting	left foot kick start
Carburettor	single – Amal or Bing
Electrics	6v, 50/70 watt
Clutch	single-plate, dry
Gearbox	hand-change, 4-speed
Final	exposed shaft

FRAME & WHEELS

Type	pressed steel construction, duplex cradle design
Front forks	pressed steel parallelogram, helical sprung, friction damped
Rear forks	without suspension
Brakes	internal expanding drums, front and rear
Tyre size	3.50 x 19" front, 4.00 x 19" rear, road pattern

DIMENSIONS

Overall length	2150mm	(84.6")
Overall width	815mm	(32.0")
Overall height	800mm	(31.4")
Wheelbase	1390mm	(54.7")
Ground clearance	110mm	(4.3")
Seat Height	720mm	(28.3")
Unladen weight	190 kg	(419 lb)
Fuel tank	12.5 litre	(2.7 gal Imp)

Performance 100 km/h (62 mph) max
250/200 km range road/off road

GEAR RATIO		MILITARY EQUIP. rear carry rack or pillion
I	= 3.00 : 1	saddle, leather panniers, and all over service livery,
II	= 1.92 : 1	and black exhaust system.
III	= 1.15 : 1	
IV	= 0.95 : 1	

MODEL ZÜNDAPP DB 200 1935

Military Service Standard production model adopted by *Reichswehr* & *Wehrmacht*, for solo despatch and general liaison. Remained in production 1935-40 (economy model 1947-51); widely used throughout World War 2.

ENGINE & TRANSMISSION
Type	Zündapp 2-stroke vertical single-cylinder
Capacity	198cc (60mm bore x 70mm stroke), twin port
Comp. ratio	6 : 1
Output	7 hp at 4000 rpm
Starting	left foot kick start
Carburettor	single, Bing 20mm Ø
Electrics	6v, 50 watt Bosch magneto
Clutch	multi-plate
Gearbox	hand-change, 3-speed
Final	exposed chain

FRAME & WHEELS
Type	bolted tubular construction, single downtube
Front forks	pressed steel parallelogram, helical sprung, friction damped
Rear forks	without rear suspension
Brakes	internal expanding drum, front and rear
Tyre size	3.00 x 19″ front and rear, road pattern

DIMENSIONS
Overall length	2000mm	(78.7″)
Overall width	750mm	(29.5″)
Overall height		
Wheelbase	1300mm	(51.2″)
Ground clearance	130mm	(5.1″)
Seat height	680mm	(26.8″)
Unladen weight	117 kg	(258 lb)
Fuel tank	12 lt	(2.6 gal Imp)
Performance	80 km/h	(50 mph) max
	2.5 lt/100 km	

GEAR RATIO		MILITARY EQUIP. rear carrier or pillion saddle,
I	= 3.00 : 1	a pair of leather panniers and overall service livery.
II	= 1.73 : 1	
III	= 1.00 : 1	

MODEL ZÜNDAPP K 800 1934

Military Service Standard production model works modified for the German armed forces, for solo/sidecar despatch, personnel carrier, reconnaissance and general liaison. Produced 1933-38. One of the heaviest military models of the period.

ENGINE & TRANSMISSION
Type	Zündapp, transverse sv flat-four
Capacity	804cc 62 x 66.6mm
Comp. ratio	5.8 : 1
Output	20 hp at 4000 rpm
Starting	left foot kick start
Carburettor	single Amal or Pallas 22mm Ø
Electrics	6v, 50/70 watt
Clutch	single plate, dry
Gearbox	hand-change, 4-speed, integral design
Final	exposed shaft

FRAME & WHEELS
Type	pressed steel duplex cradle design
Front forks	pressed steel parallelogram, helical sprung, friction damped
Rear forks	without suspension
Brakes	internal expanding drums, front and rear
Type size	3.50 or 4.00 x 19″ front and rear (& sidecar wheel)

DIMENSIONS
Overall length	2165mm	(85.2″) solo
Overall width	815mm	(32.0″) solo
Overall height	900mm	(35.4″) solo
Wheelbase	1405mm	(55.3″) solo
Ground clearance	120mm	(4.7″) solo
Seat height	720mm	(28.3″)
Unladen weight	215 kg	(474 lb)
Fuel tank	15 litre	(3 gal Imp) solo
Performance	110 km/h max (68 mph) solo	
	230 km, 200 km sidecar range	

GEAR RATIO		MILITARY EQUIP. rear carry or pillion saddle,
I	= 3.00 : 1	leather panniers, high level exhaust, all over service
II	= 1.80 : 1	livery and black exhaust system.
III	= 1.13 : 1	
IV	= 0.88 : 1	

MODEL ZÜNDAPP KS600W 1937

Military Service A standard production model works modified for German armed forces for solo/sidecar despatch, personnel carrier, reconnaissance and general liaison. Produced during 1937-41, more than 18,000 supplied, mainly with sidecar.

ENGINE & TRANSMISSION
Type	Zündapp, transverse ohv flat-twin
Capacity	597cc 75 x 67.6mm
Comp. ratio	6.5 : 1
Output	28 hp at 4700 rpm
Starting	left foot kick start

Carburettor	single Amal 25.4mm Ø
Electrics	6v, 50/70 watt, Bosch
Clutch	single-plate, dry
Gearbox	foot- or hand-change, 4-speed
Final	exposed shaft

FRAME & WHEELS
Type	pressed steel duplex cradle design
Front forks	pressed steel parallelogram, helical sprung, friction damped
Rear forks	without suspension
Brakes	internal expanding drums, front and rear
Tyre size	3.50 or 4.00 x 19″ front and rear, road pattern

DIMENSIONS
Overall length	2150mm	(84.6″) solo
Overall width	820mm	(32.2″) solo
Overall height	900mm	(35.4″) solo
Wheelbase	1390mm	(54.7″) solo
Ground clearance	125mm	(4.9″) solo
Seat height	730mm	(28.7″)
Unladen weight	205 kg	(451 lb) solo
Fuel tank	15 litre	(3.2 gal Imp)
Performance	120 km/h max (75 mph) solo	
	270 km range solo	

GEAR RATIO		MILITARY EQUIP. rear carry rack or pillion
I	= 3.00 : 1	saddle, leather panniers, various machine gun
II	= 1.80 : 1	fittings and spare wheel on sidecar, all over service
III	= 1.13 : 1	livery and black exhaust system.
IV	= 0.88 : 1	

GREAT BRITAIN

MODEL BSA MILITARY 500cc 1932

Manufacturer	BSA Motor Cycles Ltd, Small Heath, Birmingham
Military Service	Specialised model prepared to British military specifications; large capacity overhead valve, twin-cylinder model for solo despatch and police duties. After 10,000 mile reliability test, order placed, but too 'complicated' for WD use; became civilian J11 in 1934.

ENGINE & TRANSMISSION
Type	BSA, 50° V-twin ohv
Capacity	498cc 63 x 80mm
Comp. ratio	7.25 : 1
Output	22 hp at 5000 rpm
Starting	right foot kick start
Carburettor	single Amal 4/130
Electrics	6v
Clutch	multi-plate, wet
Gearbox	hand-change, 4-speed (J11; foot change)
Final	exposed chain

FRAME & WHEELS
Type	tubular construction, single downtube
Front forks	girder parallelogram, helical sprung, friction damped
Rear forks	without suspension
Brakes	internal expanding drum, 7″ dia x 1⅜″ front and rear
Tyre size	3.25 x 19″ front and rear, heavy road pattern

DIMENSIONS
Overall length		
Overall width		
Overall height		
Wheelbase	1397mm	(55.0″)
Ground clearance		
Seat height		
Unladen weight	776 kg	(352 lb)
Fuel tank	13.6 litre	(3 gal Imp)
Performance	120 km/h max(75 mph)	

GEAR RATIO		MILITARY EQUIP. rear carrier rack, small
I	= 14.3 : 1	leather panniers and overall service livery.
II	= 9.9 : 1	
III	= 6.3 : 1	
IV	= 4.8 : 1	

MODEL BSA M20 1938

Military Service Standard production model works modified for British armed forces for solo multi-terrain despatch and general liaison. During 12 months before declaration of war, BSA supplied more than 3000 motorcycles to British army (M20 and C10 trainer).

ENGINE & TRANSMISSION
Type	BSA, vertical sv single-cylinder
Capacity	496cc 82 x 94mm
Comp. ratio	4.9 : 1
Output	13 hp at 4200 rpm
Starting	right foot kick start
Carburettor	single Amal 276
Electrics	6v, magneto ignition (Lucas)
Clutch	multi-plate, wet
Gearbox	foot-change, 4-speed
Final	exposed chain

FRAME & WHEELS
Type	tubular construction, single downtube
Front forks	girder parallelogram, helical sprung, friction damped
Rear forks	without suspension
Brakes	internal expanding drums, 7″ diameter front and rear
Tyre size	3.25 x 19″ front and rear, road or cross country pattern

DIMENSIONS
Overall length	2185mm	(86.0″)

Overall width	737mm	(29.0″)
Overall height	991mm	(39.0″)
Wheelbase	1372mm	(54.0″)
Ground clearance	115mm	(4.5″)
Seat height	686mm	(27.0″)
Unladen weight	178 kg	(392 lb)
Fuel tank	16 litre	(3.5 gal Imp)
Performance	100 km/h	(62 mph) max
	50 mpg, 175 miles range	

GEAR RATIO		MILITARY EQUIP. rear carry rack or pillion
I	= 2.98 : 1	pad, canvas panniers in metal frame, masked
II	= 2.06 : 1	lighting, all over service livery.
III	= 1.32 : 1	
IV	= 1.00 : 1	

MODEL BSA MILITARY G14 1938

Military Service Standard production model works modified for military service by Netherlands Army for solo/sidecar use. NV Werkspoor at Utrecht built box-type machine gun carrying sidecar. Military BSA also procured by Eire, India, South Africa and Sweden.

ENGINE & TRANSMISSION
Type	BSA, V-twin sv
Capacity	986cc 80 x 98mm
Comp. ratio	4.5 : 1
Output	25 hp at 3800 rpm
Starting	right foot kick start
Carburettor	single Amal type 76
Electrics	6v
Clutch	multi-plate
Gearbox	hand-change, 4-speed
Final	exposed chain

FRAME & WHEELS
Type	tubular construction, single downtube
Front forks	girder parallelogram, helical sprung, friction damped
Rear forks	without suspension
Brakes	internal expanding drum, 7″ dia x 1⅜″ front and rear
Tyre size	4.00 x 18″ front and rear, heavy on/off road pattern

DIMENSIONS
Overall length		
Overall width		
Overall height		
Wheelbase	1600mm	(63.0″)
Ground clearance		
Seat height		
Unladen weight	190.5 kg	(420 lb)
Fuel tank	17 litre	(3.75 gal Imp)
Performance	104 km/h	(65 mph) max

GEAR RATIO		MILITARY EQUIP. rear carrier rack or pillion
I	= 13.7 : 1	saddle, off-road tyres, and all over service livery.
II	= 9.5 : 1	
III	= 6.0 : 1	
IV	= 4.6 : 1	

ITALY

MODEL BIANCHI 500M 1936

Manufacturer	Edoardo Bianchi, Moto Meccancia SpA, Milan
Military Service	Standard production model works modified for Italian armed forces in 1936, for solo despatch and general liaison, widely used throughout Italy and North Africa in World War 2 and after.

ENGINE & TRANSMISSION
Type	Bianchi, vertical sv single-cylinder
Capacity	496cc 82 x 94mm
Comp. ratio	5 : 1
Output	9 hp at 4000 rpm
Starting	right foot kick start
Carburettor	single Dell'Orto
Electrics	6v
Clutch	multi-plate, wet
Gearbox	hand-change, 3-speed
Final	exposed chain

FRAME & WHEELS
Type	tubular construction, single downtube design
Front forks	girder parallelogram, helical sprung, friction damped
Rear forks	plunger type, helical sprung
Brakes	internal expanding drums, front and rear
Tyre size	3.50 x 19″ front and rear, road pattern

DIMENSIONS
Overall length	2120mm	(83.4″)
Overall width	750mm	(29.5″)
Overall height	960mm	(37.7″)
Wheelbase	1380mm	(54.3″)
Ground clearance		
Seat height		
Unladen weight	170 kg	(375 lb)
Fuel tank	12 litre	(2.6 gal Imp)
Performance	75 km/h max (46 mph) max	
	260 km range, 100 km/4.5 lt	

MILITARY EQUIP. rear carry rack or pillion saddle, additional tool boxes, and all over service livery.

MODEL GILERA MILITARY LTE 1936

Manufacturer	Moto Gilera SpA, Arcore
Military Service	Standard production Mars model, works modified for Italian armed forces in 1936 for solo despatch, personnel carrier, reconnaissance and general liaison. Very similar to military Marte model, introduced in 1942, with shaft and sidecar wheel drive.

ENGINE & TRANSMISSION

Type	Gilera, vertical sv single-cylinder
Capacity	498cc 84 x 90mm
Comp. ratio	4.5 : 1
Output	12 hp at 3800 rpm
Starting	right foot kick start
Carburettor	single Dell'Orto MC 26 F
Electrics	6v, magneto ignition (Marelli MLA 49)
Clutch	multi-plate, wet
Gearbox	hand-change, 4-speed
Final	exposed chain

FRAME & WHEELS

Type	pressed steel and tubular construction, single downtube design
Front forks	girder parallelogram, helical sprung, friction damped
Rear forks	trailing rear sub-frame, helical sprung, friction damped
Brakes	internal expanding drums, front and rear
Tyre size	3.50 x 19″ front and rear, heavy road pattern

DIMENSIONS

Overall length	2200mm	(86.6″)
Overall width	800mm	(31.4″)
Overall height	1035mm	(40.7″)
Wheelbase	1450mm	(57.0″)
Ground clearance	140mm	(5.5″)
Seat height	720mm	(28.3″)
Unladen weight	190 kg	(418 lb)
Fuel tank	11.5 litre	(2.5 gal Imp)
Performance	90 km/h max (56 mph)	
	4.5 litre/100 km	

GEAR RATIO

I	= 19.16 : 1
II	= 11.70 : 1
III	= 8.79 : 1
IV	= 5.91 : 1

MILITARY EQUIP. rear carry rack or pillion saddle with folding handlebars, legshields, additional toolboxes, and all over service livery.

MODEL MOTO GUZZI GT 17 1932

Manufacturer	Moto Guzzi SpA, Mandello del Lario
Military Service	Specialised military model adopted by Italian military, for solo despatch, personnel carrier, reconnaissance and general police duties. A total of 4810 produced 1932-39; the first Moto Guzzi model built specifically for military service.

ENGINE & TRANSMISSION

Type	Moto Guzzi, horizontal single-cylinder, exhaust-over-inlet valve
Capacity	499cc 88 x 82mm
Comp. ratio	4.7 : 1
Output	13.2 hp at 4000 rpm
Starting	right foot kick start
Carburettor	single Dell'Orto MC 26 F
Electrics	6v, Marelli MLA 1 magneto
Clutch	multi-plate, dry
Gearbox	hand-change, 3-speed
Final	exposed chain

FRAME & WHEELS

Type	pressed steel and tubular construction, duplex cradle design
Front forks	girder parallelogram, helical sprung, friction damped
Rear forks	trailing rear sub-frame, helical sprung, friction damped
Brakes	internal expanding drums, front and rear
Tyre size	3.00 x 19″ front and rear

DIMENSIONS

Overall length	2235mm	(87.9″)
Overall width	925mm	(36.4″)
Overall height	1090mm	(42.9″)
Wheelbase	1520mm	(59.8″)
Ground clearance	165mm	(6.4″)
Seat height	746mm	(29.3″)
Unladen weight	196 kg	(432 lb)
Fuel tank	11.5 litre	(2.5 gal Imp)
Performance	100 km/h	(62 mph) max
	260 km range	

MILITARY EQUIP. rear carry rack or pillion saddle with handlebars, additional tool boxes, leg shields, handlebar mounted machine gun, various machine gun transport fittings, all over service livery.

MODEL MOTO GUZZI GTV 1934

Military Service	Standard production model (1934-40), adopted by Italian armed forces, Cavalleria & Bersaglieri, for solo despatch, reconnaissance, limited attack, military police and personnel carrier duties. Limited numbers remained in service during World War 2.

ENGINE & TRANSMISSION

Type	Moto Guzzi, horizontal ohv single-cylinder
Capacity	498cc 88 x 82mm
Comp. ratio	5.5 : 1
Output	18.9 hp at 4300 rpm
Starting	left foot kick start
Carburettor	single; Amal
Electrics	6v
Clutch	multi-plate, dry
Gearbox	foot-change, 4-speed
Final	exposed chain

FRAME & WHEELS

Type	pressed steel and tubular construction, duplex cradle design
Front forks	girder parallelogram, helical sprung, friction damped
Rear forks	trailing rear sub-frame, helical sprung, friction damped
Brakes	internal expanding drums, front and rear
Tyre size	3.25 x 19″ front, 3.50 x 19″ rear, road pattern

DIMENSIONS

Overall length	
Overall width	
Overall height	
Wheelbase	1400mm
Ground clearance	
Seat height	
Unladen weight	160 kg
Fuel tank	12 lt
Performance	120 km/h
	(4.5 lt/100 km)

MILITARY EQUIP. rear carrier rack or pillion saddle, additional tool boxes, leg shields, all-over service livery.

MODEL SERTUM 250 MCM 1937

Manufacturer	Moto Sertum SpA, Milan
Military Service	Standard production model (1937-40), adopted by Italian armed forces for solo despatch, reconnaissance and general liaison duties; procured with similar, but larger engined, 500cc Sertum 500 MCM model, both widely used throughout World War 2.

ENGINE & TRANSMISSION

Type	Sertum, vertical sv single-cylinder
Capacity	248cc
Comp. ratio	
Output	7 hp
Starting	right foot kick start
Carburettor	single; Amal
Electrics	6v
Clutch	multi-plate
Gearbox	hand-change, 3-speed
Final	exposed chain

FRAME & WHEELS

Type	pressed steel and tubular construction, single downtube
Front forks	girder parallelogram, helical sprung, friction damped
Rear forks	trailing sub-frame, leaf sprung, friction damped
Brakes	internal expanding drum, front and rear
Tyre size	3.50 x 19″ front and rear

DIMENSIONS

Overall length	2100mm	(82.7″)
Overall width	850mm	(33.5″)
Overall height	1000mm	(39.4″)
Wheelbase	1450mm	(57.1″)
Ground clearance		
Seat height		
Unladen weight	150 kg	(331 lb)
Fuel tank		
Performance	90 km/h	(56 mph) max

MILITARY EQUIP. rear carrier rack or pillion saddle, all over service livery.

JAPAN

MODEL SANKYO 97 1937

Manufacturer	Sankyo, Shinagawa Works, Tokyo, Japan
Military Service	Standard production model adopted for solo/sidecar despatch, personnel carrier, convoy escort and general liaison. A Harley-Davidson copy. Some 18,000 produced, becoming the major Japanese military motorcycle during the World War 2.

ENGINE & TRANSMISSION

Type	Sankyo, 45° V-twin sv
Capacity	1196cc 90 x 94mm
Comp. ratio	4.8 : 1
Output	24 hp at 4000 rpm
Starting	right foot kick start
Carburettor	single – Sankyo
Electrics	6v
Clutch	multi-plate, wet
Gearbox	hand-change, 3-speed and reverse with sidecar
Final	exposed chain

FRAME & WHEELS

Type	tubular construction, single downtube design
Front forks	leading link, helical sprung, friction damped
Rear forks	without suspension
Brakes	internal expanding drums, front and rear
Tyre size	4.75 x 18″ front and rear, road pattern

DIMENSIONS

Overall length	2591mm	(102.0″) solo
Overall width	915mm	(36.0″) solo
Overall height	1168mm	(45.9″) solo
Wheelbase	1600mm	(62.9″) solo
Ground clearance	203mm	(8.0″) solo
Seat height		
Unladen weight	280 kg	(617 lb) solo
Fuel tank		
Performance	96 km/h	(60 mph) max solo

MILITARY EQUIP. rear carry rack or pillion saddle, high level exhaust, and various fittings for sidecar mounted light machine gun.

POLAND

MODEL CWS/SOKOL MILITARY M111 1934

Manufacturer	Centralne Warsztaty Samochodowe, Warsaw
Military Service	Standard production model used by Polish military for solo/sidecar despatch, personnel carrier, convoy escort, and machine-gun platform. First produced under CWS name and later Sokol. Some 4000 were built between 1934-39, for Army, Police and Postal service.

ENGINE & TRANSMISSION

Type	CWS, sv V-twin
Capacity	995cc 83 x 92mm
Comp. ratio	5 : 1
Output	18 hp at 3000 rpm
Starting	left foot kick start
Carburettor	single CWS
Electrics	6v, 45 watt, Bosch RD (made in Poland under licence)
Clutch	multi-plate, wet
Gearbox	hand-change, 3-speed
Final	exposed chain

FRAME & WHEELS

Type	tubular construction, single downtube
Front forks	leading link, helical sprung, friction damped
Rear forks	without suspension
Brakes	internal expanding drums, front and rear
Tyre size	4.40 x 19″ front and rear (& sidecar)

DIMENSIONS

Overall length	2270mm	(89.3″) solo
Overall width	800mm	(31.6″) solo
Overall height	1135mm	(44.6″) solo
Wheelbase	1464mm	(57.6″) solo
Ground clearance		
Seat height		
Unladen weight	230 kg	(507 lb) solo
Fuel tank		
Performance	100 km/h max (62 mph) solo	
	7.5 litre/100 km solo	

MILITARY EQUIP. rear carry rack or pillion saddle, leather panniers, often used with various commercial sidecars or machine gun mounted platform, with ammunition boxes and spare wheel.

MODEL SOKOL 600 RT M211 1936

Manufacturer	Panstwowe Zakkady Inzynierii, Warsaw
Military Service	Standard production model works modified for Polish armed forces for solo/sidecar despatch, personnel carrier, reconnaissance and general liaison. Remained in production until 1939.

ENGINE & TRANSMISSION

Type	PZInz, forward-inclined sv single-cylinder
Capacity	575cc 83 x 106mm
Comp. ratio	4.6 : 1
Output	15 hp at 3900 rpm
Starting	right foot kick start
Carburettor	single Amal 26mm or Graetzin 22mm Ø
Electrics	6v, 45 watt, Bosch magneto
Clutch	multi-plate, wet
Gearbox	foot-change, 3-speed
Final	exposed chain

FRAME & WHEELS

Type	tubular construction, duplex cradle design
Front forks	girder pallelogram, helical sprung, friction damped
Rear forks	without suspension
Brakes	internal expanding drums, front and rear
Tyre size	4.00 x 19″ front and rear

DIMENSIONS

Overall length	2160mm	(85.0″) solo
Overall width	780mm	(30.7″) solo
Overall height	1000mm	(39.3″) solo
Wheelbase	1430mm	(56.2″) solo
Ground clearance		
Seat height		
Unladen weight	164 kg	(361 lb) solo
Fuel tank		
Performance	110 km/h	(68 mph) max
	4 litre/100 km	

MILITARY EQUIP. rear carry rack or pillion saddle, leather panniers, various machine gun fittings on sidecar, allover service livery.

MODEL MOJ 130 1938

Manufacturer	Fabryka Maszyn & Odlewnia Inz, Katowice
Military Service	Standard production model works modified for Polish armed forces for solo despatch and general liaison.

ENGINE & TRANSMISSION

Type	MOJ, vertical single-cylinder, two-stroke
Capacity	128cc 55 x 54mm
Comp. ratio	5.5 : 1
Output	3.5 hp at 3550 rpm
Starting	right foot kick start
Carburettor	single Graetzin
Electrics	6v, 18 watt, Bosch magneto
Clutch	multi-plate, wet
Gearbox	foot-change, 3-speed
Final	exposed chain

FRAME & WHEELS

Type	pressed steel construction, duplex cradle design

Front forks	pressed steel parallelogram, helical sprung, friction damped	
Rear forks	without suspension	
Brakes	internal expanding drums, front and rear	
Tyre size	3.00 x 19″ front and rear, road pattern	

DIMENSIONS

Overall length	1895mm	(74.6″)
Overall width	750mm	(29.5″)
Overall height	900mm	(35.4″)
Wheelbase		
Ground clearance	1225mm	(48.2″)
Seat height		
Unladen weight	70 kg	(154 lb)
Fuel tank		
Performance	65 km/h	(40 mph)
	2.5 litre/100 km	

MILITARY EQUIP. rear carry rack and all over service livery.

SWEDEN

MODEL	HUSQVARNA 500A 1922
Manufacturer	Husqvarna Vapenfabriks AB, Husqvarna
Military Service	Standard production model works modified for Swedish armed forces in 1922, for sidecar despatch, reconnaissance and general liaison. 299 machines supplied in 1922 and a further 416 machines in 1923.

ENGINE & TRANSMISSION

Type	HVA, V-twin sv
Capacity	990cc 79 x 101mm
Comp, ratio	5 : 1
Output	8 hp at 3500 rpm
Starting	right foot kick start
Carburettor	single Schebler
Electrics	6v, Bosch magneto
Clutch	multi-plate, wet, foot operated
Gearbox	hand-change, 3-speed
Final	exposed chain

FRAME & WHEELS

Type	tubular construction, duplex cradle design
Front forks	girder parallelogram, double helical sprung, friction damped
Rear forks	without suspension
Brakes	internal expanding drums, rear only
Tyre size	3.00 x 28″ all three wheel, road pattern

DIMENSIONS

Overall length		
Overall width		
Overall height		
Wheelbase		
Ground clearance		
Seat height		
Unladen weight	160 kg	(352 lb)
Fuel tank	12 litre	(2.6 gal Imp)
Performance	100 km/h	(62 mph) max

MILITARY EQUIP. rear carry rack or pillion saddle, spare wheel on sidecar, leather panniers and all over service livery.

MODEL	SUECIA ARME-TYPE 1937
Manufacturer	Suecia Verken Motor AB, Orelljunga
Military Service	Standard production model works modified for Swedish armed forces in 1937, for solo/sidecar despatch, personnel carrier, reconnaissance and general liaison.

ENGINE & TRANSMISSION

Type	MAG, vertical sv single-cylinder
Capacity	496cc 82 x 94mm
Comp, ratio	5 : 1
Output	11 hp at 3600 rpm
Starting	right foot kick start
Carburettor	single Amal 76/001
Electrics	6v, coil ignition (Bosch)
Clutch	multi-plate, wet
Gearbox	foot-change, 4-speed, Burman separate unit
Final	exposed chain

FRAME & WHEELS

Type	tubular construction, single downtube
Front forks	girder parallelogram, helical sprung, friction damped
Rear forks	without suspension
Brakes	internal expanding drums, front and rear
Tyre size	3.00 x 26″ front and rear, road pattern

DIMENSIONS

Overall length	
Overall width	

Overall height		
Wheelbase	1420mm	(55.9″) solo
Ground clearance		
Seat height	700mm	(27.5″) solo
Unladen weight	165 kg	(363 lb) solo
Fuel tank		
Performance	65 km/h	(40 mph) max

MILITARY EQUIP. rear carry rack or pillion saddle, various commercial sidecar designs, all over service livery.

SWITZERLAND

MODEL	CONDOR 641 ARMEE 1927
Military Service	Standard production model works modified for Swiss armed forces with standard sidecar, for despatch and general liaison, and personnel carrier duties. From 1930, widely used alongside Condor model 752 Armee, with improved MAG sv engine.

ENGINE & TRANSMISSION

Type	MAG, 45° V-twin, inlet-over-exhaust valves
Capacity	992cc 82 x 94mm
Comp, ratio	5 : 1
Output	10 hp nominal
Starting	right foot kick start
Carburettor	single semi-automatic
Electrics	6v, 30 watt Bosch magneto
Clutch	multi-plate, wet
Gearbox	foot-change, 3-speed
Final	exposed chain

FRAME & WHEELS

Type	tubular construction, single downtube
Front forks	girder parallelogram, double helical sprung, friction damped
Rear forks	without rear suspension
Brakes	block brakes upon auxiliary rims front and rear
Tyre size	710 x 85mm all three wheels

DIMENSIONS

Overall length		
Overall width		
Overall height		
Wheelbase		
Ground clearance		
Seat height		
Unladen weight	290 kg	(639 lb) with sidecar
Fuel tank	11 litre	(2.4 gal Imp) with sidecar
Performance	80 km/h	(50 mph) max with sidecar
	(5½ lt/100 km)	

MILITARY EQUIP. rear carrier rack or pillion saddle, full electric lighting, fully sprung single seat sidecar upon tubular chassis with 4 point fixing to motorcycle, spare wheel behind sidecar seat, overall service livery.

MODEL	CONDOR 752 ARMEE 1930
Military Service	Standard production model works modified for Swiss armed forces with standard sidecar, for despatch and general liaison, and personnel carrier duties. Remained in production until mid-1930s; mostly replaced by similar Universal 1000cc model in 1942.

ENGINE & TRANSMISSION

Type	MAG, 45° V-twin, sv
Capacity	992cc 82 x 94mm
Comp, ratio	5 : 1
Output	10 hp nominal
Starting	right foot kick start
Carburettor	single
Electrics	6v, 30 watt Bosch magneto
Clutch	multi-plate, wet
Gearbox	foot-change, 3-speed
Final	exposed chain

FRAME & WHEELS

Type	tubular construction, single downtube
Front forks	girder parallelogram, helical sprung, friction damped
Rear forks	without suspension
Brakes	internal expanding drums, front and rear
Tyre size	710 x 90mm or 27 x 4″ all three interchangeable wheels

DIMENSIONS

Overall length		
Overall width		
Overall height		
Wheelbase		
Ground clearance		
Seat height		
Unladen weight	300 kg	(661 lb) with sidecar

Fuel tank	14 litre	(3 gal Imp) with sidecar
Performance	85 km/h	(53 mph) max with sidecar
	5½ lt/100 km	

MILITARY EQUIP. rear carrier rack or pillion saddle, full electric lights, fully sprung single seat sidecar upon tubular chassis with 4 points fixing to motorcycle, spare wheel behind sidecar seat, overall service livery.

RUSSIA

MODEL	TIM-AM600 1935
Manufacturer	Tagnarog Motorcycle Works, Tagnarog
Military Service	Standard production model works modified for Russian forces for solo/sidecar despatch, personnel carrier, reconnaissance and general liaison. Produced between 1935-43, the first Russian motorcycle to adopt a tubular frame.

ENGINE & TRANSMISSION

Type	TIM, forward inclined sv single-cylinder
Capacity	595cc 85 x 108mm
Comp, ratio	5 : 1
Output	16.5 hp at 3800 rpm
Starting	right foot kick start
Carburettor	single TIM
Electrics	6v, 45 watt
Clutch	multi-plate, wet
Gearbox	hand-change, 4-speed, separate unit
Final	exposed chain

FRAME & WHEELS

Type	tubular construction, single downtube
Front forks	girder parallelogram, helical sprung, friction damped
Rear forks	without suspension
Brakes	internal expanding drums, front and rear
Tyre size	4.50 x 18″ front and rear

DIMENSIONS

Overall length		
Overall width		
Overall height		
Wheelbase	1420mm	(55.9″)
Ground clearance	125mm	(4.9″)
Seat height		
Unladen weight	185 kg	(408 lb)
Fuel tank	17 litre	(3.7 gal Imp)
Performance	95 km/h max	(59 mph)

MILITARY EQUIP. rear carry rack or pillion saddle, leather panniers, machine gun mounted on handlebars (option), all over service livery.

MODEL	PMZ A750 1935
Manufacturer	Podolsky Motorcycle Works, Podolsky
Military Service	Standard production model adopted by Russian armed forces, for solo and sidecar despatch, personnel carrier, reconnaissance and general police duties. Remained in production until 1939 (with Harley-Davidson influence); replaced by M-72 (BMW R71 copy).

ENGINE & TRANSMISSION

Type	PMZ, sv V-twin
Capacity	747cc 70 x 97mm
Comp, ratio	5 : 1
Output	15 hp at 3600 rpm
Starting	kick start
Carburettor	single PMZ
Electrics	6v, 45 watt
Clutch	multi-plate, wet
Gearbox	hand-change, 4-speed
Final	exposed chain

FRAME & WHEELS

Type	pressed steel duplex cradle design
Front forks	pressed steel leading link, leaf sprung, friction damped
Rear forks	without suspension
Brakes	internal expanding drums, front and rear
Tyre size	4.50 x 18″ front and rear

DIMENSIONS

Overall length		
Overall width		
Overall height		
Wheelbase	1395mm	(54.9″) solo
Ground clearance	112mm	(4.4″) solo
Seat height		
Unladen weight	220 kg	(485 lb) solo
Fuel tank	21 litre	(4.6 gal Imp)
Performance	100 km/h max	(62 mph) solo

MILITARY EQUIP. rear carry rack or pillion saddle, leather panniers, machine gun mounted on sidecar, all over service livery.

CHAPTER THREE

Second World War – 1939–45

The following specifications are for 48 of the best known motor-cycles in military service during World War 2, and described in Chapter 3. Each model is cross-referenced below to the relevant page number in Chapter 3.

Austria
Puch 250-S4 1940 *p 79*

Belgium
FN Tricar 12A SM-T3 1039 *p 119*
Sanolea H 1939 *p 119*

France
Motobecane B1V2 1940 *p 119*
Peugeot P53 1939 *p 119*
Peugeot 135 1939 *p 119*
Terrot RDA 1939 *p 119*
Terrot RGMA 1939 *p 119*

Germany
Ardie VF125 1939 *p 80*
Ardie RBZ200 1939 *p 80*
BMW R75 1940 *p 79*
DKW RT 125 1939 *p 78*
NSU 125 ZDB 1939 *p 78*
Phänomen AHOJ 1939 *p 78*
Zündapp KS 750 1940 *p 79*

Great Britain
Ariel W/NG 1940 *p 95*
BSA B30 1940 *p 100*
Excelsior Welbike Mk-II 1942 *p 102*
James ML 1942 *p 102*
Matchless G3L 1941 *p 97*
Norton Big Four 1939 *p 95*
Norton 16H 1939 *p 97*
Royal Enfield WD/C 1940 *p 101*
Royal Enfield WD/CO 1942 *p 101*
Royal Enfield WD/RE 1942 *p 101*
Triumph 3HW 1941 *p 100*
Velocette MAF 1942 *p 95*

Italy
Benelli 500 Motocarro 1942 *p 94*
Gilera Mercurio 1942 *p 94*
Gilera VL Marte 1942 *p 94*
Moto Guzzi Alce 1939 *p 91*
Moto Guzzi Trialce 1940 *p 93*
Moto Guzzi 500U 1940 *p 93*
Moto Guzzi Airone 1940 *p 93*

Japan
Kurogane Sanrinsha 1939 *p 119*

Sweden
Monark m/42 ohv 1942 *p 122*
NV Military 1000cc 1943 *p 123*

USA
Cushman 53 Autoglide 1944 *p 103*
Harley-Davidson WLA 1939 *p 104*
Harley-Davidson ELA 1939 *p 115*
Harley-Davidson XA 1942 *p 115*
Indian 841 1942 *p 115*
Indian 340 1939 *p 116*
Indian 640-A 1939 *p 117*
Indian 640-B 1939 *p 117*
Simplex Servi-Cycle 1942 *p 103*

USSR
IZH-9 1940 *p 119*
M-72 1941 *p 119*

AUSTRIA

MODEL	PUCH TYPE 250-S4 1940
Manufacturer	Steyr-Daimler-Puch AG, Graz, Austria
Military Service	Standard production model works modified for military service, adopted by Austrian military, subsequently widely used by the Germans, for solo lightweight despatch and general liaison.

ENGINE & TRANSMISSION

Type	Puch, vertical split-single, two-stroke
Capacity	248cc 2 x 45 x 78mm
Comp. ratio	6.5 : 1
Output	10.5 hp at 4300 rpm
Starting	right foot kick start
Carburettor	single – Solex
Electrics	6v
Clutch	single plate, dry, within rear wheel hub
Gearbox	hand-change, 4-speed
Final	exposed chain

FRAME & WHEELS

Type	tubular construction, duplex cradle design
Front forks	pressed steel parallelogram, helical sprung, friction damped
Rear forks	without suspension
Brakes	internal expanding drums, front and rear
Tyre size	3.00 x 19″ front and rear, road pattern

DIMENSIONS

Overall length	2000mm	(78.7″)
Overall width	800mm	(31.4″)
Overall height		
Wheelbase	1350mm	(53.1″)
Ground clearance	130mm	(5.1″)
Seat height	720mm	(28.3″)
Unladen weight	128 kg	(282 lb)
Fuel tank	12.5 litre	(2.7 Imp gal)
Performance	100 km/h	(62 mph) max
	(3.1 lt/100 km)	

GEAR RATIO

I	= 2.75 : 1	MILITARY EQUIP. rear carry rack, leather
II	= 1.50 : 1	panniers and all over service livery.
III	= 1.06 : 1	
IV	= 0.76 : 1	

BELGIUM

MODEL	FN TRICAR (12A SM-T3) 1939
Manufacturer	Fabrique Nationale SA, Herstal
Military Service	Specialised military tricycle, based on FN M12 sidecar outfit, developed for multi-terrain duties for personnel or equipment transportation. Also built with extended chassis and steering wheel (T8). Approximately 450 supplied 1939-40, and used by *Wehrmacht*.

ENGINE & TRANSMISSION

Type	FN, transverse sv, flat-twin
Capacity	992cc 90 x 78mm
Comp. ratio	5 : 1
Output	22 hp at 4000 rpm
Starting	left foot kick start
Carburettor	single Amal
Electrics	6v, 45/70 watt, coil ignition
Clutch	single-plate
Gearbox	hand-change, 4-speed and reverse with high/low ratio
Final	exposed chain and car-type axle to rear two wheels

FRAME & WHEELS

Type	tubular construction extended to meet various requirements
Front forks	girder parallelogram, helical sprung, friction damped
Rear forks	leaf sprung rear body
Brakes	internal expanding drum, all three wheels
Tyre size	12 x 45mm front, 14 x 45mm rear two, heavy cross-country pattern, solid disc-type wheels

DIMENSIONS

Overall length		
Overall width		
Overall height		
Wheelbase	2025mm	(79.7″)
Ground clearance		
Seat height		
Unladen weight	425 kg	(937 lb)
Fuel tank	19 litre	(4.1 Imp gal)
Performance		

MILITARY EQUIP. with various superstructures for personnel, ammunition transport or a anti-aircraft machine gun (5 soldiers or 550 kg payload), spare wheel, masked lighting, all overall service livery.

MODEL	SAROLEA H 1939
Manufacturer	Sarolea SA, Herstal
Military Service	Specialised military model developed for Belgian

army; a multi-terrain heavyweight sidecar outfit for personnel and equipment transportation. Some 300 supplied 1939-40, subsequently used by German troops. The Belgian Forces also procured standard production Sarolea 350 & 600cc models.

ENGINE & TRANSMISSION

Type	Sarolea, sv, flat-twin
Capacity	978cc 88 x 80mm
Comp. ratio	5 : 1
Output	20 hp at 4000 rpm
Starting	left foot kick start
Carburettor	single – Amal
Electrics	6v, 70 watt
Clutch	single-plate, dry
Gearbox	right hand-change, 3-2 & reverse
Final	exposed shafts to rear and sidecar wheels

FRAME & WHEELS

Type	tubular construction, duplex cradle design
Front forks	girder parallelogram, helical sprung, friction damped
Rear forks	without suspension
Brakes	internal expanding drums, all three wheels
Tyre size	12 x 45 all three wheels, heavy cross country pattern

DIMENSIONS

Overall length	(Dimensions not available)	
Overall width		
Overall height		
Wheelbase	1500mm	(59.0″) w/sc
Ground clearance		
Seat height		
Unladen weight	545 kg	(1202 lb) w/sc
Fuel tank	22 litre	(4.8 Imp gal)
Performance	82 km/h	(51 mph) max w/sc
		220/120 km range road/off road

MILITARY EQUIP. rear carry rack or pillion saddle, crash bars and sump guard, spare wheel, capstan on sidecar wheel for self-recovery, high level exhaust system, and various fittings for either sidecar mounted machine gun, ammunition boxes, radio equipment, or ambulance service.

FRANCE

MODEL	MOTOBECANE B1V2 1940
Manufacturer	Usines Motoconfort, Pantin, Seine
Military Service	Standard production model works modified for French armed forces in 1940, for solo lightweight despatch and general liaison duties.

ENGINE & TRANSMISSION

Type	Motobecane, vertical single-cylinder, two-stroke
Capacity	99.8cc 46 x 60mm
Comp. ratio	
Output	
Starting	right foot kick start
Carburettor	single Gurtner R17/25
Electrics	6v
Clutch	multi-plate, wet
Gearbox	hand-change, 3-speed
Final	exposed chain

FRAME & WHEELS

Type	tubular construction, single downtube
Front forks	girder parallelogram, helical sprung, friction damped
Rear forks	without suspension
Brakes	internal expanding drums, front and rear
Tyre size	600 x 65mm front and rear, road pattern

DIMENSIONS

Overall length	1860mm	(73.2″)
Overall width	650mm	(25.5″)
Overall height	900mm	(35.4″)
Wheelbase	1200mm	(47.2″)
Ground clearance		
Seat height		
Unladen weight	60 kg	(132 lb)
Fuel tank	8 litre	(1.75 Imp gal)
Performance	50 km/h	(31 mph) max
		350 km range

MILITARY EQUIP. rear carry rack, masked lighting, all over service livery.

MODEL	PEUGEOT P53 1939
Manufacturer	Cycles Peugeot, Paris
Military Service	Standard production model works modified for military service by French armed forces in 1939, for lightweight despatch and general liaison duties.

ENGINE & TRANSMISSION

Type	Peugeot, single-cylinder, two-stroke
Capacity	100cc 46 x 60mm
Comp. ratio	
Output	
Starting	right foot kick start
Carburettor	single Gurtner R17
Electrics	6v, magneto-Dynamo
Clutch	multi-plate, wet

Gearbox hand-change, 3-speed
Final exposed chain

FRAME & WHEELS
Type tubular construction, single downtube
Front forks girder parallelogram, helical sprung, friction damped
Rear forks without suspension
Brakes internal expanding drums, front and rear
Tyre size 600 x 65mm front and rear

DIMENSIONS
Overall length	1850mm	(72.8")
Overall width	650mm	(25.5")
Overall height	880mm	(34.6")
Wheelbase	1280mm	(50.3")
Ground clearance		
Seat height		
Unladen weight	40 kg	(88 lb)
Fuel tank	12 litre	(2.6 Imp gal)
Performance	50 km/h max	(31 mph)
	350 km range	

MILITARY EQUIP. rear carry rack, masked lighting, all over service livery.

MODEL PEUGEOT 135 1939

Military Service Standard production model works modified for French armed forces in 1939, for solo despatch and general liaison duties.

ENGINE & TRANSMISSION
Type Peugeot, vertical single-cylinder
Capacity 350cc 72 x 85mm
Comp. ratio
Output
Starting right foot kick start
Carburettor single Amal 6/010
Electrics 6v, magneto ignition
Clutch multi-plate, wet
Gearbox hand-change, 4-speed
Final exposed chain

FRAME & WHEELS
Type tubular construction, single downtube
Front forks girder parallelogram, helical sprung, friction damped
Rear forks without suspension
Brakes internal expanding drums, front and rear
Tyre size 3.50 x 26" front and rear, road pattern

DIMENSIONS
Overall length	2150mm	(84.6")
Overall width	700mm	(27.5")
Overall height	1000mm	(39.3")
Wheelbase	1400mm	(55.1")
Ground clearance	130mm	(5.1")
Seat height		
Unladen weight	150 kg	(330 lb)
Fuel tank	11 kg	(2.4 Imp gal)
Performance	90 km/h	(56 mph) max
	280 km range	

MILITARY EQUIP. rear carry rack or pillion saddle, panniers, masked lighting, all-over service livery.

MODEL TERROT RDA 1939

Manufacturer Ets Terrot, Dijon
Military Service Standard production model works modified for French armed forces in 1939, for solo/sidecar despatch, and general liaison duties.

ENGINE & TRANSMISSION
Type Terrot, vertical sv, single-cylinder
Capacity 498cc 84 x 90mm
Comp. ratio 5.4 : 1
Output 12 hp at 4000 rpm
Starting right foot kick start
Carburettor single Amac 6/001
Electrics 6v
Clutch multi-plate, wet
Gearbox foot-change, 4-speed
Final exposed chain

FRAME & WHEELS
Type tubular construction, single downtube
Front forks girder parallelogram, helical sprung, friction damped
Rear forks without suspension
Brakes internal expanding drum, front and rear
Tyre size 4.00 x 27" front and rear, road pattern

DIMENSIONS
Overall length	2330mm	(91.7") solo
Overall width	740mm	(29.1") solo
Overall height	1040mm	(40.9") solo
Wheelbase	1420mm	(55.9") solo
Ground clearance	110mm	(4.3") solo
Seat height		
Unladen weight	160 kg	(352 lb) solo
Fuel tank	18 litre	(3.9 Imp gal)
Performance	95 km/h	(60 mph) max solo
	280 km range	

GEAR RATIO
I	= 2.78 : 1	
II	= 1.75 : 1	
III	= 1.25 : 1	
IV	= 1.00 : 1	

MILITARY EQUIP. rear carrier rack or pillion saddle, leather panniers, allover service livery, and black exhaust system.

MODEL TERROT MODEL RGMA 1939

Manufacturer
Military Service Standard production model works modified for French solo/sidecar despatch, general liaison and military police duties.

ENGINE & TRANSMISSION
Type Terrot vertical ohv, single-cylinder
Capacity 498cc 84 x 90mm
Comp. ratio 6.2 : 1
Output
Starting right foot kick start
Carburettor single Amal 6/011
Electrics 6v
Clutch multi-plate, wet
Gearbox foot-change, 4-speed
Final exposed chain

FRAME & WHEELS
Type tubular construction, single downtube
Front forks girder parallelogram, helical sprung, friction damped
Rear forks without suspension
Brakes internal expanding drums, front and rear
Tyre size 4.00 x 27" front and rear, road pattern

DIMENSIONS
Overall length	2200mm	(86.6 ") solo
Overall width	900mm	(35.4") solo
Overall height	1050mm	(41.3") solo
Wheelbase	1400mm	(55.1") solo
Ground clearance	120mm	(4.7") solo
Seat height		
Unladen weight	150 kg	(330 lb) solo
Fuel tank		
Performance	110 km/h	(68 mph) max solo

GEAR RATIO
I	= 2.78 : 1	
II	= 1.75 : 1	
III	= 1.25 : 1	
IV	= 1.00 : 1	

MILITARY EQUIP. rear carry rack or pillion saddle, panniers, masked lighting, leg shields, all-over service livery.

GERMANY

MODEL ARDIE VF125 1939

Manufacturer Ardie Werke GmbH, Nuremberg
Military Service Standard production model, works modified for military service, used for solo despatch and general liaison. More than 9000 of these machines were produced 1939-45, and most of these were supplied to the *Wehrmacht*.

ENGINE & TRANSMISSION
Type Ardie, forward-inclined single-cylinder, two-stroke
Capacity 123cc 51 x 60mm
Comp. ratio 6.75 : 1
Output 5 hp at 4500 rpm
Starting left foot kick start
Carburettor single Bing: AJ 1/14
Electrics 6v, Bosch magneto
Clutch multi-plate, wet
Gearbox hand-change, 3-speed
Final exposed chain

FRAME & WHEELS
Type tubular construction, single downtube
Front forks pressed steel parallelogram, helical sprung, friction damped
Rear forks without rear suspension
Brakes internal expanding drum, front and rear
Tyre size 2.50 x 19" front and rear, road pattern

DIMENSIONS
Overall length	1920mm	(75.6")
Overall width	690mm	(27.2")
Overall height		
Wheelbase	1250mm	(49.2")
Ground clearance	150mm	(6.0")
Seat height	670mm	(26.4")
Unladen weight	68 kg	(150 lb)
Fuel tank	10.5 litre	(2.3 Imp gal)
Performance	75 km/h	(47 mph)
	(2.2 lt/100 km)	

GEAR RATIO
I	= 32.2 : 1	
II	= 16.0 : 1	
III	= 9.2 : 1	

MILITARY EQUIP. rear carrier rack, leather panniers, masked lighting, hand pump, and all-over service livery.

MODEL ARDIE RBZ200 1939

Military Service Standard production model, works modified for military service, used by *Wehrmacht* for solo despatch and general liaison.

ENGINE & TRANSMISSION
Type Ardie, forward-inclined single-cylinder, two-stroke
Capacity 197cc 61 x 68mm
Comp. ratio 5.8 : 1
Output 7 hp at 5000 rpm
Starting right foot kick start
Carburettor single: Amal 4/025 LH
Electrics 6v
Clutch multi-plate, wet
Gearbox hand-change, 3-speed
Final exposed chain

FRAME & WHEELS
Type pressed steel and tubular construction, single downtube
Front forks pressed steel parallelogram, helical sprung, friction damped
Rear forks without suspension

Brakes internal expanding drum, front and rear
Tyre size 3.00 x 19" front and rear, road pattern

DIMENSIONS
Overall length	2000mm	(78.7")
Overall width	740mm	(29.1")
Overall height		
Wheelbase	1310mm	(51.6")
Ground clearance	130mm	(5.1")
Seat height	680mm	(26.8")
Unladen weight	119 kg	(262 lb)
Fuel tank	13.5 litre	(3 Imp gal)
Performance	85 km/h	(53 mph) max
	(3.4 lt/100 km)	

GEAR RATIO
I	= 18.9 : 1	
II	= 8.8 : 1	
III	= 6.6 : 1	

MILITARY EQUIP. rear carrier rack, leather panniers, masked lighting, hand pump, and all-over service livery.

MODEL BMW MODEL R75 1940

Manufacturer Bayerische Motoren Werke AG, Munich
Military Service Specialised military model developed for German army; a multi-terrain heavyweight sidecar outfit for personnel and equipment transportation, limited attack and convoy control. Produced 1940-44, a total of 16,510 supplied.

ENGINE & TRANSMISSION
Type BMW, transverse ohv flat-twin
Capacity 746cc 78 x 78mm
Comp. ratio 5.7 : 1
Output 26 hp at 4400 rpm
Starting left foot kick start
Carburettor two Graetzin Sa 24
Electrics 6v, 50/70 watt
Clutch single plate, dry
Gearbox left foot- and right hand-change, 4+3 and reverse speed
Final exposed shaft, sidecar wheel shaft-drive

FRAME & WHEELS
Type pressed steel and tubular construction
Front forks telescopic, helical sprung
Rear forks without suspension
Brakes internal expanding drums, front and rear, hydraulic operation drive wheel
Tyre size 4.50 x 16" all three wheels, heavy cross country pattern

DIMENSIONS
Overall length	2400mm	(94.4") w/sc
Overall width	1730mm	(68.1") w/sc
Overall height	1000mm	(39.3") w/sc
Wheelbase	1444mm	(56.8")
Ground clearance	150mm	(5.9")
Seat height		
Unladen weight	420 kg	(925 lb)
Fuel tank	24 litre	(5.2 Imp gal)
Performance	92 km/h max	(57 mph)
	340 km road range	

GEAR RATIO
I	= 3.22 : 1	road
II	= 1.83 : 1	road
III	= 1.21 : 1	road
IV	= 0.90 : 1	road
R	= 2.41 : 1	road
I	= 4.46 : 1	off road
II	= 2.54 : 1	off road
III	= 1.67 : 1	off road

MILITARY EQUIP.rear carry rack or pillion saddle, leather panniers, masked lighting, high level exhaust, spare wheel and machine gun fittings on sidecar, all over service livery.

MODEL DKW RT 125 1939

Manufacturer Auto Union AG, Zschopau/Sachsen
Military Service Standard production model procured by the *Wehrmacht* for solo despatch and general liaison; one of the very few motorcycles to be assembled throughout the war, and eventually widely copied worldwide.

ENGINE & TRANSMISSION
Type DKW, vertical single-cylinder, two-stroke
Capacity 123cc 52 x 58mm
Comp. ratio 6 : 1
Output 4.3 hp at 4000 rpm
Starting left foot kick start
Carburettor single Amal, Bing or Graetzin
Electrics 6v, 35/45 watt
Clutch multi-plate, wet
Gearbox foot-change, 3-speed
Final exposed chain

FRAME & WHEELS
Type tubular construction, single downtube
Front forks pressed steel parallelogram, single helical sprung
Rear forks without rear suspension
Brakes internal expanding drums, front and rear
Tyre size 2.50 x 19" front and rear

DIMENSIONS
Overall length	1940mm	(76.3")
Overall width	650mm	(25.5")
Overall height	900mm	(35.4")

Wheelbase	1230mm	(48.4″)
Ground clearance	145mm	(5.7″)
Seat height		
Unladen weight	91 kg	(200 lb)
Fuel tank	9 litre	(2 gal Imp)
Performance	72 km/h	(45 mph) max
	(360 km range)	

GEAR RATIO	MILITARY EQUIP. rear carry rack, leather panniers, masked lighting, hand pump, all over service livery and black exhaust system.
I = 3.16 : 1	
II = 1.49 : 1	
III = 1.00 : 1	

MODEL NSU 125 ZDB 1939

Manufacturer	Neckarsulmer Fahrzeugwerke AG, Neckarsulm
Military Service	Standard production model, procured by *Wehrmacht* for solo despatch and general liaison, widely used throughout the war alongside Ardie VF125, DKW RT125, Phänomen AHOJ 125, etc.

ENGINE & TRANSMISSION

Type	NSU, vertical single-cylinder, twin-port two-stroke
Capacity	122cc 50 x 62mm
Comp, ratio	7.5 : 1
Output	4.8 hp at 4500 rpm
Starting	left foot kick start
Carburettor	single Amal E 68/16, Bing AJ 1/16 N or Graetzin Kf 16 A
Electrics	6v, Bosch W 225 T 1
Clutch	multi-plate, wet
Gearbox	foot-change, 3-speed
Final	exposed chain

FRAME & WHEELS

Type	tubular construction, single downtube design
Front forks	pressed steel construction, helical sprung, friction damped
Rear forks	without rear suspension
Brakes	internal expanding drums, front and rear
Tyre size	2.50 x 19″ front and rear, road pattern

DIMENSIONS

Overall length	1980mm	(78.0″)
Overall width	680mm	(26.8″)
Overall height		
Wheelbase	1280mm	(50.4″)
Ground clearance	130mm	(5.2″)
Seat height	700mm	(27.6″)
Unladen weight	82 kg	(181 lb)
Fuel tank	11 litre	(2.4 Imp gal)
Performance	70 km/h	(43 mph)
	(2.5 lt/100 km)	

GEAR RATIO	MILITARY EQUIP. rear carrier rack, leather panniers, masked lighting, hand pump, allover service livery.
I = 17.8 : 1	
II = 10.4 : 1	
III = 7.9 : 1	

MODEL PHÄNOMEN AHOJ 1939

Manufacturer	Phänomen-Werke, Gustav Hiller AG, Zittau
Military Service	Standard production model, works modified for military service, one of several lightweight models adopted by the *Wehrmacht*, the Phänomen was unusual in having a sprung rear wheel. Widely used throughout the war for solo despatch and general liaison duties.

ENGINE & TRANSMISSION

Type	Sachs, vertical single-cylinder, two-stroke
Capacity	124cc 54 x 54mm
Comp, ratio	6.5 : 1
Output	4.2 hp at 4700 rpm
Starting	left foot kick start
Carburettor	single Sachs
Electrics	6v, 35/45 watt
Clutch	multi-plate, wet
Gearbox	foot-change, 3-speed
Final	exposed chain

FRAME & WHEELS

Type	tubular construction, single downtube
Front forks	swinging pressed steel fork, pivoted under headstock, rubber sprung
Rear forks	pressed steel swinging fork, rubber sprung, friction damped
Brakes	internal expanding drums, front and rear
Tyre size	2.50 x 19″ front and rear, road pattern

DIMENSIONS

Overall length	1885mm	(74.2″)
Overall width	690mm	(27.1″)
Overall height	940mm	(37.0″)
Wheelbase	1220mm	(48.0″)
Ground clearance	170mm	(6.7″)
Seat height	680mm	(26.7″)
Unladen weight	83 kg	(183 lb)
Fuel tank	10 litre	(2.2 gal Imp)
Performance	75 km/h	(47 mph) max
	(2.6 lt/100 km)	

GEAR RATIO	MILITARY EQUIP. rear carrier rack, masked lighting, high level exhaust system, and overall service livery.
I = 26.1 : 1	
II = 13.6 : 1	
III = 7.6 : 1	

MODEL ZÜNDAPP KS 750 1940

Manufacturer	Zündapp Werke GmbH, Nuremburg
Military Service	Specialised military model developed for *Wehrmacht*; a multi-terrain heavyweight sidecar outfit for personnel and equipment transportation, limited attack and convoy control. Produced 1940-44, a total of 18.635 supplied.

ENGINE & TRANSMISSION

Type	Zündapp, transverse ohv flat-twin
Capacity	751cc 75 x 85mm
Comp, ratio	6.2 : 1
Output	26 hp at 4000 rpm
Starting	left foot kick start
Carburettor	single Solex 30 BFR (H)
Electrics	6v, 50/70 watt
Clutch	single plate, dry
Gearbox	left-hand & right foot-change, 4+1 & reverse speed
Final	exposed shaft, sidecar wheel shaft-drive

FRAME & WHEELS

Type	pressed steel and tapered tubular construction, duplex cradle
Front forks	girder parallelogram, helical sprung
Rear forks	without suspension
Brakes	internal expanding drums, all three wheels, hydraulic operation drive wheels
Tyre size	4.50 x 16″ all three wheels, heavy cross country pattern

DIMENSIONS

Overall length	2385mm	(93.8″) w/sc
Overall width	1650mm	(64.9″) w/sc
Overall height	1010mm	(36.7″) w/sc
Wheelbase	1410mm	(55.5″) w/sc
Ground clearance	160mm	(6.2″) w/sc
Seat height	785mm	(30.9″) w/sc
Unladen weight	420 kg	(925 lb) w/sc
Fuel tank	24 litre	(5.2 Imp gal)
Performance	92 km/h road (57 mph) max	
	340 km, road range	

GEAR RATIO	MILITARY EQUIP. rear carry rack or pillion saddle, leather panniers, masked lighting, high level exhaust, spare wheel and machine gun fittings on sidecar, all over service livery.
I = 4.83 : 1 road	
II = 2.29 : 1 road	
III = 1.43 : 1 road	
IV = 1.00 : 1 road	
R = 7.52 : 1 road	

GREAT BRITAIN

MODEL ARIEL W/NG 1940

Manufacturer	Ariel Motors Ltd, Selly Oak, Birmingham
Military Service	Standard production model widely used for military service, for solo despatch, reconnaissance and general liaison. 1940-44 a total of 47,599 supplied to British & Allied Forces. Many remained in European & Scandinavian military use until late 1950s.

ENGINE & TRANSMISSION

Type	Ariel, vertical ohv, single-cylinder
Capacity	346cc 72 x 85mm
Comp, ratio	6.5 : 1
Output	17 hp at 5800 rpm
Starting	right foot kick start
Carburettor	single Amal 275
Electrics	6v, magneto ignition
Clutch	multi-plate, wet
Gearbox	foot-change, 4-speed (Burman)
Final	exposed chain

FRAME & WHEELS

Type	tubular construction, single downtube
Front forks	girder type parallelogram, helical sprung, friction damped
Rear forks	without suspension
Brakes	internal expanding drums, 6.5″ diameter front & 7″ rear
Tyre size	3.25 x 19″ front and rear, road pattern

DIMENSIONS

Overall length	2134mm	(84.0″)
Overall width	762mm	(30.0″)
Overall height	1067mm	(42.0″)
Wheelbase	1397mm	(55.0″)
Ground clearance	127mm	(5.0″)
Seat height	724mm	(28.5″)
Unladen weight	171 kg	(376 lb)
Fuel tank	11 litre	(2.4 Imp gal)
Performance	110 km/h	(68 mph) max
	80 mpg, 210 miles range	

GEAR RATIO	MILITARY EQUIP. rear carry rack or pillion pad, canvas panniers, additional tool box, longer prop stand hinged below saddle, masked lighting, all over service livery.
I = 18.1 : 1	
II = 12.0 : 1	
III = 8.7 : 1	
IV = 5.75 : 1	

MODEL BSA B30 1940

Manufacturer	BSA Cycles Ltd, Birmingham
Military Service	Standard production model works modified for military service, based upon pre-war B29, for solo multi-terrain despatch and general liaison, remained experimental only (contract replaced by M20), but provided foundation for successful post-war B31 off-road competition model.

ENGINE & TRANSMISSION

Type	BSA, vertical ohv, single-cylinder
Capacity	348cc 71 x 88mm
Comp, ratio	7.2 : 1
Output	15 hp at 4850 rpm
Starting	right foot kick start
Carburettor	single Amal
Electrics	6v, magneto ignition
Clutch	multi-plate, wet, four rings, three Ferodo and one cork inserts
Gearbox	foot-change, 4-speed
Final	exposed chain

FRAME & WHEELS

Type	tubular construction, single downtube
Front forks	girder parallelogram, helical sprung, friction damped
Rear forks	without suspension
Brakes	internal expanding, 7″ drums front and rear
Tyre size	3.25 x 19″ front and rear, heavy road pattern

DIMENSIONS

Overall length	2019mm	(79.5″)
Overall width	724mm	(28.5″)
Overall height	927mm	(36.5″)
Wheelbase	1346mm	(53.0″)
Ground clearance	153mm	(6.0″)
Seat height		
Unladen weight	154 kg	(339 lb) full tank
Fuel tank	10.2 litre	(2.25 Imp gal)
Performance	120 km/h	(75 mph)
	80 mpg, 180 miles range	

GEAR RATIO	MILITARY EQUIP. rear carry rack or pillion pad, canvas panniers, masked lighting, sump guard, all over service livery.
I = 17.1 : 1	
II = 12.0 : 1	
III = 7.8 : 1	
IV = 6.0 : 1	

MODEL EXCELSIOR WELBIKE MK-II 1942

Manufacturer	Excelsior Motor Co Ltd, Birmingham
Military Service	Specialised military model developed for British Airb orne troops. Total of 3840 machines supplied from late 1942. The Brockhouse Corgi was introduced as a modified post-war version.

ENGINE & TRANSMISSION

Type	Villiers Junior, horizontal single-cylinder, two-stroke
Capacity	98cc 50 x 50mm
Comp, ratio	6 : 1
Output	1.5 hp
Starting	
Carburettor	single: Villiers
Electrics	6v, flywheel magneto ignition
Clutch	single-plate, dry
Gearbox	single-speed
Final	exposed chain

FRAME & WHEELS

Type	tubular construction, collapsible steering column, handle bars, saddle
Front forks	without suspension
Rear forks	without suspension
Brakes	internal expanding drum, rear wheel only
Tyre size	2.25 x 12.5″ front and rear, road pattern

DIMENSIONS

Overall length	1321mm	(52.0″) reduce to: 1295mm (51.0″)
Overall width	559mm	(22.0″) reduce to: 305mm (12.0″)
Overall height	787mm	(31.0″) reduce to: 381mm (15.0″)
Wheelbase	1003mm	(39.5″)
Ground clearance	102mm	(4.0″)
Seat height		
Unladen weight	32 kg	(70 lb)
Fuel tank	3.6 litre	(0.8 Imp gal)
Performance		

MILITARY EQUIP. A collapsible 'parascooter' designed to be packed into a cylindrical container for parachute use.

MODEL JAMES ML 1942

Manufacturer	James Cycle Co Ltd, Birmingham
Military Service	Specialised military model prepared for British airborne troops. Total of 6040 produced 1942-44. Popularly known as the Clockwork Mouse the machine could be easily manhandled for parachute use.

ENGINE & TRANSMISSION

Type	Villiers 9D, vertical single-cylinder, two-stroke
Capacity	122cc 50 x 62mm
Comp, ratio	6.5 : 1
Output	3.3 hp at 4000 rpm
Starting	right foot kick start
Carburettor	single Villiers 3/1
Electrics	6v
Clutch	multi-plate, wet
Gearbox	hand-change, 3-speed
Final	exposed chain

FRAME & WHEELS

Type	tubular construction, single downtube
Front forks	pressed steel parallelogram, helical sprung, friction damped
Rear forks	without rear suspension
Brakes	internal expanding drum, 4″ diameter front and 3.6″ diameter rear
Tyre size	2.75 x 19″ front and rear, road pattern

DIMENSIONS

Overall length	1854mm	(73.0″)
Overall width	889mm	(35.0″) 16″ folded
Overall height		
Wheelbase	1219mm	(48.0″)
Ground clearance		
Seat height		
Unladen weight	72.2 kg	(157 lb)
Fuel tank	6.4 litre	(1.4 Imp gal)
Performance	65 km/h	(40 mph)

GEAR RATIO	MILITARY EQUIP. rear carrier rack, masked lighting, folding handlebars and foot rests, and over-all service livery.
I = 2.92 : 1	
II = 1.63 : 1	
III = 1.0 : 1	

MODEL MATCHLESS G3L 1941

Manufacturer	Associated Motor Cycles Ltd, Plumstead, London
Military Service	Specialised military model developed for British Army; a solo machine for despatch and general liaison duties. Replaced former G3 of 1939. Produced 1941-45 more than 63,000 and many provided post-war years service.

ENGINE & TRANSMISSION

Type	AMC, air-cooled vertical ohv, single-cylinder
Capacity	348cc 69 x 93mm
Comp, ratio	5.9 : 1
Output	16 hp at 5500 rpm
Starting	right foot kick start
Carburettor	single Amal 275/IJ
Electrics	6v, magneto ignition
Clutch	multi-plate, wet
Gearbox	foot-change, 4-speed
Final	exposed chain

FRAME & WHEELS

Type	tubular construction, single downtube
Front forks	telescopic, helical sprung, hydraulic damping
Rear forks	without suspension
Brakes	internal expanding drums, 7″ diameter front and rear
Tyre size	3.25 x 19″ front and rear

DIMENSIONS

Overall length	2096mm	(82.5″)
Overall width	762mm	(30.0″)
Overall height	1042mm	(41.0″)
Wheelbase	1296mm	(51.0″)
Ground clearance	152mm	(6.0″)
Seat height	711mm	(28.0″)
Unladen weight	149 kg	(328 lb)
Fuel tank	13.5 litre	(3 Imp gal)
Performance	110 km/h	(68 mph) max
	76 mpg, 225 miles range	

GEAR RATIO
I = 3.19 : 1
II = 2.11 : 1
III = 1.28 : 1
IV = 1.00 : 1

MILITARY EQUIP. rear carry rack, canvas panniers, additional tool-boxes, masked lighting, all-over service livery.

MODEL NORTON BIG FOUR 1939

Manufacturer	Norton Motors Ltd, Birmingham
Military Service	Standard production model developed for military service; procured by British & Allied Forces for sidecar despatch, personnel and ammunition carrier duties. A total of 4737 supplied.

ENGINE & TRANSMISSION

Type	Norton, vertical sv, single-cylinder
Capacity	633cc 82 x 120mm
Comp, ratio	4.8 : 1
Output	14.5 hp at 4000 rpm
Starting	right foot kick start
Carburettor	single Amal 276
Electrics	6v, magneto ignition
Clutch	multi-plate, wet
Gearbox	foot-change, 4-speed
Final	exposed chain, shaft-drive to sidecar wheel

FRAME & WHEELS

Type	tubular construction, single downtube
Front forks	girder parallelogram, helical sprung, friction damped
Rear forks	without suspension
Brakes	internal expanding drums, 7″ diameter front and rear
Tyre size	4.00 x 18″ all three wheels, heavy cross country pattern

DIMENSIONS

Overall length	2184mm	(86.0″)
Overall width	1689mm	(66.5″)
Overall height	1168mm	(46.0″)
Wheelbase	1371mm	(54.0″)
Ground clearance	127mm	(5.0″)
Seat height		
Unladen weight	308 kg	(679 lb)
Fuel tank	14 litre	(3 Imp gal)
Performance	90 km/h	(56 mph) max

GEAR RATIO
I = 23.6 : 1
II = 15.3 : 1
III = 9.4 : 1
IV = 6.4 : 1

MILITARY EQUIP. rear carry rack or pillion saddle, masked lighting, spare wheel and clips between machine and sidecar to carry a Bren gun. Ammunition box at back of sidecar.

MODEL NORTON 16H 1939

Military Service	Standard production model used by British & Allied Forces for solo, occasional sidecar, despatch, military police, reconnaissance, convoy control and escort duties. Of the 100,000 Nortons supplied during the war, the 16H was the most numerous.

ENGINE & TRANSMISSION

Type	Norton, vertical sv, single-cylinder
Capacity	490cc 79 x 100mm
Comp, ratio	4.9 : 1
Output	14 hp at 4500 rpm
Starting	right foot kick start
Carburettor	single Amal 276
Electrics	6v, magneto ignition (Lucas)
Clutch	multi-plate, wet
Gearbox	foot-change, 4-speed
Final	exposed chain

FRAME & WHEELS

Type	tubular construction, single downtube
Front forks	girder type parallelogram, helical sprung, friction damped
Rear forks	without suspension
Brakes	internal expanding drums, 7″ diameter front and rear
Tyre size	3.25 x 19″ front and rear, heavy road pattern

DIMENSIONS

Overall length	2172mm	(85.5″)
Overall width	762mm	(30.0″)
Overall height	991mm	(39.0″)
Wheelbase	1372mm	(54.0″)
Ground clearance	114mm	(4.5″)
Seat height	737mm	(29.0″)
Unladen weight	176 kg	(388 lb)
Fuel tank	11 litre	(2.4 Imp gal)
Performance	110 km/h	(68 mph) max
	50 mpg, 175 miles range	

GEAR RATIO
I = 2.98 : 1
II = 1.77 : 1
III = 1.21 : 1
IV = 1.00 : 1

MILITARY EQUIP. rear carry rack or pillion pad, canvas panniers, masked lighting, all over service livery.

MODEL ROYAL ENFIELD WD/C 1940

Manufacturer	Enfield Cycle Co Ltd, Redditch
Military Service	Standard production model works modified for military service, used by British and Allied forces for solo despatch and general liaison but gradually superseded by ohv WD/CO version.

ENGINE & TRANSMISSION

Type	Enfield, vertical sv, single-cylinder
Capacity	346cc 70 x 90mm
Comp, ratio	5 : 1
Output	9.5 hp at 4500 rpm
Starting	right foot kick start
Carburettor	single Amal 276
Electrics	6v, magneto ignition (Lucas)
Clutch	multi-plate, wet
Gearbox	foot-change, 4-speed
Final	exposed chain

FRAME & WHEELS

Type	tubular construction, single downtube, duplex cradle
Front forks	girder parallelogram, helical sprung, friction damped
Rear forks	without suspension
Brakes	internal expanding, 6″ drums front and rear
Tyre size	3.25 x 19″ front and rear, heavy road pattern

DIMENSIONS

Overall length	2159mm	(85.0″)
Overall width	724mm	(28.5″)
Overall height	965mm	(38.0″)
Wheelbase	1346mm	(53.0″)
Ground clearance	107mm	(4.2″)
Seat height		
Unladen weight	160 kg	(353 lb) full tank
Fuel tank	13.6 litre	(3 Imp gal)
Performance	88 km/h	(55 mph)
	64 mpg, 190 miles range	

GEAR RATIO
I = 17.6 : 1
II = 10.7 : 1
III = 8.0 : 1
IV = 5.9 : 1

MILITARY EQUIP. rear carry rack, canvas panniers, masked lighting, all-over service livery.

MODEL ROYAL ENFIELD WD/CO 1942

Military Service	Standard production model works modified for military service, used by British and Allied armed forces, for solo despatch and general liaison. Total of 29,037 machines supplied 1942-44. (Alongside WD/C 350cc side valve version).

ENGINE & TRANSMISSION

Type	Enfield, vertical ohv, single-cylinder
Capacity	346cc 70 x 90mm
Comp, ratio	5.75 : 1
Output	14 hp at 4800 rpm
Starting	right foot kick start
Carburettor	single Amal 276
Electrics	6v, magneto ignition (Lucas)
Clutch	multi-plate, wet
Gearbox	foot-change, 4-speed
Final	exposed chain

FRAME & WHEELS

Type	tubular construction, single downtube, duplex cradle
Front forks	girder parallelogram, helical sprung, friction damped
Rear forks	without suspension
Brakes	internal expanding drums, 6″ diameter front & 7″ rear
Tyre size	3.25 x 19″ front and rear, heavy road pattern

DIMENSIONS

Overall length	2159mm	(85.0″)
Overall width	698mm	(27.5″)
Overall height	1016mm	(40.0″)
Wheelbase	1422mm	(56.0″)
Ground clearance	127mm	(5.0″)
Seat height		
Unladen weight	154 kg	(340 lb)
Fuel tank	12.5 litre	(2.75 Imp gal)
Performance	110 km/h	(68 mph) max
	73 mpg, 200 miles range	

GEAR RATIO
I = 18.60 : 1
II = 11.20 : 1
III = 7.90 : 1
IV = 5.65 : 1

MILITARY EQUIP. rear carry rack, canvas panniers, masked lighting, all-over service livery.

MODEL ROYAL ENFIELD WD/RE 1942

Military Service	Standard production model works modified for British airborne troops, popularly known as Flying Flea. Produced 1942-44 nearly 8000 supplied. Widely used by paratroops, the machine could be easily manhandled on landing.

ENGINE & TRANSMISSION

Type	Royal Enfield, vertical, single-cylinder, two-stroke
Capacity	126cc 54 x 55mm
Comp, ratio	
Output	2.6 hp
Starting	right foot kick start
Carburettor	single
Electrics	6v, flywheel magneto
Clutch	multi-plate
Gearbox	hand-change, 3-speed
Final	exposed chain

FRAME & WHEELS

Type	tubular construction, single downtube
Front forks	girder parallelogram, rubber-band sprung, friction damping
Rear forks	without rear suspension
Brakes	internal expanding drum, front and rear
Tyre size	2.75 x 19″ front and rear, road pattern

DIMENSIONS

Overall length	1880mm	(74.0″)
Overall width	864mm	(34.0″) 16.0″ folded
Overall height		
Wheelbase	1219mm	(48.0″)
Ground clearance		
Seat height		
Unladen weight	62.1 kg	(137 lb)
Fuel tank		
Performance	65 km/h	(40 mph)

MILITARY EQUIP. rear carrier rack, masked lighting, folding handlebars and foot rests, and over-all service livery.

MODEL TRIUMPH 3HW 1941

Manufacturer	Triumph Engineering Co, Ltd, Warwick
Military Service	Standard production Tiger 80 model works modified for military service from 1941, mainly by Royal Navy, for soldier despatch and general liaison. A side-valve version, model 3SW, was used by WRNS.

ENGINE & TRANSMISSION

Type	Triumph, vertical ohv, single-cylinder
Capacity	343cc 70 x 89mm
Comp, ratio	6.7 : 1
Output	17 hp at 5200 rpm ohv/10 hp at 4800 rpm sv
Starting	right foot kick start
Carburettor	single Amal 276
Electrics	6v, magneto ignition
Clutch	multi-plate, wet
Gearbox	foot-change, 4-speed
Final	exposed chain

FRAME & WHEELS

Type	tubular construction, single downtube, duplex cradle
Front forks	girder parallelogram, helical sprung, friction damped
Rear forks	without suspension
Brakes	internal expanding drums, 7″ front and rear
Tyre size	3.25 x 19″ front and rear, heavy road pattern

DIMENSIONS

Overall length	2057mm	(81.0″)
Overall width	762mm	(30.0″)
Overall height	1016mm	(40.0″)
Wheelbase	1334mm	(52.5″)
Ground clearance	140mm	(5.5″)
Seat height	689mm	(27.0″)
Unladen weight	161 kg	(355 lb)
Fuel tank	14 litre	(3 Imp gal)
Performance	115 km/h	(71 mph) max

GEAR RATIO
I = 3.06 : 1
II = 2.12 : 1
III = 1.34 : 1
IV = 1.00 : 1

MILITARY EQUIP. rear carry rack or pillion pad, canvas panniers, masked lighting, integral cast rocker covers (aluminium shortage), all over service livery.

MODEL VELOCETTE MAF 1942

Manufacturer	Veloce Ltd, Hall Green, Birmingham
Military Service	Specialised military model (development of 1940 model MDD/WD based upon civilian MAC), specified by British armed forces for solo despatch and general liaison. In total some 5000 were supplied from 1942, with many going to the RAF.

ENGINE & TRANSMISSION

Type	Veloce, verttical ohv, single-cylinder
Capacity	349cc 50 x 96mm
Comp, ratio	
Output	14.9 hp at 5500 rpm
Starting	right foot kick start
Carburettor	single Amal 276
Electrics	6v, magneto ignition
Clutch	multi-plate, wet
Gearbox	foot-change, 4-speed
Final	exposed chain

FRAME & WHEELS

Type	tubular construction, single downtube, duplex cradle
Front forks	girder parallelogram, helical sprung, friction damped
Rear forks	without suspension
Brakes	internal expanding drums, 6" diameter front and rear
Tyre size	3.25 x 19" front and rear, road pattern

DIMENSIONS

Overall length	2159mm	(85.0")
Overall width	711mm	(28.0")
Overall height	965mm	(38.0")
Wheelbase	1321mm	(52.0")
Ground clearance	127mm	(5.0")
Seat height		
Unladen weight	154 kg	(340 lb)
Fuel tank	11.4 litre	(2.5 Imp gal)
Performance	110 km/h	(68 mph) max
	65.6 mpg, 165 miles range	

GEAR RATIO
I = 18.17 : 1
II = 9.6 : 1
III = 7.3 : 1
IV = 5.5 : 1

MILITARY EQUIP. rear carry rack or pillion pad, canvas panniers, masked lighting, cast iron timing chest and gearbox end plates, reversed gear change to fall in line with other makes, all over service livery.

ITALY

MODEL BENELLI 500 MOTOCARRO 1942

Manufacturer	Moto Benelli SpA, Pesaro
Military Service	Standard production multi-purpose tricycle, widely used as general-purpose carrier and prime mover of 47mm anti-tank gun.

ENGINE & TRANSMISSION

Type	Benelli, forward-inclined ohc, single-cylinder
Capacity	493cc 85 x 87mm
Comp, ratio	5 : 1
Output	13 hp at 4000 rpm
Starting	right foot kick start
Carburettor	single: Dell'Orto
Electrics	6v, 40 watt, coil ignition
Clutch	multi-plate, wet
Gearbox	foot-change, 4-speed
Final	exposed chain to rigid axle for two rear wheels

FRAME & WHEELS

Type	tubular construction, single downtube, extended members for platform
Front forks	girder parallelogram, helical sprung, friction damped
Rear forks	leaf sprung rear platform (wooden box design)
Brakes	internal expanding drum, all three wheels
Tyre size	3.50 x 19" all three wheels, road pattern

DIMENSIONS

Overall length	3420mm	(134.6")
Overall width	1120mm	(44.1")
Overall height	1130mm	(44.5")
Wheelbase	2170mm	(85.4")
Ground clearance		
Seat height		
Unladen weight	325 kg	(717 lb)
Fuel tank		
Performance	65 km/h	(40 mph) max

MILITARY EQUIP. open-box body for ammunition and general equipment (425 kg payload), all-over service livery.

MODEL GILERA MERCURIO 1942

Manufacturer	Moto Gilera SpA, Arcore
Military Service	Specialised military tricycle used by Italian armed forces for personnel or equipment carrying.

ENGINE & TRANSMISSION

Type	GIlera, vertical ohv, single-cylinder
Capacity	499cc 84 x 90mm
Comp, ratio	5.5 : 1
Output	18 hp at 4100 rpm
Starting	right foot kick start
Carburettor	single
Electrics	6v, Marelli magneto
Clutch	multi-plate, wet
Gearbox	hand-change, 4-speed
Final	exposed shaft to rigid axle for rear two wheels

FRAME & WHEELS

Type	pressed steel and tubular construction
Front forks	girder parallelogram, helical sprung, friction damped
Rear forks	leaf sprung rear body
Brakes	internal expanding drum, all three wheels
Tyre size	4.50 x 17" front, 6.00 x 13" rear two wheels, heavy road pattern

DIMENSIONS

Overall length	3930mm	(154.7")
Overall width	1540mm	(60.6")
Overall height	1380mm	(54.3")
Wheelbase	2220mm	(87.4")
Ground clearance		
Seat height		
Unladen weight	605 kg	(1334 lb)
Fuel tank	16 litre	(3.5 Imp gal)
Performance		

MILITARY EQUIP. with various superstructures for personnel, ammunition transport or machine gun (1495 kg payload), spare wheel, masked lighting, all-over service livery.

MODEL GILERA VL MARTE (1942)

Military Service	Specialised military sidecar model for Italian armed forces, derived from solo Gilera LTE model. Used as personnel and equipment carrier.

ENGINE & TRANSMISSION

Type	Gilera, vertical sv, single-cylinder
Capacity	499cc 84 x 90mm
Comp, ratio	5 : 1
Output	14 hp at 4800 rpm
Starting	right foot kick start
Carburettor	single: Dell'Orto
Electrics	6v, 45 watt, magneto ignition
Clutch	multi-plate, wet
Gearbox	foot- or hand-change, 4-speed
Final	exposed shaft to rear/sidecar wheels; (sidecar drive could be disengaged)

FRAME & WHEELS

Type	tubular construction, single downtube, 5 point sidecar mounting
Front forks	girder parallelogram, helical sprung, friction damped
Rear forks	helical sprung rear sub-frame, friction damped (s/a sidecar wheel)
Brakes	internal expanding drum, all three wheels
Tyre size	3.25 x 19" all three wheels, road pattern

DIMENSIONS

Overall length	2300mm	(90.6")
Overall width	1600mm	(63.0")
Overall height	1020mm	(40.2")
Wheelbase	1430mm	(56.0")
Ground clearance		
Seat height		
Unladen weight	300 kg	(661 lb)
Fuel tank	14 litre	(3.0 Imp gal)
Performance	90 km/h	(56 mph)

MILITARY EQUIP. single seat sidecar with spare wheel, rear carrier rack or pillion saddle, all-over service livery; could also be used as solo machine.

MODEL MOTO GUZZI ALCE 1939

Manufacturer	Moto Guzzi SpA, Mandello del Lario
Military Service	Specialised military model procured by Italian military (Cavalleria & Bersaglieri) for solo/sidecar despatch, reconnaissance, military police and personnel carrier duties. Produced 1939-45, a total of 6390 solo and 669 sidecar outfits supplied.

ENGINE & TRANSMISSION

Type	Moto Guzzi, horizontal exhaust-over-inlet valve, single-cylinder
Capacity	499cc 88 x 82mm
Comp, ratio	4.7 : 1
Output	13.2 hp at 4000 rpm
Starting	right foot kick start
Carburettor	single Dell'Orto MC 26 F
Electrics	6v, magneto ignition (Marelli MLA 49)
Clutch	multi-plate, dry
Gearbox	hand-change, 4-speed
Final	exposed chain

FRAME & WHEELS

Type	pressed steel and tubular construction, duplex cradle
Front forks	girder type parallelogram, helical sprung, friction damped
Rear forks	trailing rear sub frame, helical sprung, friction damped
Brakes	internal expanding drums, forward and rear
Tyre size	3.50 x 19" front and rear, heavy road pattern

DIMENSIONS

Overall length	2220mm	(87.4")
Overall width	790mm	(31.1")
Overall height	1065mm	(41.9")
Wheelbase	1450mm	(57.0")
Ground clearance	200mm	(7.8")
Seat height	710mm	(27.9")
Unladen weight	180 kg	(396 lb)
Fuel tank	13.5 litre	(3 Imp gal)
Performance	95 km/h max	(60 mph)

GEAR RATIO
I = 5.07 : 1
II = 2.84 : 1
III = 1.52 : 1
IV = 1.00 : 1

MILITARY EQUIP. rear carry rack or pillion saddle, pillion handlebars, leg shields, machine gun fittings, ski attachments (snow patrol), all-over service livery.

MODEL MOTO GUZZI AIRONE 1940

Military Service	Standard production model, works modified for military service, for solo despatch and general liaison until 1946.

ENGINE & TRANSMISSION

Type	Moto Guzzi, horizontal ohv, single-cylinder
Capacity	247cc 70 x 64mm
Comp, ratio	6 : 1
Output	9.5 hp at 4800 rpm
Starting	right foot kick start
Carburettor	single Cozette SB 22
Electrics	6v, Marelli BL magneto
Clutch	multi-plate, dry
Gearbox	foot-change, 4-speed
Final	exposed chain

FRAME & WHEELS

Type	pressed steel and tubular construction, duplex cradle design
Front forks	girder parallelogram, helical sprung, friction damped
Rear forks	trailing rear sub frame, helical sprung, friction damped
Brakes	internal expanding drums, forward and rear
Tyre size	3.00 x 19" front and rear, road pattern

DIMENSIONS

Overall length		
Overall width		
Overall height		
Wheelbase	1370mm	(53.9")
Ground clearance		
Seat height		
Unladen weight	135 kg	(298 lb)
Fuel tank	11 litre	(2.4 Imp gal)
Performance	90 km/h	(56 mph)
	(3.3 lt/100 km)	

MILITARY EQUIP. rear carrier rack or pillion pad, leg shields, masked lighting, and all-over service livery.

MODEL MOTO GUZZI TRIALCE 1940

Military Service	Specialised military tricycle model developed for Italian army, derived from the Alce motorcycle for general load carrying and machine gun mounting. Produced 1940-43 and widely used throughout the war.

ENGINE & TRANSMISSION

Type	Moto Guzzi, horizontal exhaust-over-inlet valve, single-cylinder
Capacity	499cc 88 x 82mm
Comp, ratio	4.7 : 1
Output	13.2 hp at 4000 rpm
Starting	right foot kick start
Carburettor	single Dell'Orto MC 26 F
Electrics	6v, Marelli MLA magneto ignition
Clutch	multi-plate, dry
Gearbox	hand-change, 4-speed
Final	exposed chain to rigid axle for rear two wheels

FRAME & WHEELS

Type	pressed steel and tubular construction
Front forks	girder parallelogram, helical sprung, friction damped
Rear forks	leaf sprung rear body (1942: horizontally hinged frame introduced)
Brakes	internal expanding drum, all three wheels
Tyre size	3.50 x 19" all three wheels

DIMENSIONS

Overall length	2825mm	(111.2")
Overall width	1240mm	(48.8")
Overall height	1050mm	(41.3")
Wheelbase	1880mm	(74.0")
Ground clearance	210mm	(8.3")
Seat height		
Unladen weight	355 kg	(783 lb)
Fuel tank	16 litre	(3.5 Imp gal)
Performance	74 km/h	(50 mph) max

GEAR RATIO
I = 5.07 : 1
II = 2.84 : 1
III = 1.52 : 1
IV = 1.00 : 1

MILITARY EQUIP. with various superstructures for personnel, ammunition transport or machine gun (445 kg payload), spare wheel, masked lighting, all over service livery.

MODEL MOTO GUZZI 500U 1942

Military Service	Specialised military heavyweight tricycle developed for Italian army for personnel and equipment.

ENGINE & TRANSMISSION

Type	Moto Guzzi, horizontal ohv single-cylinder
Capacity	499cc 88 x 82mm
Comp, ratio	5.5 : 1
Output	17.8 hp at 4300 rpm
Starting	right foot kick start
Carburettor	single Dell'Orto 2 MC 25
Electrics	6v
Clutch	multi-plate, dry
Gearbox	hand-change, 4-speed
Final	chain to rigid axle for two rear wheels

FRAME & WHEELS

Type	pressed steel and tubular construction, extended I section
Front forks	pressed steel parallelogram, helical sprung, friction damped
Rear forks	leaf sprung rear platform
Brakes	internal expanding drum, all three wheels
Tyre size	3.5 x 19" front, 6.00 x 16" rear, road pattern (also available with heavier disc-type front wheel and 6.00 x 16" tyre)

DIMENSIONS

Overall length	3580mm	(140.9")
Overall width	1498mm	(59.0")
Overall height	2025mm	(79.7")
Wheelbase	2300mm	(90.6")
Ground clearance		
Seat height		
Unladen weight	1620 kg	(1367 lb)
Fuel tank	16 litre	(3.5 Imp gal)
Performance	60 km/h	(37 mph) max
	(7 lt/100 km)	

MILITARY EQUIP. various superstructures for personnel, ammunition and equipment carrier, (1,000 kg payload), leg shields, spare wheel and all-

over service livery. At least one example prepared as Anti-Aircraft machine gun mount.

JAPAN

MODEL	KUROGANE 'SANRINSHA' 1939
Manufacturer	Nippon Nainenki Seiko Co, Tokyo
Military Service	Standard production tricycle used by Japanese armed forces for personnel or equipment transportation. Various versions produced by several factories (Iwasaki, Toyo Kogyo, etc), with single & V-twin engines, widely used throughout Pacific operations.

ENGINE & TRANSMISSION

Type	Kurogane, 45° sv, V-twin
Capacity	750cc 70 x 97mm
Comp. ratio	5 : 1
Output	23 hp
Starting	right foot kick start
Carburettor	single
Electrics	6v, 35/45 watt
Clutch	multi-plate, wet
Gearbox	hand-change, 3-speed & reverse
Final	exposed shaft to car-type rear axle

FRAME & WHEELS

Type	pressed steel construction, extended for various requirements
Front forks	pressed steel parallelogram, helical sprung, friction damped
Rear forks	leaf sprung rear body
Brakes	internal expanding drum, all three wheels
Tyre size	4.75 x 18″ all three wheels, heavy road pattern, disc-type wheels

DIMENSIONS

Overall length	2730mm	(107.4″)
Overall width	1220mm	(48.0″)
Overall height	1220mm	(48.0″)
Wheelbase	1900mm	(74.8″)
Ground clearance		
Seat height		
Unladen weight	540 kg	(1191 lb)
Fuel tank		
Performance		

MILITARY EQUIP. with various superstructures for personnel, ammunition and water carrier, (5 soldiers or 550 kg payload), spare wheel, masked lighting, and all over service livery.

SWEDEN

MODEL	MONARK m/42 ohv 1942
Manufacturer	AB Cykelfabriken Monark, Varberg
Military Service	Specialised military model prepared for Swedish armed forces, for multi-terrain solo despatch and general liaison. 3,000+ supplied and remained in service until mid-60s. Also produced with side-valve engine.

ENGINE & TRANSMISSION

Type	Albin/HVA, vertical ohv, single-cylinder
Capacity	495cc 79 x 101mm
Comp. ratio	6.4 : 1
Output	20 hp at 4000 rpm
Starting	right foot kick start
Carburettor	single Amal 276
Electrics	6v, magneto ignition (Bosch W 175-T)
Clutch	multi-plate, wet
Gearbox	foot-change, 3-speed
Final	exposed chain

FRAME & WHEELS

Type	pressed steel and tubular construction, rear wheel sub-frame
Front forks	girder parallelogram, helical sprung, friction damped
Rear forks	plunger design, helical sprung
Brakes	internal expanding drums, 185mm diameter front and rear
Tyre size	3.50 x 19″ front and rear, heavy road pattern

DIMENSIONS

Overall length	2120mm	(83.4″)
Overall width	740mm	(29.1″)
Overall height	940mm	(37.0″)
Wheelbase	1410mm	(55.5″)
Ground clearance	145mm	(5.7″)
Seat height	760mm	(29.9″)
Unladen weight	200 kg	(440 lb)
Fuel tank	13.5 litre	(3 Imp gal)
Performance	110 km/h	(68 mph) max

MILITARY EQUIP. rear carry rack or pillion saddle, leather panniers, additional masked lighting, all over service livery.

MODEL	NV MILITARY 1000cc 1943
Manufacturer	Nymans Verkstäder, Uppsala
Military Service	Specialised military model developed for Swedish army; a multi-terrain heavyweight sidecar outfit for personnel and equipment carrier, limited production only before project was abandoned. (NV supplied a 125cc lightweight for military use in 1953).

ENGINE & TRANSMISSION

Type	Albin/NV, ohv, V-twin
Capacity	990cc 79 x 101mm
Comp. ratio	6.4 : 1
Output	36 hp at 4000 rpm
Starting	right foot kick start
Carburettor	single Amal
Electrics	6v
Clutch	multi-plate, wet
Gearbox	hand-change, 3-2 & reverse
Final	exposed shaft to rear and sidecar wheel

FRAME & WHEELS

Type	pressed steel and tubular construction, single downtube
Front forks	telescopic, helical sprung, hydraulic damping
Rear forks	without suspension
Brakes	internal expanding drums, all three wheels, hydraulic operation
Tyre size	5.00 x 16″ all three wheels, cross country pattern

DIMENSIONS

Overall length	2400mm	(94.4″) w/sc
Overall width	1640mm	(64.5″) w/sc
Overall height	1090mm	(42.9″) w/sc
Wheelbase	1480mm	(58.2″) w/sc
Ground clearance	200mm	(7.8″) w/sc
Seat height		
Unladen weight	500 kg	(1102 lb) w/sc
Fuel tank	25 litre	(5.5 Imp gal) w/sc
Performance	100 km/h	(62 mph) max w/sc

GEAR RATIO

I	= 10.6 : 1	road	
II	= 6.9 : 1	road	
III	= 5.2 : 1	road	
R	= 12.8 : 1	road	
I	= 28.0 : 1	off road	
II	= 18.0 : 1	off road	
III	= 13.6 : 1	off road	
R	= 34.0 : 1	off road	

MILITARY EQUIP. pillion saddle, high level exhaust, spare wheel and machine gun fittings on sidecar, and all over service livery.

USA

MODEL	CUSHMAN 53 AUTOGLIDE 1944
Manufacturer	Cushman Motor Works, Lincoln, Nebraska
Military Service	Specialised lightweight military model prepared for American airborne troops. A total of 4734 supplied 1944-45.

ENGINE & TRANSMISSION

Type	Husky 16M71, fan-cooled sv, single-cylinder
Capacity	244cc 66.7 x 69.9mm
Comp. ratio	
Output	4.6 hp at 3600 rpm
Starting	left foot kick start
Carburettor	single
Electrics	6v, 35/45 watt, magneto ignition
Clutch	centrifugal clutch
Gearbox	hand-change, 2-speed
Final	exposed chain

FRAME & WHEELS

Type	pressed steel and tubular construction
Front forks	reinforced tubes, without suspension
Rear forks	without suspension
Brakes	internal expanding drum, rear wheel only
Tyre size	6.00 x 6″ front and rear, road pattern

DIMENSIONS

Overall length	1956mm	(77.0″)
Overall width	584mm	(23.0″)
Overall height	965mm	(38.0″)
Wheelbase	1448mm	(57.0″)
Ground clearance	170mm	(6.7″)
Seat height		
Unladen weight	116 kg	(255 lb)
Fuel tank	7.6 litre	(2 US gal)
Performance	64 km/h	(40 mph) max (100 mile range)

GEAR RATIO

I	= 15.2 : 1	
II	= 5.0 : 1	

MILITARY EQUIP. parachute attachment rings and rear pintle hook, side stand, and all-over service livery.

MODEL	HARLEY-DAVIDSON WLA 1939
Manufacturer	Harley-Davidson Motor Co, Milwaukee, Wisconsin
Military Service	Standard production model widely used for despatch, escort, convoy control and military police. 89,000+ built 1939-44; 60,000+ to US forces, remainder mainly British & Commonwealth many used until late 1950s.

ENGINE & TRANSMISSION

Type	Harley-Davidson, sv V-twin
Capacity	740cc 69.85 x 96.85mm
Comp. ratio	6 : 1
Output	23 hp at 4500 rpm
Starting	right foot kick start
Carburettor	single Schebler
Electrics	6v, coil ignition
Clutch	multi-plate, wet
Gearbox	hand-change, 3-speed
Final	exposed chain

FRAME & WHEELS

Type	tubular construction, duplex cradle
Front forks	leading link, helical sprung, friction damped
Rear forks	without suspension
Brakes	internal expanding drum, front and rear
Tyre size	4.00 x 18″ front and rear

DIMENSIONS

Overall length	2235mm	(88.0″)
Overall width	920mm	(36.25″)
Overall height	1041mm	(41.0″)
Wheelbase	1460mm	(57.5″)
Ground clearance	102mm	(4.0″)
Seat height		
Unladen weight	242 kg	(535 lb)
Fuel tank	12.5 litre	(2.7 Imp gal)
Performance	96 km/h	(60 mph) (119 mile range)

GEAR RATIO

I	= 2.47 : 1	
II	= 1.57 : 1	
III	= 1.00 : 1	

MILITARY EQUIP. rear carry rack, leather panniers, front and rear crash bars, wind screen, a scabbard for Thompson machine gun or rifle mounted on right front fork leg, crank case guard, all over service livery and black exhaust system.

MODEL	HARLEY-DAVIDSON ELA 1939
Military Service	Standard production model used for sidecar despatch, escort and military police. Supplied 1939-42 to US forces, Defence-Aid & Lend-Lease (mainly British & Commonwealth). Very similar to Harley-Davidson UA military sidecar outfit, with larger 1200cc V-twin engine.

ENGINE & TRANSMISSION

Type	H-D, sv 42° V-twin
Capacity	987cc 84.1 x 88.9mm
Comp. ratio	6 : 1
Output	
Starting	right foot kick start
Carburettor	single Schebler
Electrics	6v
Clutch	multi-plate, wet
Gearbox	hand-change, 3-speed
Final	exposed chain

FRAME & WHEELS

Type	tubular construction, duplex cradle
Front forks	leading link, helical sprung, friction damped
Rear forks	without suspension
Brakes	internal expanding drums, all three wheels
Tyre size	4.50 x 18″ all three wheels, heavy road pattern

DIMENSIONS

Overall length	2426mm	(95.5″) w/sc
Overall width	1753mm	(69.0″) w/sc
Overall height	1079mm	(42.4″) w/sc
Wheelbase	1511mm	(59.4″) w/sc
Ground clearance	105mm	(4.1″) w/sc
Seat height		
Unladen weight	386 kg	(850 lb) w/sc
Fuel tank	15.1 litre	(3.3 Imp gal) w/sc
Performance	88 km/h	(55 mph) w/sc 112 mile range

MILITARY EQUIP. rear carry rack or pillion saddle, front and rear crash bars, leg shield and windscreen, spare wheel and machine gun fittings on sidecar, all over service livery and black exhaust system.

MODEL	HARLEY-DAVIDSON XA 1942
Military Service	Specialised military model developed for American Forces; a multi-terrain solo despatch and general liaison duties. More than 1000 built before project abandoned. XS model with sidecar wheel drive also prepared, but remained experimental.

ENGINE & TRANSMISSION

Type	H-D, transverse sv, flat-twin
Capacity	739cc 77.8 x 77.8mm
Comp. ratio	5.7 : 1
Output	23 hp at 4500 rpm
Starting	right foot kick start
Carburettor	twin Schebler, single air filter
Electrics	6v, coil ignition
Clutch	single plate, dry
Gearbox	right-hand & left foot-change, 4-speed
Final	exposed shaft

FRAME & WHEELS

Type	tubular construction, duplex cradle
Front forks	leading link, helical sprung, friction damped
Rear forks	plunger type, helical sprung, undamped
Brakes	internal expanding drums, front and rear
Tyre size	4.00 x 18″ front and rear, heavy road pattern

DIMENSIONS

Overall length	2286mm	(90.0″)
Overall width	914mm	(35.9″)
Overall height	1022mm	(40.2″)
Wheelbase	1511mm	(59.4″)
Ground clearance		
Seat height		
Unladen weight	238 kg	(525 lb)
Fuel tank	15.2 litre	(3.3 Imp gal)
Performance	96 km/h	(60 mph) max

MILITARY EQUIP. rear carry rack, leather panniers, additional masked lighting, windscreen and legshields, front and rear crash bars, all over service livery.

MODEL   INDIAN 841 1942

Manufacturer	Indian Motorcycle Co, Springfield, Massachusetts
Military Service	Specialised military model developed for American Forces; a multi-terrain machine for solo despatch and general liaison duties. More than 1000 built before U.S. Government reconsidered the contract and the project was abandoned.

ENGINE & TRANSMISSION

Type	Indian, transverse 90°, sv V-twin
Capacity	744cc 73 x 88.9mm
Comp. ratio	6 : 1
Output	24 hp at 4000 rpm
Starting	left foot kick start
Carburettor	twin Schebler single filter
Electrics	6v
Clutch	single plate, dry
Gearbox	foot-change (heel & toe), 4-speed
Final	exposed shaft drive

FRAME & WHEELS

Type	tubular construction, duplex cradle
Front forks	parallelogram, helical sprung, friction damped
Rear forks	plunger type, helical sprung, undamped
Brakes	internal expanding drums, front and rear
Tyre size	4.00 x 18″ front and rear, heavy road pattern

DIMENSIONS

Overall length	2305mm	(90.75″)
Overall width	934mm	(36.75″)
Overall height	1029mm	(40.5″)
Wheelbase	1499mm	(59.0″)
Ground clearance		
Seat height		
Unladen weight	256 kg	(564 lb)
Fuel tank		
Performance	96 km/h	(60 mph) max

MILITARY EQUIP. rear carry rack, leather panniers, additional masked lighting, all-over service livery.

MODEL   INDIAN 340 1939

Military Service	Standard production model works modified for military use, originally prepared for French army in 1939 but subsequently used by US and other Allied Forces (mainly British & Commonwealth), for sidecar despatch, convoy escort and military police duties.

ENGINE & TRANSMISSION

Type	Indian, sv V-twin
Capacity	1206cc 82.55 x 112.71mm
Comp. ratio	
Output	30 hp at 4000 rpm
Starting	right foot kick start
Carburettor	single Schebler
Electrics	6v
Clutch	multi-plate, wet
Gearbox	hand-change, 3-speed
Final	exposed chain

FRAME & WHEELS

Type	tubular construction, single downtube
Front forks	trailing link, leaf sprung, friction damped
Rear forks	plunger type, helical sprung, undamped
Brakes	internal expanding drums, all three wheels
Tyre size	4.50 x 18″ all three wheels, heavy road pattern

DIMENSIONS

Overall length	2477mm	(97.5″) w/sc
Overall width	2248mm	(88.5″) w/sc
Overall height	1118mm	(44.0″) w/sc
Wheelbase	1562mm	(61.4″) w/sc
Ground clearance	133mm	(5.2″) w/sc
Seat height		
Unladen weight	383 kg	(845 lb) w/sc
Fuel tank	13.2 litre	(3.5 U.S. gal) w/sc
Performance	88 km/h	(55 mph) max

MILITARY EQUIP. rear carry or pillion saddle, leather panniers, front and rear crash bars, spare wheel and machine gun fittings on sidecar, all over service livery and black exhaust system.

MODEL   INDIAN 640-A 1939

Military Service	Standard production model works modified for military service use and supplied 1939-42 to US & Allied armed forces (mainly British & Commonwealth), for solo despatch, etc. At least some 18,600 produced. Re-designated as the 741-A.

ENGINE & TRANSMISSION

Type	Indian, sv V-twin
Capacity	493cc 63.5 x 77.9mm
Comp. ratio	
Output	15 hp at 4000 rpm
Starting	right foot kick start
Carburettor	single Schebler
Electrics	6v
Clutch	multi-plate, wet
Gearbox	hand-change, 3-speed
Final	exposed chain

FRAME & WHEELS

Type	tubular construction, single downtube
Front forks	girder parallelogram, helical sprung, friction damped
Rear forks	without suspension
Brakes	internal expanding drums, front and rear
Tyre size	3.50 x 18″ front and rear, heavy road pattern

DIMENSIONS

Overall length	2238mm	(88.125″)
Overall width	851mm	(33.5″)
Overall height	1010mm	(39.75″)
Wheelbase	1442mm	(56.75″)
Ground clearance		
Seat height		
Unladen weight	209 kg	(460 lb)
Fuel tank		
Performance	88 km/h	(55 mph) max

MILITARY EQUIP. rear carry rack, leather panniers, front and rear crash bars, all-over service livery, and black exhaust system.

MODEL   INDIAN 640-B 1939

Military Service	Standard production model works modified for military use, supplied 1939-42 to US & Allied armed forces (mainly British & Commonwealth), for solo despatch, etc.

ENGINE & TRANSMISSION

Type	Indian, sv V-twin
Capacity	744cc 73 x 88.9mm
Comp. ratio	
Output	24 hp at 4000 rpm
Starting	right foot kick start
Carburettor	single Schebler
Electrics	6v
Clutch	multi-plate, wet
Gearbox	hand-change, 3-speed
Final	exposed chain

FRAME & WHEELS

Type	tubular construction, single downtube
Front forks	girder parallelogram, helical sprung, friction damped
Rear forks	without suspension
Brakes	internal expanding drums, front and rear
Tyre size	4.00 x 18″ front and rear, heavy road pattern

DIMENSIONS

Overall length	2286mm	(90.0″)
Overall width	32.5mm	(826″)
Overall height	1169mm	(46.0″)
Wheelbase	1448mm	(57.0″)
Ground clearance	127mm	(5.0″)
Seat height		
Unladen weight	245 kg	(540 lb)
Fuel tank	13.2 litre	(2.9 Imp gal)
Performance	96 km/h	(60 mph)
	147 mile range	

MILITARY EQUIP. rear carry rack, leather panniers, front and rear crash bars, all-over service livery, and black exhaust system.

MODEL   SIMPLEX SERVI-CYCLE (1942)

Manufacturer	Simplex, New Orleans, Louisiana
Military Service	Standard production model, works modified for American airborne troops. A total of 654 delivered 1942-43.

ENGINE & TRANSMISSION

Type	Simplex, vertical single-cylinder, two-stroke, twin spark plugs
Capacity	194cc
Comp. ratio	
Output	4 hp at 4000 rpm
Starting	push start
Carburettor	single: butterfly design
Electrics	6v, flywheel magneto
Clutch	centrifugal drum
Gearbox	foot-change, variable-ratio pulleys
Final	exposed V-belt, idler/tensioner on secondary belt

FRAME & WHEELS

Type	tubular construction, duplex loops
Front forks	leading link, parallelogram, helical sprung
Rear forks	without suspension
Brakes	internal expanding drum, rear wheel only
Tyre size	2.25 x 26″ front and rear, road pattern

DIMENSIONS

Overall length	1778mm	(70.0″)
Overall width	711mm	(28.0″)
Overall height	965mm	(38.0″)
Wheelbase	1422mm	(56.0″)
Ground clearance		
Seat height		
Unladen weight	74.8 kg	(165 lb)
Fuel tank		
Performance	48 km/h	(30 mph)

MILITARY EQUIP. rear carrier rack, parachute attachment rings, rear pintle hook, head-lamp, and all over service livery.

MODEL   IZH-9 1940

Manufacturer	Izhevsk Motorcycle Works, Ustinov
Military Service	Standard production model works modified for Soviet armed forces in 1940, for solo lightweight despatch and general liaison duties.

ENGINE & TRANSMISSION

Type	Izh, vertical single-cylinder, twin-port, two-stroke
Capacity	293cc 74 x 68mm
Comp. ratio	5.8 : 1
Output	9 hp at 4000 rpm
Starting	right foot kick start
Carburettor	single
Electrics	6v
Clutch	multi-plate, wet
Gearbox	hand-change, 3-speed
Final	exposed chain

FRAME & WHEELS

Type	pressed steel and tubular construction, single downtube
Front forks	girder parallelogram, helical sprung, friction damped
Rear forks	without suspension
Brakes	internal expanding drums, front and rear
Tyre size	3.25 x 19″ front and rear, road pattern

DIMENSIONS

Overall length		
Overall width		
Overall height		
Wheelbase	1370mm	(53.9″)
Ground clearance	105mm	(4.1″)
Seat height		
Unladen weight	137 kg	(302 lb)
Fuel tank	14 litre	(3 Imp gal)
Performance	90 km/h	(55 mph)

MILITARY EQUIP. rear carry rack or pillion pad, panniers, masked lighting, all-over service livery.

MODEL   M-72 1941

Manufacturer	Iskra Zavad Plant, Moscow
Military Service	Specialised military model based on BMW R71, for solo/sidecar despatch, convoy control, personnel carrier and military police duties. Remained in military service until 1956, when superseded by K-750, with improved engine and revised suspension.

ENGINE & TRANSMISSION

Type	IZP, transverse sv, flat-twin
Capacity	746cc 78 x 78mm
Comp. ratio	5.5 : 1
Output	22 hp at 4600 rpm
Starting	left foot kick start
Carburettor	twin K-37
Electrics	6v
Clutch	single-plate, dry
Gearbox	hand-change, 4-speed
Final	exposed shaft

FRAME & WHEELS

Type	tubular construction, duplex cradle
Front forks	telescopic, helical sprung, hydraulic damping
Rear forks	plunger type, helical sprung, undamped
Brakes	internal expanding drums, 200mm diameter front and rear
Tyre size	3.75 x 19″ front and rear

DIMENSIONS

Overall length	2130mm	(83.8″) solo
Overall width	815mm	(32.0″) solo
Overall height	960mm	(37.7″) solo
Wheelbase	1400mm	(55.1″) solo
Ground clearance	135mm	(5.3″) solo
Seat height		
Unladen weight	205 kg	(451 lb) solo
Fuel tank	22 litre	(4.8 Imp gal) solo
Performance	105 km/h	(65 mph) max solo

GEAR RATIO

I	= 3.60 : 1
II	= 2.28 : 1
III	= 1.70 : 1
IV	= 1.30 : 1

MILITARY EQUIP. rear carry rack or pillion saddle, spare wheel and machine gun fittings on sidecar, all over service livery.

CHAPTER FOUR

Post-War Production – 1946–66

The following specifications are for 40 of the best known motorcycles and motorised tricycles in military service in the twenty years following World War 2. Those mentioned in the text are cross referenced below. All are listed on the following pages in alphabetical order by country.

Austria
Puch 250SG 1956 *p 149*
Puch 175MCH 1959 *p 149*

Belgium
FN Military M13 1951
FN AS24 1959 *p 149*
Gillet-Herstal 500 AB 1951
Sarolea AS350 1951

Czechoslovakia
Jawa 350 Military 554/05 1963 *p 130*

France
Terrot Military HCT 1951
Terrot Military RGST 1951 *p 149*

Germany (East)
EMW R35 1946

Germany (West)
BMW R51 1950 *p 140*
BMW R25 1950 *p 141*
DKW Military RT 175VS 1955 *p 141*
Maico M250/3 1961 *p 141*
Triumph BDG 250SL 1955 *p 141*

Great Britain
AJS 18CS 1956 *p 140*
BSA A65 1962 *p 140*
James J10 Comet 1949 *p 136*
Matchless G3LS 1961 *p 140*
Triumph TRW 1948 *p 136*
Triumph T100 1955 *p 137*
Triumph Military 3TA 1963 *p 137*

Italy
Bianchi MT61 1961 *p 149*
Gilera Saturno 500 Militare 1950 *p 149*
Gilera 175 Militare 1956
Moto Guzzi Superalce 1946
Moto Guzzi 250 Airone Sport 1952 *p 149*
Moto Guzzi 500 Falcone Turismo 1953 *p 149*
Moto Guzzi 125 Sturnello 1960
Moto Guzzi 3 x 3 1960 *p 149*

Norway
Tempo Taifun Militaer 1969 *p 149*

Sweden
Monark MC 252
Monark MC356A 1963 *p 147*
NV MOD.38 1955

Switzerland
Condor A580-1 1948 *p 142*
Condor A250 1959 *p 142*

USA
Indian 148M 1947 *p 133*
Indian 149M 1953 *p 133*
Harley-Davidson G 1950 *p 133*

USSR
M-72 to K750 M 1941-77 *p 131*

AUSTRIA

MODEL   PUCH 250 SG 1956

Manufacturer   Steyr-Daimler-Puch AG, Graz
Military Service   Standard production model, works modified for military service, adopt by Austrian armed forces for solo despatch and occasional pillion use upon surfaced roads only.

ENGINE & TRANSMISSION
Type	Puch, two-stroke, split-single
Capacity	248cc 2 x 45 x 78mm
Comp. ratio	6.2 : 1
Output	13.8 hp at 5800 rpm
Starting	left foot kick start
Carburettor	single Puch 32mm Ø
Electrics	6v, 45/60 watt (Bosch W 225 T 1)
Clutch	multi-plate, wet
Gearbox	foot-change, 4-speed
Final	enclosed chain

FRAME & WHEELS
Type	tubular and pressed steel construction (single downtube)
Front forks	telescopic, helical sprung, hydraulic damping
Rear forks	trailing, helical sprung, hydraulic damping
Brakes	internal expanding drum, 180mm diameter 40mm wide, front and rear
Tyre size	3.50 x 16″ front and rear, road pattern

DIMENSIONS
Overall length	1985mm	(78.1″)
Overall width	645mm	(25.3″)
Overall height	920mm	(36.2″)
Wheelbase	1345mm	(52.9″)
Ground clearance	140mm	(5.5″)
Seat height	735mm	(28.9″)
Unladen weight	155 kg	(341 lb)
Fuel tank	13 litre	(2.8 Imp gal)
Performance	105 km/h	(65 mph) max

GEAR RATIO
I	= 19.5 : 1
II	= 10.6 : 1
III	= 77.1 : 1
R	= 5.4 : 1

MILITARY EQUIP. rear carrier rack or pillion saddle, canvas pannier bags, hand pump, all over service livery.

MODEL   PUCH 175 MCH 1959

Military Service   Standard production model, works modified for military service, adopt by Austrian armed forces for solo despatch and occasional pillion use multi-terrain restricted distance service.

ENGINE & TRANSMISSION
Type	Puch, two-stroke, split-single
Capacity	172cc 2 x 42 x 62 mm
Comp. ratio	7 : 1
Output	10 hp at 5800 rpm
Starting	left foot kick start
Carburettor	single Puch 24mm Ø
Electrics	6v, 40/50 watt (Bosch W 225 T 1)
Clutch	multi-plate, wet
Gearbox	foot-change, 4-speed
Final	enclosed chain

FRAME & WHEELS
Type	tubular and pressed steel construction (single downtube)
Front forks	telescopic, helical sprung, hydraulic damping, 110mm travel
Rear forks	trailing, helical sprung, hydraulic damping, 90mm travel
Brakes	internal expanding drum, 160mm diameter 35mm wide, front and rear
Tyre size	3.25 x 19″ front and rear, trials pattern

DIMENSIONS
Overall length	2030mm	(80.0″)
Overall width	750mm	(29.5″)
Overall height	1030mm	(40.5″)
Wheelbase	1320mm	(52.0″)
Ground clearance	190mm	(7.5″)
Seat height	775mm	(30.5″)
Unladen weight	135 kg	(298 lb)
Fuel tank	11.5 litre	(2.5 Imp gal)
Performance	78 km/h	(48 mph) max

GEAR RATIO
I	= 30.01 : 1
II	= 16.55 : 1
III	= 11.75 : 1
R	= 8.2 : 1

MILITARY EQUIP. rear carriage rack or pillion pad, fuel tank-top bag, canvas pannier bags, hand pump, all over service livery.

BELGIUM

MODEL   FN MILITARY M13 1951

Manufacturer   Fabrique Nationale, Herstal, Belgium
Military Service   Standard production model works modified for military service, adopted by Belgian armed forces for solo despatch, escort, military police and general liaison. Between June and December 1951, a total of 1030 of these machines were supplied.

ENGINE & TRANSMISSION
Type	FN, air cooled vertical cylinder, side valves
Capacity	450cc (84.5mm bore x 80mm stroke)
Comp. ratio	5 : 1
Output	12 hp at 3500 rpm
Starting	right foot kick start
Carburettor	single Amal
Electrics	6v, Lucas or Miller mag-dyno
Clutch	multi-plate, wet operation
Gearbox	right foot-change, 4-speed, separate unit
Final	exposed chain, upper guard only

FRAME & WHEELS
Type	tubular single loop design
Front forks	rigid forks rubber sprung
Rear forks	without suspension
Brakes	internal expanding drum front and rear
Tyre size	3.50 x 26″ front and rear

DIMENSIONS
Overall length	2200mm	(86.6″)
Overall width	830mm	(32.6″)
Overall height	1030mm	(40.5″)
Wheelbase	1280mm	(50.3″)
Ground clearance	200mm	(7.8″)
Seat height		
Unladen weight	140 kg	(308 lb)
Fuel tank		
Performance	100 km/h	(63 mph)

MILITARY EQUIP. rear carry rack or pillion pad, leather panniers, front crash bars, all-over service livery.

MODEL   FN AS24 1959

Manufacturer   Fabrique Nationale SA, Herstal
Military Service   Specialised military model, built under licence, for Belgian airborne troops. A folding tricycle for parachute use, taking one minute to become operational. About 500 produced for Belgian army and export.

ENGINE & TRANSMISSION
Type	FN, vertical two-stroke twin
Capacity	243.5cc (mounted above rear axle)
Comp. ratio	
Output	15 hp at 5300 rpm
Starting	
Carburettor	single
Electrics	6v, magneto ignition (no other electrical equipment)
Clutch	multi-plate
Gearbox	hand-change, 4-speed
Final	exposed chain

FRAME & WHEELS
Type	tubular and box-section construction
Front forks	Front and rear suspension provided by single front and two rear 'Lypsoid' tyres (with steering wheel)
Rear forks	
Brakes	internal expanding drum, rear two wheels only
Tyre size	22 x 12″ all three wheels, heavy road pattern

DIMENSIONS
Overall length	1836mm	(72.3″) when 'folded' (1040mm)
Overall width	1640mm	(64.6″) when 'folded' (1640mm)
Overall height	900mm	(35.5″) when 'folded' (770mm)
Wheelbase	1270mm	(50.0″)
Ground clearance		
Seat height		
Unladen weight	220 kg	(485 lb)
Fuel tank		
Performance	57 km/h	(35 mph) max

MILITARY EQUIP. various models providing transport for four (bench seat across frame), driver plus 250 kg load, also fire fighting and other special equip. Exp. model with half-track conversion, and two wheeled trailer.

MODEL   GILLET-HERSTAL 500 ESTATETTE AB 1951

Manufacturer   Gillet SA, Herstal, Belgium
Military Service   Standard production model works modified for military service, adopted by Belgian armed forces in 1951, for solo despatch and general liaison duties. Also available as 400cc version.

ENGINE & TRANSMISSION
Type	Gillet, air cooled vertical single cylinder, side valves
Capacity	489cc (77mm bore x 105mm stroke)
Comp. ratio	5.5 : 1
Output	14 hp at 4200 rpm
Starting	left foot kick start
Carburettor	single Amal 24mm Ø
Electrics	6v, 40 watt
Clutch	multi-plate, wet operation
Gearbox	right foot-change, 4-speed, integral design
Final	exposed chain, upper guard only

FRAME & WHEELS
Type	tubular single loop design
Front forks	telescopic, hydraulic damping

Rear forks	plunger type rear suspension, helical sprung	
Brakes	internal expanding drum, front and rear, 180mm diameter 30mm wide	
Tyre size	3.50 x 26″ front and rear, road pattern	

DIMENSIONS

Overall length	2050mm	(80.7″)
Overall width	720mm	(28.3″)
Overall height	1080mm	(42.5″)
Wheelbase	1380mm	(54.3″)
Ground clearance	160mm	(6.2″)
Seat height		
Unladen weight	170 kg	(374 lb)
Fuel tank	17 litre	(3.7 Imp gal)
Performance	110 km/h	(68 mph)

GEAR RATIO

		MILITARY EQUIP. rear carry rack or pillion pad, leather panniers, front crash bars, all-over service livery.
I	= 12.8 : 1	
II	= 8.2 : 1	
III	= 5.9 : 1	
IV	= 4.5 : 1	

MODEL SAROLEA MILITARY AS350 1951

Manufacturer	Sarolea SA, Herstal, Belgium
Military Service	Standard production model works modified for military service, adopted by Belgian armed forces in 1951, for solo despatch and general liaison duties. Also available as 400cc version.

ENGINE & TRANSMISSION

Type	Sarolea, air cooled vertical single cylinder, side valves
Capacity	348cc (75mm bore x 79mm stroke)
Comp, ratio	5 : 1
Output	10 hp at 4200 rpm
Starting	right foot kick start
Carburettor	single Amal
Electrics	6v
Clutch	multi-plate, wet operation
Gearbox	right foot-change, 4-speed, separate unit
Final	exposed chain, upper guard only

FRAME & WHEELS

Type	tubular single loop design
Front forks	telescopic, hydraulic damping
Rear forks	plunger type rear suspension, helical sprung
Brakes	internal expanding drum, front and rear, 180mm diameter 25mm wide
Tyre size	3.25 x 26″ front and rear, road pattern

DIMENSIONS

Overall length	2120mm	(83.4″)
Overall width	700mm	(27.5″)
Overall height	1100mm	(43.3″)
Wheelbase	1400mm	(55.1″)
Ground clearance		
Seat height		
Unladen weight	130 kg	(286 lb)
Fuel tank	13 litre	(2.8 Imp gal)
Performance	90~ km/h	(56 mph)

GEAR RATIO

		MILITARY EQUIP. rear carry rack or pillion pad, leather panniers, front crash bars, all over service livery.
I	= 13.5 : 1	
II	= 9.5 : 1	
III	= 6.9 : 1	
IV	= 5.7 : 1	

CZECHOSLOVAKIA

MODEL JAWA 350 MILITARY 554/05 1963

Manufacturer	Zbrojovka F. Janecek, Prague
Military Service	Standard production model procured by Finnish and Swedish military in 1963; a solo multi-terrain machine with the option of ski use, for despatch and general liaison all year. Also supplied in 250cc form.

ENGINE & TRANSMISSION

Type	Jawa, vertical-twin, two-stroke
Capacity	344cc 58 x 65mm
Comp, ratio	8 : 1
Output	18 hp at 4750 rpm
Starting	left foot kick start
Carburettor	single Jikov 2924 SBD
Electrics	6v, 45 watt
Clutch	multi-plate, wet
Gearbox	foot and hand-change, 4-speed
Final	enclosed chain
Note: Also refer to sections for Sweden and Finland – Chapter 4	

FRAME & WHEELS

Type	pressed steel and tubular construction, single downdown
Front forks	telescopic, hydraulic damping, 150mm travel
Rear forks	trailing, hydraulic damping
Brakes	internal expanding drum, front and rear, 160mm Ø hand and foot control
Tyre size	3.00 x 21″ front, 3.50 x 19″ rear, trials pattern

DIMENSIONS

Overall length	1980mm	(77.9″)
Overall width	670mm	(26.3″)
Overall height	1025mm	(40.3″)
Wheelbase	1318mm	(51.8″)
Ground clearance		
Seat height		
Unladen weight	160 kg	(4.24 lb)
Fuel tank	13.5 litre	(3 Imp gal)
Performance	120 km/h	(75 mph)

GEAR RATIO

I	= 13.42 : 1
II	= 7.44 : 1
III	= 5.36 : 1
IV	= 4.24 : 1

MILITARY EQUIP. rear carry rack, fuel tank leather bag, additional masked lighting, optional ski attachments (snow patrol), all-over service livery.

FRANCE

MODEL TERROT TYPE MILITARY HCT (1951)

Manufacturer	Ets Terrot, Dijon, France
Military Service	Standard production model works modified for military service, adopted by French armed forces in 1951, for solo despatch and general liaison duties.

ENGINE & TRANSMISSION

Type	Terrot, air cooled vertical single cylinder, side valves
Capacity	346cc (70mm bore x 90mm stroke)
Comp, ratio	5 : 1
Output	8 hp at 4000 rpm
Starting	right foot kick start
Carburettor	single Amac 5/012
Electrics	6v
Clutch	multi-plate, wet operation
Gearbox	right foot-change, 4-speed, separate unit
Final	exposed chain, upper guard only

FRAME & WHEELS

Type	tubular single loop design
Front forks	telescopic, hydraulic damping, 90mm travel
Rear forks	without suspension
Brakes	internal expanding drum, front and rear
Tyre size	3.50 x 26″ front and rear

DIMENSIONS

Overall length		
Overall width		
Overall height		
Wheelbase	1400mm	(55.1″)
Ground clearance	110mm	(4.3″)
Seat height		
Unladen weight	160 kg	(353 lb)
Fuel tank	18 litre	(4 Imp gal)
Performance	100 km/h	(62 mph)

MILITARY EQUIP. rear carry rack, leather panniers, front crash bars, all over service livery.

MODEL TERROT MILITARY RGST 1951

Manufacturer	Ets Terrot, Dijon
Military Service	Standard production model works modified for military service by French forces in 1951, for solo despatch, escort, military police and general liaison.

ENGINE & TRANSMISSION

Type	Terrot, vertical ohv single cylinder
Capacity	498cc 84 x 80mm
Comp, ratio	6.6 : 1
Output	21 hp at 4800 rpm
Starting	right foot kick start
Carburettor	single Amac 6/024, 27mm 27mm Ø
Electrics	6v, 35 watt
Clutch	multi-plate, wet
Gearbox	foot-change, 4-speed
Final	exposed chain

FRAME & WHEELS

Type	tubular single loop design
Front forks	telescopic, hydraulic damping, 110mm travel
Rear forks	plunger type rear suspension, helical sprung, 40mm travel
Brakes	internal expanding drum, front and rear
Tyre size	3.25 x 26″ front, 3.75 or 4.00 x 27″ rear road pattern

DIMENSIONS

Overall length		
Overall width	780mm	(30.7″)
Overall height		
Wheelbase	1460mm	(57.4″)
Ground clearance	120mm	(4.7″)
Seat height		
Unladen weight	180 kg	(399 lb)
Fuel tank	16 litre	(3.5 Imp gal)
Performance	130 km/h	(80 mph)

GEAR RATIO

		MILITARY EQUIP. rear carry rack, leather panniers, front crash bars, all service livery.
I	= 2.78 : 1	
II	= 1.75 : 1	
III	= 1.25 : 1	
IV	= 1.00 : 1	

GERMANY (EAST)

MODEL EMW R35 1946

Manufacturer	EMW Motor Works, Eisenach
Military Service	Standard production model works modified for military service, adopted by East German armed forces in 1946, for solo despatch and general liaison duties. (A pre-war BMW model).

ENGINE & TRANSMISSION

Type	EMW, vertical ohv, single-cylinder
Capacity	340cc 72 x 84mm
Comp, ratio	5.5 : 1
Output	14 hp at 5200 rpm
Starting	right foot kick start
Carburettor	single SUM
Electrics	6v, 45 watt (Bosch W 175 T 1)
Clutch	single-plate, dry

Gearbox	hand-change, 4-speed
Final	exposed shaft

FRAME & WHEELS

Type	pressed steel construction
Front forks	telescopic, hydraulic damping
Rear forks	plunger type rear suspension
Brakes	internal expanding drum, 160mm diameter front & 180mm rear
Tyre size	3.50 x 19″ front and rear, road pattern

DIMENSIONS

Overall length	2150mm	(84.6″)
Overall width	725mm	(28.5″)
Overall height	960mm	(37.7″)
Wheelbase	1400mm	(55.1″)
Ground clearance		
Seat height	750mm	(29.5″)
Unladen weight	170 kg	(374.7 lb)
Fuel tank	12 litre	(2.6 Imp gal)
Performance	95 km/h	(60 mph)
		0.35 litre/mile

GEAR RATIO

		MILITARY EQUIP. rear carry rack and leather panniers, all-over service livery.
I	= 3.60 : 1	
II	= 2.18 : 1	
III	= 1.35 : 1	
IV	= 1.00 : 1	

GERMANY (WEST)

MODEL BMW R51 1950

Manufacturer	Bayerische Motoren-Werke AG, Munich
Military Service	Standard production model works modified for general police and military service, European armed forces for solo despatch and general liaison. Austria, France and the Netherlands. Replaced by further developed R51/3, and later R50 models.

ENGINE & TRANSMISSION

Type	BMW, transverse ohv flat-twin
Capacity	494cc 68 x 68mm
Comp, ratio	6.3 : 1
Output	24 hp at 5800 rpm
Starting	left foot kick start
Carburettor	two Bing
Electrics	6v, Noris MD
Clutch	single plate, dry
Gearbox	foot-change, 4-speed
Final	exposed shaft

FRAME & WHEELS

Type	tubular double loop
Front forks	telescopic, internal helical sprung, hydraulic damping
Rear forks	plunger design, internal helical sprung, without damping
Brakes	internal expanding drums front and rear, 200mm diameter front
Tyre size	3.50 x 19″ front and rear, road pattern

DIMENSIONS

Overall length		
Overall width		
Overall height		
Wheelbase	1448mm	(57.0″)
Ground clearance	127mm	(5.0″)
Seat height	711mm	(28.0″)
Unladen weight	185 kg	(400 lb)
Fuel tank	14 litre	(3 Imp gal)
Performance	140 km/h	(87 mph) max

GEAR RATIO

		MILITARY EQUIP. rear carrier rack, a pair of leather pannier bags, overall service livery and the option of handlebar or frame mounted screen or fairing.
I	= 2.77 : 1	
II	= 1.75 : 1	
III	= 1.31 : 1	
IV	= 1.00 : 1	

MODEL BMW R25 1950

Military Service	Standard production model works modified for general service, by several European military and police forces for solo despatch and general liaison. Austria, France and the Netherlands. Replaced by further developed R26 and R27 versions.

ENGINE & TRANSMISSION

Type	BMW, vertical ohv single-cylinder
Capacity	247cc 68 x 68mm
Comp, ratio	6.5 : 1
Output	12 hp at 5600 rpm
Starting	left foot kick start
Carburettor	single Bing
Electrics	6v, Noris C
Clutch	single-plate, dry
Gearbox	foot-change, 4-speed
Final	exposed shaft

FRAME & WHEELS

Type	tubular double loop
Front forks	telescopic, internal helical sprung, without damping
Rear forks	plunger design, internal helical sprung, without damping
Brakes	internal expanding drums front and rear
Tyre size	3.25 x 19″ front and rear, road pattern

DIMENSIONS

Overall length		
Overall width		
Overall height		
Wheelbase	1323mm	(54.0″)
Ground clearance	102mm	(4.0″)

Seat height | 711mm | (28.0″)
Unladen weight | 140 kg | (300 lb)
Fuel tank | 12 litre | (2.6 Imp gal)
Performance | 95 km/h | (60 mph) max

GEAR RATIO | MILITARY EQUIP. rear carrier rack, a pair of
I = 3.96 : 1 | leather pannier bags, high level exhaust system and
II = 1.95 : 1 | over-all service livery.
III = 1.32 : 1
IV = 1.00 : 1

MODEL — DKW MILITARY RT 175 VS 1955

Manufacturer | Auto-Union GmbH, Ingolstadt
Military Service | Standard production model works modified for military service by West German armed forces, for solo despatch and general liaison. Supplied between 1955-58, and superseded by Maico M 250/B.

ENGINE & TRANSMISSION
Type | DKW, vertical two-stroke single-cylinder
Capacity | 174cc 62 x 58mm
Comp. ratio | 6.2 : 1
Output | 9.6 hp at 5000 rpm
Starting | left foot kick start
Carburettor | single Bing 24mm Ø
Electrics | 6v
Clutch | multi-plate, wet
Gearbox | foot-change, 4-speed
Final | enclosed chain

FRAME & WHEELS
Type | pressed steel and tubular single loop design
Front forks | leading link, hydraulic damping
Rear forks | trailing, helical damping
Brakes | internal expanding drum, front and rear
Tyre size | 3.25 x 19″ front and rear

DIMENSIONS
Overall length | 1975mm | (77.7″)
Overall width | 660mm | (25.9″)
Overall height | 926mm | (36.4″)
Wheelbase | 1278mm | (50.3″)
Ground clearance | 120mm | (4.7″)
Seat height |
Unladen weight | 135 kg | (298 lb)
Fuel tank | 15 litre | (3.3 Imp gal)
Performance | 95 km/h | (60 mph)

GEAR RATIO | MILITARY EQUIP. rear carry rack, leather
I = 3.19 : 1 | panniers, crash bars, all-over service livery.
II = 1.86 : 1
III = 1.33 : 1
IV = 1.00 : 1

MODEL — MAICO M250/B 1961

Manufacturer | Maico Fahrzeugfabrik GmbH, Ammerbuch
Military Service | Standard production model procured by West German Army in 1961, for solo multi-terrain despatch and general liaison. Total of 10,000 supplied 1961-65, also exported.

ENGINE & TRANSMISSION
Type | Maico, single-cylinder, two-stroke
Capacity | 247cc 67 x 70mm
Comp. ratio | 7 : 1
Output | 14.5 hp at 5200 rpm
Starting | left foot kick start
Carburettor | single Bing 26mm Ø
Electrics | 6v
Clutch | multi-plate, wet
Gearbox | foot-change, 4-speed
Final | enclosed chain

FRAME & WHEELS
Type | tubular construction, single downtube
Front forks | telescopic, hydraulic damping
Rear forks | trailing, helical sprung
Brakes | internal expanding drum, front and rear
Tyre size | 3.25 x 18″ front, 3.50 x 18″ rear, trials pattern

DIMENSIONS
Overall length | 2010mm | (79.1″)
Overall width | 800mm | (31.4″)
Overall height | 1075mm | (42.3″)
Wheelbase | 1330mm | (52.3″)
Ground clearance | 140mm | (5.5″)
Seat height |
Unladen weight | 165 kg | (363 lb)
Fuel tank | 16 litre | (3.5 Imp gal)
Performance | 96 km/h | (59 mph)

GEAR RATIO | MILITARY EQUIP. rear carry rack, high level
I = 3.275 : 1 | exhaust, sump guard, braced handlebars, headlamp
II = 1.945 : 1 | protection, all over service livery.
III = 1.335 : 1
IV = 1.000 : 1

MODEL — TRIUMPH BDG 250 SL 1955

Manufacturer | Triumph-Werke AG, Nuremburg
Military Service | Standard production model works modified for military service, by West German armed forces in 1955, for solo despatch and general liaison duties.

ENGINE & TRANSMISSION
Type | TWN, vertical two-stroke, split-single
Capacity | 248cc 2 x 45 x 78mm
Comp. ratio | 6.2 : 1
Output | 12 hp at 4600 rpm
Starting | left foot kick start
Carburettor | single Bing 26mm Ø
Electrics | 6v

Clutch | multi-plate, wet
Gearbox | foot-change, 4-speed
Final | enclosed chain

FRAME & WHEELS
Type | pressed steel and tubular construction (single downtube)
Front forks | telescopic, hydraulic damping
Rear forks | plunger type rear suspension, helical sprung
Brakes | internal expanding drum, front and rear
Tyre size | 3.25 x 19″ front and rear, road pattern

DIMENSIONS
Overall length | 2080mm | (81.8″)
Overall width | 760mm | (29.9″)
Overall height | 985mm | (38.7″)
Wheelbase | 1330mm | (52.3″)
Ground clearance | 122mm | (4.8″)
Seat height |
Unladen weight | 160 kg | (352 lb)
Fuel tank | 14 litre | (3 Imp gal)
Performance | 100 km/h | (62 mph)

GEAR RATIO | MILITARY EQUIP. rear carry rack or pillion
I = 3.25 : 1 | saddle, leather panniers, all-over service livery.
II = 1.80 : 1
III = 1.33 : 1
IV = 1.00 : 1

GREAT BRITAIN

MODEL — AJS 18CS 1956

Manufacturer | Associated Motor Cycles, Plumstead, London
Military Service | Standard production scrambling competition model, adopted for solo multi-terrain despatch and general liaison by Swedish armed forces in 1956, and South African border patrol in 1962, demonstrating the full flexibility of this robust design.

ENGINE & TRANSMISSION
Type | AMC, ohv vertical single-cylinder
Capacity | 497cc 86 x 85.5mm
Comp. ratio | 8.7 : 1
Output | 33 hp at 6200 rpm
Starting | right foot kick start
Carburettor | single - Amal 389
Electrics | 6v, magneto ignition (Lucas)
Clutch | multi-plate, wet
Gearbox | foot-change, 4-speed
Final | exposed chain

FRAME & WHEELS
Type | tubular construction, duplex cradle design
Front forks | telescopic, helical sprung, hydraulic damping
Rear forks | trailing, helical sprung, hydraulic damping
Brakes | internal expanding drum, front and rear, 7″ diameter
Tyre size | 3.00 x 21″ (3.50 x 19″ 1958 option) front, 4.00 x 19″ rear, off road

DIMENSIONS
Overall length | 2164mm | (85.2″)
Overall width | 711mm | (28.0″)
Overall height |
Wheelbase | 1402mm | (55.2″)
Ground clearance | 165mm | (6.5″)
Seat height | 826mm | (32.5″)
Unladen weight | 147 kg | (324 lb)
Fuel tank | 9.1 litre | (2 Imp gal)
Performance |

GEAR RATIO | MILITARY EQUIP. rear carry rack, canvas
I = 3.24 : 1 | panniers, crash bars, braced handlebars, ski
II = 2.44 : 1 | attachment option (Sweden), and all other service
III = 1.56 : 1 | livery.
IV = 1.00 : 1

MODEL — BSA A65 1962

Manufacturer | BSA Cycles Ltd, Small Heath, Birmingham
Military Service | Standard production model works modified for public service; procured by civilian and military police departments worldwide, supplied in various specifications, providing solo despatch, escort and general liaison.

ENGINE & TRANSMISSION
Type | BSA, ohv vertical-twin
Capacity | 654cc 75 x 74mm
Comp. ratio | 7.5 : 1
Output | 38 hp at 5800 rpm
Starting | right foot kick start
Carburettor | single: Amal 389 monbloc (twin option)
Electrics | 6v
Clutch | multi-plate, wet
Gearbox | foot-change, 4-speed
Final | exposed chain

FRAME & WHEELS
Type | tubular construction, single downtube
Front forks | telescopic, helical sprung, hydraulic damping
Rear forks | pivoted/trailing, helical sprung, hydraulic damping
Brakes | internal expanding drum, 8″ dia x 1¼″ front, 7″ dia x 1½″ rear
Tyre size | 3.25 x 18″ front, 3.5 x 18″ rear, road pattern

DIMENSIONS
Overall length |
Overall width |
Overall height |
Wheelbase | 1397mm | (55.0″)
Ground clearance |
Seat height |
Unladen weight | 177 kg | (390 lb)
Fuel tank | 18 litre | (4 Imp gal)
Performance | 161 km/h | (100 mph)

GEAR RATIO | MILITARY EQUIP. rear carrier rack, solo saddle,
I = 11.1 : 1 | front and rear crash bars, panniers and service
II = 7.2 : 1 | livery.
III = 5.1 : 1
IV = 4.3 : 1

MODEL — JAMES J10 COMET 1949

Manufacturer | James Cycle Co Ltd, Greet, Birmingham
Military Service | Standard production model works modified for RAF/Air Ministry for messenger service.

ENGINE & TRANSMISSION
Type | Villiers Mk 1F, vertical-single, two-stroke
Capacity | 99cc 47 x 57mm
Comp. ratio | 8 : 1
Output | 2.8 hp at 4000 rpm
Starting | right foot kick start
Carburettor | single Villiers 6/0
Electrics | 6v
Clutch | multi-plate, wet
Gearbox | foot-change, 2-speed
Final | exposed chain

FRAME & WHEELS
Type | tubular construction, single down tube
Front forks | tubular parallelogram, single helical sprung
Rear forks | without suspension
Brakes | internal expanding drum, 4″ diameter front and 5″ diameter rear
Tyre size | 2.50 x 19″ front and rear, road pattern

DIMENSIONS
Overall length | 2007mm | (79.0″)
Overall width | 648mm | (25.5″)
Overall height | 851mm | (33.5″)
Wheelbase | 1181mm | (46.5″)
Ground clearance | 119mm | (4.7″)
Seat height | 724mm | (28.5″)
Unladen weight | 58 kg | (128 lb)
Fuel tank | 8 litre | (1.75 Imp gal)
Performance | 64 km/h | (40 mph) max

GEAR RATIO | MILITARY EQUIP. rear carry rack and a pair of
I = 1.54 : 1 | leather panniers, leg shields, handlebar mounted
II = 1.00 : 1 | windscreen, and all-over service livery.

MODEL — MATCHLESS G3LS 1961

Military Service | Standard production model works modified for various armed forces during 1949-63, for solo despatch and general liaison duties. Netherlands, South Africa, Australia etc.

ENGINE & TRANSMISSION
Type | AMC, ohv vertical single-cylinder
Capacity | 349cc 69 x 93mm
Comp. ratio | 6.3 : 1
Output | 16 hp at 5600 rpm
Starting | right foot kick start
Carburettor | single Amal type 76
Electrics | 6v, magneto ignition (Lucas)
Clutch | multi-plate, wet
Gearbox | foot-change, 4-speed
Final | exposed chain

FRAME & WHEELS
Type | tubular construction, single downtube
Front forks | telescopic, hydraulic damping
Rear forks | trailing, helical sprung, load adjustable
Brakes | internal expanding drum, front and rear, 7″ diameter
Tyre size | 3.25 x 19″ front and rear, road pattern

DIMENSIONS
Overall length | 2190mm | (86.2″)
Overall width | 711mm | (28.0″)
Overall height |
Wheelbase | 1403mm | (55.2″)
Ground clearance | 140mm | (5.5″)
Seat height | 788mm | (31.0″)
Unladen weight | 172 kg | (380 lb)
Fuel tank | 13.6 litre | (3 Imp gal)
Performance | 95 km/h | (60 mph)

GEAR RATIO | MILITARY EQUIP. rear carry rack, panniers, all-
I = 2.56 : 1 | over service livery.
II = 1.70 : 1
III = 1.22 : 1
IV = 1.00 : 1

MODEL — TRIUMPH TRW 1948

Manufacturer | Triumph Motor Co Ltd, Coventry
Military Service | Specialised military model selected by British army, for solo despatch, reconnaissance and general liaison duties. Remained in service until 1969, when replaced by Triumph 500, based upon the standard production Tiger 100 model. Also used in Canada.

ENGINE & TRANSMISSION
Type | Triumph, sv, vertical-twin
Capacity | 499cc 63 x 80mm
Comp. ratio | 6 : 1
Output | 18 hp at 5000 rpm
Starting | right foot kick start
Carburettor | single Solex type 26 WH-Z
Electrics | 6v, 35 watt, magneto ignition
Clutch | multi-plate, wet
Gearbox | foot-change, 4-speed
Final | exposed chain

FRAME & WHEELS

Type	single loop, tubular construction
Front forks	telescopic, hydraulic damping
Rear forks	without suspension
Brakes	internal expanding drum, 7″ diameter front and rear
Tyre size	3.25 x 19″ front, 4.00 x 19″ rear, road pattern

DIMENSIONS

Overall length	2096mm	(82.5″)
Overall width	724mm	(28.5″)
Overall height	1042mm	(41.0″)
Wheelbase	1346mm	(53.0″)
Ground clearance	159mm	(6.2″)
Seat height	787mm	(31.0″)
Unladen weight	170 kg	(375 lb)
Fuel tank	14 litre	(3 Imp gal)
Performance	88 km/h	(55 mph)

GEAR RATIO
I = 2.91 : 1
II = 2.21 : 1
III = 1.42 : 1
IV = 1.00 : 1

MILITARY EQUIP. rear carry rack and canvas panniers, crash bars, siameze exhaust on to the right, all-over service livery.

MODEL TRIUMPH T100 1955

Military Service	Standard production model modified for police departments, civil and military worldwide and supplied in various versions, providing solo despatch, escort and general liaison. Superseded Triumph TR5 and replaced by Triumph T110 machines.

ENGINE & TRANSMISSION

Type	Triumph, ohv, vertical-twin
Capacity	499cc 63 x 80mm
Comp, ratio	8 : 1
Output	32 hp at 6500 rpm
Starting	right foot kick start
Carburettor	single: Amal 376
Electrics	6v, magneto ignition
Clutch	multi-plate, wet
Gearbox	foot-change, 4-speed
Final	exposed chain

FRAME & WHEELS

Type	tubular construction, single down tube
Front forks	telescopic, helical sprung, hydraulic damping
Rear forks	pivoted/trailing, helical sprung, hydraulic damping
Brakes	internal expanding drum, 8″ dia front, 7″ dia rear
Tyre size	3.25 x 19″ front, 3.50 x 19″ rear, standard road pattern

DIMENSIONS

Overall length	
Overall width	
Overall height	
Wheelbase	55.75″
Ground clearance	5.00″
Seat height	30.5″
Unladen weight	375 lb
Fuel tank	4 Imp gal
Performance	95 mph (60 mpg)

GEAR RATIO
I = 2.44 : 1
II = 1.69 : 1
III = 1.19 : 1
IV = 1.00 : 1

MILITARY EQUIP. rear carrier rack, solo saddle, front and rear crash bars, panniers, all-over service livery.

MODEL TRIUMPH MILITARY 3TA 1963

Military Service	Standard production model works modified for military service by Dutch armed forces in 1963, for solo despatch and general liaison duties. A total of 1100 machines supplied.

ENGINE & TRANSMISSION

Type	Triumph, ohv, vertical-twin
Capacity	349cc 58.25 x 65.5mm
Comp, ratio	7.5 : 1
Output	18.5 hp at 6500 rpm
Starting	right foot kick start
Carburettor	single: Amal
Electrics	6v, coil ignition
Clutch	multi-plate, wet
Gearbox	foot-change, 4-speed
Final	exposed chain

FRAME & WHEELS

Type	tubular construction, single downtube
Front forks	telescopic, hydraulic damping
Rear forks	trailing, helical sprung, 2.5″ travel
Brakes	internal expanding drum, front and rear, 7″ diameter
Tyre size	3.25 x 17″ front and rear

DIMENSIONS

Overall length	2057mm	(81.0″)
Overall width	686mm	(27.0″)
Overall height		
Wheelbase	1340mm	(52.75″)
Ground clearance	127mm	(5.0″)
Seat height	724mm	(28.5″)
Unladen weight	152 kg	(340 lb)
Fuel tank	16 litre	(3.5 Imp gal)
Performance	120 km/h	(75 mph)

GEAR RATIO
I = 2.41 : 1
II = 1.74 : 1
III = 1.17 : 1
IV = 1.00 : 1

MILITARY EQUIP. rear carry rack and panniers, solo saddle, crash bars, all-over service livery.

ITALY

MODEL BIANCHI MT61 1961

Manufacturer	Edoardo Bianchi, Moto Meccancia SpA, Milan
Military Service	Specialised military model procured by Italian army in 1961; a solo multi-terrain machine for despatch, reconnaissance and general liaison. Replaced by Moto Guzzi machines when factory ceased production in 1967.

ENGINE & TRANSMISSION

Type	Bianchi, vertical ohv single
Capacity	318cc 74 x 74mm
Comp, ratio	6.2 : 1
Output	10.5 hp
Starting	right foot kick start
Carburettor	single, Dell'Orto
Electrics	6v
Clutch	multi-plate, wet
Gearbox	foot-change, 5-speed
Final	exposed chain

FRAME & WHEELS

Type	tubular construction, single downtube design
Front forks	telescopic, hydraulic damping, helical sprung
Rear forks	trailing arm, hydraulic damping, helical sprung
Brakes	internal expanding drum, front and rear
Tyre size	3.25 x 18″ front and rear, heavy cross country pattern

DIMENSIONS

Overall length	2030mm	(79.9″)
Overall width	760mm	(29.9″)
Overall height	1050mm	(41.3″)
Wheelbase	1330mm	(52.3″)
Ground clearance		
Seat height		
Unladen weight	195 kg	(430 lb)
Fuel tank		
Performance	88 km/h	(55 mph)

MILITARY EQUIP. rear carry rack or pillion saddle, high level exhaust and mudguards, front crash bars and leg shields.

MODEL GILERA SATURNO 500 MILITARE 1950

Manufacturer	Moto Gilera SpA, Arcore
Military Service	Standard production model works modified for Italian armed forces for solo despatch, escort, military police, and general liaison. Remained in limited service throughout 1950s.

ENGINE & TRANSMISSION

Type	Gilera, vertical ohv single
Capacity	498cc 84 x 90mm
Comp, ratio	6 : 1
Output	22 hp at 5000 rpm
Starting	right foot kick start
Carburettor	single Dell'Orto RDF 28
Electrics	6v, Marelli MCR/4D magneto
Clutch	multi-plate, wet
Gearbox	foot-change, 4-speed
Final	exposed chain

FRAME & WHEELS

Type	tubular single loop design
Front forks	telescopic, hydraulic damping
Rear forks	trailing, helical sprung
Brakes	internal expanding drums front and rear
Tyre size	3.00 x 19″ front, 3.25 x 19″ rear, road pattern

DIMENSIONS

Overall length	2160mm	(85.0″)
Overall width	750mm	(29.5″)
Overall height	1020mm	(50.2″)
Wheelbase	1470mm	(57.8″)
Ground clearance	130mm	(5.1″)
Seat height		
Unladen weight	198 kg	(436 lb)
Fuel tank	14 litre	(3 Imp gal)
Performance	128 km/h	(80 mph)

GEAR RATIO
I = 2.18 : 1
II = 1.31 : 1
III = 1.04 : 1
IV = 0.88 : 1

MILITARY EQUIP. rear carry rack or pillion saddle, crash bars, all-over service livery.

MODEL GILERA GT 175 MILITARE 1956

Manufacturer	Moto Gilera SpA, Arcore, Italy
Military Service	Standard production model works modified for military service, adopted by Italian armed forces in 1956, for solo despatch and general liaison duties.

ENGINE & TRANSMISSION

Type	Gilera, air cooled vertical single cylinder, overhead valves
Capacity	173cc (60mm bore x 61mm stroke)
Comp, ratio	6.5 : 1
Output	7.5 hp at 6000 rpm
Starting	right foot kick start
Carburettor	single Dell'Orto MA 18 B
Electrics	6v, 45 watt
Clutch	multi-plate, wet operation
Gearbox	right foot-change, 4-speed, integral design
Final	exposed chain, upper guard only

FRAME & WHEELS

Type	pressed steel and tubular construction (duplex cradle)
Front forks	telescopic, hydraulic damping
Rear forks	trailing, helical sprung
Brakes	internal expanding drum, front and rear
Tyre size	2.50 x 19″ front, 2.75 x 19″ rear, road pattern

DIMENSIONS

Overall length	2000mm	(78.7″)
Overall width	680mm	(26.7″)
Overall height	970mm	(38.1″)
Wheelbase	1300mm	(51.1″)
Ground clearance	160mm	(6.2″)
Seat height		
Unladen weight	109 kg	(240 lb)
Fuel tank	13 litre	(2.8 Imp gal)
Performance	95 km/h	(59 mph)

GEAR RATIO
I = 2.78 : 1
II = 1.86 : 1
III = 1.26 : 1
IV = 1.00 : 1

MILITARY EQUIP. rear carry rack, solo saddle, front crash bars, hand pump, all-over service livery.

MODEL MOTO GUZZI 500 SUPERALCE 1946

Manufacturer	Moto Guzzi SpA, Mandello del Lario, Italy
Military Service	Specialised military model procured by Italian army for solo/sidecar service; produced 1946-57 (based upon war-time Alce model) to provide despatch, escort, reconnaissance, military police and liaison duties.

ENGINE & TRANSMISSION

Type	Moto Guzzi, horizontal air cooled single cylinder, overhead valves
Capacity	498cc (88mm bore x 82mm stroke)
Comp, ratio	5.5 : 1
Output	18.5 hp at 4300 rpm
Starting	right foot kick start
Carburettor	single Dell'Orto MD 27 F
Electrics	6v
Clutch	multi-plate, dry operation
Gearbox	right foot change, 4-speed, integral design
Final	exposed chain, upper guard only

FRAME & WHEELS

Type	pressed steel and tubular duplex construction
Front forks	parallelogram, helical sprung, friction damped
Rear forks	trailing, helical sprung, friction damped rear sub-frame
Brakes	internal expanding drum, front and rear
Tyre size	3.50 x 19″ front and rear, road pattern

DIMENSIONS

Overall length	2220mm	(87.4″) solo
Overall width	790mm	(31.1″) solo
Overall height	1065mm	(41.9″) solo
Wheelbase	1455mm	(57.2″) solo
Ground clearance	210mm	(8.2″) solo
Seat height		
Unladen weight	195 kg	(429 lb) solo
Fuel tank	12.5 litre	(2.7 Imp gal)
Performance	110 km/h (230 km range)	(68 mph) solo

GEAR RATIO
I = 5.07 : 1
II = 2.84 : 1
III = 1.52 : 1
IV = 1.00 : 1

MILITARY EQUIP. rear carry rack, pillion saddle with additional handlebars, leg shields, all-over service livery.

MODEL MOTO GUZZI AIRONE SPORT 1952

Manufacturer	Moto Guzzi SpA, Mandello del Lario, Italy
Military Service	Standard production model, works modified for Italian police and armed forces, for solo despatch, escort and general liaison duties. Widely replaced the 1939-46 version with 9.5 hp at 4800 rpm output and original girder front forks.

ENGINE & TRANSMISSION

Type	Moto Guzzi, horizontal ohv single cylinder
Capacity	247cc (70 x 64mm)
Comp, ratio	7 : 1
Output	13.5 hp at 6000 rpm
Starting	left foot kick start
Carburettor	single Cozette SB 22
Electrics	6v, Marelli MCR 4-G
Clutch	multi-plate, dry
Gearbox	foot-change, 4-speed
Final	exposed chain

FRAME & WHEELS

Type	pressed steel and tubular duplex construction
Front forks	telescopic, helical sprung, hydraulic damping
Rear forks	helical sprung rear sub-frame, friction damped
Brakes	internal expanding drum, front and rear
Tyre size	3.25 x 19″ front and rear, road pattern

DIMENSIONS

Overall length		
Overall width		
Overall height		
Wheelbase	1370mm	(53.9″)
Ground clearance		
Seat height		
Unladen weight	150 kg	(331 lb)
Fuel tank	13.5 litre	(2.9 Imp gal)
Performance	92 km/h	(57 mph) max (1 litre per 30 km

MILITARY EQUIP. rear carrier rack or pillion pad, handlebar mounted screen, leg shields front crash bars and all over service livery.

MODEL	MOTO GUZZI 500 FALCONE 'TURISMO' 1953	
Military Service	Standard production model, works modified for Italian police and armed forces, for solo despatch, escort and general liaison duties. Widely used alongside the 'Sport' version and later both replaced by Nuovo Falcone model.	

ENGINE & TRANSMISSION

Type	Moto Guzzi, horizontal ohv single	
Capacity	498cc 88 x 82mm	
Comp, ratio	5.5 : 1	6.5 : 1; sport
Output	18.8 hp at 4300 rpm	23 hp sport
Starting	left foot kick start	
Carburettor	single Dell'Orto MD 27 F	SS 29 A sport
Electrics	6v, Marelli MCR 4 E magneto	
Clutch	multi-plate, dry	
Gearbox	foot-change, 4-speed	
Final	exposed chain	

FRAME & WHEELS

Type	pressed steel and tubular duplex construction
Front forks	telescopic, helical sprung, hydraulic damping
Rear forks	helical sprung rear sub-frame, friction damped
Brakes	internal expanding drum, front and rear
Tyre size	3.5 x 19″ front and rear, road pattern

DIMENSIONS

Overall length		
Overall width		
Overall height		
Wheelbase	1500mm	(59.0″)
Ground clearance		
Seat height		
Unladen weight	170 kg	(374.7 lb)
Fuel tank	17.5 litre	(3.8 Imp gal)
Performance	120 km/h	(75 mph) max
	(4.5 litre per 100 km)	

GEAR RATIO	
I = 2.29 : 1	MILITARY EQUIP. rear carrier rack or pillion pad, handlebar mounted screen, leg shield front crash bars and all-over service livery. A special version with enclosed engine and mudguards prepared for the Vatican Guard.
II = 1.71 : 1	
III = 1.31 : 1	
IV = 1.00 : 1	

MODEL	MOTO GUZZI 125 STORNELLO 1960
Manufacturer	Moto Guzzi SpA, Mandello del Lario, Italy
Military Service	Standard production model works modified for military service, adopted by Italian armed forces in 1960, for solo despatch and general liaison duties.

ENGINE & TRANSMISSION

Type	Moto Guzzi, air cooled inclined single cylinder, overhead valves
Capacity	124cc (52mm bore x 58mm stroke)
Comp, ratio	8 : 1
Output	6.8 hp
Starting	left foot kick start
Carburettor	single Dell'Orto ME 18 BS
Electrics	6v, Marelli CW 225 LV
Clutch	multi-plate, dry operation
Gearbox	right foot-change, 4-speed, integral design
Final	exposed chain, upper guard only

FRAME & WHEELS

Type	duplex cradle, tubular construction
Front forks	telescopic, hydraulic damping
Rear forks	trailing, helical sprung
Brakes	internal expanding drum, front and rear
Tyre size	2.50 x 17″ front, 2.75 x 17″ rear, road pattern

DIMENSIONS

Overall length	1900mm	(74.8″)
Overall width	720mm	(28.3″)
Overall height	1030mm	(40.5″)
Wheelbase	1250mm	(49.2″)
Ground clearance	160mm	(6.2″)
Seat height		
Unladen weight	92 kg	(202 lb)
Fuel tank	12.5 litre	(2.7 Imp gal)
Performance	100 km/h	(62 mph)

GEAR RATIO	
I = 3.04 : 1	MILITARY EQUIP. rear carry rack and leather panniers, crash bars and leg shields, windscreen, all-over service livery.
II =1.81 : 1	
III = 1.29 : 1	
IV = 1.00 : 1	

MODEL	MOTO GUZZI 3 x 3 1960
Military Service	Specialised military tricycle model, prepared 1959-60 for use in mountainous regions, some 500 supplied 1961-62, to Italian Alpine troops. This V-twin engine provided the foundation for the Moto Guzzi V-twin motorcycle model range that shortly followed.

ENGINE & TRANSMISSION

Type	Moto Guzzi, ohv transverse 90° V-twin
Capacity	753cc 80 x 75mm
Comp, ratio	6.5 : 1
Output	20 hp at 4000 rpm
Starting	electric start
Carburettor	single Weber 26 IMB 1 or 26 IMB 4
Electrics	6v, Marelli MT 48 A magneto
Clutch	multi-plate, dry
Gearbox	hand-change, 6-forward/1-reverse
Final	exposed shaft, 2 lockable diffs (centre and rear)

FRAME & WHEELS

Type	pressed steel and tubular construction
Front forks	single telescopic leg, hydraulic damping, with steering wheel acting-through reduction gears
Rear forks	rubber sprung swinging rear arms
Brakes	internal expanding drum, hydraulic control on all 3 wheels
Tyre size	6.00 x 15″ all 3 wheels (with demountable tracks for rear two)

DIMENSIONS

Overall length	3000mm	(118.1″)
Overall width	1570mm	(61.8″) max
Overall height	1420mm	(55.9″)
Wheelbase	2030mm	(79.9″)
Ground clearance		
Seat height		
Unladen weight	1000 kg	(2204 lb)
Fuel tank	53 litre	(11.6 Imp gal)
Performance	50 km/h	(31 mph) max
	(15 litre per 100 km)	

GEAR RATIO	
I = 12.92 : 1	MILITARY EQUIP. adjustable rear track width, rear idler wheels, payload of 500 kg, torque dividing diff. (1/5: front and 4/5 rear two), additional masked lighting, spare wheel, overall service livery.
II = 5.97 : 1	
III =3.10 : 1	
IV = 1.93 : 1	
V =1.31 : 1	
VI = 1.00 : 1	

NORWAY

MODEL	TEMPO TAIFUN MILITAER 1961
Manufacturer	Jonas Øglaend As, Sandnes
Military Service	Standard production model procured by Norwegian army in 1961, for solo despatch and general liaison; a total of 650 supplied 1961-66. Proposed military service until 1993.

ENGINE & TRANSMISSION

Type	Sachs, vertical, two-stroke, single
Capacity	175cc 62 x 58mm
Comp, ratio	6.5 : 1
Output	10 hp at 5250 rpm
Starting	left foot kick start
Carburettor	single – Bing 24mm Ø
Electrics	6v, 45 watt, Bosch magneto
Clutch	multi-plate, wet
Gearbox	foot-change, 4-speed
Final	enclosed chain

FRAME & WHEELS

Type	pressed steel and tubular construction, single downtube design
Front forks	telescopic, hydraulic damping, helical sprung
Rear forks	trailing, helical sprung, hydraulic damping
Brakes	internal expanding drum, front and rear
Tyre size	3.25 x 19″ front and rear, road pattern

DIMENSIONS

Overall length	2110mm	(83.0″)
Overall width	650mm	(25.6″)
Overall height	1040mm	(40.9″)
Wheelbase	1290mm	(50.8″)
Ground clearance	190mm	(7.5″)
Seat height		
Unladen weight	102 kg	(225 lb)
Fuel tank	11 litre	(2.4 Imp gal)
Performance	95 km/h	(59 mph)
		300 km range

GEAR RATIO	
I = 3.22 : 1	MILITARY EQUIP. folding rear carry rack, canvas panniers, headlamp protection, black exhaust system and all-over service livery.
II = 1.85 : 1	
III = 1.24 : 1	
IV = 0.95 : 1	

SWEDEN

MODEL	MONARK MC 252 1955
Manufacturer	AB Cykelfabiken Monark, Varberg, Sweden
Military Service	Standard production Blue Arrow model works modified for military service, adopted by Swedish armed forces for solo multi-terrain despatch and general liaison. Introduced in 1955 and remained in service until mid 1960s, when superseded by Monark MC 356.

ENGINE & TRANSMISSION

Type	ILO, air cooled vertical twin cylinder, two-stroke
Capacity	244cc (52mm bore x 58mm stroke)
Comp, ratio	6.8 : 1
Output	15.1 hp at 6000 rpm
Starting	left foot kick start
Carburettor	single Amal
Electrics	6v
Clutch	multi-plate, wet operation
Gearbox	left foot-change, 4-speed, integral design
Final	enclosed chain, rubber gaiters and enclosed rear hub

FRAME & WHEELS

Type	pressed steel and tubular construction
Front forks	telescopic, hydraulic damping
Rear forks	trailing, helical sprung
Brakes	internal expanding drum, front and rear
Tyre size	3.25 x 19″ front and rear, cross country pattern

DIMENSIONS

Overall length	2090mm	(82.2″)
Overall width	730mm	(28.7″)
Overall height	1050mm	(41.3″)
Wheelbase	1360mm	(53.5″)
Ground clearance	160mm	(6.2″)
Seat height		
Unladen weight	165 kg	(363 lb)
Fuel tank	14 litre	(3 Imp gal)
Performance	100 km/h	(62 mph)

MILITARY EQUIP. rear carry rack and small leather panniers, high level exhaust, headlamp protection, all over service livery.

MODEL	MONARK MC 356 A 1963
Manufacturer	AB Cykelfabriken Monark, Varberg
Military Service	Standard production model procured by Swedish army in 1963; works modified for solo multi-terrain despatch and general liaison use.

ENGINE & TRANSMISSION

Type	Jawa, two-stroke, vertical twin
Capacity	344cc 58 x 65mm
Comp, ratio	8 : 1
Output	20 hp at 4740 rpm
Starting	left foot kick start
Carburettor	single Jikov 2926 SBD
Electrics	6v, 45 watt
Clutch	multi-plate, wet
Gearbox	foot-change, 4-speed
Final	enclosed chain

FRAME & WHEELS

Type	tubular construction, single downtube
Front forks	leading link, hydraulic damping
Rear forks	trailing, helical sprung
Brakes	internal expanding drum, front and rear
Tyre size	3.50 x 21″ front, 3.50 x 19″ rear, trials pattern

DIMENSIONS

Overall length	2100mm	(82.6″)
Overall width	820mm	(32.2″)
Overall height		
Wheelbase	1360mm	(53.5″)
Ground clearance	110mm	(4.3″)
Seat height		
Unladen weight	175 kg	(385 lb)
Fuel tank	13 litre	(2.8 Imp gal)
Performance	120 km/h	(75 mph)

GEAR RATIO	
I = 14.3 : 1	MILITARY EQUIP. rear carry rack, additional masked lighting, high level mudguards, all-over service livery.
II = 8.9 : 1	
III = 6.4 : 1	
IV = 4.5 : 1	

MODEL	NV Mod 38 1955
Manufacturer	Nymans Verkstäder, Uppsala, Sweden
Military Service	Standard production trials model works modified for solo multi-terrain military service; a successful entry in the International Six Days Trial from 1951, procured in limited numbers with AJS (GB), Jawa (CS), Monark (S), and Triumph (GB) off-road models.

ENGINE & TRANSMISSION

Type	DKW, vertical single cylinder, two-stroke
Capacity	246cc (70 x 64mm)
Comp, ratio	6.3 : 1
Output	14.1 hp at 4700 rpm
Starting	left foot kick start
Carburettor	single: Bing
Electrics	6v, 55/70 watt
Clutch	multi-plate, wet operation
Gearbox	left foot-change, 4-speed, unit construction
Final	enclosed chain, rubber gaitors and pressed steel hub case

FRAME & WHEELS

Type	tubular construction, single downtube, duplex cradle
Front forks	telescopic, helical sprung, hydraulic damping
Rear forks	trailing, helical sprung, hydraulic damping
Brakes	internal expanding drums, 180mm Ø front and 160mm Ø rear
Tyre size	3.00 x 19″ front, 3.25 x 19″ rear, cross country pattern

DIMENSIONS

Overall length		
Overall width		
Overall height		
Wheelbase	1360mm	(53.5″)
Ground clearance		
Seat height		
Unladen weight	155 kg	(341.7 lb)
Fuel tank	18 litre	(3.9 Imp gal)
Performance	110 km/h	(68 mph)

MILITARY EQUIP. rear carrier rack, small canvas panniers, high level exhaust system, headlamp protection bar, and overall service livery.

SWITZERLAND

MODEL	CONDOR A580-1 1948
Manufacturer	Condor SA, Courfaivre
Military Service	Specialised military model procured by Swiss army in 1948, for solo and sidecar despatch, escort, military police and general liaison. A total of 4420 supplied 1948-54, and remained in service until 1977.

ENGINE & TRANSMISSION

Type	Condor, transverse sv, flat-twin
Capacity	577cc 70 x 75.2mm
Comp, ratio	6 : 1
Output	19.8hp at 4400 rpm
Starting	right foot kick start
Carburettor	single OBA type 20
Electrics	6v
Clutch	single-plate, dry
Gearbox	foot-change, 4 x 2 speed
Final	exposed shaft

FRAME & WHEELS

Type	duplex cradle, tubular construction
Front forks	telescopic, hydraulic damping
Rear forks	rigid rear frame (plunger type suspension adopted in 1953)
Brakes	internal expanding drum, front and rear
Tyre size	3.50 x 19″ front and rear, road and trials pattern

DIMENSIONS

Overall length	2220mm	(87.4″) solo
Overall width	800mm	(31.4″) solo
Overall height	1050mm	(41.3″) solo
Wheelbase	1450mm	(57.0″) solo
Ground clearance	160mm	(6.2″) solo
Seat height	730mm	(28.7″) solo
Unladen weight	240 kg	(529 lb) solo
Fuel tank	14 litre	(3 Imp gal) solo
Performance	105 km/h	(65 mph) solo

GEAR RATIO

I	= 3.38 : 1	road
II	= 2.15 : 1	road
III	= 1.54 : 1	road
IV	= 0.99 : 1	road
I	= 6.00 : 1	off road
II	= 3.82 : 1	off road
III	= 2.74 : 1	off road
IV	= 1.76 : 1	off road

MILITARY EQUIP. rear carry rack or pillion saddle, crash bars, additional lighting, all-over service livery.

MODEL   CONDOR A250 1959

Military Service	Specialised military model adopted by Swiss armed forces in 1959, for solo despatch and general liaison duties. Revised in 1965 and 1968, a total of 573 machines supplied.

ENGINE & TRANSMISSION

Type	Condor, vertical ohv single-cylinder
Capacity	248cc 58 x 68mm
Comp, ratio	7.8 : 1
Output	13 hp at 6000 rpm
Starting	right foot kick start
Carburettor	single Amal-Monobloc 376, with choke
Electrics	6v, 60-90 watt, Bosch magneto
Clutch	single-plate, dry
Gearbox	foot-change, 4-speed
Final	enclosed shaft

FRAME & WHEELS

Type	duplex cradle, tubular construction
Front forks	telescopic, hydraulic damping
Rear forks	trailing, helical sprung
Brakes	internal expanding drum, front and rear, 180mm diameter 35mm wide
Tyre size	3.25 x 18″ front and rear, road pattern

DIMENSIONS

Overall length	2050mm	(80.7″)
Overall width	690mm	(27.1″)
Overall height	1050mm	(41.3″)
Wheelbase	1350mm	(53.1″)
Ground clearance	180mm	(7.0″)
Seat height	800mm	(31.4″)
Unladen weight	190 kg	(418 lb)
Fuel tank	14 litre	(3 Imp gal)
Performance	110 km/h	(68 mph)

GEAR RATIO

I	= 5.29 : 1
II	= 3.24 : 1
III	= 2.34 : 1
IV	= 1.59 : 1

MILITARY EQUIP. pillion seat, leather panniers, additional masked lighting, tyre pump, sub-machine gun support bracket, all-over service livery.

USA

MODEL   HARLEY-DAVIDSON G 1950

Manufacturer	Harley-Davidson Motor Co, Milwaukee, Wisconsin
Military Service	Standard production model (Servicar), adopted by America armed forces to provide messenger service, convoy control and police operations. (Later Model GE remained in production until 1974).

ENGINE & TRANSMISSION

Type	Harley-Davidson, 45° sv, V-twin
Capacity	740cc 69.85 x 96.85mm
Comp, ratio	4.75 : 1
Output	23 hp at 4600 rpm
Starting	right foot kick start
Carburettor	single: Schebler
Electrics	6v, coil ignition
Clutch	multi-plate, wet
Gearbox	hand-change, 3-speed
Final	exposed chain to rigid axle and two rear wheels

FRAME & WHEELS

Type	tubular construction, duplex cradle
Front forks	leading link, helical sprung, friction damped

Rear forks	without rear suspension	
Brakes	internal expanding drum, all three wheels	
Tyre size	5.00 x 16″ all three wheels, road pattern	

DIMENSIONS

Overall length	2718mm	(107.0″)
Overall width	1321mm	(52.0″)
Overall height	1315mm	(51.75″)
Wheelbase	1562mm	(61.5″)
Ground clearance	114mm	(4.5″)
Seat height		
Unladen weight	1102 kg	(500 lb)
Fuel tank	12.80 litre	(3.38 US gal)
Performance	72 km/h	(45 mph)
		(35 mpg, 120 ,miles range)

GEAR RATIO

High	= 5.85 : 1	MILITARY EQUIP. closed-box rear body (above rear axle), for general equipment and larger postal items, additional hazard lights, all-over service livery. Payload of 500 lb.
Low	= 14.4 : 1	

MODEL   INDIAN 148M 1947

Manufacturer	Indian Motorcycle Co, Springfield, Massachusetts
Military Service	Standard production model procured by United States military in 1947; a solo lightweight adopted as suitable for parachute use by the airborne troops.

ENGINE & TRANSMISSION

Type	Indian, vertical sv, single-cylinder
Capacity	221cc 63.5 x 69.9mm
Comp, ratio	4.75 : 1
Output	6.3 hp at 4800 rpm
Starting	left foot kick start
Carburettor	single
Electrics	6v, Geneto magneto
Clutch	multi-plate, wet
Gearbox	foot-change, 3-speed
Final	exposed chain

FRAME & WHEELS

Type	tubular single loop
Front forks	girder type, parallelogram, helical sprung, friction damped
Rear forks	without suspension
Brakes	internal expanding drum, front and rear
Tyre size	3.00 x 18″ front and rear

DIMENSIONS

Overall length	1969mm	(77.5″)
Overall width	711mm	(28.0″)
Overall height	933mm	(36.7″)
Wheelbase	1270mm	(50.0″)
Ground clearance	140mm	(5.5″)
Seat height		
Unladen weight	114 kg	(250 lb)
Fuel tank	10.5 litre	(2.75 US gal)
Performance	72 km/h	(45 mph)
		(250 mile range)

MILITARY EQUIP. rear carry rack, crash bars, parachute attachment rings, and all service livery.

MODEL   INDIAN 149M 1953

Military Service	Standard production model procured by United States military in 1953 a solo lightweight suitable for parachute use and adopted by airborne troops to replace Indian 148A model.

ENGINE & TRANSMISSION

Type	Indian, vertical ohv, single-cylinder
Capacity	292cc 69.8 x 76.2mm
Comp, ratio	7 : 1
Output	9 hp at 6000 rpm
Starting	left foot kick start
Carburettor	single
Electrics	6v, Geneto magneto
Clutch	multi-plate, wet
Gearbox	foot-change, 4-speed
Final	exposed chain

FRAME & WHEELS

Type	tubular single loop design
Front forks	telescopic, hydraulic damping
Rear forks	without suspension
Brakes	internal expanding drum, front and rear
Tyre size	3.25 x 18″ front and rear, road pattern

DIMENSIONS

Overall length	2184mm	(86.0″)
Overall width	737mm	(29.0″)
Overall height	965mm	(38.0″)
Wheelbase	1359mm	(53.5″)
Ground clearance	127mm	(5.0″)
Seat height		
Unladen weight	141 kg	(310 lb)
Fuel tank	14 litre	(4.75 US gal)
Performance	97 km/h	(60 mph)
		300 mile range

MILITARY EQUIP. rear carry rack, crash bars, parachute attachment rings, and all service livery.

USSR

MODEL   M-72 to K-750M 1941-77

Manufacturer	State motorcycle Works thoughout USSR
Military Service	Military motorcycles based on BMW flat-twin format, available in solo and sidecar versions for despatch, general liaison and transportation duties. Replaced by Dnieper MT-12 (See next Chapter).

ENGINE & TRANSMISSION

Type	BMW-type transverse sv, flat-twin
Capacity	746cc 78 x 78mm
Comp, ratio	5.5 : 1 – 6.0 : 1
Output	22 hp at 4600 rpm – 26 hp at 4900 rpm
Clutch	single-plate, dry
Gearbox	hand-change, 4-speed
Final	exposed shaft

Brief specifications 1941-1977, of Soviet military motorcycle M-72 and K750; superseded by Dnieper MT-12.

Model	M-72	M-72M	M-72K	M-72H	K-750	K-750M
Years of production	1941–1956	1956–1960	1954–1960	1956–1959	1959–1963	1963–1977
Manufacturers	MMZ, IMZ, GMZ, ZMZ, K-O, KMZ	IMZ	IMZ	KMZ	KMZ	KMZ
Cubic capacity	746cc	746cc	746cc	746cc	746cc	746cc
Comp. ratio	5.5	5.5	5.5	5.5	6.0	6.0
Output hp/rpm	22hp at 4,600rpm	22hp at 4,600rpm	27hp at 5,000rpm	22hp at 4,600rpm	26hp at 4,900rpm	26hp at 4,900rpm
Ignition	Coil G11	Coil G11A	magento	Coil G11A	Coil G11A	Coil G414
Max. speed solo km/h	105	105	–	–	–	–
Max. speed with sidecar km/h	85	85	120	90	90	90
Fuel consumption 1/100 km	5.9–40	7.5–50	–	6.0-45	6.0-45	6.0-45
Front suspension	telescopic	telescopic	telescopic	leading-link	leading link	telescopic
Rear suspension	plunger	plunger	plunger	plunger	swinging arm	swinging arm
Wheelbase	1400mm	1400mm	1400mm	1450mm	1450mm	1450mm
Dry Wt. solo kg.	205	211	190	204	204	209
Dry Wt. with sidecar kg.	336	340	227	335	315	318

MMZ: Minsk Motorcycle Plant, IMZ: Izhevsk Motorcycle Plant, GMZ: Gorkiy Motorcycle Plant, ZMZ: Zavod Motorcycle Plant, KMZ: Kiyev Motorcycle Plant

CHAPTER FIVE

Contemporary Design

The following specifications are 28 of the best known motorcycles in military service between 1967 and 1990.

Austria
Puch 250 MCH 1969 *p 177*

Canada
Bombardier Military 250 1978 *p 171*

Czechoslovakia
Jawa 350 Military 634-5-16 1978 *p 177*

Finland
Winha 340 Automatic 1977-78 *p 173*

France
Peugeot SX8 AR 1979 *p 177*

Germany (East)
MZ ES250/2A 1969 *p 177*

Germany (West)
BMW R60/5 1969 *p 157*
BMW R80/7 1977 *p 157*
BMW K100RT 1984 *p 159*
BMW R65GS 1988 *p 157*
Hercules K 125BW 1981 *p 155*
Maico M250/M 1975 *p 156*

Great Britain
Armstrong MT 500 1984 *p 170*
BSA B40WD 1967 *p 170*

Italy
Moto Guzzi V7 1967 *p 153*
Moto Guzzi Nuovo Falcone 1970 *p 154*
Moto Guzzi 850-T3 1973 *p 154*
Moto Guzzi V50-11 1980 *p 154*

Japan
Honda CB400T 1978 *p 160*
Susuki GS400 1978 *p 160*
Yamaha DT250MX 1980 *p 160*

Spain
Bultaco Commander MOD 224 1981 *p 177*

Sweden
Hagglunds XM 74 1974 *p 176*
Husqvarna MC 256A MT 1967 *p 175*
Husqvarna MC 258 MT 1980 *p 176*

Switzerland
Condor A350 1973 *p 177*

USA
Harley-Davidson FLH 1967 *p 173*

USSR
Dnieper MT-12 1977 *p 150*

AUSTRIA

MODEL	PUCH 250 MCH 1969
Manufacturer	Steyr-Daimler-Puch AG, Graz
Military Service	Standard production model works modified for military service, by Austrian armed forces in 1969, for solo multi-terrain despatch and general liaison duties.

ENGINE AND TRANSMISSION

Type	Puch, split-single, two-stroke
Capacity	248cc 2 x 45 x 78mm
Comp, ratio	6.2 : 1
Output	14 hp at 5500 rpm
Starting	left foot kick start
Carburettor	single Puch 32mm bore
Electrics	6v
Clutch	multi-plate, wet
Gearbox	foot-change, 4-speed
Final	exposed chain

FRAME & WHEELS

Type	duplex cradle, single downtube, tubular construction
Front forks	telescopic, hydraulic damping, 170mm travel
Rear forks	trailing, helical sprung, load adjustable, 80mm travel
Brakes	internal expanding drums, 160mm diameter front and rear
Tyre size	3.50 x 19" front and rear, on and off road pattern

DIMENSIONS

Overall length	2060mm	(81.1")
Overall width	850mm	(33.3")
Overall height	1100mm	(43.3")
Wheelbase	1350mm	(53.1")
Ground clearance	190mm	(7.4")
Seat height	800mm	(31.4")
Unladen weight	155 kg	(341 lb)
Fuel tank	12.3 litre	(3.2 Imp gal)
Performance	100 km/h	(62 mph) max

MILITARY EQUIP. canvas panniers, braced handlebars, extra long side stand for off road use, all-over service livery.

CANADA

MODEL	BOMBARDIER MILITARY 250 1978
Manufacturer	Bombardier Limited, Valcourt, Quebec, Canada
Military Service	Standard production trials model works modified for military service, for multi-terrain despatch and general liaison. Ordered by Canadian armed forces in 1978 and USA in 1982. BSA assembled version prepared for British and Belgian military in 1979.

ENGINE AND TRANSMISSION

Type	Bombardier-Rotax, single-cylinder, two-stroke
Capacity	247cc 74 x 57.5mm
Comp, ratio	10 : 1
Output	26 hp at 7500 rpm
Starting	left foot kick start, in gear operation
Carburettor	Bing 32mm diameter, oil impregnated foam air filter
Electrics	12v, 130 watt, Bosch solid state ignition
Clutch	multi-plate, wet
Gearbox	foot-change, 5-speed
Final	exposed chain

FRAME & WHEELS

Type	duplex cradle, tubular construction, oil in tapered backbone
Front forks	telescopic, hydraulic damping, 250mm travel
Rear forks	trailing, helical sprung, load adjustable
Brakes	internal expanding drums, front and rear
Tyre size	3.00 x 21" front, 4.00 x 18" rear, cross country pattern

DIMENSIONS

Overall length	2130mm	(83.8")
Overall width	860mm	(33.8")
Overall height	1140mm	(44.8")
Wheelbase	1397mm	(55.0")
Ground clearance	230mm	(9.0")
Seat height	840mm	(33.0")
Unladen weight	130 kg	(286 lb)
Fuel tank	16 litre	(3.5 Imp gal)
Performance	(145 mph)	90 km/h max
	125 mile range	

MILITARY EQUIP. rear carry rack and panniers, high level exhaust and mudguards, braced handlebars, all-over service livery, and black engine and exhaust finish.

CZECHOSLOVAKIA

MODEL	JAWA 350 MILITARY 634-5-16 1978
Manufacturer	Zbrojovka F. Janecek, Prague
Military Service	Standard production model works modified for military service, by Czechoslovak armed forces in 1978, for solo and with sidecar despatch and general liaison duties. Proposed service life until 1999.

ENGINE AND TRANSMISSION

Type	Jawa, twin-cylinder, two-stroke
Capacity	344cc 58 x 65mm
Comp, ratio	9.2 : 1
Output	22 hp at 5000 rpm
Starting	left foot kick start
Carburettor	single JIkov 2926 SBD
Electrics	6v, 75 watt, PAL magneto
Clutch	multi-plate, wet
Gearbox	foot-change, 4-speed
Final	enclosed chain

FRAME & WHEELS

Type	duplex cradle, tubular construction
Front forks	telescopic, hydraulic damping, 150mm travel
Rear forks	trailing, helical sprung, 80mm travel
Brakes	internal expanding drums, 160mm diameter front and rear
Tyre size	3.25 x 18" front, 3.50 x 18" rear, road pattern

DIMENSIONS

Overall length	2080mm	(81.8") solo
Overall width	710mm	(27.9") solo
Overall height	1130mm	(44.4") solo
Wheelbase	1360mm	(53.5") solo
Ground clearance	130mm	(5.1") solo
Seat height	810mm	(31.8") solo
Unladen weight	156 kg	(343 lb) solo
Fuel tank	16.2 litre	(3.5 Imp gal)
Performance	120 km/h	(75 mph) max solo

GEAR RATIO

I	= 3.16 : 1	MILITARY EQUIP. rear carry rack and panniers, additional masked lighting, front crash bars, all-over service livery.
II	= 1.88 : 1	
III	= 1.33 : 1	
IV	= 1.00 : 1	

FINLAND

MODEL	WINHA 340 AUTOMATIC 1977-78
Manufacturer	Polar Metal Plast, Rovaniemi
Military Service	Specialised military model developed for Finnish armed forces; solo multi-terrain model for despatch and general liaison duties.

ENGINE AND TRANSMISSION

Type	Kohler 340 2AX, fan-cooled twin-cylinder, two-stroke
Capacity	338cc 62 x 56mm
Comp, ratio	7 : 1
Output	30 hp at 7000 rpm
Starting	right hand pull cord
Carburettor	Walbro WD 33
Electrics	12v, 100 watt
Clutch	automatically engaged centrifugal clutch
Gearbox	Kohler Variomatic torque converter
Final	exposed chain

FRAME & WHEELS

Type	duplex cradle, tubular construction
Front forks	Ceriani, telescopic, hydraulic damping, 36mm diameter
Rear forks	trailing, Girling, helical sprung, load adjustable
Brakes	internal expanding drums, front and rear
Tyre size	21 x 3" front, 18 x 4" rear, trials pattern

DIMENSIONS

Overall length	2240mm	(88.1")
Overall width	800mm	(31.4")
Overall height	1270mm	(50.0")
Wheelbase	1540mm	(60.6")
Ground clearance	300mm	(11.8")
Seat height	820mm	(32.2")
Unladen weight	114 kg	(251 lb)
Fuel tank	12.5 litre	(2.7 Imp gal)
Performance	120 km/h	(74 mph) max

MILITARY EQUIP. high level exhaust system, high level mudguards, braced handlebars, ski attachments, and all-over service livery and black engine finish.

FRANCE

MODEL	PEUGEOT SX8 AR 1979
Manufacturer	Cycles Peugeot, Valentigney
Military Service	Standard production model works modified for military service by French armed forces in 1979, for solo despatch and general liaison duties.

ENGINE AND TRANSMISSION

Type	Peugeot, single-cylinder, two-stroke
Capacity	79.6cc 48 x 44mm
Comp, ratio	9.6 : 1
Output	8 hp at 6500 rpm
Starting	left foot kick start
Carburettor	Peugeot 20mm diameter
Electrics	6v, magneto flywheel ignition
Clutch	multi-plate, wet
Gearbox	foot-change, 5-speed
Final	exposed chain

FRAME & WHEELS

Type	duplex cradle, tubular construction
Front forks	telescopic, hydraulic damping, 130mm travel
Rear forks	trailing, helical sprung, 80mm travel, load adjustable
Brakes	internal expanding drums, 120mm diameter front and rear
Tyre size	2.75 x 21″ front, 3.00 x 21″ rear, trial pattern

DIMENSIONS

Overall length	2000mm	(78.7″)
Overall width	800mm	(31.4″)
Overall height		
Wheelbase	1260mm	(49.6″)
Ground clearance	310mm	(12.2″)
Seat height		
Unladen weight	77 kg	(169 lb)
Fuel tank	14.5 litre	(3.1 Imp gal)
Performance	75 km/h	(46 mph) max
	300 km range	

MILITARY EQUIP. rear carry rack, high level exhaust and mudguards, braced handlebars, all-over service livery, and black engine and exhaust finish.

GERMANY (EAST)

MODEL — MZ ES250/2A 1969

Manufacturer	VEB Motorradwerke Zschopau
Military Service	Standard production model works modified for military service, by East German military for solo/sidecar despatch and general liaison. Introduced late '60s to replace MZ ES250/1A and superseded mid '70s by MZ TS250/A with telescopic front forks.

ENGINE AND TRANSMISSION

Type	MZ, single-cylinder, two-stroke
Capacity	243cc 65 x 69mm
Comp, ratio	8.5 : 1
Output	17.5 hp at 5300 rpm
Starting	left foot kick start
Carburettor	single BVF 28mm N 1-1
Electrics	6v, 60 watt, coil ignition
Clutch	multi-plate, wet
Gearbox	foot-change, 4-speed
Final	enclosed chain

FRAME & WHEELS

Type	pressed steel and tubular construction, single loop design
Front forks	leading link, hydraulic damping, 142mm travel
Rear forks	trailing, hydraulic damping, load adjustable, 115mm travel
Brakes	internal expanding drums, 160mm diameter front and rear
Tyre size	3.25 x 16″ front, 3.50 x 16″ rear, road pattern

DIMENSIONS

Overall length	2090mm	(82.2″) solo
Overall width	862mm	(33.9″) solo
Overall height	1060mm	(41.7″) solo
Wheelbase	1325mm	(52.1″) solo
Ground clearance	170mm	(6.6″) solo
Seat height		
Unladen weight	156 kg	(343 lb)
Fuel tank	16 litre	(3.5 Imp gal)
Performance	120 km/h	(75 mph) max

GEAR RATIO

I = 2.77 : 1
II = 1.63 : 1
III = 1.23 : 1
IV = 0.92 : 1

MILITARY EQUIP. rear carry rack or pillion seat, left side canvas pannier, all-over service livery.

GERMANY (WEST)

MODEL — BMW R60/5 1969

Military Service	Standard production model works modified for general service, by armed forces throughout the world, including Austria, Belgium, France, Netherlands, Switzerland and West Germany, for solo escort, despatch and military police.

ENGINE AND TRANSMISSION

Type	BMW, transverse ohv flat-twin cylinder
Capacity	599cc 73.5 x 70.6mm
Comp, ratio	9.2 : 1
Output	40 hp at 6400 rpm
Starting	left foot kick start
Carburettor	two Bing 26mm bore
Electrics	12v
Clutch	single plate, dry
Gearbox	foot-change, 4-speed
Final	enclosed shaft

FRAME & WHEELS

Type	duplex cradle, tubular construction
Front forks	telescopic, hydraulic damping
Rear forks	trailing, helical sprung, load adjustable
Brakes	internal expanding drums, front and rear
Tyre size	3.25 x 19″ front, 4.00 x 18″ rear, road pattern

DIMENSIONS

Overall length	2100mm	(82.6″)
Overall width	740mm	(29.1″)
Overall height	850mm	(33.4″)
Wheelbase	1385mm	(54.5″)
Ground clearance	165mm	(6.4″)
Seat height	810mm	(31.8″)
Unladen weight	210 kg	(462.9 lb)
Fuel tank	24 litre	(6.3 Imp gal)
Performance	167 km/h	(103 mph) max

GEAR RATIO

I = 3.89 : 1
II = 2.57 : 1
III = 1.87 : 1
IV = 1.50 : 1

MILITARY EQUIP. rear carry rack for two way radio, leather panniers, additional lighting, wind screen, crash bars, siren, all over service livery.

MODEL — BMW R80/7 1977

Military Service	Standard production model works modified for armed forces throughout the World, including Austria, Belgium, Netherlands, France, West Germany and Switzerland, for solo escort and military police.

ENGINE AND TRANSMISSION

Type	BMW, transverse ohv flat-twin
Capacity	785cc 84.8 x 70.6mm
Comp, ratio	8.2 : 1
Output	50 hp at 6500 rpm
Starting	electric and left foot kick start
Carburettor	twin Bing 32mm bore
Electrics	12v, 280 watt Bosch alternator, solid state ignition
Clutch	single plate, dry
Gearbox	foot-change, 5-speed
Final	enclosed shaft

FRAME & WHEELS

Type	duplex cradle, tubular construction
Front forks	telescopic, hydraulic damping, 200mm travel
Rear forks	trailing, helical sprung, load adjustable, 125mm travel
Brakes	twin hydraulic disc front 260mm dia, drum brake rear 200mm dia
Tyre size	3.25 x 19″ front, 4.00 x 18″ rear, road pattern

DIMENSIONS

Overall length	2210mm	(87.0″)
Overall width	746mm	(29.2″)
Overall height	810mm	(31.8″)
Wheelbase	1465mm	(57.6″)
Ground clearance		
Seat height	820mm	(32.2″)
Unladen weight	198 kg	(436 lb)
Fuel tank	24 litre	(6.3 Imp gal)
Performance	170 km/h	(105 mph) max

GEAR RATIO

I = 4.4 : 1
II = 2.86 : 1
III = 2.07 : 1
IV = 1.67 : 1
V = 1.5 : 1

MILITARY EQUIP. rear carry rack for two way radio, plastic panniers, additional lighting, windscreen, front and rear crash bars, siren, all over service livery.

MODEL — BMW K100 RT 1984

Military Service	Standard production model works modified for armed forces throughout the World, including Belgian, French, Swiss, etc, for solo escort and military police.

ENGINE AND TRANSMISSION

Type	BMW, liquid-cooled ohv horizontal in-line-four
Capacity	987cc 67 x 70mm
Comp, ratio	10.2 : 1
Output	90 hp at 8000 rpm
Starting	electric start
Carburettor	four Bosch LE-Jetronic 34mm Ø
Electric	12v, 460 watt, digital ignition system, Bosch VZ-51L
Clutch	single plate, dry
Gearbox	foot-change, 5-speed
Final	enclosed shaft

FRAME & WHEELS

Type	tubular space frame, integral engine support
Front forks	telescopic, hydraulic damping, 185mm travel
Rear forks	trailing, helical sprung, 110mm travel
Brakes	twin hydraulic discs front, single disc rear, 285mm diameter
Tyre size	100/90 x 18″ front, 130/90 x 17″ rear, standard road tubeless

DIMENSIONS

Overall length	2220mm	(87.4″)
Overall width	916mm	(36.0″)
Overall height		
Wheelbase	1516mm	(59.6″)
Ground clearance		
Seat height	810mm	(31.8″)
Unladen weight	254 kg	(556 lb)
Fuel tank	22 litre	(4.9 Imp gal)
Performance	215 km/h	(135 mph) max

GEAR RATIO

I = 4.50 : 1
II = 2.96 : 1
III = 2.30 : 1
IV = 1.88 : 1
V = 1.67 : 1

MILITARY EQUIP. rear carry rack for two way radio, leather or plastic panniers, full fairing or screen, additional lights, siren, crash bars, all over service livery.

MODEL — BMW R65GS 1988

Manufacturer	Bayerische Motorenwerke AG, Munich
Military Service	Standard production model works modified for general police service, and adopted by Danish armed forces in 1988, for solo multi-terrain despatch and general liaison. A second version with 48hp was also prepared for Denmark and the Netherlands.

ENGINE AND TRANSMISSION

Type	BMW, transverse ohv flat-twin
Capacity	650cc 82 x 61.5mm
Comp, ratio	8.4 : 1
Output	27 hp at 5500 rpm
Starting	electric
Carburettor	two Bing 26mm Ø
Electrics	12v, 280 watt
Clutch	single plate, dry
Gearbox	foot-change, 5-speed
Final	enclosed shaft

FRAME & WHEELS

Type	tubular duplex cradle
Front forks	telescopic, hydraulic damping, 200mm travel
Rear forks	trailing, hydraulic damping, 170mm travel
Brakes	single hydraulic disc 260mm Ø, internal expanding drum 200mm Ø rear
Tyre size	3.00 x 21″ front, 4.00 x 18″ rear, trials pattern

DIMENSIONS

Overall length	2230mm	(87.7″)
Overall width	1000mm	(39.3″)
Overall height		
Wheelbase	1465mm	(57.6″)
Ground clearance		
Seat height	860mm	(33.8″)
Unladen weight	198 kg	(436 lb)
Fuel tank	19.5 litre	(4.2 Imp gal)
Performance	146 km/h	(90 mph) max

GEAR RATIO

I = 4.40 : 1
II = 2.86 : 1
III = 2.07 : 1
IV = 1.67 : 1
V = 1.50 : 1

MILITARY EQUIP. rear carry rack and leather panniers, high level exhaust and mudguards, braced handlebars, engine crash bars, all over service livery.

MODEL — HERCULES K 125 BW 1981

Manufacturer	Nurnberger Hercules-Werke GmbH, Nuremburg
Military Service	Standard production model works modified for military service by West German armed forces in 1970, for solo multi-terrain despatch and liaison. 15,000 machines delivered by 1984.

ENGINE AND TRANSMISSION

Type	Sachs, single-cylinder, two-stroke
Capacity	122cc 54 x 54mm
Comp, ratio	9 : 1
Output	13 hp at 7000 rpm
Starting	left foot kick start
Carburettor	single Bing 24mm diameter
Electrics	6v, Bosch magneto
Clutch	Sachs multi-plate, wet
Gearbox	foot-change, 5-speed
Final	exposed chain

FRAME & WHEELS

Type	duplex cradle, tubular construction
Front forks	telescopic, hydraulic damping, 140mm travel
Rear forks	trailing, helical sprung, 90mm travel
Brakes	internal expanding drums, 140mm diameter front and rear
Tyre size	3.25 x 18″ front, 3.50 x 18″ rear, trials pattern

DIMENSIONS

Overall length	2035mm	(80.1″)
Overall width	930mm	(36.6″)
Overall height	1060mm	(41.7″)
Wheelbase	1295mm	(50.9″)
Ground clearance		
Seat height	810mm	(31.8″)
Unladen weight	130 kg	(286 lb)
Fuel tank	15 litre	(3.3 Imp gal)
Performance	100 km/h	(62 mph) max
	300 km range	

GEAR RATIO

I = 4.60 : 1
II = 2.73 : 1
III = 1.85 : 1
IV = 1.39 : 1
V = 1.15 : 1

MILITARY EQUIP. folding rear carry rack, left side pannier, high level exhaust right side, braced handlebars, crash bars, all over service livery and black engine finish.

MODEL — MAICO MODEL M250/M 1975

Military Service	Standard production model works modified for military service, by West German armed forces in 1975, for solo despatch and general liaison duties. 10,000 machines supplied.

ENGINE AND TRANSMISSION

Type	Maico MC/GS, single-cylinder, two-stroke
Capacity	247cc 67 x 70mm
Comp, ratio	
Output	17 hp at 6000 rpm
Starting	left foot kick start
Carburettor	Single Bing
Electrics	6v, Bosch HKZ
Clutch	multi-plate, wet
Gearbox	foot-change, 5-speed
Final	exposed chain

FRAME & WHEELS

Type	duplex cradle, tubular construction
Front forks	telescopic, hydraulic damping, 180mm travel
Rear forks	trailing, helical sprung, load adjustable
Brakes	internal expanding drums, 136mm Ø front and 160mm rear
Tyre size	3.15 x 18″ front, 4.00 x 18″ rear, cross country pattern

DIMENSIONS

Unladen weight	130 kg	(286 lb)

Fuel tank 17 litre (3.7 Imp gal)
Performance 140 km/h (87 mph) max

MILITARY EQUIP. rear carry rack and leather panniers, all over service livery and black engine and exhaust finish.

GREAT BRITAIN

MODEL ARMSTRONG MT 500 1984

Manufacturer CCM-Armstrong Limited, Bolton
Military Service Specialised military model for British armed forces, for solo multi-terrain despatch, reconnaissance and general liaison. A total of 2300 machines were supplied between 1984-87, to replace Bombardier 250cc.

ENGINE AND TRANSMISSION
Type Rotax, ohv single-cylinder
Capacity 485cc 89 x 77.4mm
Comp. ratio 8.2 : 1
Output 32 hp at 6200 rpm
Starting left foot kick start
Carburettor single Amal 34mm diameter
Electrics 12v, 190 watt, solid state ignition, auto advance
Clutch multi-plate, wet
Gearbox foot-change, 5-speed
Final exposed chain

FRAME & WHEELS
Type welded tubular and box section, oil carrying, sealed taper bearings
Front forks telescopic, hydraulic damping, sealed heavy duty, 241mm travel
Rear forks trailing, helical sprung, load adjustable
Brakes internal expanding drums, 140mm diameter front and 160mm rear
Tyre size 90/90 x 21″ front, 4.00 x 18″ rear, trials pattern

DIMENSIONS
Overall length 2210mm (87.0″)
Overall width 790mm (31.1″)
Overall height 1160mm (45.6″)
Wheelbase
Ground clearance 216mm (8.5″)
Seat height 930mm (36.6″)
Unladen weight 150 kg (330 lb)
Fuel tank 13.6 litre (3 Imp gal)
Performance 145 km/h (90 mph) max
200 mile range

GEAR RATIO
I = 2.909 : 1
II = 2.000 : 1
III = 1.400 : 1
IV = 1.117 : 1
V = 0.913 : 1

MILITARY EQUIP. rear carry rack and canvas panniers, high level exhaust and mudguards, braced handlebars, sump guard, all over service livery and black engine finish.

MODEL BSA B40WD 1967

Manufacturer BSA Motor Cycles Ltd, Small Heath, Birmingham
Military Service Standard production model works modified for military service, following 10,000 mile reliability test. British army placed an order for 2000, for solo despatch and military police duties. Also used by Australia, Belgium, Denmark, etc.

ENGINE AND TRANSMISSION
Type BSA, vertical ohv single-cylinder
Capacity 343cc 79 x 70mm
Comp. ratio 5 : 1
Output 18 hp at 6000 rpm
Starting right foot kick start
Carburettor single: butterfly valve
Electrics 6v
Clutch multi-plate, wet
Gearbox foot-change, 4-speed
Final enclosed chain

FRAME & WHEELS
Type tubular construction, single downtube
Front forks telescopic, hydraulic damping, helical sprung
Rear forks trailing, hydraulic damping, helical sprung
Brakes internal expanding drum, 7″ dia front, 6″ dia rear
Tyre size 3.25 x 18″ front, 4.00 x 18″ rear, heavy road pattern

DIMENSIONS
Overall length 2057mm (81.0″)
Overall width 163mm (29.5″)
Overall height 1092mm (43.0″)
Wheelbase 1359mm (53.5″)
Ground clearance 178mm (7.0″)
Seat height
Unladen weight 162 kg (358 lb)
Fuel tank 13.6 litre (3 Imp gal)
Performance 88 km/h (55 mph) max

MILITARY EQUIP. canvas panniers held in metal frames, full fairing (white) for police escort duties, overall service livery.

ITALY

MODEL MOTO GUZZI V7 1967

Manufacturer Moto Guzzi SpA, Mandello del Lario
Military Service Standard production model works modified for general police service, adopted by Italian armed forces in 1967, for solo escort, despatch and military police. Also adopted by military in Africa.

ENGINE AND TRANSMISSION
Type Moto Guzzi, transverse 90° ohv, V-twin
Capacity 703cc 80 x 70mm
Comp. ratio 9 : 1
Output 50 hp at 6300 rpm
Starting electric start (left foot kick start option)
Carburettor two Dell'Orto VHB 29mm CD
Electrics 12v, 300 watt, coil ignition
Clutch single plate, dry
Gearbox foot-change, 4-speed
Final enclosed shaft

FRAME & WHEELS
Type duplex cradle, tubular construction
Front forks telescopic, hydraulic damping
Rear forks trailing, helical sprung, load adjustable
Brakes internal expanding drums, front and rear
Tyre size 4.00 x 18″ front and rear, road pattern

DIMENSIONS
Overall length 2230mm (87.7″)
Overall width 795mm (31.2″)
Overall height 1050mm (41.3″)
Wheelbase 1445mm (56.8″)
Ground clearance 150mm (5.9″)
Seat height
Unladen weight 243 kg (535.7 lb)
Fuel tank 20 litre (4.3 Imp gal)
Performance 170 km/h (105 mph) max

GEAR RATIO
I = 11.33 : 1
II = 7.61 : 1
III = 5.97 : 1
IV = 4.56 : 1

MILITARY EQUIP. rear carry rack, plastic panniers, two way radio, windscreen, additional lighting, siren, crash bars, all-over service livery.

MODEL MOTO GUZZI NUOVO FALCONE 1970

Military Service Specialised model (1970-76) developed for public service, to replace earlier Falcone model (1950-67). Widely used by Italian military and various police departments for solo escort, despatch and general liaison duties. Also procured by military in Ghana and Yugoslavia.

ENGINE AND TRANSMISSION
Type Moto Guzzi, horizontal ohv, single-cylinder
Capacity 498cc 88 x 82mm
Comp. ratio 6.8 : 1
Output 26.2 hp at 4800 rpm
Starting left foot kick start
Carburettor single Dell'Orto VHB 29 A
Electrics 12v, 150 watt
Clutch multi-plate, wet
Gearbox foot-change, 4-speed
Final exposed chain

FRAME & WHEELS
Type duplex cradle, tubular construction
Front forks telescopic, hydraulic damping
Rear forks trailing, helical sprung, load adjustable
Brakes internal expanding drums, front and rear
Tyre size 3.50 x 18″ front and rear, road pattern

DIMENSIONS
Overall length 2170mm (85.4″)
Overall width 770mm (30.3″)
Overall height 1040mm (40.9″)
Wheelbase 1450mm (57.0″)
Ground clearance
Seat height
Unladen weight 214 kg (471 lb)
Fuel tank 18 litre (3.9 Imp gal)
Performance 130 km/h (80 mph) max

MILITARY EQUIP. rear carry rack for pillion seat or two way radio, metal or plastic panniers, windscreen, crashbars/leg shields, all-over service livery.

MODEL MOTO GUZZI 850-T3 1973

Military Service Standard production model, works modified for public service by Italian military police and numerous police departments worldwide. In 1975, 1000cc automatic version, V-1000 Convert model, introduced also for public service, but not as widely successful.

ENGINE AND TRANSMISSION
Type Moto Guzzi, transverse 90° ohv, V-twin
Capacity 844cc 83 x 78mm
Comp. ratio 9.5 : 1
Output 68.5 hp at 7000 rpm
Starting electric start
Carburettor twin Dell'Orto type VHB 30
Electrics 12v, Bosch W 225 T
Clutch single plate, dry
Gearbox foot-change, 5-speed
Final enclosed shaft

FRAME & WHEELS
Type tubular structure, duplex cradle
Front forks telescopic, helical sprung, sealed hydraulic dampers
Rear forks trailing, adjustable helical sprung, hydraulic damping
Brakes Twin hydraulic front discs (300mm Ø), single interconnected rear (242mm)
Tyre size 100/90 H – 18″ front, 110/90 H – 18″ rear, road pattern

DIMENSIONS
Overall length 2200mm (86.6″)
Overall width 780mm (30.7″)
Overall height 1060mm (41.7″)
Wheelbase 1470mm (57.8″)
Ground clearance 150mm (5.9″)
Seat height
Unladen weight *243 kg (535.7 lb)
Fuel tank 24 litre (5.3 Imp gal)
Performance 195 km/h (121 mph) max
(1.6 litre/100 km)
* without military accessories

GEAR RATIO
I = 2.000 : 1
II = 1.388 : 1
III = 1.047 : 1
IV = 0.869 : 1
V = 0.750 : 1

MILITARY EQUIP. rear carrier rack for optional radio equipment, handlebar mounted screen, front and rear crashbars, panniers, leg shields, police lights, two sirens, and overall service livery.

MODEL MOTO GUZZI V50-II 1980

Manufacturer
Military Service Standard production model works modified for general police service by Dutch armed forces in 1980 (to replace ageing Mk-I model), for solo despatch and general liaison duties. A smaller 350cc model, the V35, supplied the Yugoslav military in late 1970s.

ENGINE AND TRANSMISSION
Type Moto Guzzi, 90° ohv, V-twin
Capacity 490cc 74 x 57mm
Comp. ratio 10.8 : 1
Output 45 hp at 7500 rpm
Starting electric start, left foot kick start option
Carburettor twin Dell'Orto VHB 24 F
Electrics 12v, solid state ignition
Clutch single plate, dry
Gearbox foot-change, 5-speed
Final enclosed shaft

FRAME & WHEELS
Type duplex cradle, tubular construction
Front forks telescopic, hydraulic damping
Rear forks trailing, helical sprung, load adjustable
Brakes hydraulic disc brakes front and rear, inter-linked operation
Tyre size 3.00 x 18″ front, 3.50 x 18″ rear, road pattern

DIMENSIONS
Overall length 2080mm (81.8″)
Overall width 750mm (29.5″)
Overall height 1035mm (40.7″)
Wheelbase 1395mm (54.9″)
Ground clearance 175mm (6.8″)
Seat height
Unladen weight 152 kg (335 lb)
Fuel tank 16.5 litre (3.6 Imp gal)
Performance 170 km/h (105 mph) max

GEAR RATIO
I = 17.35 : 1
II = 11.02 : 1
III = 8.12 : 1
IV = 6.64 : 1
V = 5.78 : 1

MILITARY EQUIP. rear carry rack for pillion seat or two way radio, metal or plastic panniers, windscreen, crashbars with leg shields, all-over service livery.

JAPAN

MODEL HONDA CB400T 1978

Manufacturer Honda Motor Co Ltd, Shibuya Ku, Tokyo
Military Service Standard production model modified, delivery, for South African armed forces in 1978 and Danish in 1982, for solo despatch and general liaison type duties.

ENGINE AND TRANSMISSION
Type Honda, ohc parallel-twin
Capacity 395cc 70.5 x 50.6mm
Comp. ratio 9.3 : 1
Output 43 hp at 9500 rpm
Starting electric and right foot kick start option
Carburettor twin Honda CV
Electrics 12v, AC generator, solid state ignition
Clutch multi-plate, wet
Gearbox foot-change, 5-speed
Final exposed chain

FRAME & WHEELS
Type duplex cradle, tubular construction
Front forks telescopic, hydraulic damping
Rear forks trailing, helical sprung, load adjustable
Brakes single hydraulic disc front, internal expanding rear drum
Tyre size 3.60 x 19″ front, 4.10 x 18″ rear, road pattern

DIMENSIONS
Overall length 2130mm (83.8″)
Overall width 730mm (28.7″)
Overall height
Wheelbase 1390mm (54.7″)
Ground clearance 165mm (6.4″)
Seat height
Unladen weight 180 kg (396 lb)
Fuel tank 14 litre (3 Imp gal)
Performance 145 km/h (90 mph) max

GEAR RATIO
I = 2.73 : 1
II = 1.85 : 1
III = 1.41 : 1
IV = 1.14 : 1
V = 0.96 : 1

MILITARY EQUIP. rear carry rack panniers, front and rear crash bars, all over service livery.

MODEL SUZUKI GS400 1978

Manufacturer Suzuki Motor Co Ltd, Hamamatsu
Military Service Standard production model modified on delivery for

Australian armed forces in 1978, for solo despatch, military police and general liaison duties. 447 machines supplied.

ENGINE AND TRANSMISSION

Type	Suzuki, dohc parallel-twin
Capacity	398cc 65 x 60mm
Comp. ratio	
Output	36 hp at 8500 rpm
Starting	electric and right foot kick start option
Carburettor	twin Mikuni BS34, constant vacuum
Electrics	12v, 200 watt
Clutch	multi-plate, wet
Gearbox	foot-change, 6-speed
Final	exposed chain

FRAME & WHEELS

Type	duplex cradle, tubular construction
Front forks	telescopic, hydraulic damping
Rear forks	trailing, helical sprung, 5 way adjustable
Brakes	single hydraulic disc front, internal expanding drum rear
Tyre size	3.00 x 19″ front, 3.50 x 18″ rear, road pattern

DIMENSIONS

Overall length	2085mm	(82.0″)
Overall width	836mm	(32.9″)
Overall height	1110mm	(43.7″)
Wheelbase	1384mm	(54.4″)
Ground clearance	155mm	(6.1″)
Seat height		
Unladen weight	172 kg	(379 lb)
Fuel tank	14 litre	(3 Imp gal)
Performance	145 km/h	(90 mph) max

MILITARY EQUIP. rear carry rack for two way radio, leather panniers, front and rear crash bars, siren and additional warning lights, all over service livery.

MODEL   YAMAHA DT250MX 1980

Manufacturer	Yamaha Motor Co Ltd, Hamakita-Shi Shizuoka-Ken
Military Service	Standard production model modified, upon arrival, for Danish armed forces in 1980, for solo multi-terrain despatch and general liaison duties. Also adopted by South African border patrols.

ENGINE AND TRANSMISSION

Type	Yamaha, single-cylinder, two-stroke
Capacity	246cc 70 x 64mm
Comp. ratio	6.7 : 1
Output	23 hp at 6000 rpm
Starting	right foot kick start
Carburettor	single VM28-SS
Electrics	6v, flywheel magneto, solid state ignition
Clutch	multi-plate, wet
Gearbox	foot-change, 5-speed
Final	exposed chain

FRAME & WHEELS

Type	tubular duplex cradle
Front forks	telescopic, hydraulic damping
Rear forks	trailing, helical sprung, single shock absorber
Brakes	internal expanding drums, front and rear
Tyre size	3.00 x 21″ front, 4.00 x 18″ rear, trials pattern

DIMENSIONS

Overall length	2145mm	(84.4″)
Overall width	875mm	(34.4″)
Overall height	1140mm	(44.8″)
Wheelbase	1415mm	(55.7″)
Ground clearance	245mm	(9.6″)
Seat height	860mm	(33.8″)
Unladen weight	119 kg	(262 lb)
Fuel tank	12 litre	(2.6 Imp gal)
Performance	145 km/h	(90 mph) max

MILITARY EQUIP. rear carry rack for two way radio, high level exhaust and mudguards, fuel tank enlarged from 8 to 12 litres, all over service livery and black engine and exhaust finish.

SPAIN

MODEL   BULTACO COMMANDER MOD 224 1981

Manufacturer	Bultaco SA, Barcelona
Military Service	Standard military model for Spanish armed forces, for solo multi-terrain despatch, reconnaissance and general liaison. Available in 250 and 350cc versions, first offered for military service in 1981.

ENGINE AND TRANSMISSION

Type	Bultaco, single-cylinder, two-stroke
Capacity	238cc 71 x 60mm
Comp. ratio	9 : 1
Output	14.1 hp at 5500 rpm
Starting	left foot kick start
Carburettor	single Amal 2600, 27mm diameter
Electrics	6v, magneto flywheel ignition
Clutch	multi-plate, wet
Gearbox	foot-change, 5-speed
Final	exposed chain

FRAME & WHEELS

Type	duplex cradle, tubular construction
Front forks	telescopic, hydraulic damping, 165mm travel
Rear forks	trailing, Betor (gas) damping, 90mm travel

Brakes	internal expanding drums, 140mm diameter front and rear	
Tyre size	2.75 x 21″ front, 4.00 x 18″ rear, trials pattern	

DIMENSIONS

Overall length	1960mm	(77.1″)
Overall width	830mm	(32.6″)
Overall height	1095mm	(43.1″)
Wheelbase	1270mm	(50.0″)
Ground clearance	305mm	(12.0″)
Seat height	840mm	(33.0″)
Unladen weight	101 kg	(222 lb)
Fuel tank	9 litre	(2 Imp gal)
Performance	130 km/h	(80 mph) max

GEAR RATIO		MILITARY EQUIP. rear carry rack for two way
I	= 3.484 : 1	radio, high level exhaust, sub-machine gun support bracket, panniers or spare fuel containers, all-over service livery and black engine finish.
II	= 2.262 : 1	
III	= 1.600 : 1	
IV	= 1.218 : 1	
V	= 1.000 : 1	

SWEDEN

MODEL   HÄGGLUNDS XM 74 1974

Manufacturer	AB Hägglund & Söner, Ornsköldsvik
Military Service	Specialised military model developed for Swedish army; solo multi-terrain model for despatch and general liaison duties. Limited production before primary drive problems brought project to halt, and contract completed by Husqvarna (Mod. MC 258A MT).

ENGINE AND TRANSMISSION

Type	Bombardier-Rotax 347, single-cylinder, two-stroke
Capacity	345cc 76 x 76mm
Comp. ratio	9 : 1
Output	24 hp at 5300 rpm
Starting	right foot kick start, with decompression valve
Carburettor	single Tillotson HR
Electrics	12v, 140 watt, solid state ignition, no battery
Clutch	automatically engaged centrifugal unit
Gearbox	Häggland-DAF variomatic torque converter, 24.6:1 to 6.1:1
Final	enclosed shaft

FRAME & WHEELS

Type	welded steel backbone, integral fuel tank and air intake
Front forks	Cerani telescopic, hydraulic damping, heavy duty
Rear forks	single rear arm, helical sprung, load adjustable
Brakes	internal expanding drums, front and rear
Tyre size	3.00 x 21″ front, 4.00 x 18″ rear, cross country pattern (pressed steel wheels)

DIMENSIONS

Overall length	2210mm	(87.0″)
Overall width	900mm	(35.4″)
Overall height	1110mm	(43.7″)
Wheelbase	1410mm	(55.5″)
Ground clearance	237mm	(9.3″)
Seat height	810mm	(31.8″)
Unladen weight	139 kg	(306 lb)
Fuel tank	16 litre	(3.5 Imp gal)
Performance	130 km/h	(80 mph) max

MILITARY EQUIP. high level exhaust, high level mudguards, braced handlebars, additional lighting, ski attachments.

MODEL   HUSQVARNA MC 256A MT 1967

Manufacturer	Husqvarna Motorcyklar AB, Odeshog
Military Service	Standard production model works modified for military service, adoped by Swedish armed forces in 1967, for solo multi-terrain despatch and general liaison duties. A total of 1100 machines supplied between the 1967-68 period.

ENGINE AND TRANSMISSION

Type	HVA, air cooled vertical single cylinder, two stroke
Capacity	245cc 69.5mm bore x 64.5mm stroke
Comp. ratio	8.9 : 1
Output	15.4 hp
Starting	left foot kick start
Carburettor	single Bing 22/5
Electrics	12v, 53 watt
Clutch	multi-plate, wet operation
Gearbox	right foot-change, 4-speed, unit design
Final	exposed chain – upper guard only

FRAME & WHEELS

Type	tubular construction, single loop
Front forks	telescopic, hydraulic damping
Rear forks	trailing, helical sprung
Brakes	internal expanding drums, front and rear
Tyre size	3.00 x 21″ front, 4.00 x 18″ rear, cross country pattern

DIMENSIONS

Overall length	2200mm	(86.6″)
Overall width	830mm	(32.6″)
Overall height	1130mm	(44.4″)
Wheelbase	1380mm	(54.3″)
Ground clearance	230mm	(9.0″)
Seat height	810mm	(31.8″)
Unladen weight	130 kg	(286.6 lb)
Fuel tank	12.4 litre	(2.72 Imp gal)
Performance	130 km/h	(62 mph) max

MILITARY EQUIP. rear carry rack on mudguard, high level exhaust system, additional masked

---

lighting, dual seat saddle, all-over service livery and black engine finish.

MODEL   HUSQVARNA MC 258A MT 1980

Manufacturer	Husqvarna Motorcyklar AB, Odeshog
Military Service	Specialised military model developed for Swedish army; solo multi-terrain model for despatch and general liaison duties. First 1000 supplied in 1980 (following failure of Hägglund XM-74 project). Further 2000 supplied in 1981. Proposed military service until 1999.

ENGINE AND TRANSMISSION

Type	HVA, single-cylinder, two-stroke
Capacity	250cc 69.5 x 64.5mm
Comp. ratio	11.8 : 1
Output	20 hp
Starting	left foot kick start
Carburettor	single Mikuni WM 32
Electrics	12v, 140 watt, SEM solid state ignition
Clutch	automatically engaged centrifugal design
Gearbox	HVA automatic 4-speed
Final	exposed chain

FRAME & WHEELS

Type	tubular construction, single loop
Front forks	telescopic, hydraulic damping
Rear forks	trailing, helical sprung, load adjustable
Brakes	internal expanding drums, 160mm diameter front and rear
Tyre size	3.50 x 21″ front, 4.40 x 17″ rear, trials pattern

DIMENSIONS

Overall length	2220mm	(87.4″)
Overall width	860mm	(33.8″)
Overall height	1200mm	(47.2″)
Wheelbase	1480mm	(58.2″)
Ground clearance	280mm	(11.0″)
Seat height	900mm	(35.4″)
Unladen weight	130 kg	(286 lb)
Fuel tank		
Performance	110 km/h	(68 mph) max
	300 km range	

MILITARY EQUIP. rear carry rack, high level exhaust and mudguards, braced handlebars, all-over service livery, and black engine and exhaust finish.

SWITZERLAND

MODEL   CONDOR A350 1973

Manufacturer	Condor SA, Courfaivre
Military Service	Specialised military model supplied to the Swiss armed forces in 1973, for solo despatch and general liaison duties. 3000 supplied to replace the ageing Condor A580-1 model (Chapter 4).

ENGINE AND TRANSMISSION

Type	Ducati-Condor, vertical ohc single-cylinder
Capacity	340cc 76 x 75mm
Comp. ratio	8.2 : 1
Output	16.6 hp at 5000 rpm
Starting	left foot kick start
Carburettor	single Dell'Orto type VHB 27 AD
Electrics	6v, 70 watt
Clutch	multi-plate, wet
Gearbox	foot-change, 5-speed
Final	exposed chain

FRAME & WHEELS

Type	duplex cradle, tubular construction
Front forks	telescopic, hydraulic damping
Rear forks	trailing, helical sprung
Brakes	internal expanding drums, 200mm diameter front and rear
Tyre size	3.25 x 18″ front, 3.50 x 18″ rear, road pattern

DIMENSIONS

Overall length	2120mm	(83.4″)
Overall width	825mm	(32.4″)
Overall height	1160mm	(45.6″)
Wheelbase	1400mm	(55.1″)
Ground clearance	170mm	(6.6″)
Seat height		
Unladen weight	177 kg	(390 lb)
Fuel tank		
Performance	140 km/h	(87 mph) max

GEAR RATIO		MILITARY EQUIP. rear carry rack, leather
I	= 19.43 : 1	panniers, sub-machine support brackets, additional masked lighting, all-over service livery.
II	= 12.04 : 1	
III	= 8.77 : 1	
IV	= 6.30 : 1	
V	= 5.92 : 1	

USA

MODEL   HARLEY-DAVIDSON FLH 1967

Manufacturer	Harley-Davidson Motorcycles, Milwaukee
Military Service	Standard production model works modified for general police service, by armed forces throughout the World, for solo escort, despatch and general liaison duties. Final European military service in Belgium and the Netherlands from 1967.

ENGINE AND TRANSMISSION

Type	Harley-Davidson, 45° ohv V-twin
Capacity	1207cc 87.3 x 100.8mm
Comp. ratio	8 : 1

Output	66 hp at 5600 rpm
Starting	electric
Carburettor	single 38mm bore
Electrics	12v
Clutch	multi-plate, dry
Gearbox	foot- or hand-change, 4-speed (3 and reverse option)
Final	exposed chain

FRAME & WHEELS

Type	duplex cradle, tubular construction
Front forks	telescopic, hydraulic damping
Rear forks	trailing, hydraulic damping, load adjustable
Brakes	internal expanding drums, front and rear
Tyre size	5.10 or 5.00 x 16" front and rear, road pattern

DIMENSIONS

Overall length	2337mm	(92")
Overall width	889mm	(35")
Overall height	1016mm	(40")
Wheelbase	1524mm	(60")
Ground clearance	165mm	(6.5")
Seat height		
Unladen weight	299 kg	(659 lb)
Fuel tank	13.2/18.9 litre	(3.5/5 US gal)
Performance	177 km/h	(110 mph) max

GEAR RATIO

I	= 3.73 : 1
(high gear)	

MILITARY EQUIP. rear carry rack, plastic panniers, two way radio, wind screen, additional lighting, siren, crash bars, all-over service livery.

USSR

MODEL	DNIEPER MT-12 1977
Manufacturer	Kiev Motorcycle Works, Kiev
Military Service	Specialised military model works modified for general police and military service during late 1970s, to replace ageing K-750 model, for sidecar despatch, convoy, personnel carrier, and general liaison. Service life expected until 1999.

ENGINE AND TRANSMISSION

Type	KMZ, transverse sv flat twin
Capacity	746cc 78 x 78 mm
Comp. ratio	6 : 1
Output	26 hp at 4900 rpm
Starting	left foot kick start
Carburettor	twin K-302
Electrics	6v
Clutch	single plate, dry
Gearbox	foot-change, 4-speed and reverse
Final	enclosed shaft

FRAME & WHEELS

Type	duplex cradle, tubular construction
Front forks	telescopic, hydraulic damping
Rear forks	trailing, helical sprung, load adjustable
Brakes	internal expanding drums, front and rear
Tyre size	3.75 x 19" front and rear

DIMENSIONS

Overall length	2430mm	(95.6") (w/sc)
Overall width	1700mm	(66.9") (w/sc)
Overall height	1100mm	(43.3") (w/sc)
Wheelbase	1510mm	(59.4") (w/sc)
Ground clearance	125mm	(4.9") (w/sc)
Seat height		
Unladen weight	350 kg	(772 lb) (w/sc)
Fuel tank	19 litre	(4.1 Imp gal) (w/sc)
Performance	90 km/h	(56 mph) max (w/sc)
	6.2 litre/100 km	

GEAR RATIO

I	= 3.6 : 1
II	= 2.28 : 1
III	= 1.70 : 1
IV	= 1.30 : 1
R	= 3.67 : 1

MILITARY EQUIP. rear carry rack for two way radio, panniers, sidecar mounted spare wheel, additional lighting, windscreen, front and rear crash bars, siren, all-over service livery.

Above: **May 1913, an 'Aerial machine-gun' mounted upon the handlebars of an Eysink 3.5 hp model. Although the Netherlands remained neutral during the First World War, the Eysink factory of Amersfoort supplied a number of these purpose-built machine-gun carriers. The ammunition case is mounted alongside the front forks.** *(Mick Woollett)*

Above: **1915 NSU 7 hp sidecar model prepared for military service. The majority of motorcycles procured by the German armed forces during the First World War were supplied by NSU, and the 7 hp model was of particular importance.** *(Sven-Olof Persson)*